Butterfly's Sisters

Butterfly's Sisters

THE GEISHA IN
WESTERN CULTURE

YOKO KAWAGUCHI

YALE UNIVERSITY PRESS | NEW HAVEN AND LONDON

For Simon

For information about this and other Yale University Press publications, please contact:
U.S. Office: sales.press@yale.edu   www.yalebooks.com
Europe Office: sales @yaleup.co.uk   www.yaleup.co.uk

Set in Arno Pro by IDSUK (DataConnection) Ltd
Printed in Great Britain by the MPG Books Group

Library of Congress Cataloging-in-Publication Data

Kawaguchi, Yoko.
  Butterfly's Sisters / Yoko Kawaguchi.
    p. cm.
  Includes bibliographical references and index.
  ISBN 978–0–300–11521–5 (cl:alk. paper)
  1. Geishas—History. 2. Civilization, Western. I. Title.
  GT3412.K36 2010
  792.702'80952—dc22

                                                            2010017516

A catalogue record for this book is available from the British Library.

10 9 8 7 6 5 4 3 2 1

Contents

Illustrations

Acknowledgements

This book has been many years in gestation, and I would like to thank my numerous friends who have lent me their warm support through the various stages of its development. I am grateful to Dr John Pikoulis for giving me the opportunity at a very early stage to present some of my ideas in the form of a series of lectures for the Department for Continuing Education, Cardiff University. The late Maureen Lawrence also kindly invited me to give a talk for the Friends of Welsh National Opera, at which I became so enthusiastic that I overshot my allotted time by twenty minutes before I got to my first musical example. The encouragement from the many Friends over the years has been very important to me. I would also like to thank my husband's colleagues at Welsh National Opera for the warm welcome and generous help they have always extended to me.

I would like to thank Robert Baldock and Phoebe Clapham, my editors at Yale University Press, London, for giving me the opportunity to write this book, and the editorial department for their patience and expertise in seeing the project through to the end. I owe a deep debt of gratitude to Professor Peter Davidson and Professor Jane Stevenson, who generously read through a draft of this book. Their practical advice and emotional support have been invaluable to me, while the intellectual stimulus they have provided has helped to push me to aim towards their own high standard of scholarship. The unflagging support of Mike and Alice Sharland, my agents, has been crucial to me in getting to the end of this project. I would also like to thank Iwata Tatsuji and his family for their warm hospitality in Tōkyō, when I needed to get some vital research done at several major libraries in that city.

I am grateful to the following libraries and their staff for making their resources available to me: the British Library, London; the Bodleian Library and the Bodleian Japanese Library, Oxford; Cambridge University Library; the London Library; the National Art Library at the Victoria & Albert Museum, London; the Theatre Collections Reading Room at the Victoria & Albert Museum, London; Cardiff Central Library; Cardiff University Library; Glasgow University Library; the National Diet Library of Japan, both its Main Library in Tōkyō and its Kansai-kan; Tōkyō Metropolitan Library; Ōsaka Prefectural Library; Aichi Prefectural Library; the Tsubouchi Memorial Theatre Museum at Waseda University, Tōkyō; and Nagasaki University Library.

My parents, as ever, have given me their unstinting support, and the love and kindness of the extended Rees and Powling clans have seen me over the toughest hurdles. I am extremely grateful to Dr Kamila Hawthorne, Dr Tracy Tye and, above all, Dr Ian Hughes, for restoring to me my health and the precious ability to enjoy life to the full. To my husband Simon Rees, whose inquiring mind, critical insight and relish for language have always been the primary inspiration in my life, I owe my deepest, heartfelt thanks.

Introduction

As a Japanese girl growing up in North America in the 1960s and '70s, I used to be greatly irritated that the geisha appeared to be one of the chief images associated with Japan and its culture. That mincing, simpering personification of female subservience to the male infuriated me. I was annoyed at the persistence of such an anachronistic image of Japan. I hated, moreover, the insinuation that the Japanese were being disingenuous about the true nature of the geisha's occupation. At the same time, I felt that the geisha was being held up to me as a standard of exotic glamour that I could not possibly hope to live up to.

But then what did I know about real Japanese geishas? What I was reacting against was a western construct – a western image of oriental femininity based upon reports (some more accurate than others) of the Japanese pleasure quarters, of which geishas were denizens, and upon western impressions of the Japanese generally, of their culture and their womenfolk, all of which had been brought back by generations of visitors to Japan.

The present book *Butterfly's Sisters* is about the development of a western cultural image of the feminine east. It will look at how the Japanese geisha has been depicted in a range of popular media in the west since the middle of the nineteenth century, when Japan opened its doors to wider contact with the rest of the world after more than two centuries of self-imposed isolation. Works that will be examined in this book range from painting, sculpture and photography to fiction, drama, musical comedy, opera, dance and motion pictures. I will be considering the reasons why the geisha should have taken hold of the western imagination as she has done, and how certain images of the geisha have come to be perpetuated in the west. I will also be looking at the connection between western images of the geisha and western ideas of other classes of Japanese women.

The geisha's rise to worldwide renown was not as straightforward as might now be imagined. What was known in the west even during the centuries of Japan's isolation, which lasted from the first half of the seventeenth century to the middle of the nineteenth, was that the social system of that country accommodated a class of licensed prostitutes who inhabited officially sanctioned brothel quarters. Reports of such women appeared in the few accounts of Japan published in the west during that period, mostly by employees of the Dutch East India Company (Verenigde Oostindische Compagnie), which, along with a small number of Chinese merchants, constituted the only foreign presence in Japan during those centuries. The VOC maintained a trading post on Dejima (otherwise known as Deshima), a tiny, man-made, fan-shaped island off the shore of the port town of Nagasaki, while the Chinese had their own walled quarter on land nearby. Foreigners were restricted to their respective trading posts, and they were only allowed to leave them under special circumstances. Since they were also prohibited from bringing their own womenfolk with them into Japan, they had no choice, if they wanted female companionship, but to ask for a professional courtesan to be sent from the official brothel quarter in town. Many of the accounts produced by employees of the VOC of their life on Dejima are candid about the arrangement that ensured a steady supply of women to the trading post.

When in the middle of the nineteenth century Japan opened the newly constructed port of Yokohama to sea traffic from abroad, the Japanese authorities attempted to set up in that town a system of regulated prostitution similar – though not identical – to the one which had operated for so long in Nagasaki. The difference was that in former times foreigners in Nagasaki had been forbidden to visit the brothel quarter in person and had had to wait for the women to come to them, while now, in Yokohama, they were being enticed to visit its brand-new brothel quarter so they might dissipate their pent-up energies within its confines. Sex was not the only pleasure on offer in the brothel quarter. Patrons were able to eat and drink while enjoying entertainment put on by professional female musicians and dancers. Known as geishas or *geiko*, these female entertainers were a relatively new addition to the brothel quarters of Japan. It was only in the 1730s, once the heyday of the well-educated, highly cultured (and most expensive) *tayū* class of courtesan was over, that geishas first made their appearance. Their role was to divert brothel-house patrons while they waited for their appointed courtesan to become available. There were also male entertainers whose role was similarly to entertain waiting patrons with amusing banter, song and dance; indeed, the term geisha was originally used of both sexes, although it gradually came to designate female performers specifically (although in many parts of Japan they continued to be known as *geiko*), while the men were called *otoko geisha* (male geisha), *hōkan* or *taikomochi*.

For the new foreign communities that sprang up in the handful of Japanese port towns now opened to commerce with the west, predominantly made up of men as they were, a major preoccupation was indeed women, specifically, local women who were willing to sleep with westerners. The chief concern of many incomers was simply how they might identify such women and go about acquiring a mistress for themselves. Others within the foreign community, such as western military commanders and doctors attached to foreign troops stationed in Japan, to say nothing of Christian missionaries, were more worried about the consequences of such contact on the morals but even more on the physical well-being of their fellow countrymen, in the light of the constant threat of a widespread outbreak of venereal disease. In this respect, the western concern over how prostitution was being dealt with by the Japanese authorities in Japan's ports was not vastly different from concern in countries across Europe and North America over how their public officials were dealing with the proliferation of prostitution on their doorstep. Prostitution, and its effects on both the moral and physical health of men, especially young men, became an urgent, much-discussed social issue in many western countries during the nineteenth century.

What, however, was controversial to the minds of western commentators was the manner in which the Japanese authorities chose to tackle the problem: through regulation, both at the supply end (by setting up one officially sanctioned, monitored brothel quarter per city) and the demand end (by channelling would-be consumers of prostitution exclusively to these quarters). Many western observers – particularly churchmen and missionaries, not surprisingly – objected to this approach to prostitution on moral grounds. It was detrimental, they cried, to the moral well-being of men (whether local or foreign visitors) that the authorities, who ought to be trying to improve public morality and setting the right examples, should condone prostitution in any form whatsoever. But other sections of the western community in Japan attacked regulated prostitution from another direction: as an imposition placed on their personal liberty in a blatant attempt on the part of the Japanese authorities to restrict their activities. In any case, the official Japanese plan to control the amount of contact and the nature of the contact which took place between foreign incomers and local women ultimately failed, not least because there turned out to be a significant number of young women not already involved in legalised prostitution who were nonetheless willing to enter into relationships with foreign men, usually for monetary gain, whether for themselves or for the sake of their families. These girls were often referred to within the foreign community as 'mousmee', from the Japanese term *musume*, meaning daughter and, more generally, any young woman. Plenty of local brokers emerged, willing to act as go-betweens to bring interested parties together. The Japanese authorities ended up tolerating these arrangements, just as they had for many centuries tolerated other infringements of official regulations, such as pleasure quarters in many Japanese cities which were not strictly legal.

The apparent abundance of willing candidates contributed to the debate among westerners about the morality of Japanese women. When western visitors to Japan came across young Japanese women, they often found it difficult to know how to read their demeanour, their gestures, indeed, their general behaviour. Because casual visitors were not often afforded the opportunity to meet women of the well-to-do classes, the women they did encounter tended to be those who worked in what would now be called the hospitality industry. These included geishas, as well as teahouse waitresses and servants at inns and hostelries. Yet despite the outgoing, eager-to-please friendliness towards strangers which these women had of necessity to cultivate as part of their job, it was frequently remarked by western visitors how much modesty they managed to retain at the same time. So were most of these girls truly chaste and virtuous? they wondered. Or was dissembling a widespread habit among Japanese women? Western commentators looked to other Japanese practices, bathing, for example, for evidence of sexual immorality among the Japanese. Meanwhile, the word 'mousmee' (with its many spelling variants), carrying with it implications of sexual looseness, quickly entered the English language, as well as the French. While the term has fallen out of usage in English, French retains the word *mousmé* to mean a female companion or, more specifically, a mistress.

Meanwhile, back in Europe and in North America, a fascination with things Japanese took hold of the public imagination, as more and more examples of Japanese arts and crafts came to be imported from the Far East. The interest in Japanese art had first emerged among a clutch of artists and art collectors in London and Paris in the late 1850s and early 1860s, but as consumerism took off in the west in the second half of the nineteenth century with the rise of the department store in large cities, goods produced in Japan, as well as articles manufactured in the west in a so-called Japanese style, became increasingly available and affordable to an ever wider section of the general public. This broadening of interest in Japan contributed to the popularisation of the image of the geisha. In artistic circles, connoisseurs of Japanese art such as Edmond de Goncourt discussed how the brothel quarters of Japan had been depicted by the great Japanese *ukiyoe* artists in their woodblock prints. But there was probably no single work which played a bigger role in first spreading the idea of the geisha in the west than the hit musical comedy *The Geisha*, which was premiered at Daly's Theatre, London, in the spring of 1896, and went on to be staged all over Europe in translation. The producer of the show was the shrewd theatre manager George Edwardes, who had formerly worked for the theatre impresario Richard D'Oyly Carte on the earlier Savoy Operas of Gilbert and Sullivan, including the Japanese-themed *The Mikado* (1885). Edwardes knew how to use the contemporary fad for Japonisme to his advantage. In *The Geisha* he was able to draw in large audiences by adroitly blending risqué subject matter with innocuous theatrical spectacle.

In Japan itself, a new imperial regime supplanted the Tokugawa Shogunate in 1868, bringing to an end the Shogunate's two-and-a-half-century rule over the country. Many social reforms were implemented, including changes to legislation governing prostitution. One of the effects of these changes was the attrition of the higher classes of courtesan, and the rise in prominence of the geisha. Demand for the most expensive and exclusive entertainment was now met by the most highly polished, well-trained geishas, while many others lower down the rungs of prestige catered to less well heeled patrons. Meanwhile, outside Japan, the geisha, of whom it was widely known that most entered their profession, like prostitutes and courtesans, by being indentured into service, came gradually to represent all the powerless victims of the Japanese system of legalised prostitution.

But the geisha was also supposed to be trained to be agreeable to men, so that while she could be considered to be a victim of a barbaric system of social oppression (which allowed her family to barter her freedom with geisha houses for an advance of money), she was in another sense the epitome of ideal womanhood: on the one hand a selfless daughter or sister ready to sacrifice herself for the sake of her impoverished family and, on the other, a woman conditioned specifically to be pleasing to men. In this regard, the geisha was often seen in the west not so much as an exceptional sort of Japanese woman but as typical, or even exemplary, albeit one who had her powers of forbearance more severely tested than many of her fellow countrywomen. The eminent Japanologist Basil Hall Chamberlain related in the second edition of his compendium of information on Japan *Things Japanese* (1891) that a 'well-known author' of books on Japan had wondered in a letter to him whether the suppressing of women by Japanese society could be altogether a bad thing if it produced such gentle, obliging, uncomplaining examples of the sex, so unlike the 'diamond-hard' women of America, the 'superb, calculating, penetrating Occidental Circe[s] of our more artificial society'.[1]

The development of the image of the geisha in the west since the middle of the nineteenth century is interesting for the way it reflects changing western anxieties regarding female sexuality in general. The present book *Butterfly's Sisters* takes up five key moments in the past century and a half when the geisha has been in the cultural consciousness, and explores how the geisha served as a focus for western social angst about female sexuality and women's role in society. While the first chapter of *Butterfly's Sisters* looks at western discussions of the treatment of women within Japanese society, the second chapter examines the ways in which nineteenth-century artists and writers on art responded to the idea of Japanese courtesans and geishas. For many, such as the Australian-born artist Mortimer Menpes, heavily influenced by the idea of 'art for art's sake' as advocated by his mentor James McNeill Whistler, the geisha was a fellow artist, an exemplar of woman's genius for re-creating herself. For others, however, a woman's talent for remaking herself anew each day was a reflection of nature's fearsome power to bring about change. There was a clash between the idea that eternal, unchanging ideals of female beauty did exist and the idea of women as dangerous seething cauldrons of the forces of nature. In the view of writers such as Edmond de Goncourt and J.-K. Huysmans, Japanese woodblock artists captured perfectly the dual characteristic of woman: her elegant decorous beauty and her insatiable appetites.

Chapter Three takes up the subject of the temporary portside 'marriages' between westerners and local Japanese women, and examines how attitudes to the temporary Japanese 'wife' change from Pierre Loti's widely read novel *Madame Chrysanthème* (1887) to André Messager's 1893 opera based on the novel, and then through the four-stage evolution of the Madame Butterfly story, from a piece of Nagasaki gossip about a teahouse girl related by an American missionary to her brother, the writer John Luther Long, to his novella about the geisha girl Cho-Cho-San, to the dramatisation of Long's story by the American theatre impresario David Belasco, and finally the immortal opera *Madama Butterfly* by the composer Giacomo Puccini and his librettists Giuseppe Giacosa and Luigi Illica.

The fourth chapter delves into the influence in the west of two former geishas from Japan who rose to fame in America and Europe as stage actresses at the beginning of the twentieth century. Kawakami Sadayakko (or Sada Yacco, as her name was commonly rendered in the west) spent nine gruelling months between 1899 and 1900 touring cities across America with her husband Kawakami Otojirō's troupe of Japanese actors. With the encouragement of Sir Henry Irving, whom the Kawakamis met in Boston, the company next crossed the Atlantic and put on a run of performances in London, where they were then engaged by the American dancer and theatre impresario Loie Fuller for what turned out to be a triumphant appearance at the Exposition Universelle which was being held in Paris in the summer of 1900. Sadayakko returned to Europe with her husband in the spring of 1901 for a subsequent year-long tour. The second of the two Japanese women to make a name for herself in the west as an actress was Madame Hanako, born Ōta Hisa. She toured Europe extensively from 1904 until the outbreak of the First World War, and was famous from London to Moscow. Both women became popular celebrities of the day, having dresses, perfumes, liqueurs and even cigarettes named after them.

Both Sadayakko and Madame Hanako derived their acting skills from the rigorous training they had had in traditional dance from a very young age. Sadayakko had been intended from earliest childhood for a career as a geisha, while in Hanako's case, dance had initially been no more than a pleasurable hobby until family circumstances forced her to put her training to professional use, first as a child actor and later as a geisha. Considering that both women had been geishas in Japan before becoming professional actresses in the west, it was, perhaps, ironic that many of the stage roles which they were given to play were those of geishas. The Japanese-language plays in which they appeared were mainly adapted from kabuki and noh plays and from Japanese legends, but they were carefully devised to appeal to western audiences unfamiliar with Japanese customs, literature, stage traditions or, indeed, language. The plays largely succeeded with stage spectacle: with colourful dances and over-the-top death scenes, often involving suicide by dagger. But it was stage spectacle quite unlike anything western audiences had seen before. The women's unfamiliar style of performance added fuel to the debate among critics, writers and artists across Europe and America over what counts as realism in drama (and, indeed, whether realism on stage was desirable at all). Sadayakko's abrupt shifts of mood from dispassionate calm to passionate frenzy perplexed as much as they thrilled audiences. The actress's many admirers included the French writer André Gide, the British artist Charles Ricketts, the British theatre critic and writer Max Beerbohm, and the American dancers Isadora Duncan and Ruth St Denis. Picasso painted her, and an eleven-year-old Jean Cocteau carried a vivid impression of her performance away with him from the Exposition Universelle. Rodin tried to get Sadayakko to model for him, but failed. He later had better luck with Madame Hanako, and they became good friends. Rodin went on to execute nearly sixty busts and masks of Madame Hanako, as he strived to capture the dramatic stage expressions for which she became so famous throughout Europe, especially the look she employed in her death scenes, variously mixing rage, anguish and bitter regret with bewilderment and resignation. The Russian theatre directors Konstantin Stanislavsky, a close friend of Isadora Duncan, and Vsevolod Meierkhol'd (Meyerhold) shared Rodin's enthusiasm for Madame Hanako's acting style.

Madame Hanako's theatre career waned, however, after the First World War broke out in 1914. Public enthusiasm for her sensational exoticism evaporated, and she finally returned to Japan for good in 1921. By that time, the mood in Britain towards Japan was souring. Japan's relations with the United States and

Britain deteriorated rapidly through the 1920s and '30s, sinking to the nadir of the days of the Second World War. It was not until the 1950s that Japan and the Japanese began once more to appear in American and British popular culture as something other than a hated enemy. Chapter Five of *Butterfly's Sisters* first looks at the pre-war novel *Kimono* (1921), a popular book of its day written by John Paris, who uses the image of the Yoshiwara pleasure quarter of Tōkyō to paint the Japanese as a sinister, devious and ruthless race. The chapter then considers various post-war depictions of Japan under Allied occupation in popular works such as the hit Broadway play *The Teahouse of the August Moon*, which ran for two and a half years from 1953 to 1956 and was later adapted for cinema, and novels such as Elliott Chaze's *The Stainless Steel Kimono* (1947), James A. Michener's *The Bridges at Toko-Ri* (1953) and *Sayonara* (1954), and *Cry for Happy* (1958) by George Campbell, the last three of which were also turned into successful motion pictures. All of these works use images of Japanese women to suggest to the American public Japan's new place in the world. With tensions rising between the United States and Communist countries such as the Soviet Union and China, Japan was increasingly portrayed, not as a dependency of the United States, but as a supporting partner, acquiescent to American leadership. One thing the well-established popularity of Puccini's *Madama Butterfly* had done was to create a template for the loving, guileless Japanese geisha girl; the Madame Butterfly prototype helped to fix the idea of Japanese women (if not the men) as caring and honest and, above all, sympathetic to Americans. Curiously enough, by employing the image of geishas, writers were able to sanitise for their domestic readers their portrayal of the sex trade in contemporary Japan. Geishas were depicted as quaintly risqué, but possessing Old World courtesy, good manners and consideration. They stood for an idealised traditional Japan, suggesting that the Japanese were not such a threat to the west as long as they did not try to imitate – or try to rival – western nations. Chapter Five will examine how American writers portrayed geishas not as home-wreckers, but as models of old-fashioned feminine virtue, by bringing up the geisha's association with ideas of self-sacrifice, duty to the family and respect for the male sex. Just as in the nineteenth century, Japanese women were taken up by conservatives in the west as exemplars of family-oriented values, which western women, with their insatiable demand for independence, were supposed to be abandoning.

The final chapter of *Butterfly's Sisters* looks at works of popular culture which show western women (and in one case a man) identifying themselves in one way or another with the geisha. In these cases, the image of the geisha acts as a medium through which the western protagonist comes to understand what it means to be a woman. The first example is the Paramount motion picture *My*

Geisha (1962), in which Shirley MacLaine plays a successful Hollywood comedienne who pretends to be a real Japanese geisha and tricks her movie-director
husband into casting her in the role of Madame Butterfly in his film version of
the opera, which he has gone to the trouble of travelling all the way to Japan to
shoot for greater authenticity. Her deception nearly costs her her marriage, until
a genuine geisha, one whom the American actress has hired to coach her on
Japanese mannerisms so she could pass herself off as a geisha in front of her
husband, gives her a lesson on the importance of being attentive to the needs of
men. The role of Cio-Cio-San, which MacLaine's character covets so much,
serves as a reminder of the unhappiness that lies in wait for the woman abandoned (for whatever reason) by her man. The successful career woman whose
life is unfulfilled because she does not have a stable relationship with a man of
her own is also the theme of the 1987 screen hit *Fatal Attraction*, in which the
female protagonist Alex Forrest, a high-flying editor with a New York publishing
firm, becomes obsessed with a relationship which was originally intended to be
nothing more than a one-night stand. Alex, played by Glenn Close, has a fixation
with Puccini's opera *Madama Butterfly*. The film suggests that a woman's
capacity to be faithful becomes a destructive force when it is not directed into a
legitimate channel, that is to say, wedlock. Just as Alex remains thwarted because
she unfortunately chooses a man who is, ultimately, unattainable, so the character of Cio-Cio-San, with whom Alex identifies, comes to stand for the deluded
'other woman', who yearns for the legitimacy which is denied her. In the
acclaimed stage play *M. Butterfly* (1988), by the American playwright David
Henry Hwang, it is the male protagonist, a French diplomat based in Peking,
who has a Madame-Butterfly-type obsession with the object of his passion who
ultimately eludes him. In this case, the passion must remain unrequited because
the Frenchman is doubly deluded: he refuses to accept that the object of his love
is in reality neither a woman, as he had believed, but a man, nor the model
oriental woman, modest, defenceless and innocent, who needs a strong western
man to protect her and make her happy, but a Chinese spy who has been taking
advantage of the diplomat's blind love to get him to work on behalf of the
Communists. In the end, the Frenchman emulates Butterfly and kills himself
(although with a knife rather than a dagger), thus immolating himself as a
martyr on the altar of his feminine ideal, the oriental woman who would rather
die than acknowledge that her love had been misplaced.

A book on the image of the geisha in the west cannot pass by Arthur Golden's
recent international bestseller *Memoirs of a Geisha* (1997) without a word. Even as
the novel harks back to a long-gone age, to the time before the Second World War,
when women and girls were still being indentured to long years of service
in geisha houses, *Memoirs* shares contemporary concerns about career and

relationships with works such as *My Geisha* and *Fatal Attraction*. Unlike the protagonist of either of the two films, Sayuri, the geisha heroine of *Memoirs*, manages both to have a career and to secure a man. But Sayuri's successes are those defined within the narrow world of geishas; even though she has been sold against her will to a geisha house in her childhood, she soon grows to accept that what counts as success among her fellow geishas is meaningful to her also. She goes on to beat off her rivals to become one of the most sought-after geishas of them all, and she wins the man she loves, who happens financially to be in a position to be able to buy her her freedom. He is also already married, but this does not discommode Sayuri in the least, for she is perfectly satisfied with being installed as his mistress. Indeed, the situation even has its advantages, as she persuades her lover to let her go to New York, where she starts a teahouse/restaurant. They meet at leisure whenever he is in town, which is often, because he is an important Japanese industrialist. For his part, Sayuri's protector is happy to make her his after he has witnessed her use deception to see off an unwanted lover, his own friend who unwittingly became the chief obstacle of their union. *Memoirs of a Geisha* is a curiously hybrid work, for along with its intention to portray the abuses which young girls encountered in the Japanese pleasure quarters of old, it tries at the same time to be a coming-of-age saga charting its heroine's triumph over adversity, and even a romance novel as well, complete with happy ending, in which the heroine finally gets her implausibly good-looking, kind-hearted (albeit already married) man. Ultimately, the novel glamorises the victims of a business the abuses of which it has supposedly set out to expose. Not surprisingly, the pop superstar Madonna was attracted to the glamour, and in the final years of the 1990s she adopted a geisha-look as her latest stage persona. Her model from *Memoirs of a Geisha*, moreover, was not the priggish heroine Sayuri but her chief rival, the talented but wilful, lascivious and spiteful star geisha Hatsumomo.

The geisha has thus been cast in many different lights in the west over the past century and a half. Numerous contradictory characteristics have been ascribed to her: modesty, sexual uninhibitedness, affectation, sincerity, docility, obsequiousness, weak-mindedness, selflessness, courage, and both childishness and motherliness. She has been held up as a model of the type of woman who selflessly puts her family before her own desires and as the prototypical, self-obsessed celebrity entertainer. Meanwhile, in Japan the ancient practice of indenturing women and girls to service in brothels and geisha houses ended after the Japanese Diet, the national legislature, passed the Anti-Prostitution Act in 1956, criminalising the abetting of prostitution. Tolerated prostitution zones – the latest, and last, metamorphosis of the brothel quarters of ancient times – disappeared for good from Japanese cities in 1958. With the rapid westernisation of taste in the 1960s, the demand for the geisha's kind of entertainment dwindled away. Only the exclusive end of the geisha business now survives, catering to a small coterie of aficionados. Becoming a geisha in Japan is a career choice these days, not something women are forced into by poverty as in past times. Nevertheless it remains a profession which trades on a woman's ability to be pleasant and pleasing to others (namely, men), rather than promoting the importance of being independent-minded and assertive. The subject of geishas is still drawn into discussions over the contentious issue of how women should conduct themselves in relation to men.

The geisha is only one of several competing images which have been employed by westerners over the last century and a half to convey ideas of various aspects of the Japanese national character. The samurai, for one, was useful as a reminder that the Japanese appeared also to possess an aggressive and bellicose streak. With Japan's emergence in the last decade of the nineteenth century as a serious regional power in east Asia – one with which Britain considered it expedient to enter into a military alliance in 1902 in order to contain the activities of Russia – it was not always the case that Japan was portrayed for public consumption (at least in Britain) as a weak, feminised entity. More recently, the sumo wrestler, represented as a lumbering ball of fat, has been adopted by western political cartoonists as a symbol of Japanese corporate greed, suggesting aggressiveness mixed with structural unwieldiness, although such comparisons do not stop to ask what, if any, relation exists between Japanese business practices and the Japanese custom of creating wrestlers who traditionally combine physical corpulence with muscularity and agility. But the samurai and the sumo wrestler (to say nothing of the ninja) will have to wait for another occasion. Now is the turn of the geisha as seen through western eyes.

Japanese names are given surname first throughout this book.

CHAPTER ONE

Were They or Weren't They? Geishas and Early Western Perceptions of the Morality of Japanese Women

'The Japanese woman is the crown of the charm of Japan,' crooned Henry Norman, the travelling commissioner for the *Pall Mall Gazette* and the *Daily Telegraph*, in a collection of his articles about Japan which was published in 1892 under the title *The Real Japan*. Whether it was the most aristocratic of noble-women or the 'frailest and most unfortunate' of her sisters, Japanese women of every social standing and condition, according to Norman, possessed alike 'an indefinable something which is fascinating at first sight and grows only more pleasing on acquaintance'.[1] Notwithstanding the suggestion in the title of Norman's book that he was clearing away a tangle of mistaken beliefs about Japan which had already accrued since the opening of the hitherto little known country to international trade in the middle of the nineteenth century – while at the same time seeing through the misinformation the Japanese were keen to spread about themselves; despite, that is, Norman's claim to originality, his enthusiastic commendation of Japanese womanhood was, by the time he was writing, a commonplace repeatedly heard from the mouths – and pens – of travellers just returned from Japan.

How had this idea taken such firm root, overcoming prejudices about race as well as differing criteria of beauty? There was a time, in the middle of the nineteenth century, when intrepid westerners, living in foreign enclaves in those few ports which the Tokugawa Shogunate had recently been forced to open to western shipping, welcomed the attentive ministrations of local women (even though the favours were usually bought in exchange for money or gifts of goods) as a pleasing change from the scowling rudeness of hostile samurai, the evasive reticence of their higher-placed masters from whom concessions had to be won, and the fawning pleasantries of merchants whose sincerity it seemed more prudent to suspect than not. The appearance of Commodore Matthew C. Perry and his squadron of American battleships at the mouth of Edo (Tōkyō) Bay in the summer of 1853 had effectively led to the Tokugawa Shogunate suspending its policy of international isolation which it had maintained since 1639. In response to Perry's veiled aggression, a number of Japanese ports were grudgingly opened to American ships, starting with Shimoda in 1854 and Hakodate, on the northern island of Hokkaidō, in 1855. In 1859, Yokohama, Nagasaki and Hakodate were opened to trade with the British, the French and the Russians, as well as with the Americans. The Netherlands, which had long had a commercial presence in Nagasaki, gained new access to Yokohama and Hakodate.

Within Japan, however, this strategy, which was perceived as an indication of the Shogunate's increasing weakness by its critics, eroded confidence among certain powerful circles within the ruling warrior class (the *bushi*) in the ability of a doddering regime to ward off foreign threats to Japanese sovereignty. Opponents of the Tokugawa Shogunate aligned themselves with the imperial faction in Kyōto. During this period when anti-western sentiments were running high, residents of foreign concessions, which were located within treaty ports but remained outside Japanese jurisdiction, often felt they were living in an isolated outpost of western civilisation, similar in many ways to a frontier fort in the American West. In the autumn of 1867 the fifteenth and last *shōgun* of the Tokugawa dynasty, Tokugawa Yoshinobu, abdicated and after a great deal of political manoeuvring, the restoration of imperial rule was declared on 9 December in the third year of Keio (3 January 1868 according to the western calendar) in the name of the fifteen-year-old emperor Mutsuhito, known posthumously by his reign name Meiji. The imperial court was effectively moved from Kyōto, where it had been situated since 794, to Tōkyō, as Edo, the Tokugawa Shogunate's seat of government, was renamed in the summer of 1868. Against the expectations of many of the emperor's followers, his ministers actively looked to the west in order to rapidly modernise the country. In 1868 the newly constructed port of Kōbe was inaugurated, and Ōsaka, Niigata and Tōkyō were eventually added to the list of ports open to western trade.

By this time, there were regular passenger services linking Japanese ports with China as well as with the continental United States. In 1864 the British shipping firm Peninsular and Oriental set up one such service between Shanghai and Yokohama. Three years later, the American firm the Pacific Mail Steamship Company started a service between San Francisco and Yokohama. Once the first transcontinental railroad route across the United States opened and the Suez Canal was completed, both in 1869, around-the-world travel no longer remained in the realms of fantasy. More and more tourists joined the merchants, missionaries, diplomats and military personnel who resided in the foreign settlements in

Japanese ports. Yokohama became firmly established as a port of call for Americans travelling westwards, as well as for Europeans travelling eastwards towards the North American continent.

Henry T. Finck, the music editor of the *New York Evening Post* who was also an enthusiastic international traveller, wrote in 1895 that the 'principal attraction' Japan had to offer to tourists was its womenfolk 'with their picturesque costumes and ways'.[2] Visitors to Japan, like Finck, had their expectations shaped by the voluminous amount of literature about Japan which was already available in the west, much of it written by those who had preceded them there in what, perhaps, had been a more adventurous age. By the 1880s, commercially available photographs, sold as souvenirs, helped to fix a set of visual images of Japan, its society and people. These images differed from Japanese *ukiyoe* prints of previous ages, those products of the artistic imagination which were avidly collected in the west, in that they possessed at least some contemporary referentiality, even if they tended still to emphasise the more traditional aspects of Japanese life, those features which marked Japan's difference from the west. One area of subject matter where *ukiyoe* prints crossed over with late nineteenth-century souvenir photographs was that of the inhabitants of the legal pleasure (or brothel) quarter.

Of the existence in Japan of courtesans and government-sanctioned pleasure quarters there was early knowledge in the west, mainly through the published writings of the employees of the Dutch East India Company (Verenigde Oostindische Compagnie, or VOC for short). François Caron, for example, who arrived in Japan in 1619 as a ship's cook's assistant and rose to become head of the Dutch trading post twenty years later, reported that brothels and prostitutes were legally recognised in Japan. The German naturalist and physician Engelbert Kaempfer, who, as an employee of the VOC, was in Nagasaki for several years in the last decade of the seventeenth century, wrote in his posthumously published *History of Japan* (1727) how he had been informed by one of his Japanese sources that the town possessed its own '*Bawdy Houses Quarters*', which lay to the south of the town 'on a rising hill, call'd *Mariam*'. The district consisted of two streets, along which stretched 'the handsomest private buildings of the whole Town, all inhabited by Bawds'. Kaempfer explained how very young girls were 'purchas'd' from their parents for a fixed term of years, either ten or twenty, and then brought up by their new master. The girls began as waiting-maids to full-fledged courtesans, from whom they would receive instruction in the arts of dance and music, as well as that of writing graceful letters, and 'all other respects [required] to qualify them for the way of life they are oblig'd to lead'. A brothel could have from seven to as many as thirty women, all 'very commodiously lodg'd in handsome apartments'. The most beautiful, accomplished and popular ones could expect to be housed and dressed in even greater splendour at the expense of the men who succeeded in winning their favours.[3]

By 'Mariam' Kaempfer was referring to the Maruyama district of Nagasaki. Together with the adjoining district of Yoriai, Maruyama had been chosen in the early 1640s to become the town's official brothel quarter or *yūkaku*. In his account of Japan, Kaempfer described the quarter, as a '*Kesiematz*', or *keisei-machi*. *Keisei*, a Japanese term for a courtesan or prostitute, literally meaning 'leaning (or crumbling) fortifications', alludes to a famous Chinese song by Li Yannian, court musician to the Chinese emperor Wudi, who reigned from 141 to 87 BC. Li Yannian sings of a woman so beautiful that a single glance from her is enough to raze a walled city, a second to lay waste to an entire nation.[4] The Maruyama-Yoriai area was on the outskirts of Nagasaki, and a number of brothels had already sprung up there in the middle of farmland before the area was officially designated a brothel quarter. Once it became Nagasaki's *yūkaku*, all of the town's courtesans were ordered to relocate to Yoriai. The Tokugawa Shogunate's preferred method of tackling the proliferation of prostitution was by attempting to bring it under regulatory control in exchange for official protection. Japan's rulers were probably less interested in the sexual morality of individuals than in maintaining public order within Japan's towns and cities. In any case, the keystone of their strategy was the setting up of legally recognised pleasure/brothel quarters. Previous regimes had made attempts to restrict prostitutes to a particular district within a city, one as early as 1193. In 1397 a pleasure district was approved for Kyōto, and the licensing of courtesans was briefly introduced in 1528. The number of legally recognised pleasure quarters began to increase in the late sixteenth and early seventeenth centuries, as a succession of overlords sought to consolidate their control over the whole of Japan. In 1585, the chief warlord Toyotomi Hideyoshi granted his official sanction to the pleasure districts which already existed in his capital Ōsaka. Four years later he gave permission for the construction of Japan's first purpose-built *yūkaku* in Kyōto. Known as the Nijō-Yanagimachi quarter, it was located to the south of the imperial palace, and all the city's courtesans were compelled to live and work there. With the city's rapid expansion, the brothel quarter was moved further south in 1602 and was called the Rokujō-Misujimachi quarter. In 1641 it was moved yet again by official order, this time slightly to the west. Thereafter, the quarter was known by the nickname Shimabara. Shimabara was originally enclosed on all sides by a wall and a moat, and had only one gateway, although a second was built in 1732.

The city of Edo had its own famous brothel quarter, the Yoshiwara. After the Tokugawa clan became the de facto rulers of Japan at the beginning of the seventeenth century, the new Shogunate formally granted permission (and land) in 1617 for an officially sanctioned brothel quarter to be established in its capital Edo. Called Yoshiwara, this *yūkaku* was located to the east of Edo Castle, in a formerly marshy area west of the Sumida River – the word Yoshiwara originally meant 'rushy field', but in 1626 the name was changed to designate 'a field of good fortune'. Yoshiwara opened for business in 1618, but in 1656 was ordered to relocate. A fire in 1657 destroyed most of the district, hastening the move. The *yūkaku* was rebuilt to the north of the city, beyond the Asakusa temple district, and called Shin-yoshiwara, the 'new Yoshiwara'. The original site was thereafter referred to as Moto-yoshiwara, or the 'former Yoshiwara'. Edo's Yoshiwara, Kyōto's Shimabara, and the Shinmachi district in Ōsaka were the three most prestigious legal brothel quarters under the Tokugawa regime. The courtesans of Kyōto had the reputation of being the most feminine, and those of Edo the most spirited. But it was Ōsaka, long the commercial capital of Japan, which boasted the most luxurious and elegantly appointed brothels. Even in the late nineteenth century, the American tourist Henry Finck was informed by his Japanese guide that the prettiest and most popular geishas of Kyōto went to find work in Ōsaka.

However, during the long reign of the Tokugawa Shogunate (which lasted from 1603 to 1867), the Yoshiwara, Shimabara and Shinmachi districts were all out of bounds to foreigners. Indeed, most of the country was closed off to foreigners by 1639. The Portuguese had been the first Europeans to reach Japan, arriving in 1543. In 1609 the Dutch East India Company established a trading settlement on the small island of Hirado, off the north-western coast of the western island of Kyūshū. The English East India Company set up its own trading post there in 1613. Europeans had initially been received favourably by some of Japan's most powerful overlords who were vying with each other for overall domination of the country – Japan had been rent by internecine warfare for more than a century. But as Catholic missionaries succeeded in gaining ever more converts, Europeans came to be regarded as a destabilising influence on the country. The Tokugawa Shogunate, once it had established control over the whole of Japan and set up its seat of government at Edo in 1603, began applying measures aimed at curtailing the activities of Catholic missionaries. This culminated in 1639 in the expulsion of the Portuguese from Japan. Fearful at the same time that the local lords of Kyūshū would become too powerful through foreign trade, the Shogunate also imposed restrictions on the trading operations of the Dutch and the English. In 1623 the English East India Company withdrew from Japan, finding trade unprofitable. After 1639 only the Dutch and the Chinese were permitted to maintain a limited presence in the country. In 1641, the Dutch trading post was moved to Dejima (or Deshima), a fan-shaped artificial island off Nagasaki originally built in 1634 to confine the Portuguese. Company employees were prohibited from leaving the island at will. From 1688 onwards, the Chinese too were restricted to their own separate compound, which was on land, close to Nagasaki's harbour.

All foreign women were banned from Japanese soil, but special provisions were made for the entertainment of the inhabitants of the Dutch and Chinese quarters, to the profit of the brothels of Maruyama and Yoriai. Engelbert Kaempfer, who was with the VOC trading settlement at Dejima between 1690 and 1692, had to have Nagasaki's brothel quarter described to him because he, along with all other foreigners, was not permitted to move freely about town. Among the women registered with brothels in the quarter there was a separate class of prostitutes who were licensed to meet specifically with either Chinese or European clients. These women were among the few locals who were granted access by the Japanese authorities to the restricted areas where foreigners resided. Prostitutes were allowed to go to Dejima from around 1645 onwards. At first this was only at night-time, but from 1700 they were permitted to stay throughout the day. Initially it was the lowest-ranking women in the brothels who fraternised with the 'barbarians'. It was not until 1782 that a highest-ranking *tayū*-class courtesan deigned to attend on an *opperhoofd*, the head of the VOC trading settlement.

Engelbert Kaempfer noted that the '*Kaimono Tskai*' (*kaimono tsukai*) – a term which in Japanese literally means someone charged with the task of doing the shopping – did not merely supply the inhabitants of Dejima with food, drink and other necessities, as well as obtaining samples of the limited selection of Japanese merchandise foreigners were allowed to purchase for themselves. The '*Kaimono Tskai*' procured women. According to Kaempfer, the privilege of working as a '*Kaimono Tskai*' belonged to about seventeen local families in Nagasaki. The Swedish botanist Carl Peter Thunberg, who was with the VOC trading settlement on Dejima as a physician from 1775 to 1777, recalled that a Japanese was on hand on the island to take requests from any Company employee who wanted a female companion for the night. This man would return in the evening with a suitable girl and her young servant, or '*Kalbro*' (*kamuro*). According to Thunberg, a courtesan had to be kept for at least three days, and arrangements could be made to prolong her stay on Dejima almost indefinitely. Her own food and drink were fetched daily from town by her servant girl, who also prepared her meals, made tea, tidied rooms and ran errands. Thunberg added that for every day the woman spent on the island a fee had to be paid to 'the lady's husband'. The courtesan herself expected expensive presents, luxuries such as new robes and personal ornaments.[5]

Manners and Customs of the Japanese, a compendium published in Britain in 1841 of information gleaned predominantly from accounts of Japan composed by VOC employees, sympathetically evokes the inconvenience, to say nothing of the loneliness, with which westerners must have had to contend from day to day, stuck on their tiny island. The inhabitants of Dejima, the book argues, needed the women as personal attendants as much as anything else, especially at night-time, since all other Japanese were required by the Japanese authorities to leave the island at sunset. Who else could these poor men rely upon to boil up a kettle for an evening cup of tea? (Actually the VOC brought over male Javanese servants from Batavia, modern-day Jakarta, their power base in east Asia.) *Manners and Customs* is also candidly open about children born to westerners and local women, noting the observation made by Hendrik Doeff, *opperhoofd* of Dejima from 1803 to 1817, that infants were being nursed by their mothers on Dejima, though women were prohibited from actually giving birth there. *Manners and Customs* informed its readers that whilst the fathers were permitted less and less direct contact with their sons as they grew up, they were allowed to provide for their boys' education, and even to buy them a government position when they reached adulthood.[6]

It was not long after *Manners and Customs of the Japanese* was published that Japan faced enormous changes. In 1858 the Tokugawa Shogunate signed a trade treaty with the United States, which, among other things, committed it to open new ports to American shipping. The list included Kanagawa, but the Shogunate decided it would rather build a new port than let the Americans into the established one at Kanagawa, which was also an important posting station on the main arterial road that linked Kyōto and Edo. To this end, the Shogunate chose to develop Yokohama, which had up to then been nothing more than a small fishing hamlet. As a way of making the brand-new town more attractive to foreign incomers (as well as to deflect western criticism of the Shogunate's unilateral decision not to honour its treaty commitment to open Kanagawa), a brothel quarter was included in the plans.

The decision to build a *yūkaku* in Yokohama was made in 1858. Those who applied for permission to set up brothels in the new quarter included experienced brothel proprietors such as Suzuki Zenjirō, from nearby Kanagawa, and Iwakiya Sakichi, of the Shinagawa district of Edo. The Shogunate lent money towards the enterprise and contributed the land. The new brothels were supposed to be ready for business by the summer of 1859, when the port of Yokohama was due to be opened formally to western shipping. Construction, however, was not finished on time, and the brothel proprietors were allowed (in the face of some opposition from certain official quarters in Edo) temporarily to rent three of the twenty-four tenement buildings the Shogunate had erected to house foreigners.

The official Miyozaki site was finally ready in the autumn. Yokohama was spread along the seafront: its eastern half was taken up by the foreign settlement, while the western area was comprised of Japanese residences and businesses. The Miyozaki brothel quarter was set inland, among rice fields in an area of reclaimed marshland to the south of the new town. The quarter was surrounded by a moat, as were the Shimabara quarter in Kyōto and the Shin-yoshiwara in Edo. Sole access was by a single bridge and gate. Within two years, there were seventy licensed brothels, as well as nineteen geisha houses and five teahouses. One of the most prominent and lavish of the brothels was the Gankirō, which was run by Iwakiya Sakichi from Edo. The Gankirō catered to both a Japanese and foreign clientele, but in strictly segregated areas. The Shogunate had decided to follow a strategy similar to the one they had formerly implemented in Nagasaki, that is to say, to permit foreigners controlled access only to specially licensed prostitutes. The prostitutes at the Gankirō were therefore split into two distinct categories: those who saw only Japanese clients, and those who fraternised only with foreigners.

Brothel proprietors appear to have encountered difficulties recruiting women for the latter group. Although the nearby port of Kanagawa had a *yūkaku* with courtesans of different classes, it was said that the brothel proprietors of Miyozaki had to resort to hiring women who were the lowest kind of prostitute, those called *meshimori onna*, who worked, not in the brothel quarter, but from inns and hostelries. The original Miyozaki quarter was destroyed in the great Yokohama Fire of 1866, after which it was rebuilt in what is now the general area of Nakaku Suehirochō, Chojamachi and Isesakichō, and was renamed Yoshiwara. This quarter in turn burnt down in 1871, after which the brothel quarter was moved to Takashimachō. One of the most famous of all the brothels in Takashimachō was the 'Jinpooro' (Jinpūrō), which was also known among the international seafaring fraternity as the 'Nectarine' and the 'Number Nine'. It is mentioned in Rudyard Kipling's poem 'McAndrew's Hymn' (started in 1893 and published the following year), in which the poem's narrator, the Scottish chief engineer on a cargo liner, addresses his God with reflections on his past life. In 1882 the 'Jinpooro' relocated to the Shingane Eirakuchō area of Yokohama, and in Kanagawa opened a second brothel aimed at foreigners. By 1886 the entire Yokohama brothel quarter had been moved to the new Shingane Eirakuchō site.[7]

Descriptions survive of the original Gankirō brothel. C. Pemberton Hodgson, who served as British consul at Nagasaki and Hakodate from 1859 to 1860, and Edward Barrington de Fonblanque both wrote of the escorted tours they were given around the establishment. According to De Fonblanque, the Gankirō (which he spelt Gankeroo), was a 'magnificent building, all lacquer and carving and delicate painting':

This was the court-yard; – *that* was to be a fish-pond with fountains (the building was still incomplete at this time); in this room refreshments might be procured – *that* was the theatre; *those* little nooks into which you entered by a sliding panel in the wall were dormitories, encumbered with no unnecessary furniture; *there*, affixed to the walls, was the tariff of charges, which I leave to the imagination; and in that house, across the court, seated in rows on the verandah, were the moosmes themselves.[8]

C. Pemberton Hodgson, in his published account of his Japanese experiences, writes of the Gankirō's 'grand saloons', which he found to be fine rooms with 'fountains, fish, trees, and flowers, marble and old lacquer ornaments'. The central staircase was broad and made of marble.[9]

De Fonblanque describes being taken around the Gankirō by two 'officers', who showed off the sights 'with as much pride as if they were exhibiting an ancient temple sacred to their dearest gods'. Hodgson was astounded that, similarly, a government official, a 'Yakonin' (*yakunin*), acted as his guide around the brothel. Then, there were the women. The 'Gankeroo', De Fonblanque reported, provided, for the amusement and pleasure of foreigners, 'painted *moosmes*, dressed in gorgeous robes and *coiffées* in the most wonderful manner'. Whereas Hodgson in his book calls such women 'kānkrō' (possibly from the name of the brothel Gankirō), De Fonblanque applies to them the general Japanese word for a young girl: *musume*.[10] Hodgson, to his discomfiture, was obliged to follow the custom of the place and 'select, or, at any rate, make the pretence of selecting' one or another of these girls as his companion for the occasion:

> There were three rows of wooden boxes, some hundred mats long, with a passage of half a mat between them; each row was subdivided into narrow horse-stalls, little rooms with a small window or aperture towards the passage; and in each of these stalls was a female. At a given signal, either a clap of the hands or a shrill cry, all the inhabitants rose from their cages, like dogs from their kennels, and put out their well-dressed heads. The visitor had to pass through a hedge, not of hawthorn or tea-trees, but of females. . . . When an object has been selected, and its value estimated, the temporary proprietor retires, and may either have a room worthy of Sardanapalus, or a garret fit for such monstrosities.[11]

The likening of Japanese prostitutes to caged animals being put up for sale was an analogy that was to be employed over and over again by western writers, especially when they were describing the Japanese custom of *harimise*, whereby women of the *yūkaku*, in all but the most exclusive establishments, sat behind large slatted windows in full view of the street, so that potential customers (as well as curious onlookers) were able to take a good look at them. Hodgson gives a description of just such a scene in his book, although it is not clear whether he actually witnessed it for himself or was describing it from hearsay:

> Every evening these poor creatures, made up with all their splendid finery and mockery of dress, painted and powdered, with their little teacups and pipes before them, are seated in a row, on their clean mats, within a square room which opens on the street, and is separated from it only by a wooden 'grille,' through which the gallants and passers-by may at leisure examine them, and then enter and make a vile bargain with the proprietor.[12]

Hodgson left the Gankirō after having smoked his pipe in one of the grand halls and having listened to music performed by 'Gāyǎshāǎs'. He was, he declared, thoroughly disgusted with what he had seen. Not all western consular and military officials, however, shared Hodgson's dismay and disapproval of the Miyozaki quarter. Far from it. Before the Miyozaki site was even built, the Dutch vice-consul Dirk de Graeff van Polsbroek, who was finalising trade arrangements for foreign merchants in Yokohama, raised the issue of access to prostitutes with the Shogunate. De Graeff also requested, though unsuccessfully, that women be allowed to be taken out to foreign ships docked in the harbour. The Prussian writer Rodolphe (Rudolf) Lindau, who served as the Swiss consul in Yokohama, was alluding to De Graeff when he wrote in his 1864 book about his time in Japan that the construction of the '*Yankiro*' was first proposed by a foreign consul who was keen to find a way of preventing the frequent brawls which broke out between western sailors and Japanese men in the streets of Yokohama.[13]

Lindau reported how young women – courtesans, singers and dancers – were always available in the brothel quarter for hire by the day, week or month. In his book, he referred to the entire Yokohama brothel quarter, Miyozaki, as the '*Yankiro*', describing it as '*le quartier des* maisons de thé'. Lindau helped build up the association of the word 'Gankiro' with heady pleasures other than those strictly carnal, and the Swiss politician Aimé Humbert, who arrived in Japan in 1863 in order to negotiate a trade treaty with the Shogunate, later applied the name Gankiro, in his 1870 publication on Japan, to the chief house of entertainment in the Japanese capital's Shin-yoshiwara district (which, in reality, was still closed to foreigners), characterising it as '*le casino du beau monde*'.[14] But from the time Yokohama's Miyozaki brothel quarter first opened, there was speculation among westerners as to whether the auxiliary female staff who worked in the quarter, in particular the musicians and the dancers, ever doubled as prostitutes. This was the beginning of the long-running debate over the precise nature of the geisha's occupation. The British consul C. Pemberton Hodgson felt it necessary to draw a clear line of distinction between courtesans and geishas with regard to sexual behaviour. He had himself been entertained at the Gankirō by 'Gāyăshāăs', who had sung for him and played native instruments, and he assured his readers that these 'singing-girls' or 'tea-house girls', as he variously described geishas, were virtuous. 'Gāyăshāăs' could be found in any town in Japan, and were available for hire for parties. They would even come (though in groups of three) to entertain at private residences. But although it was 'part of their profession to assist at the orgies of the Pans and Nymphs', Hodgson wrote, 'Gāyăshāăs' were respectable and no Japanese would presume to take liberties with them.[15]

Aimé Humbert also raises the matter of the sexual conduct of geishas in his book on Japan. He concludes that they were not immoral and were to be distinguished in this respect from street-musicians and dancers at fairs. The point on which he diverged from Hodgson was on whether or not geishas were allowed to attend clients at private residences. Humbert maintained that they were restricted to appearing – and only when expressly summoned – at professional entertainment venues (teahouses, restaurants and the like) which were under the careful eye of the police.[16] Rodolphe Lindau went so far as to assert that women who were either a '*ghéko*' (*geiko*), by which he meant a musician, or an '*o-doori*' (*odoriko*), a danseuse, took a vow of chastity. He added, however, that transgressions were usually looked upon indulgently by the geisha-house proprietor, except in cases where the girl became careless about her formal engagements. While thus insinuating that a Yokohama geisha might not be any less immoral than outright courtesans (though perhaps slightly more discreet), Lindau insisted that when he himself attended a dinner at a Nagasaki teahouse, the singing and dancing girls (as well as the courtesans themselves) were all so modestly behaved that they could have been taken for honest daughters of the bourgeoisie.[17] This is in contrast to the lurid description which Comte Raymond de Dalmas, a French ornithologist, gave in his 1885 book on Japan, of what he claimed to be a typical Japanese dinner party at a '*tchaia*' (*chaya*), or teahouse. Japanese orgies, Dalmas reported, lasted up to five hours. Seductive, young '*gaicha*' were on hand to spur on the evening's revelries with lascivious dances in which even the youngest of the girls participated. Dalmas dwells with relish on the idea of the Japanese love of pleasure. He bestows a bestial quality on his visions of Japanese excess – debauches which are accompanied by abominable '*cris inhumains*', that is to say, Japanese singing.[18]

The discrepancy between Lindau's account and Dalmas's suggests something more than simply that Lindau might have attended a watered-down version of traditional Japanese teahouse entertainment, much sanitised for the benefit of western sensibilities. It reflects the contradictions which westerners felt they were seeing in the behaviour of the Japanese. For while, on the one hand, the Japanese were remarked upon for possessing a highly sophisticated, even over-refined, system of etiquette, by which every aspect of their conduct towards one other appeared to be determined, it had, on the other hand, become a commonplace since the sixteenth century to charge the Japanese with lewdness. In the opinion of the Jesuit missionary Alessandro Valignano, one of the bad qualities of the Japanese race was 'that they are much addicted to sensual vices and sins'.[19] When it came to the subject of Japanese women, there was some disagreement over whether Japanese society expected women to be modest and chaste or whether it condoned licentiousness in thought and intention so long as women preserved the veneer of decorum. Much of the argument for one or the other was, however, predictably based on observation of the class of women whom travellers were most likely to encounter on the road: women who worked in eateries and inns.

Engelbert Kaempfer, who twice had the opportunity of travelling from Nagasaki to Edo as part of the entourage of the *opperhoofd* (or head) of the Dutch trading post on his annual (later to become less frequent) journey of homage to the *shōgun*, relates in his *History of Japan* that wherever there were 'great and small Inns, tea-booths, and cook-shops', 'numberless wenches' would emerge from them around noontime, dressed up and with their faces painted, ready with smiles and winning words to entice passers-by to enter their particular establishment. The Swedish botanist Carl Peter Thunberg, who in the last quarter of the eighteenth century was accorded the same privilege as Kaempfer of making the journey to Edo, reported that a port as small as '*Dsino Kameru*' (Shimo Kamagari) had no fewer than fifty lewd women, that '*Kaminoseki*' had two houses which together contained eighty, and that '*Miterai*' (Mitarai) possessed more than four houses of pleasure. Far from such establishments being merely tolerated by the authorities and local inhabitants, Thunberg observed, they were often housed in the most impressive buildings in the entire village.[20] These sights appeared to refute the claim made by earlier employees of the VOC, such as the former *opperhoofd* François Caron, that prostitution in Japan was confined to the brothel quarters. Kaempfer commended Caron for his gallant attempt to defend the view that Japanese women were generally chaste (after all, Kaempfer noted, Caron himself had a Japanese 'lady'), but Kaempfer maintained nonetheless that Caron had been sadly deluded. Although Kaempfer did point out that as far as Nagasaki's *yūkaku* was concerned, women were usually sold to its brothels as children, when they were still too young to be able to exercise any control over their future, he suggested that when it came to inns and taverns outside the official brothel quarters, women were themselves not unforthcoming in satisfying a market for which demand remained consistantly high. Kaempfer was convinced, moreover, that there was no inn in Japan that did not double as a 'bawdy-house'.²¹

Kaempfer was correct in so far as many inns did employ prostitutes, although it was by no means true that they all did. The Tokugawa Shogunate's numerous attempts to stamp out illicit prostitution in ports and posting stations proved ineffectual. After 1718 the Shogunate tacitly conceded that prostitution might help draw more custom to inns and serve as a source of much-needed extra income: many innkeepers along the arterial, long-distance highways which radiated from Edo complained of the financial strain they were under due to the fact that posting stations, where these inns were located, were required to shoulder the expense of maintaining horses for government business. Thereafter, inns were allowed to keep, apart from actual female servants, prostitutes ostensibly known as 'serving women' (*meshiuri onna* or, more popularly, *meshimori onna*). The number was initially limited to two per establishment, although greater leniency was officially granted later to inns which were situated in certain specific posting stations near the capital Edo. Before long, *meshimori onna* had spread widely throughout Japan, and were to be found in posting stations all along the country's major arterial routes. In spite of the Shogunate's efforts to exercise its authority over prostitution, infringements of the regulations were common: inns not entitled to have *meshimori onna* often underhandedly employed their female staff in that capacity, while hostels which did have them flouted restrictions limiting their number. Inevitably there were clandestine *meshimori onna* who sold their favours illicitly in towns off the main highways, and in such port towns as were not legally permitted to have prostitutes (*jorō*) working in them.²² But whether or not this was because fewer women in Japan than in the west felt prostitution to be either repugnant or shameful, as Kaempfer implies, was another matter.

Opinion remained divided among nineteenth-century visitors to Japan. C. Pemberton Hodgson characterised 'Gāyǎshǎǎs' as being perfectly good and virtuous, yet in the very next sentence he was voicing his view that '[a]ny of these women, and . . . nearly any woman in Japan, may be bought *for a time* by a foreigner, certainly by a Japanese noble'.²³ On the other hand, George Smith, the bishop of Victoria (Hong Kong), who visited Japan in 1860, did not doubt the chastity of the young Japanese women who worked in taverns. Smith had certainly read Carl Peter Thunberg's account of Japan, for he frequently refers to Thunberg in his own book, which was published in 1861. But if Smith had taken note of Thunberg's observation as to the prevalence of lewd women in the towns along the main highways and sea routes of Japan, he was not at all apprehensive that he might accidentally injure his own reputation by imprudently entering some wayside teahouse. He informed his readers that he had been reassured that serving women in 'public hotels' in Japan were hired for their decorum as much as for their beauty. As far as he was concerned, he did not feel it necessary to query this. He was unabashed about describing the attention he received from the serving girls at one refectory where he had stopped off for some refreshments. It was true the girls had been somewhat painted, their complexions 'enhanced' with 'pearl-dust and rouge' and their lips 'stained with a dark purple crimson'. But the bishop thoroughly enjoyed the experience of having a bevy of charming women make a great deal of fuss over him. He was delighted to find himself surrounded by kneeling 'waiting-damsels', who vied vivaciously to be the first to serve him, holding up to his lips spoonfuls of boiled egg, carefully seasoned, and other dainty morsels.[24]

J.J. Rein, who compiled a weighty study of Japanese customs for the Prussian government, felt he needed to explain in all solemnity that the Japanese serving girl was expected to receive guests 'with laughter, playfulness and jest', behaviour which could easily be misinterpreted by visitors unfamiliar with the customs of the country. Westerners were all too ready to dismiss 'her strikingly trusting and childishly naïve demeanour' as nothing more than insincere dissembling, but in doing so they were making a mistake.[25] Pemberton Hodgson made the point that there were teahouses in Japan 'where all the "Moosmes," or maids, are either the daughters of the proprietor, or their respectable servants', and that these were not to be mistaken for other sorts of establishment which kept women of dubious reputation. But fatally, Hodgson neglected to inform his readers by what external indications a stranger might successfully tell the one from the other.[26] Both the idea of teahouses and of the 'moosmes' who served in them were laden with ambiguity for foreign visitors to Japan. The term 'moosme' – from *musume*, a Japanese word which in its narrow sense denotes daughter, but is also used more generally to mean any young unmarried woman – was, in the second half of the nineteenth century, widely applied by westerners to the young women who waited on them in Japanese teahouses, restaurants and inns. Some writers, such as De Fonblanque, used it as well of women found in less innocent establishments. Later on, young women who entered into concubinage with foreigners were also commonly referred to as *musume*, distinguishing them from the 'professionals', the prostitutes who were registered at the local brothel quarter. Owing to such associations, the term *musume* came increasingly to suggest, among westerners at least, a young woman with loose morals.[27]

The nature of Japanese teahouses also attracted much discussion. Rodolphe Lindau noted in 1864 that foreigners were already in the habit of referring to most places of public resort in Japan as teahouses. He explained in his account of Japan that a proper Japanese teahouse was known as '*tcha-ïa*' (*chaya*) and was no more (if no less) scandalous a haunt than cafés were in the west. At the same time, Lindau himself added to the confusion by describing Japanese brothels (which he calls 'djorojas', after the Japanese word for brothel *jorōya*) as '*maisons de thé*'.[28] The intrepid traveller Isabella Bird, who journeyed to Japan in 1878 (for the sake of her health, of all things), chided those people who indiscriminately called all Japanese houses of entertainment 'tea-houses'. She informed her readers that a teahouse was 'a house at which you can obtain tea and other refreshments, rooms to eat them in, and attendance'. Those located at a popular tourist site might be large, in some instances three storeys high, and were often gaily decorated with brightly coloured bunting, flags and lanterns. Quieter establishments were to be found alongside major roads, offering tired travellers tea and simple food, as well as rooms in which one could respectably stretch one's weary legs and take some rest.[29]

This confusion about Japanese teahouses was not surprising. The Japanese word for teahouse, *chaya*, was traditionally used by the Japanese to refer to a variety of institutions: everything from the humble wayside stall that served tea to thirsty travellers (known more commonly as *chamise* from the middle of the nineteenth century onwards); imposing inns called *tatebajaya*, where noblemen could rest their horses between posting stations (some examples of which survived into the late nineteenth century); cheerful public houses found near popular beauty spots and temples and shrines, providing sightseers and pilgrims with liquid refreshments and snacks; the *mizujaya* which offered such delicacies as tea flavoured with salted cherry blossom, along with sweets and cakes, and occasionally beautiful waitresses who could be procured for a tryst; and fancy restaurants (*ryōrijaya*) where men took their (male) friends, relatives and business associates for meals and entertainment provided by geishas. In cities, there were, during the eighteenth century, teahouses called *deaijaya*, which were used for discreet sexual assignations. Towards the end of the nineteenth century and into the twentieth, there were also (particularly in Tōkyō) popular teahouses known as the *machiaijaya* to which clients could call out a favourite geisha for sex (or leave the choice of geisha to the discretion of the proprietress).[30] Inside legal brothel quarters such as the Shin-yoshiwara in Edo/Tōkyō, teahouses called *hikitejaya* specialised in providing refreshments and entertainment to patrons before they were escorted on to one of the prestigious brothels when their chosen courtesan was ready to receive them. It was in the *hikitejaya* that the geishas of the brothel quarters primarily performed their music and dance. These geishas were supposed to live by their art, the business of selling sex being the prerogative of courtesans and prostitutes. The institution of *hikitejaya* existed in the Shin-yoshiwara until the pleasure quarter was razed in the firestorm that consumed the greater part of Tōkyō after the city was struck by a massive Allied air raid on the night of 9 March 1945.

During the long reign of the Tokugawa Shogunate, the conduct expected of geishas differed from city to city. For instance, the geishas of the Shin-yoshiwara quarter in Edo were expected to support themselves exclusively by their art. Unlike those in either Kyōto or Ōsaka, these geishas were strictly differentiated from both the high-class courtesans and lower-class prostitutes of the brothel quarter and were forbidden to take business away from either. A surveillance office (*kenban*) was established in the Shin-yoshiwara quarter in 1779 to make sure this rule was observed. *Kenban* administrators also saw to it that the geishas of the brothel quarter behaved decorously, and were dressed decently and modestly. Unlike the courtesans and prostitutes, who tied their obi in front, geishas tied theirs at the back.[31] Men from the *kenban* escorted geishas to the teahouses and those brothels to which they had been summoned to provide entertainment.

It was only in the 1730s that geishas began to emerge as a distinct class from within the ranks of prostitutes and courtesans of the brothel quarters of Japan. Some of the first appeared in the rich merchant city of Ōsaka, where they were known as *geiko*, as they were also – and still are – called in Kyōto. Prostitution in Japan before then had had a long history of association with music and dance. Since at least the tenth century, there had been prostitutes who were accomplished dancers and musicians, and were therefore distinguished from the common kind who only sold their bodies. Highly talented prostitutes were often called upon to provide auspicious songs and dances at banquets attended by courtiers and government officials. During subsequent centuries, the number of prostitutes who were truly accomplished in music and dance declined, but their popularity was reignited around the beginning of the seventeenth century by a dancer named O-Kuni. She was said to have originally been a shrine maiden at the ancient shrine of Izumo in the west of Japan. By 1603, however, she was in Kyōto and becoming famous. She performed a wide variety of dances, ranging from children's dances (*yayako odori*) to Buddhist chants (*nenbutsu odori*). But it was for those dances in which she dressed up in male clothes that she won particular notoriety. Wearing a sword at her side and with her hair cut short, she performed sexually suggestive dances with a male partner who was dressed in the guise of a female prostitute. Before long, dances of the type performed by O-Kuni and her troupe were being referred to as *kabuki odori*, after the verb 'kabuku', which meant to dress flamboyantly and behave in an outrageous or licentious manner.[32] This style of dancing was quickly taken up by professional courtesans, some of whom then assumed masculine, macho-sounding names. By the second decade of the seventeenth century, courtesans were setting up a temporary stage three times a year at the crossroads between Shijō and Kawaramachi, two major thoroughfares in central Kyōto. Sometimes, fifty or sixty women would dance in unison. Many of their dances were notoriously lascivious, but the courtesans also performed the refined and contemplative plays of the noh tradition. Courtesans were the first to popularise the *shamisen*, which was introduced to mainland Japan in the middle of the sixteenth century as a modified form of the snakeskin-bellied stringed instrument of the Ryūkyū Islands, the *jabisen*. The popularity of dancing courtesans soon spread to Edo, and the rowdy crowds which such performances attracted provided Japan's rulers with a convenient excuse for confining prostitutes in officially recognised brothel quarters. In 1629 the Tokugawa government banned women from performing in public. The public stage, thereafter, officially became the exclusive domain of male actors and male musicians. With encouragement from the Shogunate, *kabuki odori* rapidly took on much more of a dramatic character, and before long evolved into kabuki theatre.

During the late seventeenth century and into the eighteenth, the licensed brothel quarters of Edo, Kyōto and Ōsaka prided themselves on their most exclusive, highly cultured courtesans, the *tayū*. Mastery of musical instruments such as the *shamisen*, *koto*, flute and hand-drums, as well as of song and dance, usually formed part of their arsenal of accomplishments (others might include calligraphy, painting, poetry and even the ancient board games *go* and *shōgi*) with which they might divert their patrons, who were usually lords of regional fiefdoms (*daimyō*) or else the very richest of merchants. But as the Shogunate kept squeezing wealth out of the senior nobility so as to prevent them from accumulating too much power and influence, there was less and less money for the *daimyō* to lavish on their favourite courtesans. The *tayū* had all but disappeared from Japan by the middle of the eighteenth century. It was only after the heyday of the prestigious *tayū* that geishas came into their own as the chief providers of musical entertainment and dance in Japan's brothel quarters.

In Kyōto, where there were several pleasure districts apart from the official brothel quarter Shimabara, licensed teahouses in these areas found it good for business to employ talented musicians and dancers to entertain their customers while they ate and drank. *Geiko* in Kyōto are to the present day associated with these districts, five of which are still in existence, including two in the famous Gion section of the city. Likewise, Edo had geishas outside the official Shin-yoshiwara brothel quarter. From the middle of the eighteenth century onwards, the unofficial but immensely popular pleasure district of Fukagawa became especially famous for its stylish and quick-witted geishas.[33] These geishas were known as *machi geisha*, or town geishas, as opposed to *kuruwa geisha*, the geishas who were registered with geisha houses in the Shin-yoshiwara. *Machi geisha* too were said to derive their origins from dancers, in their case from *odoriko*, who were both prostitutes and performers but who remained outside the jurisdiction of the Shin-yoshiwara quarter and did not belong to brothels. The *machi geisha* of Fukagawa retained the *odoriko's* custom of dressing in an extremely youthful manner: even when they were approaching forty, they continued to wear clothes and coiffures appropriate for virginal girls in their teens. They were said to dress like young women because, ostensibly at least, they were not expected to acquire a protector, while courtesans who had a protector followed the custom of married women and blackened their teeth. Blackened teeth marked out women as sexually experienced adults.[34]

By the middle of the eighteenth century, numerous unofficial pleasure quarters were well established, along with Fukagawa, in Edo. Such districts were known as *okabasho* (similar areas in Kyōto and Ōsaka were generally called *sotomachi*). *Okabasho* establishments were popular, since those of the Shinyoshiwara were perceived increasingly as being formal, stuffy and old-fashioned. Many unauthorised pleasure districts were located (to the horror of westerners visiting Japan in the nineteenth century) close to temples and shrines popular with pilgrims and worshippers. Because temples and shrines directly administered the area in their immediate vicinity, brothels located within such enclaves escaped the jurisdiction of local municipal authorities. In Edo, pleasure quarters also sprang up in areas where traffic naturally converged, especially in districts leading into the metropolis: Senju to the north, Itabashi to the north-west, Naitō-shinjuku to the west, and Shinagawa to the south. These pleasure quarters had semi-official status. The highway that ran through Shinagawa, a district which skirts the Bay of Edo (Tōkyō) towards the south of the metropolis, was the one which foreign officials were obliged to take when travelling between Yokohama and Edo. Shinagawa was notorious among foreigners for being particularly unruly.

For many of the geishas of the *okabasho* districts, art served largely as a pretext. Such geishas were referred to as *korobi geisha* – 'stumbling geisha' – because they were said to dance badly. 'Stumbling' was also a euphemism for prostitution. Laurence Oliphant, private secretary to Lord Elgin, who in 1858 concluded the first trade treaty between Britain and Japan, reported in his lively account of the diplomatic mission to the Far East that for more than a mile along the main thoroughfare leading through Shinagawa both sides of the road were lined with buildings notable for their deep verandas. These establishments, Oliphant wrote, 'seemed literally packed with the unfortunate victims of a system which is one of the most singular characteristics of the country'.[35] Rodolphe Lindau refers to these places as 'djoro-ïas', or brothels, although, strictly speaking, the establishments in Shinagawa were not legally entitled to employ courtesans even towards the end of the Tokugawa Shogunate's two and a half centuries in power. According to Lindau, the 'djoro-ïas' of Shinagawa served the idle young men of Edo as places of debauch.[36]

In provincial towns around Japan, there were women who – having fallen on hard times – resorted to what musical accomplishments they had mastered in more prosperous days to eke out a meagre existence for themselves and their families. Humble female musicians were present, for instance, in Nagasaki from the early eighteenth century onwards. Professional, well-trained geishas, on the other hand, are known to have travelled down to Nagasaki from Ōsaka in the early 1780s. Their arrival caused bitter resentment among local courtesans: not only were the geishas from Ōsaka better looking, better dressed, more talented and stylish, but they were not averse to selling their favours either. Attempts were made to get the local authorities to oust the incomers. But when, in 1817, the authorities did finally ban geishas other than local ones from working in Nagasaki, the home-grown talent became complacent and soon abandoned all pretence of being artistes. Brothel proprietors began to clamour for the return of well-trained geishas from Ōsaka, and the local authorities eventually acquiesced.

Thus the demi-monde in Japan was large, and varied from area to area. Along with many other aspects of Japanese society, its complexity perplexed visitors from abroad. But even as western observers were trying to make sense of the structure of Japanese society as they found it in the middle of the nineteenth century, the whole edifice began to undergo a rapid transformation, driven by the seismic political upheavals that shook the country. The new imperial regime which took over the reins of government from the Tokugawa Shogunate brought in radical social reforms. The old feudal caste system – in which the samurai took precedence and were followed, in descending order, by farmers, artisans, merchants, and finally a separate class of 'untouchables' (*eta*) at the very bottom – was abolished. In 1871, intermarriage between all classes was legalised. Commoners were given the freedom to move around the country and to choose their own profession, as well as the right to dispose of their land as they wished. Class-specific sartorial codes were dropped. In 1876, the carrying of swords, which was formerly the privilege of the samurai, was forbidden to all except military personnel serving with the new imperial armed forces, police officers and members of the nobility as part of their full court dress.

The year 1872 saw the abolition of the centuries-old tradition of indentured prostitution. In the autumn of that year, the Meiji government issued an edict which prohibited the trafficking of human beings under the pretext of indentured service. All courtesans and prostitutes were forthwith liberated from their bonds of service. The custom had been for women to join a brothel for a set number of years in exchange for a payment of a sum of money, which they were then expected to pay back from their earnings, along with the debts they incurred while in service, including living and wardrobe expenses. In the summer of 1872, an international incident occurred which threw a spotlight on this use of indentured labour in Japanese brothels. A Peruvian barque, the *Maria Luz*, which was transporting a 'cargo' of around 230 Chinese coolies from Macao to South America, where they were intended for slave labour, was undergoing emergency repairs in Yokohama Harbour when a couple of the men escaped. This raised the question of the legal status of the Chinese labourers. The captain of the *Maria Luz* brought a suit to force the coolies to fulfil their contracts of indentureship. Frederick V. Dickens, the British barrister representing the Peruvians, argued that the contracts by which these men were bound to service could not be considered a contravention of Japanese law since they constituted no more a violation of the men's personal liberty than the legitimate contracts which in Japan bound indentured courtesans to their masters.[37]

There were suggestions made at the time by the foreign press based in Yokohama that Dickens's argument shamed the Japanese government into acting on forced prostitution. A process of consultation on the reform of the country's traditional system of organised prostitution had, however, already been in progress for several years. It had been set in motion by the emperor's new ministers (particularly Etō Shinpei, the justice minister between 1872 and 1873) who were keen to demonstrate to the world that Japan was ready to join western countries in the forefront of modern nations. In any case, the immediate effect of the 1872 edict was to empty the old brothel quarters of their inmates. It seemed that the traditional *jorōya* had been put out of business for good.

But prostitution did not disappear, nor did this edict signal the end of state-licensed prostitution. Across Japan, many former courtesans and prostitutes, as well as *meshimori onna*, found themselves without means of support. Their families were often unwilling – or unable because of sheer poverty – to take them back. The municipal government of Tōkyō began almost immediately to issue licences to women who declared an interest in continuing their former profession. Licences were also granted for the running of *kashizashiki*. On paper, a proprietor of a *kashizashiki* merely rented out rooms. In actuality the rooms were let to prostitutes. The pretext was that a *kashizashiki* offered women who wanted to work as prostitutes the accommodation from which they could carry on their business. In 1873 the government of Tōkyō introduced legislation regularising the licensing of *kashizashiki*, restricting them to five areas of the city (a sixth was added three years later). Many of the old brothels in Shin-yoshiwara, as well as the inns and teahouses which flourished in the four posting stations around Tōkyō, were re-licensed as *kashizashiki*.[38] This meant that by 1876 the number of officially recognised pleasure quarters had actually increased from one to six. Women who 'wanted' to work as prostitutes had to be fifteen years of age or older. It was illegal for a proprietor of a *kashizashiki* to compel the women who rented his rooms to prostitute themselves in order to pay back debts which they owed him. Women who entered into an agreement with the proprietor of a *kashizashiki* did so on the pretext that each was acting of her own free volition. The reality was different. Money was advanced to the women's families, and the prostitutes had to work to pay it back. The circumstances which led women (or their families) to 'borrow' money from proprietors of *kashizashiki* were not very different from what they had always been. If anything, the social upheavals which accompanied the recent regime change had impoverished families who found it difficult to adapt to the new conditions. There were, of course, numerous illegal, unlicensed prostitutes too, working clandestinely in various parts of Tōkyō.

This reorganisation of the pleasure quarters meant that there was often a gap between the expectations, or preconceptions, of foreign visitors to Japan, based on reports dating from various periods during the time the Tokugawa Shogunate was still in power, and the present reality. The Swiss diplomat and trade negotiator Aimé Humbert, for instance, conjures up a sumptuous picture of the Shin-yoshiwara brothel quarter in his lively account of Japan. He evokes visions of the grandest of the Yoshiwara courtesans parading the main boulevard of the quarter, resplendent in their tastefully appointed luxurious finery. He sets scenes of refined merry-making in the salons of the main teahouse, where professional musicians and dancers perform their graceful arts and men of the world engage in witty banter with one or another of the charming denizens of the quarter. Yet Humbert, who was in Japan between 1863 and 1864 as the head of a delegation of Swiss manufacturers, notes that the Yoshiwara was at the time still firmly off bounds to foreigners. So detailed and intimate are Humbert's descriptions of the Yoshiwara that it is difficult not to believe that they were sketched from direct observation. Humbert makes clear his own personal abhorrence of the way prostitution was officially condoned in the brothel quarters of Japan. He believed the legalisation of prostitution in Japan had all to do with taxation and surveillance, and very little with the safeguarding of public health and public morality, which, in any case, the ready accessibility of pleasure quarters, he felt, did nothing to improve. Yet Humbert cannot resist the temptation to let his imagination wander freely in a forbidden pleasure garden of visual delights, a timeless realm which remained impervious to the paroxysms of historical change, of which his own presence in the country was a portent.[39]

No doubt many visitors to Japan in the last decades of the nineteenth century expected (or at least wanted) to find their fantasies of opulently dressed courtesans languorously gliding through elegant surroundings to be true. But the world of the brothel quarters depicted in eighteenth- and early nineteenth-century *ukiyoe* woodblock prints was fast disappearing. The high-ranking courtesan, or *oiran*,[40] such as Humbert describes, with her aureole of thick

1 Hand-tinted picture postcard of an *oiran* (*Scènes de la vie en Chine et au Japon*, No. 263), early twentieth century.

tortoiseshell hairpins and extravagantly embroidered kimono, accompanied by an entourage of attendants (including young girls known as *kamuro*[41]), was so familiar from *ukiyoe* prints that, in the west, she quickly became the iconic image of the Japanese *demi-mondaine*, to the extent that she was soon being mistaken for the geisha. Yet she was turning into an anachronistic figure in her native Japan. J.E. de Becker, a British lawyer who produced a scholarly historical and social study of the Shin-yoshiwara in 1899 (first published anonymously in Yokohama), reported that the former, traditional rankings of courtesans no longer applied in the quarter by the time he was writing. The women were now divided into nine categories according to how expensive they were, which largely depended on how luxurious and well appointed the establishment was to which they belonged. De Becker noted that only five of the 126 brothels in the Shin-yoshiwara quarter were currently of the first class and only four of the second class, all the rest being of the bottom rank. There no longer were many *oiran* left. Besides, prostitutes, and courtesans generally, ceased to dress according to the dictates of rank: the choice of costume was left to the inclination of the brothel owner or to the taste of the individual woman. Some still dressed in the traditional style of the *oiran*, but kimonos were not as fine in quality as they had once been. Many courtesans chose instead to appear in more delicate, figured silk crêpe kimonos in order to look younger, or they adopted the chic style of fashionable geishas, or they dressed formally in kimonos dyed a single colour and marked with a family crest.[42]

The journalist Henry Norman, who claimed to be the first non-Japanese to be permitted a tour of the Shin-yoshiwara, describes in *The Real Japan* the procession of courtesans to which Humbert refers. According to Norman, these stately parades took place in the district three times a year: at cherry-blossom time, in early summer when the irises opened, and finally in the autumn when the chrysanthemums were in bloom. Norman dwells on the ritualistic appearance of the elaborately and heavily costumed women, who took very slow, deliberate, curiously choreographed steps in their tall three-toothed pattens (*geta*). He emphasises the solemnity of these occasions, witnessed in awed silence by dense crowds, who flocked to the quarter specifically for the spectacle.[43] But in reality these processions were a dying custom throughout Japan. In former times, the highest ranking courtesans of the pleasure quarters used to walk with great ceremony from the *okiya*, the brothel where they lived, to the *ageya*, the places of entertainment to which they were summoned to meet their clients. The courtesans would be accompanied by many attendants. Such processions were called the *dōchū*. Even after the demise of the prestigious *tayū* after the middle of the eighteenth century, courtesans continued to parade up and down the thoroughfares of the brothel quarters, and process in great style from their *okiya* to the teahouses (*hikitejaya*) where they presided at banquets. When *hikitejaya* (where lower-ranking courtesans had always entertained their clients) were no longer permitted to have couples sleep together on their premises, the custom arose for attendants at the *hikitejaya* to escort patrons on to the brothel which they favoured. Courtesans no longer had a reason to commute to the teahouses, and the *dōchū* lost its practical function. Nonetheless, the parading retained its importance as a public event. But De Becker reported in 1899 that the last time one of these processions took place in the Shin-yoshiwara quarter was in 1887. In Kyōto, the practice was actually resurrected in the 1870s as a ploy to draw tourists back to the official Shimabara brothel quarter, which had been in a steep decline for nearly a century owing to the popularity of the Gion districts to the east of the city.

Whilst Aimé Humbert's descriptions of the Shin-yoshiwara quarter convey an idea of the stratification of the types of prostitute who worked there, such distinctions between the ranks of courtesans were in reality becoming blurred. Humbert describes how various categories of women were available at the Yoshiwara to suit clients of all social classes, budget and tastes, from the most exclusive intended for rich men with aesthetic leanings, to the women shown like caged animals behind wide, barred windows, and, at the very bottom of the pecking order, the slovenly women who occupied the hovels around the edges of the quarter. If Humbert's evocation of the cultured courtesan of the top class drew heavily on his imagination, so did his depictions of the lower end of the scale. Humbert dwells particularly on the prostitutes who inhabited single rooms which opened directly on to the narrow alleyways that criss-crossed the Shin-yoshiwara quarter. He muses lyrically on how this sort of setting just might make a petit bourgeois feel at home, thus entrapping him with an illusion of cheery ordinariness. What other surrounding could make a client of prostitutes fool himself into believing he had at last found true love, so that he would be driven to kill himself (as Humbert had been assured men did in Japan), together with his prostitute lover, when the realisation finally dawned that he would never be able to afford to buy her her freedom?[44] In truth, these small rooms were not peopled by Humbert's piteous, loving females, but by the most impoverished and desperate of prostitutes. They were often those who were no longer able to find work in even the shabbiest of the genteel brothels, and they tended to be older women. They were each allotted a single room, a row of which constituted one long building. These structures were characteristic of the rougher end of unofficial pleasure districts around Edo. They began to appear in the Shin-yoshiwara around the second decade of the nineteenth century when the quarter began catering to a wider, less exclusive clientele. The alleyways between the long houses were so narrow that two people could not walk abreast, and they could be blocked off at either end by pimps to trap unwary passers-by.

Women would then pull potential customers forcibly into their rooms. Brothels of this type were commonly referred to as *tsubonemise* ('apartment' brothels) or *nagayamise* ('tenement' brothels). They were otherwise known as *kirimise* because they charged customers according to how many units of time they spent with a prostitute.

The mystique of the higher-class courtesan faded all around Japan in the latter half of the nineteenth century. The appeal of the geisha, on the other hand, remained strong. In the Shin-yoshiwara, the geisha's traditional role had been to entertain patrons in *hikitejaya* teahouses while they waited for their chosen prostitutes at one of the more exclusive of the brothels to become available, but plenty of men went to the quarter specifically to be entertained by geishas and their male counterparts, male performers known as *taikomochi* or *hōkan*. Meanwhile, in Ōsaka, the traditional *yūjo* (courtesan) was officially replaced in 1878 by two classes of women: *shōgi*, who were licensed prostitutes, and the *geigi* (or *geiko*) – both alternative terms for the geisha – who were forbidden by law to prostitute themselves, a proscription, however, that was rescinded the following year. This meant that the *geigi* of Ōsaka, unlike the geishas of the Shin-yoshiwara quarter in Tōkyō, were not banned from prostitution: yet they were not licensed prostitutes, nor were they, strictly speaking, unlicensed prostitutes (*shishō*) either. A *geigi* often took a rich protector who was able to pay for her to continue with her music and dance training. He shouldered the cost of her wardrobe, and (in Kyōto especially) the expense involved in putting on seasonal public recitals. In return for the financial support, the woman became, in effect, her *danna*'s mistress, an extra-marital comforter in whose company he could put aside the burden of familial duties. The ambiguity of the *geigi*'s position continued for some time even after 1956 when geisha houses ceased to follow the ancient custom of indenturing women to service.[45]

A similar kind of ambiguity extended to the character of those women who could be hired in entertainment districts of cities, resorts and hot spring spa towns all over Japan – wherever there was a cluster of restaurants and inns – to attend a person at dinner and sing and dance for his amusement. Such women too were called geishas. These geishas were commonly available for sex. Geishas were also called out to meet clients at a special type of teahouse termed a *machiaijaya*. Known as *machiai* for short, these places were not licensed to prepare meals: if a client wanted to dine, dishes were delivered by a restaurant. *Machiai* were venues for prostitution. Nonetheless, these women, like the geishas of the Shin-yoshiwara, were required to be registered with a local geisha house, to which they were bound by contract. There were various kinds of contract which set out how a geisha's earnings were to be divided between her and the proprietor of her geisha house, as well as who was to pay for her food, board and clothes. A term was set within which time the geisha had to pay off her initial debt: the lump sum which had been advanced to her parents or guardian when she was first indentured to her geisha house. A geisha who failed to earn enough to repay her debt did not regain her freedom. Often, she was 'sold' on, along with her debt, to a different geisha house. In these ways geishas were distinguished from unregistered (illegal) prostitutes and streetwalkers, who fended for themselves. Geisha houses were organised into a local guild, which in turn formed an association with the restaurants and *machiai* (or with restaurant-inns in spa towns and other districts without *machiai* teahouses) to which the geisha houses sent their geishas. The proprietors of these restaurants and teahouses knew all the geishas within their own association, were familiar with the fee each geisha commanded, and could recommend women to first-time clients. Whenever a patron asked for a particular geisha, the proprietor would send the request on to the *kenban*, which operated as the headquarters of the geisha guild. The *kenban* acted as a clearing office in other ways. For example, a geisha's fees were included in the bill charged to a patron's account with the restaurant or *machiai*, and when the patron paid off his account, the proprietor of the establishment passed on what was owed to various geishas to the *kenban*, whence the money would be paid to the geisha houses. The *kenban* was also responsible for maintaining artistic standards, and many organised formal lessons for the geishas in their area.[46]

Machiai teahouses were popular in the last decades of the nineteenth and the first couple of decades of the twentieth centuries. After that, the novelty of the newfangled, so-called 'cafés', where waitresses doubled as prostitutes, began to draw clients away, and geishas were increasingly regarded as being out of touch with the times. On the other hand, artistic achievement was taken seriously, although the geishas who proved less adept at music or dance than their colleagues were not thereby necessarily disqualified from the profession, and standards varied from quarter to quarter. Various western writers suggested that Japanese geishas were of no more, if no less, easy virtue than actresses, ballet dancers and music hall artistes were in Europe and America. After all, socially respectable gentlemen were known to haunt the greenrooms of western theatres in pursuit of actresses and danseuses. Through the French Second Empire under Emperor Napoléon III and into the belle époque, celebrated actresses, singers and dancers such as the French soprano Hortense Schneider (who created the title roles in Jacques Offenbach's operettas *La belle Hélène* (1864) and *La Grande-Duchesse de Gérolstein* (1867)), the actress and singer Alice Ozy, the actress Jeanne de Tourbey, the dancer Céleste Mogador, the British actress Lillie Langtry and the Folies Bergère dancer Liane de Pougy among others, became just as famous for their liaisons as for their stage presence. Henry

Norman light-heartedly confessed to indulging in little innocent flirtations with geishas during his otherwise solitary meals at teahouses. He merely noted that a geisha's amours were 'left theoretically in her own hands'. He thought some geishas certainly remained chaste, while others found themselves a lover. A very popular girl might become unavailable all of a sudden, and patrons requesting her presence at their table would be told she had 'retired'. If a geisha was fortunate to win a lover who was enamoured of her enough to buy her her liberty, she usually remained, for her part, more or less faithful to him, if only out of gratitude. But some former geishas, Norman remarked, found being settled unbearably tedious, while many more were resigned to the probability that their new-found security would come to an end sooner rather than later.[47]

The enthusiastic American tourist Henry Finck was certainly not disturbed by suppositions about the geisha's 'frailty of character'. He felt it was important not to 'confound the geisha with the joro [prostitute]'. Finck was happy to admit that unless a foreigner was either a teacher or a missionary, he was quite unlikely to meet a lady of the better classes. Even if a fellow managed to forge an acquaintance with a Japanese gentleman, it was useless to expect an invitation to his home to meet his wife. The Japanese did not take their friends home. Unlike the disdainful narrator of Pierre Loti's semi-autobiographical novel *Madame Chrysanthème* (1887), who is attracted to the air of hauteur he reads into the attitude of women he assumes are better born than his own temporary 'wife', Finck was not particularly afflicted by social snobbery. He was not especially disappointed that he did not have much opportunity to observe aristocratic Japanese ladies at close quarters. In any case, he was happy to believe that the most attractive women in Japan were to be found at teahouses and restaurants, among the waiting maids and geishas, who, he had been told, were chosen specifically for their beauty and their cultural attainments. Finck feared for neither his reputation nor his moral well-being in attending dinners presided over by geishas. On the contrary, he strongly recommended the experience. For him, a 'real' Japanese banquet – sampling curious Japanese dishes while being waited on by exotic, slightly risqué geishas – was an 'indispensable' part of a tourist's itinerary while in Tōkyō. Nor did Finck think that being female should deter a tourist from availing herself of this very Japanese cultural experience. He reassured his readers that even though the Japanese themselves did not take their own womenfolk to such dinners, no 'breach of propriety' ever occurred on these occasions that might offend or upset a western lady traveller.[48] For the likes of Norman and Finck, who fancied themselves men of the world, the existence of geishas did not indicate that the Japanese were any less decent than western societies. Geishas merely pointed to a universal need for men to occasionally escape the family hearth and enjoy evenings spiced up by professional female charm.

2 'Cherry Blossom at Yoshiwara, Yokohama' (The 'Ellanbee' Japanese Series, No. 137), early twentieth century hand-tinted picture postcard.

While Henry Finck was recommending the geisha experience to fellow tourists, the outward trappings of Japan's open sex trade were becoming the object of the voyeuristic curiosity of western sightseers. They could ease their conscience (if it needed easing) by telling themselves they were merely confirming, by personal observation, what publications such as *Manners and Customs of the Japanese* had, after all, singled out as one of the most striking peculiarities of the Japanese race.[49] A description of *harimise* in the Shin-yoshiwara quarter of Tōkyō appears in the revised, fifth edition (published in 1899) of Murray's *Handbook for Travellers in Japan*, compiled by W.B. Mason and the famous Japanologist Basil Hall Chamberlain. The 'unfortunate inmates', who are 'decked out in gorgeous raiment', can be seen, according to the guidebook, sitting in rows against gold screens, and 'protected from the outside by iron bars'. An eerie orderliness is said to pervade the entire district, and readers are invited to take advantage of a sightseeing tour of the area to ponder the relative effectiveness of the various attempts made by public authorities all over the world to deal with 'one of the vexed questions of all ages'.[50] By contrast, the revised edition of *Terry's Guide to the Japanese Empire*, which was published in the United States in 1928, offers a conventional slice of Japanese picturesqueness that might appeal to a tourist's hunger for the exotic: referring to the Maruyama pleasure quarter in Nagasaki, a city which had been made all the more famous by the success of the opera *Madama Butterfly*, *Terry's Guide* informs its readers that

> when throaty voiced geisha sing the native contralto songs[,] the plaintive twanging of the samisen, the swish of silken kimonos and the soft pit-pat of tabi-shod feet are wafted out through the fragrant twilight, the effect is strikingly Oriental. . . .[51]

The relative absence of rowdy behaviour in Japanese pleasure quarters – either on the part of customers or the women themselves – certainly contributed to the picturesque attraction that these districts had for tourists from abroad. The smooth, well-organised efficiency with which the pleasure quarters appeared to be run provoked mixed, often contradictory responses from foreign observers. On the one hand, critics (among them Carl Peter Thunberg back in the second half of the eighteenth century) accused public officials in Japan of condoning, if not actively promoting, licentious behaviour among its people by recognising prostitution as a legal activity so long as it adhered to official regulations. However, many other observers noted that this policy of confining prostitution to approved areas appeared to be effective in removing undesirable activity from other parts of Japanese cities. William Elliot Griffis, who taught physics and chemistry in Japan from 1870 to 1874, declared in *The Mikado's Empire* (1876) that it was perfectly possible to live in the Japanese capital without ever becoming aware of the existence of what he called the 'moral leprosy' of prostitution. Japanese people were spared, even at night, the sight so common in major western cities of women touting for trade.[52]

In metropolises such as London, Paris and New York, it had become a common complaint by the middle of the nineteenth century that prostitutes and courtesans were brazenly flaunting their presence in public. In 1870 the *commissaire interrogateur* for the Paris police, Charles Lecour, wrote of illegal prostitutes that

> [t]hey are everywhere, in the brasseries, the cafés-concerts, the theaters and the balls. One encounters them in public establishments, railway stations, even railway carriages. There are some of them on all the promenades in front of most of the cafés. Late into the night, they circulate in great numbers on the most beautiful boulevards, to the great scandal of the public[.][53]

Gentlemen protested that they could not take their female relations along the Haymarket, the Boulevard des Italiens or Broadway without the delicate sensibilities of the ladies being insulted by the sight of prostitutes.[54]

Observations by western commentators about the state regulation of prostitution in Japan were not made in a vacuum, for prostitution was a much-discussed social issue in Europe and America during the nineteenth century. Like the Japanese, the French had been contemplating ways in which prostitutes might be identified and placed under official surveillance. The French writer Nicolas-Edme Restif de la Bretonne, in his book *Le Pornographe* (1769), had advocated segregating prostitutes in government-regulated institutions which he called *parthénions*. Conduct in the *parthénions* would be strictly monitored, and inmates would have to undergo a daily medical examination. One of Restif de la Bretonne's ideas was to make the presence of prostitution as unobtrusive as possible, and to this end he proposed that the *parthénions* should be built in less populated areas of a city – rather as the Shin-yoshiwara *yūkaku* was in Edo in the seventeenth century. What actually happened was that, for much of the nineteenth century, brothels in Paris were suffered to exist by the police. Known as *maisons de tolérance*, they were not sequestered in remote corners, as De la Bretonne had suggested they should be, but existed alongside other ordinary city premises, their only distinguishing characteristic being that their windows remained shuttered even in daytime. *Maisons de tolérance* were, however, kept under observation by the police. Their number decreased in the middle of the century when swathes of old Paris were destroyed in the 1860s to make way for Napoléon III's new boulevards, under the supervision of the civic administrator Georges-Eugène Haussmann. There was an accompanying upsurge in the number of unregistered prostitutes in the city, while surviving up-market *maisons* transformed themselves into specialist brothels, offering fantasy, discretion and luxury to rich and jaded patrons, and smaller brothels turned into *garnis*, lodging houses where (after 1866) prostitution could take place without the landlord being legally responsible for what went on in his building.[55]

The issue that made the question of being able to distinguish prostitutes from respectable women such a pressing one in nineteenth-century Europe was the fear of disease. The prostitutes who worked in Parisian *maisons de tolérance* were required to be registered with the police, and they had to submit to an annual examination for venereal disease.[56] To civic officials, each unregistered, therefore unidentified, prostitute represented an undetected potential carrier of corruption – a source of contamination that remained at large in society. It was this very same fear of venereal disease that made many western military officials posted to Japanese ports support, if not encourage, the state regulation of prostitution in Japan. Preventing the spread of syphilis among their men remained a matter of urgency for western military commanders, and this led to western demands for greater surveillance of the prostitutes in Japanese ports, rather than their eradication. In 1866 a Russian admiral issued regulations directing his men, when in Nagasaki, only to buy women who had been inspected by a Russian doctor. A brothel quarter for the use of Russian sailors had been established in 1860 in the Inasa district of the town, and the women who worked there were known among locals as *matarosu jorō*, after '*matrós*', the Russian word for 'sailor'. Meanwhile, in the brothel quarter of Yokohama, a clinic where prostitutes were inspected for venereal disease was established in 1867 on the recommendation of the British naval physician George Bruce Newton, who held an advisory position under the Tokugawa Shogunate in the very last years of its existence. Newton too seems to have been motivated by a concern to prevent syphilis from spreading among British sailors. He was helping to set up a similar clinic for the Maruyama quarter in Nagasaki when he died in 1871. The inspections do appear to have led to a decrease in the rate of infection among British sailors in Yokohama, but there were problems with compliance on the part of those who had to submit to them: in Yokohama, some of the brothel proprietors refused to have their prostitutes examined, while in Nagasaki many women themselves objected to the examinations.

What started out as a measure to safeguard the health of foreign troops stationed in Japan eventually came to be seen as a domestic health issue. In 1871 prefectural governments throughout Japan were ordered by Tōkyō to introduce health checks in all *yūkaku* under their jurisdiction. VD clinics were opened in the six pleasure quarters of Tōkyō, the one serving Shin-yoshiwara in 1873. Prostitutes there were to undergo three examinations a month. The comte de Dalmas explicitly associated the new '*bureau sanitaire*' in Shin-yoshiwara with the introduction of western-style medicine to Japan, although he considered the examinations the prostitutes underwent to be inadequate. Henry Norman describes in his book how the women were obliged to present themselves every Monday morning at the police station in Shin-yoshiwara for their health examination. Those found to have signs of venereal disease were taken by a policeman to a special hospital, which was ostensibly funded by the *kashizashiki* proprietors, but according to Norman was actually supported by a levy imposed on the women. Despite early difficulties getting brothel owners and women alike to comply with the regulations, by 1876 examinations for venereal disease were regularly being conducted on prostitutes in all officially recognised pleasure quarters across Japan.[57]

Moral corruption seemed a much more insidious problem. At a time when there was a growing fear in Europe that the moral fabric of society, as well as its health, was being undermined by prostitutes marrying into respectable families, visitors to Japan were returning with reports that this very thing was taking place in that country. For instance, Laurence Oliphant claimed in 1859 that it was not uncommon in Japan for courtesans to marry a man of rank. Five years later,

Rodolphe Lindau recollected that during his stay in Japan he had known three instances of courtesans entering polite society by making respectable marriages. There is a suggestion of the stereotypical picture of the eastern libertine picking a mistress for himself at a slave market in C. Pemberton Hodgson's description, in 1861, of 'nobles and grandees' going to one brothel or another to select their wives from a line-up of all the women the particular establishment had to offer. The hugely successful British musical comedy *The Geisha, a Story of a Tea House,* which opened in 1896, played upon this theme, featuring a clownish Japanese nobleman who forces an auction of geishas so that he can purchase another wife to add to his harem. Meanwhile, in 1862, Edward de Fonblanque, echoing the seventeenth-century Dutch East India Company employee Engelbert Kaempfer's view that courtesans were in demand in Japan as wives because they were rigorously brought up, wrote that Japanese men 'of good repute and consideration' (though not noblemen, who had to take dynastic considerations into account in their choice of bride) often married teahouse girls because their training made them excellent managers of large households, an assertion that reflected a western prejudice that what Japanese men predominantly wanted in a wife was a superior type of servant or housekeeper.[58]

Back in Europe, the blurring of the respectable and the non-respectable was a troubling idea. The mid-Victorian English surgeon William Acton, an expert in genito-urinary diseases and author of several works on subjects relating to human sexuality, warned in *Prostitution, Considered in its Moral, Social, & Sanitary Aspects, in London and other Large Cities* (1857) that 'the better inclined class of prostitutes become the wedded wives of men in every grade of society, from the peerage to the stable'.[59] The lack of concrete statistics seems to have contributed to the feeling that a secret menace was creeping through society. In the view of Alexandre Dumas *fils,* prostitutes were seducing decent society with their diseased beauty, their decadent ways and their ill-gotten riches. In December 1867, Dumas *fils* completed a preface for a new edition of his celebrated play *La Dame aux camélias,* which was premiered in 1852, being his own stage adaptation of his 1848 novel of the same title. He had modelled the heroine – a Parisian courtesan named Marguerite Gautier who sacrifices her own happiness for the sake of her lover's honour and that of his family – on Marie Duplessis, a famous Parisian *demi-mondaine* of the 1840s and one-time mistress of Dumas *fils* himself. But in his new preface, Dumas railed bitterly against what he saw as the increasing brazenness of vice. Gone were the decent, tactful, tender-hearted courtesans of earlier times, those who had bloomed so fleetingly in the liberal atmosphere of the July Monarchy – women such as Marie Duplessis. Times had changed. Dumas *fils* warned shrilly that corruption was now insinuating itself into the heart of the most highly regarded families in France. Under the reign of

Napoléon III, courtesans had become ruthless, grasping money-scroungers. At the same time, they were being accepted as wives by scions of the oldest French families so that their wealth might be used to prop up what had hitherto been an honourable inheritance. The very blood of France (*'le sang de la France'*) was becoming tainted.[60]

There was the question of whether a disgraced woman could ever – or should ever – be absolved of the guilt of her sexual transgressions or have her reputation restored, once her body had been, in the western view, irretrievably defiled. The French dancer and courtesan Céleste Vénard (or Veinard), known as Mogador, married her devoted former lover Comte Lionel de Chabrillan in 1854 and accompanied him to Australia, where he served as French consul-general at Melbourne. However, she found herself shunned by much of Melbourne society, and even when she later became a respected novelist, playwright and poet back in France, winning the esteem of both Dumas *père* and *fils*, she was never reconciled with her husband's aristocratic family (one of the earliest and best known of her own works, her memoirs, published in 1854, of her early life as a Parisian *demi-mondaine*, helped keep her former reputation fresh in people's minds). For the many western observers who could not but consider a former Japanese courtesan or geisha indelibly stained for life by her past, the one mitigating factor that lightened the infamy of her condition was the probability that she had not wilfully embraced, or carelessly fallen among, the demi-monde. It was widely pointed out in books on Japan that young women (and even girls) who were sold to brothels by impoverished (or rapacious) parents and guardians were expected to endure their fate for the sake of their families. The upbringing that all Japanese girls were supposed to receive, enjoining obedience and self-sacrifice, meant, it was maintained, that they accepted their fate without complaint or rebellion. Officially, they were bound for a fixed term of years, so, in theory, there came a time when they regained their liberty. It was widely believed in the west that former prostitutes were able to return to their families with their good name intact. Many western commentators, nonetheless, felt uneasy about whether a woman who had once been a courtesan (from whatever worthy, self-sacrificing motive) should be accorded the same respect as a woman who had never been such a thing. The seventeenth-century VOC physician and naturalist Kaempfer proposed that it showed the charitable side of Japanese society that unfortunate courtesans were allowed to marry into respectability, but Carl Peter Thunberg, writing about Japan towards the end of the eighteenth century, found it most 'curious' that some courtesans married 'extremely well' and were not deemed to be 'dishonoured'.[61] Major Henry Knollys of the Royal Artillery, who visited Japan in the 1880s, implied in his volume on his Japanese adventures that without the threat of permanent shame, women were free to behave as they wished with impunity. Unmarried girls in Japan, he declared, entered brazenly into prostitution in order to earn pin money before marriage:

> Many girls devote themselves to three or four years' immorality of set purpose, amass comfortable little sums of money, are warmly welcomed back into the domestic circle, and are regarded as models of filial duty in having thus toiled for the support of their parents. In fact the landmarks between virtue and vice are obliterated.

Knollys believed that this sort of shamelessness among young girls was a direct consequence of the sanitisation by the public authorities in Japan of the outward manifestations of prostitution, by their making sure that pleasure quarters were clean, well maintained and, above all, decorous – unlike the Haymarket or Regent Street in London. By taking away 'that which is externally offensive' about prostitution, the authorities removed its stigma, which would otherwise have had the salutary effect of convincing women of the moral repulsiveness of such activities.[62]

The new ruling class in Japan – the oligarchs, who were largely former samurai from various regional provinces who had spearheaded the movement to overthrow the Tokugawa Shogunate – seemed themselves to be failing to set a salutary example to the common people. Several important figures who had fought for the restoration of imperial rule and had subsequently risen to high ministerial positions under the new Meiji regime were known to be married to former geishas and *oiran*. They included Itō Hirobumi, who in 1885 became Japan's first prime minister, and the state councillor Kido Takayoshi. Such marriages became the subject of gossip among the foreign community. The writer Pierre Loti, who in public life was the French naval officer Julien Viaud, attended a ball in Tōkyō on 3 November 1885 hosted by the Japanese foreign minister Count Inoue Kaoru in celebration of the emperor's birthday. In *Japoneries d'automne* (1889), Loti recounts being told in the train taking foreign guests from Yokohama up to Tōkyō that the foreign minister's wife 'la comtesse Sodeska' (from the Japanese phrase '*sodesuka*' meaning 'is that so?'), whom they were to meet at the ball, had once been a 'guécha'. Having formed, therefore, the expectation of seeing a cheap strumpet dolled up in extravagant finery, Loti confesses his astonishment at finding himself graciously received instead by a lady attired very properly and stylishly *à la parisienne*. Loti appears to have based his countess on Inoue Takeko, the wife of the foreign minister, of whom there were rumours that she had once been a geisha in the Yanagibashi district of Edo, although there is no concrete evidence that either proves or disproves this.[63]

Inoue Takeko was said to have been from a good samurai family. Other ministerial wives who had formerly been geishas and courtesans were similarly reputed to have been of samurai birth. The social turmoil which accompanied the fall of the Tokugawa Shogunate signalled the financial ruin of numerous middle-ranking samurai families that had traditionally relied upon a hereditary stipend from their feudal overlords for their subsistence and had no other means of livelihood. Other samurai families that remained loyal to the Tokugawa regime to the end lost their menfolk in the fighting which broke out between the imperial forces and those who still resisted the transfer of power to the emperor. The British poet and journalist Sir Edwin Arnold, describing the staff he had employed for his household in Japan, gives a glimpse of the reversal of fortunes suffered by the former ruling class in the country. The good-natured, hard-working, beautifully mannered girl, Yoshida Tori, whom Sir Edwin had engaged in Tōkyō as a maid for his daughter, was, he informed his readers, the daughter of a samurai, 'a well-born swordsman'.[64] Where some women, like Yoshida Tori, went into domestic service, others from impoverished samurai families were recruited for the pleasure quarters. Saegusa Ayako, the second wife of the prominent politician Ōkuma Shigenobu, was born the daughter of a retainer of the *shōgun*. According to the memoirs of the wife of one of her husband's friends, Ayako had become an *oiran* at the age of sixteen or seventeen, although she was said never to have taken a lover because of her age.[65] Ryōko, the ravishingly beautiful and elegant wife of the diplomat and politician Mutsu Minemitsu, who became foreign minister in 1892 under Itō's second government, had once been a geisha in the Shinbashi district of Tōkyō. She too was from a samurai family.

But for those foreign observers inclined to be disparaging about the frantic efforts of the Japanese to absorb western practices, the jumped-up pretensions of former geishas who were now being paraded before the foreign community in Japan as the consorts of Japan's new leaders seemed to epitomise the ridiculousness of Japan's attempt to ingratiate itself with the advanced nations of the world. In the Canadian journalist and writer Sara Jeannette Duncan's novel *A Social Departure: How Orthodocia and I Went round the World by Ourselves* (1890), a satire on the vogue for globetrotting based on a voyage Duncan herself made, two lady travellers, one British and the other American, are party to rumours about the marital arrangements of eminently ranked Japanese courtiers:

> Heard to-day of another Japanese Cabinet Minister married to *geisha*, or professional dancer, which makes four. Extraordinary state of things. Example of extent to which Japanese are adopting Western civilisation. . . .[66]

Duncan here pokes fun at the high-society *mésalliances* which were the subject of scandalous gossip at home, and at the same time mocks the Japanese for being farcically indiscriminate in the way they were taking up western ways. The French artist Georges Bigot, whose savage caricatures of the Japanese in the process of westernisation were greatly influenced by his adamant opposition to any reduction in the privileges enjoyed by foreign residents in the treaty ports, satirised in his 1899 collection of sketches entitled *La Journée d'une guesha* the socially elevated former geisha who arrives at a ball sheathed in a western-style dress and on the arm of a strutting little husband in the shape of a mustachioed Japanese nobleman.[67] For Bigot, the geisha-turned-aristocratic wife is doubly an upstart: for in flaunting her married status, she tries to pass herself off as a respectable woman; and in her western ball gown, she seeks to present herself as a denizen of the advanced, civilised (that is to say, western) world.

Alice Bacon, whose *Japanese Girls and Women* (1891) was one of the first western studies devoted to the subject of the position of women in Japanese society, felt it boded ill for the future of Japan if its leaders continued to take geishas and courtesans for their wives, no matter what circumstances had led the women to enter the brothel quarter in the first place. What the situation urgently called for, in her view, was either a reform of male attitudes to women or an over-haul of the way Japanese girls were educated. Bacon readily conceded that men might find geishas more agreeable than their demure, respectable wives, since the former were trained to please men, while the chief attractions the latter had to offer were 'an unsullied name, silent obedience, and faithful service'. Bacon did distinguish between the geisha and the 'jōrō [sic], or licensed prostitute', but she believed nonetheless that the geisha was 'frail' because, sadly, she was given an unsound education which regarded manners more highly than morals. The geisha had very little incentive to behave virtuously. Surrounded by manifold temptations, she was not taught the discipline by which she might resist them.[68]

Awareness among foreign visitors to Japan that the social behaviour of the Japanese was governed by intricate rules of etiquette left many confused as to how they were to interpret the conduct of individual Japanese they encoun-tered. The issue was when (if at all) the outward behaviour of the Japanese could be judged to correspond with their inner intentions. In other words, the diffi-culty was in knowing whether their elaborate displays of courtesy were ever meant sincerely. There was a degree of prejudice against Japanese culture as one dominated by rituals which had long since lost their original meaning. Rules of etiquette as concocted by the Japanese, therefore, were taken as an indication not of the social maturity of the race but of its degeneracy. By mindlessly following the prescribed rules of behaviour set down by tradition, both men and women in Japan were saved the effort of having to think for themselves. Sara Jeannette Duncan's narrator in *A Social Departure* describes well-bred Japanese women as being like deftly handled marionettes, always ready to produce the absolutely correct facial expression for any social situation:

> [They] seemed to control a set of pretty stereotyped expressions, and when the occasion came to pull some hidden string, . . . the proper one flitted out; but always the same quick look that said surprise, or pleasure, or sympathy, or a politely repelled compliment, and never any other, never any shade or degree of feeling. I have not seen anything in conduct so exquisitely without flaw as the 'form' these little ladies exhibited towards one another . . . . all seemed part of a very old work of social art, inlaid and polished so wonderfully that one forgot to inquire its true significance.[69]

These women are no more than moving versions of the figures on Japanese fans, tea chests and other *objets d'art*. With their facial muscles never being required to express real feeling, they have long since forgotten (if they ever knew) how to feel anything for themselves. That they possess the power of speech at all strikes Duncan's narrator as being totally unnecessary. Norma Lorimer, who contributed observations on 'Japan from a Woman's Point of View' to *More Queer Things about Japan* (1904) facetiously suggested that a Japanese woman's day was filled with trivial social ceremonies demanded by etiquette because her insubstantial diet (basically rice and pickles) and her toy-like paper house with its bare furnishings obviously demanded so little in the way of housework as it was properly understood in the west:

> But from her own [point of view] she has very many important duties to perform, for she lives in a land where it is not the working of the elements of human nature which make up the vital things of life, but the observing of minute trifles.

The Japanese woman was not bored out of her wits as might be expected of a western female because one had to have some 'mental independence' in the first place to suffer from 'ennui' when one's spirit was being stifled by outside pressures. An American girl might be less polished than a Japanese one, but at least she had an active mind and was curious about her surroundings.[70]

The mask of polite reserve and courtesy that Japanese women wore – if it were indeed a mask – made it difficult for outsiders to single out the supposedly promiscuous ones. Appearances were deceptive, for girls of whom westerners might have expected outwardly lewd behaviour were observed to behave with faultless politeness. Aimé Humbert noted that open displays of indecency by individuals were hardly ever seen in Japan. Unlike Kaempfer, Humbert did not think there was anything particularly immodest about the behaviour of those female servants of teahouses who stood outside the door in order to entice customers to come inside. Women in similar occupations in the west, he thought, were often much more indecently or negligently dressed than their Japanese counterparts. The American artist John La Farge, who paid a visit to Japan in 1886, confessed he was not sure that a couple of bespectacled young women he had just seen were not actually 'gei-shas' rather than 'ladies' despite the eyeglasses which they wore, since he had been informed that modern geishas were now learning western languages and affecting an intellectual appearance. The French ornithologist the comte de Dalmas, who had been assured of the libertinism of all young Japanese women by a European doctor who claimed that he had seen perhaps only three virgins in the course of five years, was decidedly puzzled by the lack of outward signs by which he himself might pick out the supposedly rare virgin from all the other modest-looking young women in Japan.[71] Only if a woman were encountered in a special context, such as that of a teahouse, could any supposition be made about whether she might be déclassée or not. Even so, Arthur Diósy, founder of the Japan Society in London, explained that unwary western visitors to Japan tended to jump to the hasty conclusion that all Japanese women irrespective of class or background were lax in their sexual morals because foreigners mistakenly assumed from the gentle appearance of women who were found working in teahouses that the gentry in Japan happily sent their daughters away to become geishas and courtesans. Visitors from the west simply could not believe, Diósy wrote, that

> the gentle little woman, with hands like those of a duchess and a low, sweet voice, with exquisite manners and a quaint, solemn kind of dignity in her courteous obei-sances, a curious refinement in the graceful motions of her hands and arms, and delicate, quiet taste displayed in every item of her admirably becoming costume

could be the Japanese social equivalent of

> brazen 'Liza of the New Cut, in her tawdry finery, her ill-made clothing of star-tling aniline hues, her monstrous hat bedecked with hired ostrich plumes – poor 'Liza with her coarse, red hands and her hoarse voice, her manners of the gutter and her wit of the gin-palace bar[.][72]

Not that it was necessarily as easy to identify the prostitutes in a public crowd in nineteenth-century Paris or London or New York as Diósy suggested, either by their clothes or their mannerisms. John Binny wrote in 1862 of 'the troops of elegantly dressed courtesans, rustling in silks and satins, and waving in laces, promenading . . . among throngs of fashionable people' in London, and in the same year the London weekly newspaper the *Saturday Review* complained that it was not easy 'to make out the true character of a vessel from the colours under which she sails'. The French novelist and poet Arsène Houssaye, who was also director of the Comédie-Française (otherwise known as the Théâtre-Français) from 1849 to 1856 and a famous boulevardier to boot, recollected how impossible it had become towards the end of the reign of the Citizen-King Louis-Philippe to tell *coquines* apart from society women, whether it was at charity balls, at the races, or out driving in the fashionable Bois de Boulogne on the outskirts of Paris. If anything, the *demi-mondaines* were more '*chic*', a term which Houssaye believed became current among women around that time. The blurring of the outward distinctions between the respectable and the disreputable was a cause of considerable disquiet throughout European society.[73]

Just as it would have been a mistake to assume that all the women who took the air in the Bois de Boulogne in the nineteenth century were 'respectable', the German geographer J.J. Rein suggested that it was erroneous to presume that a Japanese woman must be of easy virtue just because she worked in a teahouse. Rein felt that the cause of the confusion was the teahouse girl's characteristic eagerness to please. This sort of attentiveness, he thought, was readily misconstrued as coquetry, just as many foreigners found it difficult to accept the 'strikingly trusting and childishly naïve demeanour' of ordinary Japanese women as sincere.[74] Was this childish simplicity and eagerness to please indicative of a remarkable transparency of soul, and was the foreigner guilty of excessive scepticism? Or was it affectation and artifice taken to a high degree of cynicism, and were foreigners right to be suspicious of trickery? Was the demure geisha, despite the environment in which she worked, just as sexually virtuous and altruistic in behaviour as girls whose reputation remained above suspicion? Or were childishly innocent-looking ordinary girls nonetheless enslaved to the lusts of the flesh that civilisation was supposed to tame? Pierre Loti included in his widely read novel *Madame Chrysanthème* (1887) a scene in which the French sailor Yves is mobbed by 'a band of tiny little mousmés of some twelve or fifteen years of age, who barely reached up to his waist, and were pulling him by the sleeve'. The behaviour is interpreted as an attempt to seduce the Frenchman: the girls are described as being '*voulant le mener à mal*' ('anxious to lead him astray'), and Yves is shocked '*les voyant si jeunes, si menues, si bébés, et déjà si effrontées*' ('at seeing such mere babies, so young, so tiny, already so brazen and shameless'). The comte de Dalmas similarly described young Japanese girls as having little reserve. When they did show any degree of modesty, he wrote, it was nothing but a calculated sham.[75]

The debate over how the behaviour of Japanese women ought to be interpreted reflected a wider disagreement among western commentators over the nature of

Japanese culture in general. There were those who considered the Japanese, for better or worse, to be closer to the natural state than were the races in the advanced west. For example, Japan was characterised in some quarters as an indolent, idyllic Pacific island-relict of the Golden Age – like another Tahiti, to whose people some observers thought the people of southern Japan bore a good deal of resemblance with regard to skin colour and general physique. John La Farge debated with his travelling companions whether the Japanese passion for bathing was 'a reminiscence of Polynesian ancestry', or whether it was merely due to exigencies of the local climate. Aimé Humbert wrote that a temperate climate and fertile land meant that the people of Japan did not have to work very hard to support their modest way of life. Living still in an age of innocence, they worked only so that they might live, and they lived to enjoy themselves. The Australian artist Mortimer Menpes maintained that 'the struggle for life does not exist there [i.e. in Japan] as in other countries'. It was a commonplace to describe the Japanese as a pleasure-loving race.[76]

Other commentators disagreed that the Japanese could afford to be indolent. Life in Japan was harsh, and if they lived simply, it was not because nature's bounty provided them with all they desired without the necessity of labour, but because the Japanese had learned to go without. The sixteenth-century Jesuit missionary Alessandro Valignano described in his letters to his superiors back in Europe how the Japanese, both rich and poor alike, bore with stoical patience the many physical discomforts of their way of life. They endured the cold during the winter months, and hunger was not uncommon. Engelbert Kaempfer characterised the Japanese as a race of indefatigable workers, inured to hardship and requiring very little to sustain themselves. They went about 'bare-headed and bare-legg'd', and eschewed the use of soft pillows, sleeping on the ground instead. In 1795 Carl Peter Thunberg remarked on the frugality of the Japanese, as did J.J. Rein a century later. Edward de Fonblanque wrote that '[t]hose well-built, muscular men, who stand erect at their doors, holding their little children by the hand' possessed 'a sense of liberty and self-respect never to be met with in a race of slaves or cowards'. Here was a country where men were content, like the ancient Greeks, to live simply and to defend themselves with valour. The first British minister and consul-general to Japan, Rutherford Alcock, in referring to the sparse, austere furnishings of a typical Japanese room, commented that there was 'something to admire in this Spartan simplicity of habits'. The 'universal absence of luxury' meant that people could survive on very little, and so remain self-sufficient and self-reliant. By thus avoiding dependency on outside powers to satisfy their wants, the Japanese had managed to preserve their freedom. Alcock had a generally low estimation of the state of civilisation among the Japanese when the country was finally opened up to wider international commerce. But he did consider them to be praiseworthy for having something they valued above mere material existence: their honour. In Alcock's eyes, this meant that the Japanese, for all their shortcomings, had attained a basic level of civilisation, for in his view, being civilised meant being able to be motivated by altruistic sentiments such as duty and patriotism.[77]

The flipside to this Japanese affinity with nature – this culture they had developed out of the idea of paring everything down to the bare essentials – seemed to be that they had not yet evolved the basic concept of modesty. For one thing, there seemed to be a striking lack of reticence in both speech and print. The published account of Commodore Perry's expedition to Japan mentions that books of popular literature on sale in Japanese bookshops often included 'obscene pictorial illustrations'. Rear Admiral George Henry Preble recorded in his diary that one of the gifts presented to Commodore Perry by the Japanese consisted of 'a box of obscene paintings of naked men and women'. Rutherford Alcock disapproved of what he considered to be a 'wide-spread taste for gross and obscene productions', manifested in the form of books and phallic-shaped children's toys. Raphael Pumpelly, an American geologist, informed the readers of his account of Japan that not only was there an 'immense range of light literature, illustrated with woodcuts, that often approach the obscene', but also explicit 'representations of the *phallus*', which were on open display. One example of the latter which he had come across had consisted of a group of fifteen or more shafts, all made of sandstone and standing from 'a few inches to two feet long', which had been 'erect[ed] around a central column containing a cavity either intended to hold a lantern or an incense-burner'.[78]

The Japanese appeared to have no reservations when it came to talking about sexual matters, even when women, unmarried young girls and children were present. Pumpelly reported that women went to the theatre and watched scenes of 'extreme grossness'. This struck him as an indication of the absence among the Japanese 'of that moral refinement which, with us, is considered so necessary as a safeguard for female purity'. The comte de Dalmas declared himself stupefied to have been asked on one occasion by the obsequious landlord of an inn (in front of the latter's wife and young daughters, moreover) whether 'French women were made like Japanese ones'. Then there was the time a girl hardly seven years of age had made explicit and insistent gestures to him, which the count could only interpret as an invitation for him to go and fondle the girl's servant. Dalmas explained to his readers that in Japan everyone – even the youngest girls – knew about things which were carefully kept from children in France.[79] Both Bishop George Smith and the eminent Austrian diplomat Baron Joseph Alexander von Hübner, who visited Japan between July and October 1871 in order to make a study of its people, have left accounts of how references to sex seemed to elicit not embarrassment, shame or indignation among the Japanese, but laughter and hilarity instead, particularly among women. Bishop Smith was horrified to observe women in mixed company pointing at and laughing over 'scenes which would have produced confusion and embarrassment in the female circles of Europe'.[80]

There were some, however, who warned against jumping to conclusions. Just because sexual matters were openly talked about among the Japanese, it did not necessarily follow that they behaved in a lascivious or promiscuous manner. Aimé Humbert, for instance, noted that indecent language was used by all classes of Japanese society, but felt it was a mistake to assume this frankness of speech was proof that the Japanese were especially licentious or had loose morals. The British industrial designer Christopher Dresser, who paid a whirlwind three-month visit to Japan in 1876–77 in order, among other things, to investigate the state of artistic production and manufacture in the country for the British government, discovered that unreserved conversation was not necessarily a prelude to wanton behaviour. In *Japan, its Architecture, Art and Art Manufactures* (1882), he describes a banquet he attended which had been given in the 'native' style by western diplomats at a fashionable teahouse, where, Dresser understood, Japanese government ministers held state dinners. Towards the end, he had become aware that the geishas in attendance were dropping 'strange innuendoes not admissible in English society'. Yet, Dresser noted, there had been no 'coarseness'. It was as though such talk was merely a social convention. The Victorian traveller and writer Isabella Bird felt this 'latitude of speech' was 'very offensive to English ideas of delicacy', but she did not regard it as evidence that Japanese women were not either virtuous or faithful – although she did regret that it appeared to rob Japanese children of 'that purity and innocence which are among the greatest charms of children at home'.[81]

Western opinion was likewise split about the apparent Japanese insouciance about nakedness. Bishop Smith complained in 1861 of the ubiquitous *norimono*-bearers, those sinewy men who conveyed passengers in large panniers slung on poles and commonly stripped down to their loincloths when it was warm, that their appearance offended one's sense of 'decency' (if one happened to have one), and sorely tried the delicate sensibilities of western (if not local) ladies. Two years later, Rutherford Alcock remarked that during the summer months matrons were generally to be observed 'uncovered to the waist', often with a 'copper-coloured "marmot" hanging to the breast'.[82] But it was the Japanese practice of communal bathing as well as the custom of bathing in the open during hot weather that attracted particular attention. Such practices seemed to confirm that the Japanese lacked a fundamental notion of modesty. Jorges Álvares, the first European to write a first-hand account of life in Japan (which he did at the behest of St Francis Xavier in 1547), reported that the Japanese '[did] not worry at all if their privy parts [were] seen' while they were washing themselves.[83] In the second half of the eighteenth century, Thunberg was shocked to observe that Japanese women bathed occasionally in the open, regardless of whether or not they could be seen by passers-by, and that when doing so, they did not, moreover, bother to cover their nakedness, even when they knew Dutchmen were looking at them. Eighty-five years later, Edward de Fonblanque was scandalised when, as he travelled along a road near Nagasaki on a summer's day in 1860, he found himself confronted by the sight of three generations of a single family who had all rushed out of their house 'stark naked' in order to stare at him. There had been an ancient-looking patriarch, two old women, the paterfamilias, his wife, and six or so children ranging in age from about eighteen to six. C. Pemberton Hodgson had similar experiences. He had been 'fearfully horrified' when people of both sexes came rushing out of a communal bathhouse, all in the nude, so they might gawp at him as he rode past. From such experiences, Hodgson pronounced that an 'open and undisguised licentiousness ... prevail[ed] in every rank of this people'.[84]

A more limited number of western observers found it possible to entertain the idea that even though a group of people followed practices which would be considered indecent in western society, this did not, in itself, prove that they were inherently corrupt. Captain Sherard Osborn, who commanded HMS *Furious*, the ship that took the British envoy Lord Elgin to Japan in 1858, wrote in *A Cruise in Japanese Waters* (1859) that not only did the 'ladies of Nangasaki [sic] [see] no good reason to forego their pleasurable bath because there happened to be an influx of hairy-faced strangers', but they did not hesitate to jump out of their baths and come dashing over in order to gain a close look at passing westerners. Osborn jocularly advised against Europeans going so far as to adopt such 'al-fresco habits' but he good-naturedly quoted the motto of the Order of the Garter ('*Honi soit qui mal y pense*') to recommend tolerance towards local customs. Captain Osborn noted moreover that Japanese men did not actually stop to look at bathing women.[85] Christopher Dresser too suggested in 1882 that the Japanese simply did not look at each other's nakedness with lust or lewdness – 'inconceivable as this may seem to the European mind'. The artist John La Farge declared in his book published in 1897 that the Japanese were not without their own sense of modesty: two female grooms in his employ had thought nothing of stripping down to the waist in front of him in order to wash, but they had hastily drawn their clothes back on when they noticed he was sketching them. On another occasion, one of the women had run behind a tree in horror and consternation when her hair had come undone. Even Hodgson conceded that it might only have been 'exceptional curiosity' which had prompted Japanese bathers to come running out of the bathhouse despite their state of nakedness, adding that things had changed so much even in the few years he had been in Japan that 'now, if a European attempts to draw the curtain before the [bath] house, he is received with storms of abuse, and told very plainly to go about his business'.[86]

It was not, of course, that European societies themselves had always been prudish about nudity. If Thunberg or Hodgson had ever had the opportunity of looking through, for example, the fifteenth-century book of hours, *Les Très Riches Heures du Duc de Berry*, he would have seen that the month of February is illustrated with a wintry farming scene in one corner of which there are peasants warming their exposed genitalia before an open fire, their garments drawn up to their knees.[87] Mixed bathing was not an unusual practice in late medieval Europe, not only in private residences but also in public bathhouses, with which many northern European cities were provided. A grille might physically separate the men from the women in some establishments, but bathers remained visible to one another. Just as people did in Japan, town dwellers utilised these public bathhouses not merely for purposes of personal hygiene, but for socialising. There are pictorial representations from the period of men and women not only bathing together but sharing a meal or drink while soaking in a communal tub, sometimes in the presence of a musician.

These illustrations do suggest that people associated various types of carnal pleasure with the activity of social bathing. Nonetheless, for at least one Italian, from a part of Europe where the custom of mixed bathing was less prevalent, the idea of communal bathing evoked feelings of nostalgic longing for a less corrupt age, just as notions of primitive simplicity were later applied to Japanese society by some western visitors to the Far East. In the spring of 1416, Poggio Bracciolini, a papal secretary and Renaissance humanist of Tuscan birth, wrote to his friend Niccolò Niccoli from the spa town of Baden, describing the local bathing customs. Mixed bathing was the norm there, both at public baths and in private homes. To Poggio, it seemed that the people of Baden still dwelt in a state of primitive simplicity and innocence that rightfully belonged to an earlier stage of human history, one from which Poggio himself – being a modern man – was excluded. What struck him to be 'licentiousness' appeared to be, from the point of view of the locals, nothing more than innocent convivial revelry. Perceptions of modesty changed in Europe from the sixteenth century onwards, and these shifts in perceived standards of behaviour in turn fed into the concept of cultural and social progress.[88]

Progress signified the slow and arduous climb out of the morally benighted state, coupled with the necessity of physical toil, into which humankind had been plunged since the expulsion of Adam and Eve from the Garden of Eden. For every visitor from late nineteenth-century America or Europe who was delighted not to find in Japan (because he did not seek it) evidence of that hectic modern pursuit of material gain which he had travelled halfway around the globe to escape, there were others who felt that the Japanese were guilty of not striving enough to improve themselves. Rutherford Alcock wrote, 'What they are now, they seem to have been, without change, centuries ago'. Other commentators warned against mistaking Japan for a prelapsarian Eden. C. Pemberton Hodgson commended the 'patriarchal simplicity' of the Japanese way of life and the 'primitive kindness and severity' of their government and their laws, but at the same time he described the Japanese as a remnant of the 'aborigines of creation' who had been scattered across the globe after the Great Flood. By this, Hodgson was suggesting that the Japanese had not made the same progress as the peoples of Europe. They had made no great strides in bettering themselves. In Hodgson's eyes, the Japanese were a living illustration of how the absence of true religion, of education, of freedom of speech, and of an open communion of ideas kept a race backward.[89] While Alcock considered it not quite fair to accuse the Japanese of vice when they had evidently not even reached the stage of developing either a sense of modesty or 'a consciousness of wrong doing', Edward de Fonblanque felt that no local peculiarities of custom excused them their nonchalance with regard to nakedness. He disagreed with those writers who held that 'this absence of shame [was] the natural result of perfect primitive innocence'. On the contrary, he asserted, '[w]e know too well that they have long since tasted of the forbidden tree; nay, eaten so heartily that scarcely a single fruit remains to tempt their appetites'.[90] Far from moving in the direction of moral enlightenment, the Japanese had backslid into moral turpitude. They now pursued pleasure to excess, dissipating their spare time in debauchery in the company of professional cocottes – courtesans and geishas. The comte de Dalmas asserted that entire families, including young children, went to the '*djoréa*' (brothel) in order to indulge in the sort of depraved entertainment provided by 'gaicha' and dancers. Baron von Hübner reported how, in the summer of 1871, he had been entertained on a trip to Mount Fuji by a local painter, who rounded off a virtuoso demonstration of his artistry by drawing 'erotic subjects worthy of the secret chamber at Pompeii', which elicited gleeful laughter from the many spectators, including women and girls, who had gathered round to watch.[91]

The Anglican cleric George Smith likewise cautioned against being seduced by those '[p]leasant pictures [that] are sometimes drawn of Japanese manners as resembling Arcadian scenes of innocence, simplicity and bliss'. The Japanese were merely 'content to be borne along on the tide of present sensual enjoyment and careless ease'. 'There is,' the bishop wrote, 'a palpable shamelessness in all classes and among both sexes of natives. No delicacy, no modesty, no sense of shame appears to be recognised among the courtesies of life.' He too took exception to those western commentators who wished to 'palliate this custom of promiscuous bathing in public by assuming the innocent simplicity of their primitive habits'. Aimé Humbert suggested that Europeans had difficulty accepting the proposition that their own moral and religious inhibitions might not be universal ones. But Bishop Smith sternly warned of the danger of moral relativism: moral right and wrong did not vary just because customs differed from country to country.[92] Moreover, the bishop felt that even when chastity was practised by the Japanese, it was not a reflection of virtue, because it did not emerge from a sense of moral imperative. The Japanese, the bishop insisted, were more law-abiding than other Asian peoples only because punishments were more brutal there than anywhere else. J.J. Rein suggested that, among the Japanese, obedience was inculcated from childhood by 'a wholesome fear' of parental anger. Other western commentators cynically suggested that the primary reason Japanese women were generally faithful to their spouses was because the husband had the right to exact summary punishment on an adulterous wife by putting her to the sword himself.[93]

In Gilbert and Sullivan's *The Mikado*, flirting (by men as well as by women) is a crime punishable by decapitation. W.S. Gilbert pokes fun at the British establishment – the ponderous bureaucracy which supports it and the prim social niceties which regulate it – by situating his satire in a fantastical eastern setting evocative of heady passions. Gilbert's characters are caught up in a series of legal wrangles caused by the Mikado's paradoxical laws and decrees, while the Mikado congratulates himself on his enlightened benevolence and proclaims his object to be '[t]o let the punishment fit the crime'. But punishments in Titipu are not proportionate to the gravity of the crime; indeed, they are comically cruel. Essentially the Mikado belongs in the category of the fantastical eastern despot. However, Gilbert skilfully exploits the comic potential of this stock character of western fable by ascribing to him the characteristics of the obfuscating British parliamentarian. The Mikado's officious displeasure at the inefficiency of the Lord High Executioner, who has not managed to carry out a single execution in the previous year, is all the more comical because the Mikado fundamentally remains the overblown eastern tyrant with a penchant for excessive punishments.

There were several western commentators who questioned whether the Japanese woman's eagerness to please indicated that she essentially lacked delicacy and that only the threat of severe punishment kept her from active promiscuity. They suggested rather that this complaisance was more a reflection of the Japanese woman's sense of social duty. Alice Bacon, for instance, pointed out that female virtue was understood differently in the west than in Japan. Whereas in western societies it was focused upon the idea of personal chastity, Bacon observed that the Japanese considered obedience to be the supreme virtue in women. A morally praiseworthy woman in Japan was one who was selfless. As late as 1919, Amos and Susanne Hershey, discussing the education of Japanese girls, adopted a similar point of view: the moral upbringing of the American girl was almost entirely focused on sexual morality – 'on watchfulness and resistance to the male', as well as on awareness of the dire penalties which accompanied transgressions – whereas in Japan, girls were taught that obedience and 'subserviency to the male' were the most important of all feminine virtues. These qualities actually made young Japanese women more vulnerable, and kept them unfit for the kind of social independence and freedom in dealings with the opposite sex which modern American women took for granted.[94]

There were various opinions as to whether this selflessness of Japanese women was an admirable thing or not. Many of the earliest American and British visitors to Japan in the nineteenth century compared the lot of Japanese women favourably to that endured by women in other eastern countries. Captain Osborn declared that the Japanese woman had 'succeeded in asserting her right to be treated like a rational being', escaping the fate of women in China and India who were reduced to the status of playthings to 'some fattened-up . . . mandarin, or greasy Brahmin', and Francis L. Hawks, compiler of the official account of Commodore Perry's expedition to Japan, stated that a Japanese woman was 'recognised as a companion and not merely treated as a slave'. The Japanese, Hawks noted, did not treat their women as 'chattels' or 'household drudges' as men did in China, or as 'purchased objects of . . . capricious lust' as in Turkey. Edward de Fonblanque reported that, among the labouring classes at least, a Japanese wife was 'the respected helpmate of her lord', shouldering her fair share of the burden of running not only the household but the family business, if there was one, and frequently assuming 'discretionary powers' to act, when necessary, on her spouse's behalf.[95] The Japanologist Basil Hall Chamberlain explained in *Things Japanese* (1890) that Japanese women were required to obey their father in childhood, their husband in marriage and their sons in old age, but in the second, enlarged edition of the book, which he published the following year, Chamberlain qualified this by noting that the hardships of making a living meant that women among the working classes were less subject to such control, and that the wives of peasant-farmers, artisans and small traders shared their husbands' counsels as well as their labours.[96]

On the other hand, the self-abnegating obedience which Japanese women were said to be taught from childhood hardly seemed conducive to the emergence of a proper sense of self-respect and independence in these women. William Elliot Griffis declared that

[i]f unvarying obedience, acquiescence, submission, the utter absorption of her personality into that of her husband, constitute the ideal of the perfect woman, then the Japanese married women approach so near that ideal as to be practically perfect, and in this respect are, as foreign women will cheerfully grant to them, unquestionably superior.[97]

The British journalist Henry Norman felt that the 'unequal intellectuality' which existed between a Japanese husband and his wife prevented any love from emerging out of an 'intimacy of mutual knowledge and common aspiration'. Under such circumstances, it could not be very surprising that husbands went to teahouses to seek the company of pretty, clever women who at least had been specifically trained to be entertaining to men. Norman was not the only one to blame the existence of courtesans in Japan on Japanese attitudes to wives. According to *Manners and Customs of the Japanese*, a Japanese wife was simply not recognised as 'the rational, confidential partner of [her husband's] life'. C. Pemberton Hodgson regretted that in Japan wives were not the 'sole proprietor[s] of [their husband's] affection'. He blamed this on the prevalence of arranged marriages. If inexperienced young men had little say in whom they married and marriages were not based on love, what was there to keep husbands from taking mistresses later on? At least in the choice of concubines, men were free to follow their personal inclinations.[98]

It was not just that, given the absence of rituals of courtship in Japanese society, couples presumably had little opportunity to discover before marriage whether they were compatible or not. There was no chance for romantic love to blossom – a love that fused sensuality with an active imagination, but within the proper confines of decorum.[99] The Japanese, it was observed, did not hold social gatherings, which, in the west, taught young men to treat women with respect. J.J. Rein remarked that the absence in Japan of 'social amusements that can be compared with our evening entertainments, concerts, or balls' led young men to seek diversion in 'bad company' and in 'orgies'. It was frequently said that the Japanese not only did not entertain the concept of romantic love, but they did not possess the necessary faculty of intellectual curiosity or of imagination either. The American polymath and author Percival Lowell, for instance, wrote of the 'Far Oriental' (encompassing in a broad sweep both the Chinese and the Japanese) that '[t]he delight of self-exploration, or the possibly even greater delight of losing one's self in trying to fathom femininity, is a sensation equally foreign to his temperament'. Oriental races, according to Lowell, were fundamentally uninterested in the human race: they remained indifferent to the myriad subtle differences that constitute each unique individual, nor did they recognise that the human race occupied a special place at the pinnacle of the natural order.[100] Considering humankind as no better than just another species of animal, the Japanese were unable to think about women in any terms other than the material. They did not entertain the idea of a higher level of development that involved the soul, let alone look to women for its most pure and delicate blossoming.

If Japanese men were incapable of seeing women as the mirror of what was most beautiful about the human mind and body, Japanese women were bereft of ideals to live up to. Edward de Fonblanque wrote that women were 'subjected to few restraints' before they were wed, and that the 'the grossest profligacy' on their part did not diminish their eligibility for matrimony, unlike in western countries, where brides were expected to be pure and virginal. On the other hand, in the opinion of Basil Hall Chamberlain, the low esteem in which women were held in Japan resulted in their being treated at best like babies all through their lives, indulged and protected but never allowed to mature into independent, reasoning human beings. Missionaries such as George Smith pointed to Christianity as the moral force that had shaped marriage in western societies. Bishop Smith declared that Christianity alone secured full recognition for women of their proper role in life: to be the chief dispensers of moral influence within their families, and as a wife to be the 'virtuous companion, a sympathising counsellor and an unselfish sharer of man's sorrows and joys'.[101]

Such discussions of the role of Japanese women within marriage were not without timely relevance to their western readers, for there was not such a wide divergence in marital customs between the Japanese and western societies as some writers suggested. For example, arranged marriages based on social status and family wealth were common among the bourgeoisie in nineteenth-century France. In Britain, the physician and social commentator William Acton, writing in 1857, argued that the widespread custom for young men to defer marriage until they had either built up a fortune or come into a legacy was one of the reasons why the demand for prostitutes continued to remain high. Many nineteenth-century public health authorities were agreed that under such constraints, male sexual desire needed a safe outlet. The very idea that a bond of sympathetic understanding based upon emotional compatibility should unite a married couple and become the foundation for the personal happiness and self-fulfilment of both partners (but especially the wife) was relatively new. It had found its impetus in the cult of sensibility, which arose as a movement in literature and art in the later decades of the eighteenth and the early nineteenth centuries.[102]

Some western observers felt that the Japanese were actually much more successful than western societies when it came to raising daughters to become excellent wives, mothers and housekeepers. Young women in upper middle-class America as well as in bourgeois France were, after all, largely destined for marriage.

Alice Bacon suggested that the way courtship was conducted in the west rather encouraged women to become vain and self-centred. Western girls filled their heads with 'thoughts of beaux, of coming out in society, of a brief career of flirtation and conquest', whereas Japanese maidens had no occasion to compare the relative desirability of various young gentlemen or to compete with one another to attract the attention of members of the opposite sex. In Bacon's opinion – contrary to De Fonblanque's views or those of Isabella Bird, who regretted that Japanese children seemed to be prematurely world-weary because of their exposure to the adult world from a tender age – it was the Japanese girl, rather than the European girl, who managed to preserve the 'unconscious and beautiful spirit of her childhood' up to the moment of marriage. In a similar vein, William Elliot Griffis disapproved of the calculating way European ladies carefully exposed just so much of their anatomy. He considered this much more immodest than a Japanese woman who exposed her breasts without the least 'intent to charm'.[103]

Conservative social commentators levelled accusations of vain and self-centred behaviour at western women after marriage as well as before. Glowing praise for the institution of Christian marriage, couched as a critique of Japanese society, acted as a critical commentary on the rapidly evolving role of women in society back in America and Europe. Some western writers, on the other hand, idealised the image of the family-oriented, un-self-regarding Japanese woman as a way of criticising western women for being too absorbed in themselves rather than in their families. While western observers of Japanese society deplored what they felt to be the contemptuous way in which Japanese men behaved towards their countrywomen, they tended, at the same time, to accept unquestioningly the idea that the primary sphere of activity for all women was the family. The Japanese matron, it was frequently said, was content to withdraw into the privacy of her family, making its welfare her sole concern, whereas fashionable ladies in Europe and America pursued their own pleasures outside the home, competing with one another for social distinction. Arthur Diósy was scornful of those social accomplishments which he thought western society ladies took most pride in: 'the wit and the power of repartee, the interesting small talk on the topics of the day, the amusing little affectations'. These skills, he wrote, belonged in Japan to 'tea-house waitresses and, especially, the "Accomplishment-mongers" – the *Gei-sha*, who are the professional Flirts of Japan'. The Japanese wife disdained to compete with the geisha, while the European lady of rank spent all her time in the 'overheated, overstrung conditions of Western social life', rushing about in the pursuit of excitement, pleasure and 'smartness'. In Rodolphe Lindau's view, the Japanese women who most quickly lost their most attractive quality, that is, their modesty, were those who were obliged to keep company with foreigners.[104]

In praising Japanese women for their selfless devotion to their families, the American journalist and writer Lafcadio Hearn reached further back than the Christian era to draw a parallel between the Japanese and the ancient Greeks. Hearn, who taught English literature at the nascent Imperial University of Tōkyō, and eventually became a naturalised Japanese, taking to wife the daughter of a samurai family, deeply mourned the passing of the 'old' – in his view, the real – Japan under the influence of modern western civilisation. In *Japan: An Attempt at Interpretation* (1904), Hearn described 'the Japanese woman' as a product of a pre-modern, pre-industrial society, the only type of society in which, in Hearn's view, true altruism, and hence purity of morals, could exist. To Hearn's mind it was a positive thing that traditional Japanese society had been strictly regulated and regimented. This silenced the individual's urge to assert his or her own self. Society demanded self-sacrifice instead. This was akin to 'life depicted upon old Greek vases'. And no members of Japanese society were more self-sacrificing than its women, whose lives consisted of 'working only for others, thinking only for others, happy only in making pleasure for others'. The Japanese woman, in Hearn's view, was comparable to 'the Greek type of noble woman, – to Antigoné, to Alcestis'.[105]

Parallels between Japanese society and that of the ancient Greeks had occurred to others besides Hearn, although in a slightly different context. Pierre Loti, in *Madame Chrysanthème*, described the young girls who throng around the sailor Yves as 'hétaïres de douze ou quinze ans'.[106] This reference to *hetaerae*, the courtesans of ancient Greece, is primarily intended to shock readers, but other western visitors to Japan pointed to *hetaerae* as another example of courtesans possessing superior cultural attainments. The American artist John La Farge drew upon the idea of the *hetaera* in order to describe the characteristics of the Japanese geisha (rather than the Japanese courtesan):

> They are, voluntarily, exiles from regular society and family . . . . They cultivate singing and dancing, and often poetry, and all the accomplishments and most of the exquisite politeness of their country. They are the ideals of the elegant side of woman. To them is intrusted [*sic*] the entertainment of guests and the solace of idle hours. They are the *hetairai* of the old Greeks – and sometimes they are all that that name implies.[107]

Many *hetaerae*, such as Aspasia, who was teacher, mistress and, later, wife of the Athenian leader Pericles (and is described in Plato's dialogue *Menexenus* as Socrates' teacher in rhetoric), came from Ionian colonies across the Aegean Sea, and were well educated, unlike the sheltered daughters of Athenian families, who were brought up for marriage and a life of managing their husband's household.

When J.J. Rein wrote coyly that the unfortunate inmates of the Shin-yoshiwara quarter had a mastery of 'the arts of Aspasia', he was referring to the purported intellectual attainments of the highest-ranking Japanese courtesans. Wives, burdened as they were with domestic responsibilities, were no match for the professionals who made a living from their cultural accomplishments as well as their beauty. Some Japanese courtesans managed to develop such highly refined cultural sensibilities that, according to the compiler of *Manners and Customs of the Japanese*, Japanese husbands took their wives with them to teahouses so the women could benefit from the 'conversation of their intellectual, and highly accomplished, but unfortunate and dishonoured, sisters', as well as learn to appreciate their music, dancing and singing. Had not 'the notorious Aspasia' likewise been sought out by Athenians keen for their spouses to 'share in the instruction they themselves derived from her'?[108]

But the very existence of *hetaerae* in ancient Greek society was, for the American anthropologist Lewis H. Morgan, evidence that the Greeks still had a way to go on the road to civilisation. During the nineteenth century, the high regard in which classical Greek civilisation had traditionally been held in the west began to give way to a more critical view based on ideas of social evolution and progress. Morgan, a proponent of the theory of cultural evolution, spurned the notion that either Athens or republican Rome had reached full civic maturity as a result of the moral excellence of its citizenry. Monogamy, in Morgan's view, represented the most elevated type of relationship possible between the sexes, and ensured the proper moral foundations of society. Neither the ancient Greeks nor the Romans had ever managed to achieve this 'pure morality in the intercourses of the sexes', which was now the cornerstone of enlightened modern western civilisation. Morgan considered both the Athenians and the Romans to have been fundamentally licentious, a condition which they had managed to rise above in times of exceptional adversity but to which they sank back once peace was restored. Their normative behaviour, exemplified by their tolerance of hetaerism, betrayed what Morgan considered to be vestiges of an archaic system of conjugality. They were thus tainted by a residue of barbarism.[109]

Morgan objected to the kind of idealising of classical civilisation which it did not occur to Lafacio Hearn to question. The British journalist Henry Norman cautioned against a different form of idealisation. Hearn drew his examples of noble Greek women from mythology by way of classical drama, but Norman had something to say about confusing aesthetic romanticisation with real-life attitudes. He pointed out that while the Japanese themselves idealised the concept of female self-sacrifice and had turned it into a highly sentimental literary convention, one commonly encountered in popular works of fiction and drama, they were at the same time perfectly capable of stigmatising actual women who had been forced by difficult circumstances to put the interests of their family before their personal reputation. Working in the brothel quarter, more often than not, did cast an 'ineffable stain' on the character of a girl, even when it was family poverty rather than personal cupidity (as Major Henry Knollys would have it in his *Sketches of Life in Japan*) that had impelled her to join a brothel. Norman thus warned that it was a mistake for westerners to romanticise the notion that Japanese girls frequently volunteered to enter a brothel out of sheer 'filial devotion'. Going into a brothel was a course of action not many Japanese girls would happily accept, no matter how devoted they were to their families or how obedient they had been brought up to be. Norman was equally disinclined to romanticise what became of the girls once they had entered the brothel quarter. While he did not believe they became the sort of vengeful man-eaters Aimé Humbert envisioned, swathed in robes embroidered with scenes from the underworld and exulting in the number of men they had managed to ruin, Norman did not think they were surrounded by an aura of martyrdom either. Henry Norman observed, along with Alice Bacon, that many inmates of the brothel quarter, including geishas, simply developed a practical, if somewhat hard-nosed, attitude to looking after their own interests in order to survive.[110]

William Elliot Griffis, who was a devout Christian and later became a Protestant minister back in the United States, made a cogent observation that served as a riposte both to those commentators who were self-satisfied about the state of progress in the west compared to eastern countries, and to writers who were inclined to idealise the Japanese for supposedly preserving aspects of an archaic heroism which had long been lost in the west. The social troubles the Japanese faced, Griffis pointed out charitably, were the same as those found in other countries around the world. These included prostitution. In so far as the Japanese were trying to tackle the social impact of the practice, Griffis felt that they deserved sympathy, rather than harsh criticism. The solution which the Japanese authorities had adopted – legalised brothel quarters – was far from perfect, and reflected the grave flaws that existed in their moral thinking. But it was not so depraved as to be without some redeeming features, which addressed aspects of prostitution that still remained unchecked in western societies.[111] Griffis understood the commonality of the problems that beset human societies and the fallibility of human nature.

The new imperial regime that supplanted the Shogunate was very conscious of western criticism and was anxious that the country should not appear backward to western eyes. An ordinance was issued in Yokohama in 1868 prohibiting people from appearing in public in a state of nakedness or near-nakedness; a similar ban came into force in Tōkyō in 1871. Male grooms and rickshaw men, who during summer months had only worn loincloths (and whose spectacular tattoos had attracted much excited comment among western visitors), now had to don leggings and tops all year round. Between 1872 and 1873, the government, which was intent on establishing a state-sponsored, national Shintoism, banned various representational forms of the phallus, which had hitherto been the focus of widespread folk worship among many sections of Japanese society. Phallic stones were removed from country shrines, and brothels were no longer allowed to display on their indoor altars a representation of the phallus (made of paper on a wooden frame weighed down with lead), which had traditionally been an object of worship for their inmates. This particular custom, however, seems later to have reasserted itself.[112] As for the practice of mixed bathing, it proved much more difficult to suppress. The Tokugawa Shogunate first attempted to ban it in 1791, then again in 1858. The Meiji government imposed a succession of bans, but it was only after 1900, when a regulation came into force prohibiting men and women over the age of twelve from bathing together that the practice finally began to decrease. Bathhouses eventually became segregated, although mixed bathing has continued at many hot spring spas right up to the present day.[113]

When it came to the task of rebuilding Japanese society, however, the Meiji regime, even as it abolished many of the social restrictions from the time of the Tokugawa Shogunate, reimposed a great deal of the ideology which had previously served to underpin the social hierarchy under the Shogunate. The principle of privileging the interests of the family over those of the individual – which had formerly applied only to the ruling samurai class – was now imposed upon all strata of society. The doctrine of the primacy of the family, ruled over by the paterfamilias, paralleled the state ideology of Japan as a strongly centralised nation which had the emperor as its patriarchal head. This had repercussions especially for women who belonged to those social classes in which they had customarily had to work alongside men to provide for the family, and had correspondingly enjoyed more freedom than women higher up in society. For example, many rural communities had traditionally allowed their young people a degree of choice in the selection of a marriage partner, as well as a certain amount of pre-marital sexual licence to both young men and women. But under the new civil code of 1898, the male head of the family, regardless of social class, was legally vested with authority over all other members of his family. Arranged marriages, which had formerly been customary only among the ranks of the samurai and among wealthy merchant families, became prevalent in society – ironically becoming an agent for social mobility as ambitious parents aspired to marry their daughters higher up the social ladder, for one of the changes the Meiji government introduced was the rescinding of the Tokugawa Shogunate's ban on marriage between people belonging to different castes. Unmarried girls of all classes were now firmly discouraged from associating with members of the opposite sex. The sexual integrity of women, both unmarried and married, became a matter of importance. This was reflected in the civil code, in which the offence of adultery was applied only to wives.[114]

The second half of the nineteenth century was a time of great flux throughout Japanese society. The collapse of the Tokugawa Shogunate overturned many of the old certainties. There was great economic hardship at all social levels, as well as new opportunities for enterprise. The introduction of western culture exposed people to new ideas and stimulated the exploration of new forms of artistic, literary and political self-expression, while western technology began to change the way people led their lives. But even as these changes were taking place, the Meiji regime was consolidating its control over the people. With the adoption of a constitution, which came into effect on 29 November 1890, Japan became a constitutional monarchy with a national assembly, the Diet. The ruling elite continued to pursue its agenda of building up Japan's economic and military strength. To this end, Japan's rulers wanted a disciplined, patriotic and industrious populace.

Japan's struggle to marry its own traditions to new ideas imported precipitately from the west was inevitably perceived in a different light by foreign observers. Many declared that the Japanese had to adopt a more western mentality if the country were to survive in the world. Yet at the same time, many western observers shuddered to see Japan increasingly assume the trappings of the west. Such conflicting reactions were also aroused by the perceived treatment of women in Japan. Their subordinate position in society provoked much western indignation, and yet there was loud praise for their self-abnegating behaviour. So it was with geishas: they symbolised, in western eyes, what needed reforming in Japan and yet it seemed that Japan would become a much less fascinating place if they were all to disappear.

CHAPTER TWO

Geishas as Artefact: Artifice, Ideal Beauty and the Natural Woman

Western visitors to Japan found Japanese women fascinating to look at, yet these women defied western criteria of female beauty. Though the typical Japanese woman was not as voluptuous as a Caucasian, she nonetheless possessed some curves. But the Japanese appeared to go to great trouble to disguise the natural contours of the female physique. Women flattened their chests and padded up their waists with layers of heavy brocade until their bodies looked like cylindrical parcels. Many western observers conceded that there was a certain aesthetic pleasure to be derived from beholding the end result. There was universal admiration for the tremendous artistry that went into the creation of the kimonos and accessories with which women in Japan transformed themselves. But whether these things made a Japanese woman desirable in herself remained a moot point. Some argued that the exterior look which a woman constructed around herself constituted an essential element of her being: a woman was indivisible from the image she projected to the world. Others maintained that the artifice served to disguise the true woman inside: it could conceal moral corruption under a façade of beauty, or it could disfigure the simple perfection of true beauty, whether physical or spiritual, with superfluous ornaments.

Henry Norman went to the Shin-yoshiwara pleasure quarter to witness a formal procession of the higher-ranking courtesans (*oiran*) through the avenues of the district. He found it a thoroughly alienating experience. To his eye, everything about the *oiran*'s dress was exaggerated, from the enormous bow into which her heavy brocade obi was tied in front, to the heavy pattens upon which she tottered – they were so high and heavy she could not advance without the aid of male servants who supported her on either side. Her coiffure was 'pyramidal', her face was painted 'as white as snow', her lips were tinted vermilion, and even her toenails were stained pink. Her expression – 'half contemptuous and half timid' – was frozen and immobile. The effect of this overwhelming display of artifice was to set her apart from everybody else: her attendants, the spectators, indeed from the rest of humankind. The *oiran* remained supremely indifferent to everything that was happening around her. She was utterly detached from her surroundings. It seemed to Norman that some kind of profound ritual was being conducted, as if this parade were a 'phallic ceremonial' being held in honour of Priapus.[1] It is as though the sacred and the profane had come together in the *oiran*.

Proponents of aestheticism in the west argued that a brilliant surface effect was the sole point of art. If this effect left the beholder feeling bewildered or alienated, so be it. It was degrading to art to expect it to be in some way 'meaningful', as though it were merely a tool for conveying messages, whether moral or religious. James McNeill Whistler proposed that art should be free of any didactic purpose such as 'devotion, pity, love, patriotism': art should be pre-eminently itself, 'standing alone, and appeal[ing] to the artistic sense of eye or ear'.[2] It was equally pointless to expect a work of art to refer to some kind of 'reality' beyond the work itself. Whistler, who collected Japanese *objets d'art* and had a profound appreciation of Japanese *ukiyoe*, thought it was totally unnecessary for his protégé, the Australian-born artist Mortimer Menpes, to go and see Japan for himself when all the inspiration an artist could want was to be found in the products of the Japanese imagination, that is to say, in Japanese works of art. Oscar Wilde, who assumed the mantle of public advocate for the aesthetic movement, proposed in his essay 'The Decay of Lying' that a slavish adherence to facts only killed off beauty, rendering art 'sterile'. Japan, as created in the imagination of its artists, was fascinating not because it bore any resemblance or reference to the reality of Japanese life, but because it was all 'pure invention', a flight of fancy, a remoulding of existence into 'a mode of style'.[3] The implication of this view was that when Japanese artists such as Kitagawa Utamaro and Katsushika Hokusai produced their exquisite depictions of courtesans in their woodblock prints and their paintings, they were creating images intended to please the eye and not to worry the conscience. Here was a purely imaginary world in which life was lived solely for the sake of beauty – where life blazed, in Walter Pater's expression, with a 'hard, gem-like flame'.

Mortimer Menpes did go to Japan in 1887. In his book of impressions of the country, *Japan* (1901), which was transcribed, like most of his other books, by his daughter Dorothy, one chapter is devoted to the geisha. Menpes praises the geisha for being a completely artificial construct, a product of art and the imagination. Her *raison d'être* was to be 'decorative' – to please the beholder aesthetically with a vision of beauty. Around her person were the best examples of those exquisite crafts for which Japan was so admired in the west during the nineteenth century: brocades and silks delicately figured with motifs taken from nature; finely designed and executed metalwork; fans and parasols decorated with ingenious graphic designs.

> The women are very extravagant in their dress, and some of the leading geisha-girls will often go to the length of having stencils, with elaborate designs and an immense amount of hand-work, specially cut for them, the stencils and designs being destroyed when sufficient material for one dress has been supplied. For such a unique and costly gown the geisha will of course have to pay a fabulous sum, and a sum that would astound the average English woman of fashion. But then when a geisha orders a costume she thinks it out carefully; she does not go, as we do, to a dressmaker, but to an artist.[4]

A geisha's whole ensemble was the product of artistic inspiration and highly honed craftsmanship. In the geisha Mortimer Menpes recognised a fellow artist: 'The geisha-girl is an artist: I am an artist: we understand each other.' The geisha's canvas was her own person. She, moreover, made no pretence of being anything other than totally artificial. The geisha's beauty was the beauty of the man-made – of the unnatural, even. The geisha's hair was wrought into elaborate loops and layers and gummed and stiffened with pomade until the whole coiffure shone like a mirror. Unlike western women, the geisha did not use cosmetics in order to achieve an illusion of naturalness. The British industrial designer Christopher Dresser agreed. The geisha, he noted, used a 'most potent pigment' to colour her lips the brightest of reds, accentuating the hue even more with 'lustrous touches of a green-gold bronze' applied to the central portions of the lips. '[H]appily kissing is unknown in Japan!' Dresser added.[5]

The geisha, 'grotesque' and 'fantastical', went to the trouble of drawing attention to the artificiality of her make-up by leaving portions of the nape of her neck, which the collar of her kimono exposed to view, untouched by cosmetics, creating a sharp contrast between the eerie whiteness of the painted skin and the glow of the natural skin. But this attitude to cosmetics, Menpes maintained, was not restricted to geishas: Japanese women generally did not try to disguise their use of make-up whether they were respectable or otherwise. They saw their face as a blank canvas ready for painting, and they revelled in the daily challenge of decorating it afresh.[6]

To Menpes's mind, the geisha adorned a Japanese banqueting room as a well-placed bouquet of flowers or a painting might grace a western dining room. Her every movement down to her feet and her fingers, and the exquisite poses she assumed in the course of her dancing, were all supremely decorative, since what Japanese artists excelled in, according to Menpes, was the art of placement – knowing exactly where to put every element in a composition in order to produce a beautiful effect. The geisha did not entertain with the 'accordion skirt and high kick' of Parisian dance halls such as the Moulin de la Galette in Montmartre, where the can-can took off as a craze in the early 1880s. The geisha's appeal, as Menpes saw it, was supremely aesthetic. Even as he tagged on to the conclusion of his discussion of geishas a short defence of their moral integrity, describing the geisha stripped of her finery as 'a real woman' who was 'dainty in mind' and 'highly-educated', possessing a 'great sense of honour', for Menpes their real attraction clearly lay in the acute intellectual (rather than, say, sexual) pleasure he gained from looking upon the wonderful juxtaposition of colours, textures, fabrics and ornaments, and the perfectly balanced positioning of the body which they offered to his gaze. Yet in his own drawings and paintings of Japanese scenes, which he went all the way to Japan to produce, Menpes never quite succeeded in 'absorb[ing] the spirit' of the style of Japanese artists, as Oscar Wilde was later to advise in his essay 'The Decay of Lying', so that he could break free of mere observation and create, instead, a 'Japanese effect'.[7]

3 Letter from the artist Mortimer Menpes to the actor Herbert Beerbohm Tree, with a water-colour painting of a geisha, late nineteenth/early twentieth century.

The arts and crafts which began to flow out of Japan after the opening of the country in the 1850s to wider western commerce inspired an enthusiasm among artistic circles in Europe and in America for Japanese design, to say nothing of a mania for collecting Japanese *objets d'art*. Mortimer Menpes's own mentor, Whistler, had been one of the earliest of the self-proclaimed connoisseurs of Japanese art who appeared in London and Paris in the late 1850s and 1860s. In Paris this appreciation of things Japanese was led by a circle of artists which included Félix Bracquemond, Jules Jacquemart, Manet, Fantin-Latour, Degas, Monet, Cassatt, Tissot and the Belgian painter Alfred Stevens, as well as poets, writers and critics, among them Baudelaire, Zola, Philippe Burty, Ernest Chesneau, Champfleury (pseudonym of Jules Fleury-Husson, who later became Chief of Collections at the Sèvres porcelain factory), the artist and art critic Zacharie Astruc and the brothers Edmond and Jules de Goncourt. Collectors of Japanese *objets* haunted curio shops for the latest shipments to arrive from the Far East.[8] Already in 1862, the house that Edward William Godwin, the British architect and designer, shared with the actress Ellen Terry and their young children (who grew up to become respectively the theatre director and costumier Edith Craig and the theatre designer and theorist Edward Gordon Craig) was decorated with Japanese pictures and *objets d'art*, and Godwin later went on to create furniture in a style influenced by Japanese design and for that reason called 'Anglo-Japanese'.

Before long, the fashion for decorative Japanese items percolated down through the social classes. Examples of Japanese craftsmanship were shown at international exhibitions in both London and Paris, beginning with the International Exhibition trade fair which was held in London in 1862. Japanese art was officially exhibited to the Parisian general public at the Exposition Universelle of 1867; there was another, even bigger exhibit of Japanese *objets d'art* at the 1878 Exposition.[9] In the late 1880s, the French aristocrat, aesthete and supreme arbiter of taste, Comte Robert de Montesquiou-Fezensac, who was a friend of Whistler and served as a model for J.-K. Huysmans's character Des Esseintes in the novel *A Rebours* (1884) and Proust's Baron de Charlus in *A la recherche du temps perdu*, cultivated a recherché Japanese-inspired style in interior décor. His suite of ground-floor rooms on the rue Franklin in Passy on the outskirts of Paris was elegantly decorated with Japanese hanging scrolls (*kakemono*), ornaments and fabrics, while a Japanese gardener by the name of Hata looked after his bonsai, and a Japanese valet arranged lighted Japanese lanterns outside in his rock garden. The count abandoned these rooms, however, when the Japanese taste began to spread. In Proust's *Du côté de chez Swann* (1913), the first volume of *A la recherche*, the cocotte Odette de Crécy, who tries so hard to achieve the 'smart' look, decks out her tawdry apartment with Japanese lanterns, silks and porcelain bowls which have been converted into lamp stands.

Japanese kimonos were avidly collected in the west; they appear in numerous paintings that date from the second half of the nineteenth century. Society ladies are portrayed wearing adapted kimonos as fashionable wraps donned over tea gowns. Other paintings show the artist's model in varying degrees of fancy dress, at times masquerading as a Japanese woman in notional Japanese scenes of the artist's creation. The British artist Dante Gabriel Rossetti, writing to his mother from Paris on 12 November 1864, mentioned he had been told by the propri-etress of a Japanese curio shop in the rue de Rivoli – one which his brother William occasionally visited and which was also a favourite of Whistler (this was probably La Jonque Chinoise, which opened in 1862 and was run by M and Mme Desoye) – that all of the shop's Japanese costumes had been snapped up by the artist James Tissot, who was working on no less than three 'Japanese pictures'.[10]

While some noh and kabuki robes did pass into the hands of western collec-tors, most of their acquisitions were the floor-length kimonos called *kosode*. The *kosode*, the standard item of apparel for both men and women in Japan, could be padded, unpadded, lined or unlined, according to which season the garment was intended to be worn, and the length of their square-shaped sleeves was deter-mined by the age and sex of the wearer.[11] In Japan, kimonos always were, and still are, worn left over right regardless of the sex of the wearer. An obi is wound tightly around the midriff so that the two overlapping sides of the kimono do not drift open. From the last decades of the seventeenth century onwards, women's obi became wider, much heavier and more elaborately brocaded or embroidered than those of men. A lady's formal ensemble was finished off with an *uchikake*, a kimono worn open over the *kosode*. The *uchikake* started out the same length as the *kosode*, but by the eighteenth century it had become customary to make it longer so that it trailed on the floor. Another name for the *uchikake* was the *kaidori* because the skirt of the garment was elegantly 'gathered up' and held (or tucked into a sash) when the wearer walked out of doors. Courtesans of the brothel quarters also wore *uchikake*. In their case, the garments were referred to as *shikake*, and were particularly ornate, often richly embroidered with gold and silver thread or elaborately patterned with animal, bird and flower motifs and human figures. Courtesans wore their sumptuous *shikake* even during the summer months, when other women put aside their *uchikake*.

When outdoors, courtesans held up their *shikake* with their right hand, in the same manner as married women did their *uchikake*, so that the hem of the garment did not touch the ground. The geisha, on the other hand, used her left hand. It was said that this was supposed to indicate that the geisha, unlike courtesans and matrons, remained sexually innocent. This gesture, known as *hidarizuma*, came, however, to be regarded by the general public as a mark of shame. Hanazono Utako, an articulate and progressive-minded geisha and modern dancer, who in the 1920s and '30s publicised the social discrimination faced by her fellow geishas, complained bitterly of the way in which they were effectively forced into prostitution by being prevented by law from taking on any other kind of paid work, and were then stigmatised by outdated customs such as the *hidarizuma* which society insisted they observe. But even to this day, *hidarizuma* symbolises the geisha, and Japanese brides who dress in the traditional long *uchikake* are enjoined not to hold up the hem with their left hand.[12]

Such encoded distinctions in Japanese dress more often than not went unrecognised in the west. Arthur Diósy, founder and vice-chairman of the Japan Society in London, commented satirically in 1898 on the fashion for Japanese fancy-dress costumes:

> It has happened to me more than once to be interrogated by some charming European lady, looking perfectly bewitching in a beautiful *kimono* ... and a gorgeous *obi*, and her pretty head encircled by *a dozen hair-pins* and ornaments: – 'My dress is *quite* correct, is it not?' What could I say? I own that I took refuge in ambiguity worthy of the Delphic Oracle, answering: 'Certainly, *quite* correct, but so much depends upon what particular type of Japanese you intend to represent.' – 'Ah! I *knew* I was correct. I copied all the details of the head-dress from a *lovely* Japanese fan.' I had thought as much. The Japanese *uchi-wa*, or non-folding fan, of the cheap kind so common in the Occident ... is often decorated with a highly-coloured print, a fancy portrait of some famous beauty of the *Yoshi-wara*, the purely conventional face surrounded by a halo of hair-pins.[13]

This was yet another aspect of the difficulty many people in the west had in telling Japanese *demi-mondaines* apart from ordinary women.

In Henry Norman's view, the charm of all Japanese women lay in their traditional attire. If they took to wearing western dress, Norman believed, nobody would be interested in visiting the country any longer.[14] When the Japanese woman adopted western attire, she was ugly. In the eyes too of the French novelist Pierre Loti, she was ugly once she was stripped of her long kimono and her obi twisted up into such ridiculously shaped bows. Without these artificial embellishments, she was

> nothing but a diminutive yellow being, with crooked legs and flat, unshapely bust; she has no longer a remnant of her artificial little charms, which have completely disappeared in company with her costume.[15]

Isabella Bird was disparaging about the build of Japanese women: they were physically 'below par', having a very short stature, 'round and very falling' shoulders, narrow chests and hips, and tiny hands and feet – all evidence in Miss Bird's eyes that the Japanese race was 'wearing out'. She did not regard the typical Japanese physique as offering much in the way of a model from which artists could gain an idea of the nobility of the human form. Miss Bird thought, moreover, that most Japanese women had an 'inane, vacant expression', an effect of their 'obvious lack of soul' compounded by their custom of shaving off eyebrows and blackening teeth. Edward Barrington de Fonblanque, in his 1862 book on Japan, expressed his acute disappointment at the decided lack of beauty in either the face or figure of most young Japanese women – although he conceded that they occasionally had an 'intelligent and good-natured expression', as well as good teeth. De Fonblanque wondered how it could be that the type of female beauty represented by the best Japanese artists was so different from the reality.[16]

Although the British poet and journalist Sir Edwin Arnold was delighted with the sensation that, on arriving in Japan, he had slipped into a Japanese picture that one might find, for instance, on a tea tray (he was charmed to discover that women's noses were just as he remembered seeing them depicted on Japanese *objets d'art*),[17] many other visitors to the country disagreed with De Fonblanque that there was anything appealing in the first place about the way women were portrayed in Japanese art. Considerable consensus existed among early western scholars is the field that the manner in which female physiognomy was rendered made women look deeply unattractive. This puzzled them since it was generally agreed that the Japanese excelled in depicting vegetation, birds, insects and fish. After all, as a race they were considered to have a highly strung artistic temperament. It was obvious that women were an important subject of their art, for they constantly turned up in courtly *yamatoe* (*Tosa*-style) paint-ings,[18] as well as in *ukiyoe* prints. But Marcus B. Huish, director of the Fine Art Society in London and editor of the *Art Journal*, found the conventional manner in which court ladies were portrayed in the *yamatoe* tradition decidedly insipid and ugly. Huish complained of the 'slits, very far apart, for eyes; two black bars high up on her forehead to serve the place of her shaved-off eyebrows; a long, slightly aquiline nose, and tiny mouth, and a long, oval, swollen-cheeked coun-tenance'. Likewise, the British naval surgeon William Anderson, author of the weighty, influential tome *The Pictorial Arts of Japan* (1886), deplored the inanity of expression of the noblewomen depicted in *yamatoe* paintings. He did not care much either for the awkward rendering of their figures, or for the stiff – in his view ungraceful – style in which their robes were represented. He dismissed the types of female beauty found in these paintings as 'singularly devoid of grace and character'.[19]

In the opinion of many visitors to Japan, the way in which Japanese women painted their faces did not give them much grace or character. On the contrary, it seemed to efface any physical attractions they might have been fortunate enough to have been born with. Many foreign observers may have agreed with the artist Mortimer Menpes that the application of cosmetics certainly made Japanese women look unnatural, but they did not necessarily concur with his view that this made the women look more interesting or, indeed, appealing. Around the time that the first British consul-general to Japan, Rutherford Alcock, arrived in the country in 1858, most Japanese women, both unmarried and married, still applied thick white powder (*oshiroi*) to their faces and necks.[20] The British diplomat did not care for it. He thought the powder made the women look hideously like 'painted Twelfth-night Queens done in pastry and white lead'. Art, he concluded, was employed in Japan in order to 'disfigur[e]'. By 1904, Douglas Sladen was writing that the way to distinguish a geisha from an innocent '*moosmee*' was by the colour of her complexion: 'The *geisha's* will have the fashionable whitening on it, while the *moosmee* will have her own glorious damask complexion.' Sladen thought the *moosmee* was actually prettier because she kept her own natural bloom. 'It is difficult not to pity', suggested Sladen, 'the little painted, powdered *geisha*, in her robes, as stiff as boards, of heavy brocade.'[21]

If geishas were transformed into dolls, it seemed that married women in Japan were transformed on purpose into repulsive hags. They were the ones who followed the custom Isabella Bird referred to of shaving off their eyebrows and blackening their teeth. While the tradition had for centuries been to draw in eyebrows higher up the forehead after shaving off one's own, many women in the nineteenth century did not do this, but went about browless instead. Teeth were dyed with a solution of iron filings and *sake*. This was supposed to symbolise a women's commitment to remain faithful to one man. But Rutherford Alcock thought the mouths of married women looked like 'open sepulchres'.[22] By 1873 both of these ancient practices were officially forbidden at court on the grounds that they were old-fashioned; it was only then that they were gradually abandoned by the general public.

Whatever William Anderson might have thought of the Japanese women he saw during the seven years he spent in Japan between 1873 and 1880, when it came to what he perceived as the lack of idealised feminine beauty in Japanese portraiture, he blamed – as did Marcus Huish – the artists' lack of imagination, rather than the actual appearance of Japanese women. In Anderson's estimation this was most evident in those very genres which required the imagination to soar into the realm of the ideal: in the portrayal of famous beauties from history and legend. Anderson allowed that many *ukiyoe* artists from the seventeenth century onwards became interested in representing women in a more realistic manner than *yamatoe* had traditionally attempted. Anderson, however, lamented that *ukiyoe* artists limited themselves to portraying people of the 'plebeian' classes (he happened to be wrong on this point), thereby passing over the 'more refined ideal of feminine beauty belonging to the higher social grades'.[23] Anderson's opinion reflected an implicit assumption that physical beauty was more likely to be found in the highest echelons of society, among people whose social position elevated them above the necessity of bone-grinding physical labour and the meanness of commercial activity. It was the aristocracy who were free to cultivate a noble and disinterested soul, a spirituality which would then be reflected in their person.[24] The French writer and collector of art Edmond de Goncourt, on the contrary, maintained that it was the idea of the Japanese *demi-mondaine*, the courtesan, that inspired the Japanese artist Utamaro with his unique vision of feminine beauty, one which endowed the round and dumpy Japanese figure with a svelte grace and made the flat Japanese face expressive of thoughtfulness, mischievousness, even something spiritual.[25]

Japanese artists had, of course, used courtesans and geishas as decorative motifs on magnificent standing screens (*byōbu*), hanging scrolls (*kakemono*), and woodblock prints (*ukiyoe*). *Ukiyoe*-style prints were also used to make those non-folding fans (*uchiwa*) mentioned by Diósy. Courtesans (*yūjo*), together with actors and sumo wrestlers, exemplified the urban culture that flourished in the big cities of Japan, especially in Edo and Ōsaka, after centuries of civil war finally came to an end in the early decades of the seventeenth century. Courtesans embodied the transient pleasures, fashions and fads of city life. Seventeenth-century *byōbu* capture the sensual, unencumbered movements of courtesans' bodies;[26] the courtesan's status as an outsider allowed her to flout codes of behaviour which applied to the rest of society, and when she assumed masculine dress, for example, she shrugged off the smothering layers of formal female costume and at the same time liberated herself from the strictures of acceptable female conduct. By choosing courtesans as their subject matter, Japanese artists of the seventeenth century were themselves breaking free from the strictures of artistic tradition – whether it was the austere style of ink painting inspired by Song-period Chinese art, or the indigenous *yamatoe* style of courtly painting. They turned their attention instead to contemporary manners (*fūzoku*), especially those of the common people living in the teeming cities – people who did not belong to either of the two ruling classes, the warrior (*bushi*) class or the nobility which made up the imperial court. An air of disreputableness lingered around the *ukiyoe*, and they were never really accepted among the categories of high art in Japan. This air of subversiveness gave *ukiyoe* woodblock prints their energy, exuberance and humour.

Western art traditionally had a different set of priorities. For instance, there was emphasis on the discipline of learning to draw from life. The schematic manner in which women's facial expressions were depicted in Japanese art was blamed largely on the absence in Japan of this practice. It came as something of a surprise to some visitors that the Japanese had not developed an artistic interest in the nude when – like the ancient Greeks – they had so much opportunity to observe the naked human body. Some western visitors found a certain attractive physical robustness and athleticism about many Japanese people of the common classes. Comte Raymond de Dalmas wrote appreciatively that the kimonos of Japanese women often revealed at the neckline a hint of a bosom worthy of antique statues of Venus. He also thought Japanese women possessed dainty hands and feet which were like masterpieces of sculpture, though sadly marred – since human beings were imperfect – by thick wrists and ankles.[27] The sight, however, of the naked torsos of working men – the palanquin bearers, rickshaw men and boatmen – attracted even greater admiration from some quarters, but elicited shrill protests of outraged modesty from others. The American geologist Raphael Pumpelly thought that Japanese boatmen, as well as others of the 'lower orders', were generally 'the best built men [he had ever] seen', with well-defined musculature on their arms, legs and back.[28] In August 1871, Baron Joseph Alexander von Hübner had the opportunity to scrutinise up close the bronzed, athletic bodies of the boatmen who were rowing him along the coast from Atami to Enoshima on his way to Kamakura. Writing with unfeigned admiration of the beauty of their lithe bodies, the slenderness of their hands and feet, and their supple, flowing movements, the baron compared the boatmen to classical Greek statuary:

> One must go to Japan during summer to understand Greek statuary of the golden age. The great masters of Attica and Corinth . . . constantly had before their eyes the movement of the muscles of the human body.[29]

Yet the Japanese, for all their supposed sensitivity to the beauties of nature, had never attempted to sculpt the naked human body, except in the grotesque (to the western eye) form of Buddhist divinities and spirits.

One way in which some western critics sought to explain why Japanese artists were so skilled in executing exquisitely delicate motifs taken from nature, yet so deficient in the art of depicting human anatomy, was to claim that the artistic taste for which the Japanese as a race were so famed was merely an innate instinct. An inborn taste for the picturesque, it was maintained, was in no way to be mistaken for true imagination, which the western races possessed in abundance but the Japanese fundamentally lacked. According to this line of argument, Japanese artists and artisans were dire at portraying women in any form other than that of caricature because they lacked the concept of the ideal, which is what the imagination aspires towards. Aimé Humbert suggested that naked-ness was less of a moral problem for the Japanese than for western races because the Japanese had no idea of physical beauty – Humbert exonerated the Japanese from the charge of licentiousness only to charge them with a lack of imagination. Their souls could not be corrupted by the sight of a naked body only because their imagination was no more capable of being seduced into the dangerous channels of carnality than of being lifted to the exalted heights of the ideal. This attitude of indifference towards the human physique could be contagious; Sir Edwin Arnold complained that the frankness with which the Japanese displayed their bodies had a dampening influence on his own imagination and sensibilities. The comte de Dalmas, meanwhile, was of the opinion that the Japanese lacked the mental capacity to perceive things in their totality. The Japanese knack for amassing diverse bits of information was not to be taken for intelligence. The comte felt that the Japanese fiddled with minutiæ while the bigger picture eluded their brains. He compared the Japanese to clever monkeys capable, perhaps, of taking apart a clock, but not of reassembling it. Behind these assertions lay the view that the Japanese were rather useless at abstract or meta-physical thinking.[30]

True imagination was defined by many of these commentators as a yearning after the ideal. It strove to express absolute beauty. But the Japanese fancy, it was frequently claimed, only produced bizarre, grotesque effects. Rutherford Alcock, who put together one of the first private collections of Japanese *objets d'art* in Britain and was instrumental in bringing Japanese art to the notice of the wider British public, declared that the Japanese had no concept of 'high art'. In Alcock's view, 'high art' exercised the imagination in a constructive fashion, helping to culti-vate and refine the 'higher moral faculties'. Otherwise, art just pandered to the baser human passions. The Japanese aimed only to produce effects that pleased the senses. They were content with such art that entertained them at its best with humour and wit, and, at its worst, with coarse obscenity. William Michael Rossetti wondered in his book *Fine Art, Chiefly Contemporary* (1867) whether a feeling for beauty was 'alien from the Japanese mind'. The Japanese, he wrote, seemed unable to conceive of 'beauty' either as 'an intrinsic element of art, or almost of nature'. Discussing some Japanese illustrated books, Rossetti suggested that while Japanese artists showed a compositional inventiveness, as well as a sense of unity in their designs which was unmistakably the product of an active imagination, they did not appear to possess a concept of 'moral beauty'. But Rossetti cautioned against jumping immediately to the conclusion that this artistic indifference to moral beauty was indicative of a lack of a sense of morality in daily life.[31]

Marcus Huish maintained that the Japanese artist was taught by his religion to consider the human flesh as nothing but repulsive decaying matter that was susceptible to temptation, whereas the European artist based his work on the 'conviction that the human figure [was] the most glorious piece of God's hand-iwork', which demanded meticulous study. It was in the eighteenth century that British empirical philosophers and German philosophers of aesthetics formu-lated the concept of high art as one that appealed not merely to the senses but ultimately to the reason. The influential German art historian Johann Joachim Winckelmann, the great exponent of the aesthetic superiority of classical Greek art, argued that it was through combining what an artist knew of beauty gleaned from the natural world that he was able to create an ideal beauty, a version supe-rior to anything that nature could herself produce. The nineteenth-century American art critic James Jackson Jarves, in his discussion of Japanese art, reached for Michelangelo's adage that the purpose and meaning of fine art was ' "to raise our intellect from earth to heaven" '. To represent the human body was but a means of seeking out the divine plan or, in classical terms, the Platonic ideal of feminine beauty. But the Japanese artist, ignorant of the discipline of life drawing, neglected the study of human anatomy. He did not have the most basic knowledge of the articulation of limbs, bone structure or musculature. How then could he even come close to the 'truth'? Even though the American painter John La Farge proposed that Japanese artists did possess their own concept of feminine beauty and Mortimer Menpes maintained that they aimed for a type of beauty that was not specific to one model or another but was an aggregate of sensations and images amassed over the centuries, the effect was derided by other scholars as grotesque exaggeration.[32]

There were attempts by western artists to marry the western classical tradition of the female nude with an interest in the art of the Orient. But Japan did not inspire western works of art comparable to the Turkish odalisques of Ingres or the Tahitian nudes of Gauguin. Absent is that intensity of desire to see into the lives of Japanese women, to probe the mysteries of their feminine world, to display their nakedness and vulnerability on canvas as if to possess them. In *Toilette japonaise* (1873), by the French Academic painter Marie-François Firmin-Girard, a nude woman strums a *shamisen* while sitting on the floor of a Japanese-style room crammed with Japanese *objets d'art*, with two ladies in elab-orate kimonos in attendance. While the *objets* are minutely observed and impart an exotic ambience to the painting, the nude itself is a conventionally idealised figure of a nubile occidental woman.

The American artist William Merritt Chase, who, in the late 1880s, painted numerous studies of western women wearing Japanese kimonos, produced a pastel entitled *Back of a Nude* (*c.*1888), in which the hard, flat and shiny surface of the gleaming Japanese golden screen which forms the backdrop to the painting,

4 Engraving of *Toilette japonaise*, 1873, after the original oil painting on canvas by Marie-François Firmin-Girard.

along with the stiff folds of the kimono about the model's waist, creates a contrast with the soft and supple flesh of the (Caucasian) woman, whose sharply tapering waist exemplifies an idealised western concept of female beauty. In the oil painting *The Orange Lantern* (1895) by fellow American artist Albert Herter, a nude woman with her back partially turned away from the observer sits with a gigantic spherical Japanese lantern held in her lap; the entire canvas is diffused with the muted orange and pink glow from this paper lantern, and the contours of the woman's flesh are soft, almost insubstantial in the ambient light. The flat background, with an oriental-style design of a watery stream and floating flower petals, makes the setting obscure and undefined. The orientalising effects in *The Orange Lantern* help to desexualise Herter's nude.[33] In contrast, there is nothing orientalising about *The Reading Girl* (1886–87), by the French-born artist Théodore Roussel, who worked chiefly in England and was a good friend of Whistler. His model (his mistress Hetty Pettigrew) has cast off her kimono and sash, which can be seen draped in sensuous folds on the back of the campaign chair in which she has settled down to read. She bends her head over the magazine she holds in her lap, and her long, shapely legs are stretched languorously out before her. The model's bare skin glows against the dark background of the painting. Her firm flesh is as sensually smooth and silken as her kimono. The painting was too sexually provocative for many of Roussel's contemporaries, and the scandal it caused when it was first revealed to the public at the New English Art Club in 1887 was reminiscent of the furore that erupted in 1865 at the first showing of Édouard Manet's 1863 painting *Olympia*, with its depiction of a naked young woman who seems to be announcing her sexual availability. The open and frank pose of Roussel's model harks back to Manet's painting.

Roussel does not employ a Japanese setting in *The Reading Girl*; James Tissot's attempt to do so in *Japonaise au Bain* (1864) was not successful. *Japonaise au Bain* is among the earliest of Tissot's Japanese-themed paintings, probably one of the three works Dante Gabriel Rossetti was told he was working on when Rossetti dropped into a Parisian curio shop that dealt in Japanese *objets d'art*.[34] The painting is an awkward evocation of imagined Japanese sensuality. Tissot meticulously reproduces the details of the elaborate Japanese headdress and embroidered kimono worn by the model. But the kimono is open in front and reveals a conventionally idealised, rather plump nude female body, awkwardly posed, standing gawkily on the hem of the garments with legs akimbo. Although Tissot's Caucasian model cocks her head and gazes knowingly at the viewer, while leaning invitingly against a wooden pillar, she remains strangely unengaged. One comes away with the impression that she is not doing much more than serving as a mannequin for the Japanese costume.

With *The Prodigal Son in a Foreign Land* (1880–82), Tissot was rather more successful in his attempt to evoke the eeriness of Japanese artifice as it was manifested in the geisha's costume. The painting, the subject of which is a fanciful depiction of a Japanese geisha party, constituted the second in Tissot's series of four paintings in which he set the biblical theme of the prodigal son in the context of modern decadence. In the painting, a row of dancing geishas sheathed in layers of heavily padded kimonos emerges from the gloaming into the fitful light of paper lanterns. They loom before the small figure of a bowler-hatted, mustachioed boulevardier from the west. Monumental, indistinguishable from each other by either clothes or facial expression, the geishas remain indifferent to the fate of the self-styled man of the world. Whether he continues down the path of dissipation he has chosen for himself is no concern of theirs. Tissot owes much of his effect in this painting to his use of heavy chiaroscuro, which recalls Degas's evocation, in his masterful paintings of ballet dancers and café-concert chanteuses on stage, of a sense of the surreal that is produced by the play of shadow and colour under the garish glare of artificial light in the night.[35]

Tissot's painting accords with the darker side of the spirit of the age. Creatures of the night, such as chanteuses, fascinated Charles Baudelaire, who

5 James Jacques Joseph Tissot, *The Prodigal Son in a Foreign Land*, 1880, oil on canvas.

belonged in the early 1860s to the exclusive circle of artists and writers who first started to collect Japanese art (what Baudelaire referred to as '*japonneries*' in one of his letters).[36] In the scandalous, predatory, chameleon-like women who flourished in the gaslit nocturnal world of Paris, Baudelaire felt he had caught a glimpse of 'the special beauty of evil' which lurked in modern life. These modern women transformed themselves over and over again in protean fashion, rising above the crude imperfections of nature through their use of art. They used cosmetics and dress not merely to conceal the loathsome natural functions of life. Rather, they became 'an indivisible unity' with their costume, transforming themselves into new monstrous beings.[37] Similarly, the Swiss envoy Aimé Humbert's imaginary Yoshiwara, which he described in his 1870 book on Japan, was inhabited by merciless courtesans who wear upon their backs banners (in the form of kimonos) proclaiming to the world their pitiless campaign of revenge against the male sex. Enveloped in garments portraying, for example, scenes of hell, in which the damned are being sentenced by the judge of the underworld, these women hold men in their thrall with 'a satanic power'. They gloat among themselves over the number of victims they have ruined, then rejected, and finally driven to suicide.[38]

William Michael Rossetti felt that 'atrocity' – ferocity in emotion, in action, in expression – was the chief preoccupation of Japanese art.[39] It was widely conceded in the west that something at which Japanese woodblock artists excelled was capturing the quirks of Japanese behaviour on paper. Katsushika Hokusai was especially venerated by nineteenth-century Japanophiles in Paris since the engraver Félix Bracquemond discovered a volume of Hokusai's *Manga*, a series of woodblock-printed books containing caricatures and sketches, at the shop of the printer Delâtre in 1859, perhaps even as early as 1856 as Bracquemond himself later claimed.[40] The *Manga* came to fifteen volumes altogether, and was published between 1814 and 1878. It was a design manual of sorts, offering examples of ways of depicting geological phenomena and weather, domestic architecture and household furnishings, plants and animals. *Manga* also included depictions of fictional characters from both Chinese and Japanese classics, bizarre creatures out of folklore and grotesque supernatural beings, as well as pages and pages of ordinary people caught in motion as they go about various daily activities. Hokusai's extensive range of caricatures contributed to the western consensus that the Japanese imagination was essentially fantastical in nature. The most generous comment Kenneth Clark, the magisterial British art historian of the mid-twentieth century, was able to make about *ukiyoe* bathing scenes, such as those by Torii Kiyonaga, was that they depicted a 'passing show of life', albeit of unseemly private acts which might best have been left unrecorded. Such activities, however, did not help present the human figure as a 'serious subject of contemplation', a prospect which, according to Clark, simply had not occurred to either the Chinese or the Japanese.[41]

Nineteenth-century western artists such as Manet and Degas, who were beginning to rebel against the classical idea of the nude, had the example of Japanese prints before them as they sought to depict nakedness in the context of daily life as it was led in the present world. Degas, who is known to have had a diptych of a bathhouse scene by Torii Kiyonaga hanging above his bed at one time, began to produce from the mid 1870s a great number of pictures, in a variety of media, of women clambering into or out of bathtubs or squatting over a basin. Some of these women appear to be prostitutes: the shadowy silhouette of a man often lurks in the corner of the picture, watching the woman at her ablutions. As Richard Thomson points out in his study of Degas's nudes, it is unclear 'where vice ends and respectability begins'.[42] There is nothing classically elegant or poised about Degas's nude bodies. Degas rebelled against the idealising view of the body as a vessel for the noble soul. He said he showed women 'without their coquetry, in the state of animals cleaning themselves'.[43]

The unconventional poses of Degas's women reflect *ukiyoe*'s tradition of capturing the human form at unexpected awkward moments when it is contorted by motion, often violently. Degas's women remain oblivious of, or indifferent to, the observer's gaze. Just as the women in his monotypes of the late 1870s do not feign modesty or coyness as they wash themselves or comb their hair in the presence of a man, so the women in the later pastels of the second half of the 1880s are equally unselfconscious. They energetically twist their dumpy bodies this way and that, stretch, crouch, squat, and bend over double in order to reach their toes with their towel. Degas's contemporary the dramatist Octave Mirbeau was struck by the 'terrifying sense of . . . anatomies twisted and deformed by the violent contortions to which they are submitted'.[44] A similar eye for movement characterises Degas's paintings of other women marginalised on the fringes of society – laundresses, for example, who were known to descend to casual prostitution at times of financial difficulty, and the dancers at the Opéra, including the younger students, who were known as the *petits rats de l'Opéra*.

There was a type of *ukiyoe* that particularly horrified and fascinated western artists and writers: sexually explicit compositions, which were formerly known in Japan as *waraie*, but are now more commonly called *makurae* ('pillow pictures'), or *shunga* ('spring pictures'). John Saris, who commanded the first English expedition to Japan, returned to England in 1614 with a collection of erotic books and pictures, his ownership of which became something of an open secret. This landed him in trouble with his employers, the English East India Company, and his hoard was ordered to be burned publicly so that the good reputation of the Company should remain unsullied.[45] Nineteenth-century visitors to Japan were also aware that books with *shunga* illustrations were widely available for sale. The official account of the American expedition led by Commodore Perry stated that 'popular literature with . . . obscene pictorial illustrations' could be readily obtained, although Rutherford Alcock wrote that obscene publications did not generally obtrude on one's notice unless one actively sought them out. On the other hand, the German painter Eduard Hildebrandt, who was in Japan for six weeks at the end of the summer of 1863, wrote in his memoirs that very young children could be found peddling erotic pictures and dolls in the street.[46] Foreign visitors may have been shocked to find such items for sale in Japan, but such material had a way of finding its way to Europe and America. Degas, the Goncourt brothers, Auguste Rodin (who assembled his collection of *ukiyoe* prints with advice from Edmond de Goncourt), Aubrey Beardsley (whose sexually provocative compositions, most notably the preposterous, gargantuan phalluses in his illustrations to Aristophanes' *Lysistrata*, privately published in 1896, show the influence of Japanese *shunga*), and even the eminent American collector of Japanese art William Sturgis Bigelow all owned works of this kind. The idea even in more recent times that the Japanese employ ancient *shunga* picture scrolls and erotic woodblock 'pillow books' as a kind of pornographic sex aid is reflected in works as diverse as Ian Fleming's James Bond caper *You Only Live Twice* and Saul Bellow's *Herzog*, both first published in 1964, and in both of which a Japanese woman has to resort to pulling out a 'pillow book' in order to arouse – if only physiologically – her western lover's ardour, which is flagging because he fundamentally lacks interest in her.

Edmond de Goncourt refers to Kitagawa Utamaro's output of erotica in his study of the artist, *Outamaro: Le Peintre des maisons vertes* (1891), Goncourt's first book on Japanese *ukiyoe* art.[47] As the title of the book suggests, Goncourt characterises Utamaro, who was active in the latter half of the eighteenth and first decade of the nineteenth centuries, as one of the most inspired Japanese woodblock artists to deal with the subject of the inmates of the '*maisons vertes*', a literal translation of the Japanese word *seirō* (borrowed from the Chinese), which was another term for the legal brothels of the brothel quarter. Goncourt acknowledged the wide breadth of Utamaro's repertoire, ranging from infants to insect life, but he praised Utamaro above all for the delicate, supple and sensual, yet at the same time ethereal and soulful way in which he depicted '*la grande prostituée*' of the Yoshiwara, of whose way of life Utamaro had a deep, first-hand knowledge, according to Goncourt, not only because the artist had lodged early in his career with his publisher Tsutaya Jūzaburō, who lived near the main gate of the Shin-yoshiwara quarter, but because Utamaro himself became something of a debauchee, even though he remained a hard-working artisan all his life.[48]

Goncourt believed that Utamaro had depicted himself in a famous *shunga* picture, the tenth in a series of twelve erotic illustrations which makes up Utamaro's first (and probably best known) *shunga* album *Utamakura* (1788), the title of which Goncourt translated as *Le Poème de l'oreiller*. This picture shows a couple in a voluptuous embrace, the sinuous folds of their kimonos revealing glimpses of white legs and thighs intimately intertwined. But genitalia are not depicted; intercourse is only delicately hinted at, not least by the risqué poem written on the open fan which the man holds (in a position which might very well stand in for an erect penis): 'The snipe whose beak is held fast between the two halves of a clam cannot fly away this autumn evening.' The woman has her back to the viewer, and caresses her lover's cheek with her left hand, while his left hand grips her shoulder which the dipping collar of her kimono has bared. The woman's head blocks one's view of the man's face almost completely except for one slender eye, the curve of which follows the flowing line of the woman's wide coiffure.

Despite Goncourt's claim that Utamaro meant to represent himself in this idealised portrait of the elegant and languid Japanese man about town, he admitted that there was nothing in the picture that explicitly spelt out any connection between the young man and Utamaro; the only evidence he could point to was the similarity of the pattern of the man's kimono to that worn by a

6 Kitagawa Utamaro, lovers in a private upper-storey room of a teahouse, coloured woodblock *shunga* print from the printed folding album *Utamakura*, 1788.

character who was supposed to be a representation (albeit not a naturalistic portrait) of the artist in one of Utamaro's other works.[49] Despite the lack of concrete proof, Goncourt was convinced – intuitively, he admitted – that the scene in Utamaro's *Utamakura* was a depiction of the artist himself dallying with a favourite courtesan in a Yoshiwara brothel.

There is, however, nothing in the picture to indicate that the woman is actually a courtesan, let alone that the scene occurs in the Shin-yoshiwara brothel quarter. That she is meeting a man in a teahouse for an assignation is beyond doubt, but all around Edo there were special teahouses called *deaijaya* where couples could meet for an illicit rendezvous. Many of the other illustrations in Utamaro's album *Utamakura* likewise depict townspeople conducting assignations in teahouses of this kind, rather than professional courtesans at work in the brothel quarter. In one picture, the woman can be identified from her head-covering as a waiting woman in a noble household (*oku-jochū*). Waiting women who spent all their time in the strictly segregated female living quarters of noble households were granted leave on special days to go out to pray on behalf of their mistresses at a shrine or a temple. In the popular imagination, they were sex-starved women who took advantage of their rare days out illicitly to attend the theatre and afterwards enjoy an assignation with a lover (or even a bout of sex with a lowly male attendant if no lover were forthcoming). Young unmarried women, adulterous wives, unfaithful concubines, and geishas all feature in *shunga*. Dress, hair and personal belongings help identify the social class of these women. Their emotions range from ecstatic lust to middle-aged domestic tenderness, through to detached boredom. Early examples of *shunga* generally portray women as willing, if not eager, assertive and enthusiastic, participants in love-making. It was from the third decade of the nineteenth century that images of degradation, brutality, bondage and rape began to appear.

When courtesans and geishas turn up in *shunga*, as they do in works dating from the last couple of decades of the eighteenth century and the first half of the nineteenth, they are more often than not depicted indulging in clandestine sexual liaisons. Shin-yoshiwara courtesans are shown enjoying furious, if furtive, sex with their own private lovers. Geishas are recognisable in *shunga* by their *shamisen*, and the women from the unofficial Fukagawa pleasure district by their rolled-up bedding, or *futon*, which they took with them whenever they were called out to meet a client. *Furisode shinzō* – young, recently fledged courtesans (usually aged between thirteen and sixteen) who acted as attendants to senior *oiran* – are occasionally depicted, by Torii Kiyonaga for example, in an intimate, illicit clinch with their mistress's patron. One of the unwritten rules of the Shin-yoshiwara quarter prohibited a man already in a relationship with one courtesan from having sex with another, including the young attendants with whom he might be left while his partner was called away to attend to other business.

Discussing *shunga*, Edmond de Goncourt found it extraordinary how the Japanese imagination employed images of tortured, convulsed, racked bodies to convey the idea of sexual pleasure. When, in his study of Utamaro, Goncourt wrote of 'the ardour, the fury of these copulations', 'the entanglement of bodies melted together', 'the sensual tremblings of the arms, welcoming at the same time as repulsing coitus', 'these feet with twisted toes, epileptically beating the air', 'these swoons of the women, their head tilted against the ground with "the little death" written on their faces', he chose as his example a *shunga* by Hokusai, rather than a work by Utamaro, to illustrate the terrifying and grotesque manner in which the Japanese imagination was capable of depicting the violence of sex.[50]

The print is of an *ama*, or female abalone diver, sprawled naked on a rock, with two octopuses sucking her mouth and genitalia. It was published in Hokusai's *shunga* collection, *Kinoe no komatsu* (1814), an album to which Goncourt refers again in his study of Hokusai, published in 1896. The theme of the *ama* and the octopus is not unique to Hokusai.[51] The eighteenth-century *ukiyoe* master Suzuki Harunobu depicted an *ama* being leered at from a distance by an octopus. This print, in a narrow 'pillar' format, was in the collection of the French jeweller and notable art collector Henri Vever.[52] Another version of the theme was produced by Hokusai's teacher Katsukawa Shunshō: a ferociously squinting octopus grapples an *ama*'s right ankle as she clambers on to a rock with an abalone in her hand. One of the octopus's waving tentacles is vertically positioned right below the woman's genitalia, which are veiled (but hinted at) by her parting underskirt. The woman, however, looks back placidly at the aggressive octopus, showing no sign of either fright or annoyance, or of amorous interest; the passion is all on the side of the octopus.[53] In the Hokusai picture, the woman (who is slightly less identifiable as an *ama*, being divested of her traditional red underskirt and of any abalones she may have caught) is in the throes of sexual excitement. She is not portrayed as the passive, inert object of the octopuses' attention. Her hair, which is undone to facilitate her diving, looks as though it has unravelled during sex.

Hokusai's picture is more subtle than a mere invitation to the viewer to share vicariously in the *ama*'s sexual ecstacy. Goncourt neglects to mention that the composition is in fact completely surrounded by dense script, which is tightly packed into all the available space around the two octopuses, the woman and the rocky outcrop which they occupy. Such use of writing is very characteristic of Hokusai. Early *shunga* of the eighteenth century (for example by Suzuki Harunobu) often had at the top of the page a poem or a prose description which set the scene portrayed in the picture. These insertions were called *kotobagaki*. By the 1780s, *kotobagaki* had disappeared and dialogue was being written into the pictures instead. In many of his *shunga*, Hokusai completely filled in the spaces around his figures with speech and very explicit sound effects. Where dialogue accompanies a *shunga*, it helps to clarify who the participants are and what the relationship between them is – a relationship that may very well turn out to be surprisingly different from what the viewer might have supposed. Dialogue also provides an opportunity for the woman in particular to speak her mind, which she often forcibly does; thus she escapes being reduced to a passive, mindless victim of male sexual desire. Moreover, speech often helps to distance the viewer from the action in the picture by introducing a layer of pathos, bathos or satire to the proceedings. Dialogue can no more be dispensed with in reading a *shunga* picture than it can be when reading a Rowlandson or Gillray cartoon.

The writing that surrounds the woman and the two octopuses in the Hokusai print is full of sound effects, as is typical of other *shunga* by the artist.

7 Katsushika Hokusai, an abalone diver pleasured by two octopuses, coloured woodblock *shunga* print from the illustrated book *Kinoe no komatsu*, 1814.

While Edmond de Goncourt thought the woman in the picture looked as lifeless as a cadaver, Hokusai actually provides her with a great deal of moaning and groaning, and this from pleasure rather than pain. At one point, she exclaims, 'What a good octopus you are!' The sensation of terror (if not of revulsion) which Goncourt felt melts away into further farcical surrealness when the reader realises that the larger of the two octopuses is suggesting to his companion that they take the woman back home with them to the Ryūgū, the mythical undersea palace of the dragon-god. Meanwhile, the smaller of the two – which is only being allowed to suck the woman's mouth – cheekily boasts of its (his?) sucking abilities. The picture is a grotesque satire on rampant male – and female – lust.

The image of Hokusai's *ama* lingered on, however, in nightmarish fashion in the imagination of European writers of the *fin de siècle*. J.-K. Huysmans refers to the print in his 1889 essay on the erotic works of the Belgian artist Félicien Rops, whose illustrations to *Les Diaboliques*, Barbey d'Aurevilly's collection of short stories on themes of decadent and sadistic sexuality, appeared in 1886. Huysmans thrills with horror at the picture of a woman being probed by the tentacles of a slimy octopus, her body convulsed with pain and anguish (in his view) while her face is diffused with '*la joie hystérique*' and her closed eyes make her appear as though she were already dead.[54] To Huysmans's mind, the print is virtually a sick celebration of necrophilia. Earlier in the same essay, Huysmans describes '[*la*] *hystérie mentale*' as the condition of a soul haunted by carnal thoughts at the same time as it dreads the pollution of the body.[55] He builds on Edmond de Goncourt's association of orgasm (as it is portrayed in *shunga*) with pathological convulsions and employs images of buckling limbs and writhing, straining torsos in order to describe the sexual positions depicted in *shunga*. Huysmans dwells on those pictures in which sex results in the most extreme and improbable physical contortions, as if an imagination as grotesque and violent as this were characteristic of all Japanese erotic pictures (and of the nature of sexual desire in the Japanese generally):

> With them, carnal intercourse seems to overwhelm the nervous system, to send searing flashes shooting through the bristling limbs tensed to breaking point; it tortures couples, making them clench their fists, and buckling, like an electric current, their legs so their toes writhe.[56]

The convulsions of sexual pleasure become indistinguishable from those arising from physical and mental pain.

At least, according to Huysmans, the Japanese were not hypocritical about carnal desires as the English were. He argued that physical continence only inflamed obscene thoughts – that it was those people who observed the most scrupulous physical chastity who also tended to be the most lascivious in spirit. The honest man discovers a channel in which desire can express itself. The protagonist in *A Rebours*, the aristocratic debauched former sybarite Des Esseintes, the last of a degenerate bloodline, shuts himself away in a country house so that he can lead a rarefied existence away from the necessarily coarse pleasures of the mundane world. In isolation, however, and despite his ener-vated state, Des Esseintes oscillates between deadly ennui and a frenzied craving for pleasure hitherto undiscovered. The chaste, demure heroines of Charles Dickens's novels, for example, make him think of 'the salacious seasoning, the prurient peccadilloes of which the Church disapproves'.[57] Des Esseintes yearns for pleasures that flout respectability and even morality. He enjoys the artificial – in what is as far removed as possible from the expected and the natural. But excess becomes linked in his imagination with images of disease, destruction and death, until he is wrung dry by horror and fear. In one of his nightmares, a woman turns into a beast of prey whose companion is '*la Grande Vérole*' ('the Pox'). The woman's vagina is transformed into a maw lined with sharp, devouring teeth. Female lust is avaricious, and it emasculates men. It transmits filthy, wasting diseases such as syphilis and consumption (both popularly associated with prostitutes), and passes hereditary degeneration on to children. The woman in Des Esseintes's imagination is covered with blisters, and her vagina is yet another 'hideous flesh-wound'.[58]

Huysmans sees similar images of disease in Japanese *shunga*. Female flesh looks 'lethargic' and 'white like emphysematous swellings'. Women's genitalia gape like a lesion.[59] When critics viewed Monet's *Olympia*, the colour of the woman's flesh suggested to many of them the idea of disease and putrefaction, and many viewers also assumed that the painting depicted a contemporary Parisian prostitute. Charles Baudelaire saw 'the emaciated flush of consumption' side by side with obesity, 'that hideous health of the slothful', in Constantin Guys's brothel pictures, which he greatly admired. For Huysmans, to give way to the inexorable demands of the flesh is willingly to embrace disease and submit to bodily violence. The Japanese, he declared, atone for their lust with the agony they endure during sex. Pain purifies the flame of desire, making it burn brighter and more keenly.[60]

Hokusai's image of the violated *ama* re-emerges in Pietro Mascagni's *Iris*, an opera about the fall, degradation and salvation-in-death of an innocent Japanese maiden. Premiered in 1898, *Iris* had a libretto by Luigi Illica, who later worked jointly with Giacomo Giacosa on the libretto for Puccini's *Madama Butterfly*.[61] Iris, the heroine of the piece, is a beautiful, startlingly naïve ingénue who has the misfortune to catch the eye of a well-heeled lecher named Osaka, who collaborates with the villainous proprietor of a geisha house to spirit the girl away from her wholesome country environment and take her to the Yoshiwara to have his evil way with her. Osaka seduces Iris by putting on a puppet play in which he provides the voice of 'Jor', the (fanciful) son of the sun god. In this way, he ensnares Iris – who is fatally betrayed by her own fantasies about the sublimity of love – with the power and beauty of his tenor voice.[62] Once in his power, Iris obstinately refuses to be seduced by Osaka's offers of riches and jewels (unlike Marguerite in Gounod's *Faust*), whereupon Osaka quickly loses interest in her. Kyoto, the proprietor of the geisha house, decides to make money out of her if he can and displays her in his shop window (Illica had obviously heard about the custom of *harimise*). Iris's blind father, who has pursued her to the Yoshiwara, discovers her there and publicly disowns her whereupon Iris flings herself from the high window and lands in a fetid gutter. As she lies dying, she is discovered by a horde of rag-pickers, who strip her of her remaining finery. Iris finally finds redemption and salvation in death.

The librettist Luigi Illica set familiar commonplaces about the innocent countryside and the wicked city – about natural goodness and corrupt artificiality – in the context of contrasting images of Japan: Japan as the land of flowers, and Japan as the land of ornate artifice. He evokes the idea of luxury and of opulence – of the closed oppressive world of the Yoshiwara – by calling up a profusion of grotesque Japanese artefacts – those Japanese *objets d'art* (though not necessarily the best examples of Japanese art) which were so dear to the hearts of western collectors. Illica creates a stifling, cluttered world, reflecting the hectic, restless humanity out in the streets, city-bred and city-nurtured, constantly clamouring for ever new diversions. His Yoshiwara is decked out in lacquer and gold; the only light emanates from the metallic sheen of the incense burners and the glitter of knick-knacks in enamel and cobalt. Jor, whom Osaka pretends to be, is the false sun in the sunless pleasure domes of the Yoshiwara. Jor is an elaborate fabrication, as is everything else in this realm of artificiality. When she is attracted to the glittering image of Jor, Iris takes her first step towards this world of false pleasures. Her ideas about love – gleaned from Jor's words addressed to the dying heroine of the puppet play – are as fantastical as Osaka's expectations of the novel pleasures that will be his when he finally beds Iris, whom he desires only as a change from the affected city *musumes,* of whom he has had enough. There is nothing particularly surprising about Osaka's motives: he has become bored with smart urban girls. It is no coincidence that the characters Osaka and Kyoto are named after cities, gauche and unconvincing as the names may sound. The symbolism is rather heavy-handed: Osaka has tired of the artificial glitter of the city and believes he covets the fresh, simple beauty of nature, personified in the flowery-named Iris.

Iris's own image of pleasure-as-evil is itself derived from art, not from life. Osaka tries to convince Iris he is not in fact Jor (for she remains under that misapprehension); rather, he is 'Pleasure'. Iris then recalls a screen she had seen in a temple when she was still a child. It had had a picture of a woman being violated by an octopus:

A broad lifeless shore, grey and black . . .
A young girl lay sprawled, thin in the limb, her hair all loose,
And on her lips a laugh which was a spasm . . .
From out of the lifeless sea a giant octopus raised its head . . .
And eyed the girl with an enormous crescent-shaped eye;

Overwhelmed by this terrifying sight, she fixedly stared!
From out of the lifeless sea, the monster moved its slimy tentacles,
And around her legs, her loins and her shoulders,
Then her tresses, her brow, her eyes, her thin panting chest, and her arms
It seized her and bound her!
It seized her and bound her face!
She still smiles!
She smiles and dies with a final spasm which is like a laugh . . . she smiles
And dies, dies!
The priest in a loud voice said,
'This octopus is Pleasure . . . this octopus is Death!'

Here was the east revealing its coarse carnality and repulsive sensuality, along with its contempt for life and for the sacredness of women. Japanese art is shown creating violent, gruesome images of nature and sexuality. Civilisation in Japan had only produced a culture of decadent pleasures, and the nightmare of the Yoshiwara mirrors the nightmare of the livid sea. On the other hand, the Japanese priest, in Iris's recollection, had used the image as a moral lesson about the horrors of sex, and Iris proves to have been the priest's ideal audience: she unquestioningly accepts his interpretation of the picture. Trapped in the Yoshiwara, she remembers the priest's injunction and instinctively recoils from thoughts of sexual pleasure. The opera does not suggest that there is an acceptable form of physical love: on the one hand, there is the repulsive Japanese sort of carnality embodied in the octopus; on the other, the rigorous rejection of pleasure enjoined by religion. Iris finds release and salvation only in death, in a Neoplatonic absorption of her soul into the all-encompassing life force of nature, represented by the actual sun, not Jor. Dramaturgically it is not surprising that *Iris* leaves the audience rather unpersuaded.

Notwithstanding his fascination with *shunga*, Edmond de Goncourt recognised that many of Utamaro's *ukiyoe* prints of courtesans showed them engaged in ordinary daytime activities which had nothing specifically to do with their profession – or with sex. For instance, Goncourt found Utamaro's prints of courtesans dallying with their children particularly touching, and he believed that Utamaro's skill in conveying emotions such as these maternal ones helped humanise the image of courtesans. Edmond de Goncourt, along with Balzac, Zola and Huysmans, was one of many nineteenth-century novelists who set out to study, through their fiction, the effect of prostitution on the minds and bodies of the women who fall into that way of life. In his novel *La Fille Élisa* (1877), Goncourt evoked the deadly ennui which he imagined characterised the daily lives of the unfortunate prostitutes cooped up in Parisian *maisons de tolérance*, whose shutters were required to remain closed even during daytime. The prostitutes' way of life makes them grow fat, like poultry kept in a darkened barn. Their flesh is slack, their bodies lethargic. Their brains are addled by the dreary boredom of the daytime and the drink they consume at night. Their constitution is broken by constant physical stimuli and the pleasures which they neither desire nor welcome. In Goncourt's view, prostitutes suffered from a permanent state of mental distraction; from 'a wandering mind, distracted, inattentive, empty and full of vagueness, unable to concentrate, incapable of following an argument, tormented by the need to drown out sorrow with noise, commotion and relentless chatter'.[63] Goncourt's protagonist Élisa devours romantic novels, which exercise a baleful influence on her immature, ignorant mind; prostitutes, Goncourt suggests, are less able than any other group of womankind to combat the extreme bodily sensations produced by an uncritical imagination overheated by reading. This is Edmond de Goncourt's vision of 'the violently sensual prostitution of the west',[64] against which he sets his contrasting image (drawn from the works of Utamaro) of a kind of prostitution he associates with Japan, where prostitutes strum musical instruments and are imbued with a unworldly poetic sensibility. As the description on the back of a stereograph of 'Charming *geishas* at dinner' produced by the American firm of Underwood & Underwood explained, the theme of the songs which geishas performed was usually 'vague, poetic pictures of the blossoming of flowers, the blowing of the wind, the dance of fire-flies and butterflies'.[65]

Notwithstanding the sullen defiance on the faces of Constantin Guys's sketches of prostitutes, Baudelaire had espied there an attitude of resignation which the poet associated with the Orient – a mute submission to fate that obliterates self-awareness. Lolling on their settees, Guys's prostitutes appear as stupid and stubborn as beasts; and yet they are capable, Baudelaire wrote, of assuming, at times and quite unconsciously, poses which astonished the viewer with an air 'of daring and nobility'.[66] Towards the end of 1870s, Degas, too, produced a series of about fifty monotypes in which he depicted imaginary scenes of prostitutes in similar moments of idleness, while they waited for custom – those empty moments which so intrigued writers such as Goncourt. Degas's images of the contemporary Parisian brothel, where dumpy women, naked but for shoes and stockings,[67] slump in chairs or loll on settees with their legs in the air, were a negation of those Turkish visions conjured up by the French neoclassical painter Jean Auguste Dominique Ingres (whom Degas admired so much), in which imaginary harems are inhabited by creatures who are voluptuous and seductive, and yet demand of the viewer that he turn only a chaste aesthetic eye upon them.

Henri de Toulouse-Lautrec came much closer than even Degas (by whose work he was deeply influenced) to sharing that sympathy, which Edmond de

8 'Charming *Geishas* at dinner – the correct serving of a Japanese meal, Tokyo, Japan', stereograph.

Goncourt ascribed to Utamaro, for women who worked in brothels. The German art historian Woldemar von Seidlitz, writing in 1897, suggested that Goncourt, attuned as he was to the culture of the *fin de siècle*, was ideally conditioned to appreciate the decadence of Utamaro's style, the mannered elegance of his courtesans which rejected all pretence of realism and exaggerated an unworldly, nearly morbid sensitivity of soul instead.[68] Toulouse-Lautrec, himself an enthusiastic collector of Japanese prints, eschewed Utamaro's idealising tendencies but did not exaggerate the morbid horror of degeneracy and disease which so fascinated his own contemporaries. Toulouse-Lautrec's prostitutes are not ethereally elegant or poetic, but neither are they coarse. Rather, they possess a much-tried dignity, even when they are shown in some of his paintings submitting to the humiliation of their regular genital check-ups. Just as Edmond de Goncourt had described Utamaro living in the Shin-yoshiwara quarter among the women he turned into the subjects of his pictures, so Toulouse-Lautrec claimed during 1893 and 1894 that he was living at various *maisons de tolérance* in Paris. He is known to have been on friendly terms with the proprietress of an establishment on the rue d'Amboise,[69] where he formed a close relationship with one of the prostitutes who worked there. After 1894, he became familiar with a brothel on the rue des Moulins, an infamous place notorious for the fantastical styles in which its rooms were done up in order to pander to the sexual caprices of its jaded clients. Based on his knowledge of the Shin-yoshiwara quarter, Utamaro caught what evanescent beauty was to be found among the transient pleasures which were on sale there. Drawing upon the intimate friendships he made among inmates of *maisons de tolérance*, Toulouse-Lautrec made the private moments of these women the subject of art.

In the seventeenth and eighteenth centuries, woodblock prints were the medium through which daily life in Japan was captured for posterity, but by the middle of the nineteenth, new technology was at hand to cater to the ethnographical curiosity of visitors. Towards the end of 1862 (five years before the fall of the Tokugawa Shogunate), one of the very first professional photographic studios to open in the country was established in Nagasaki. Its proprietor Ueno Hikoma set up a western-style studio for taking portraits. Many of his clients were foreigners, who could afford his high prices; besides, there was initially a widespread superstitious fear among many Japanese of having their photograph taken. Ueno also took his camera and portable darkroom out into the field, and photographed western clients out and about around Nagasaki.[70] Pierre Loti calls Ueno *the* fashionable photographer in town in his novel *Madame Chrysanthème*. Loti himself paid a visit to Ueno's studio to have his photograph taken with his seventeen-year-old Japanese 'wife' O-Kane (his model for the character of Madame Chrysanthème) and his friend Pierre Le Cor (the model for Yves, his narrator's subaltern). An account of the visit appears in Chapter 16 of the novel. The narrator Pierre and his friend Yves plan to have a portrait of themselves taken with Chrysanthème to send to their families back in France. The studio, situated in the hilly outskirts of Nagasaki, is very busy, and there is a long queue of rickshaws drawn up outside the building. A group of English sailors in white drill uniforms waits their turn in front of the camera. The studio is equipped with the same range of tired props that might be found in any contemporary photographic studio in Europe or America: the obligatory chair in 'old oak', heavily stuffed ottomans, mock-classical columns cast in plaster, and large rocks made of pasteboard. What appeared modern and chic to Japanese eyes looks hackneyed to Loti. A couple of aristocratic-looking Japanese women are having their photograph taken amidst furnishing in the style of Louis Quinze.[71]

In 1891 Ueno took a portrait of the tsarevich of Russia (who three years later became the ill-fated tsar Nicholas II) perched in a rickshaw. Among the many surviving photographs taken by Ueno are group portraits of geishas of the Inasa district of Nagasaki – these were the women who consorted with the Russians. Some of the first Japanese women ever to have been photographed appear to have been courtesans: when the daguerrotypist and artist Eliphalet Brown, Jr., who was chosen by Perry to accompany his 1853 expedition, wanted to take pictures of Japanese women, he is said to have been provided with some courtesans.[72] There was already a well-established custom for famous courtesans and teahouse waitresses to appear as subjects of *ukiyoe* (though they did not pose for them in the flesh), and after the arrival of photography, courtesans and geishas, along with kabuki actors, became popular subjects of commercially available souvenir photographs. Once the price of studio photography began to come down in the 1880s after the introduction of gelatine dry-plate photography, it became fashionable among courtesans and geishas to have their portraits done for a *carte de visite*. In *Madame Chrysanthème*, Chrysanthème has a collection of her female friends' *cartes de visite*, each with a portrait photograph taken by 'Uyeno' pasted on it.[73] Portrait photographs of this kind were available for sale to strangers at many photographic studios, and were used as a form of advertisement by courtesans and geishas. Henry T. Finck, music editor of the *New York Evening Post*, recounts how in Kyōto he visited some of the city's leading photographers so he could 'add to my collection of Japanese beauties':

> In each place they put before us a number of black lacquer trays, each containing a dozen photographs of popular geishas. You can buy not only the pictures, but the girls too – that is, you can secure their address and get them to assist at a banquet with their song, samisen, or dance.

The photographers refuse to sell him (although it appears they had no scruples showing him) private photographs of women who were not professional entertainers. This fills Finck with regret, for it seems to him that the women in the photos he cannot purchase are the most beautiful, refined and fascinating.[74] Photographs were also used in the brothel quarters to advertise the attractions of the courtesans. Instead of the women themselves being put on show behind large slatted windows, their portraits were framed and displayed outside the brothel to which they belonged. The Shimabara district in Kyōto adopted this method (called *shashinmise*) in July 1877. J.E. de Becker, who published a study of the Shin-yoshiwara district, reported that *shashinmise* took place there until 1882, after which *hikitejaya* teahouses provided photo albums for their patrons to consult before they went on to the first- or second-class brothel of their choice.[75]

Around the same time as Ueno was setting up his business in Nagasaki in 1862, another enterprising Japanese photographer was establishing his in Yokohama. Shimo'oka Renjō, born Sakurada Hisanosuke, quickly caught on to the foreign visitors' love of the exotic. He provided native 'accessories' with which his customers could have their photographs taken. He had kimonos and samurai armour for them to dress up in, and he could rustle up a westerner's fantasy of a native-style room (*zashiki*) by arranging in his studio a few *tatami*-mats and screens, even dragging in a stone lantern if desired. He had painted backdrops of typical Japanese scenery for clients to choose from and also employed, at considerable expense and difficulty, a young girl of the neighbour-hood to come and pose alongside clients if they wished it.[76]

Shimo'oka also sold souvenir photographs of Japanese people engaged in everyday tasks. Many of these were posed in the studio, rather than taken *in situ*. Picturesque genre photographs of the Japanese at work and play – as well as photographs of scenic views and famous Japanese landmarks – were sold in great numbers to foreign tourists and visitors, and were exported to the United States and to Europe, particularly to Britain and France. Pictures of this kind are now known collectively as 'Yokohama-style photographs' (*Yokohama shashin*), although their subject matter is by no means limited to Yokohama and its envi-rons. Starting with Shimo'oka's work, many of these photographs were hand-painted – with greater or less finesse, depending on the studio. Shimo'oka was said to have wanted in his youth to become a painter in the classical Japanese style, and his proficiency with the brush may have encouraged him to add colour to his work. However, the tinting of photographs was already being done as a matter of course in the west.[77]

Another photographer who produced such images of Japan in the 1860s was Felice (Felix) Beato. Of Italian descent, Beato took British nationality and began his career working with the British photographer James Robertson (who later became his brother-in-law). Beato went to the Crimea when, in the summer of 1855, Robertson took over from Roger Fenton the role of photographing the Crimean War. Over the next year, Beato produced pictures of the final stages of the conflict and its immediate aftermath. Later, in 1858, he travelled to India to record the impact of the Indian Mutiny. Then, in 1860, he joined the entourage of Sir Hope Grant, British commander in China during the Second Opium War, and was with British and French expeditionary troops as they moved in on Beijing that autumn. It was during his time in China that Beato met the British artist Charles Wirgman, who was producing illustrations of the conflict for the *Illustrated London News*.

Beato arrived in Japan some time in 1862 or the spring of 1863. In the autumn of 1864 he served as the official photographer attached to the British expedition to Shimonoseki, a port in western Japan which was bombarded by joint British, French, American and Dutch forces in retaliation for attacks by local Japanese on foreign shipping travelling through the strait between the major islands of Kyūshū and Honshū. Beato also built up a considerable reputation as a portrait photographer among the foreign community based in Yokohama. In 1864, he went into partner-ship with Wirgman producing and selling pictorial material relating to Japan.[78]

Their collaborative venture lasted from 1864 to 1867. Around 1868 Beato began to sell albums of hand-coloured Japanese photographs accompanied by explanatory material written by James William Murray. These included a two-volume set entitled *Photographic Views of Japan with Historical and Descriptive Notes*: volume 1 consisted of *Views in Japan*; and the second of *Native Types*. Beato's photographs and their accompanying texts were also available individually. Customers could make their own selection, and have them pasted into an album. The photographs were used as the basis of several of the engraved illustrations in *Our Life in Japan* (1869) by R. Mounteney Jephson and Edward Pennell Elmhirst, and in *Le Japon illustré* by the Swiss envoy Aimé Humbert, who was staying with Charles Wirgman in Yokohama in the summer of 1863.

Beato built up an extensive collection of photographs of Japanese scenery, though in 1866 he catastrophically lost his negatives in the fire that swept through Yokohama and destroyed his studio. He also photographed people of various social classes: samurai officials, nightwatchmen, firemen, palanquin bearers, rickshaw men and their passengers, merchants, street hawkers, barbers, doctors, Buddhist priests and nuns, sumo wrestlers, female street musicians, and 'Moosmies' (merely defined in the texts as 'girls'). Beato used women as models in photographs demonstrating various Japanese customs, from the way in which babies were carried on the back to the manner in which women had their hair dressed. Women were also shown eating, drinking (tea in some photos, *sake* in others), smoking the thin Japanese-style pipe, or *kiseru*, used for tobacco (not, as a common western misapprehension would have it, opium),[79] playing the *shamisen* (and other musical instruments), sitting around a brazier, and sleeping side by side under a single, thick, padded quilt. These scenes were often set up in the studio, and Beato employed teahouse girls and geishas to act them out. Not infrequently in souvenir photographs of this kind, the cosy atmosphere of the scene is heightened by the presence of a *shamisen* in the foreground or background of the composition. After all, many travel books on Japan pointed out that daughters of respectable households often learned to play the instrument too. But in *ukiyoe* prints, the *shamisen* more often than not served as a marker to signify that the woman in the picture was supposed to be a geisha. Since photographers of souvenir photographs had little alternative but to use teahouse girls, geishas, and possibly the mistresses of westerners as their models, the domesticity of such pictures is fraught with ambiguity.[80]

Domestic genre scenes of this kind became a very popular category of the Yokohama souvenir photograph. Some look quite innocent, showing women engaged in various domestic chores or out in rice- or tea-fields. Photographs of ingenuous-looking young women with dainty porcelain teacups would have reminded many westerners of the girls who staffed those Japanese teahouses which had become a staple feature of the international exhibitions held all over Europe and America. In other photographic compositions, demure young women read, write, arrange flowers, or bow deeply to each other in greeting. Still others show women at their toilette: washing; having their hair arranged by a friend or servant or colleague; or applying cosmetics. There are photographs showing women peering at their reflection in a mirror (sometimes using two hand-held mirrors), a composition which was used in *ukiyoe* but also conveniently corresponded with the long-established western iconographic emblem of vanity as a young woman – or the goddess Venus – holding a mirror in her hand. Washing and bathing (for which the Japanese were, of course, famous) were good excuses for showing female flesh. Photographs depicting women dressing, with their

9 Japanese woman checking her hair with two hand mirrors, late nineteenth-century hand-tinted photograph by Felice Beato.

10 Hand-tinted picture postcard of a Japanese woman standing on a cushion, tying/untying a sash, with her obi at her feet, early twentieth century.

thick obi coiled about their feet, are ambiguous since it is impossible to tell if the model is not in fact undressing. Pictures of gaily dressed girls being driven in or descending from a rickshaw look like innocent enough illustrations of quaint Japanese modes of transport; but when they are juxtaposed in an album with other photographs showing girls dancing, playing the *shamisen*, and in various stages of undress, they have the cumulative effect of portraying young Japanese women as women of pleasure.

Some photographs of dancing girls show elaborately costumed danseuses frozen in one or another of those dispassionate, highly stylised poses which constitute formal traditional Japanese dance. In others, however, one sees young girls, sometimes clad only in their under-kimonos (*jiban* or *juban*), kicking up their heels in a cruder, more raunchy kind of dancing, the type that took place when the *sake* and the beer had flowed freely in the banqueting room. Comte Ludovic de Beauvoir, who stopped off in Japan for a month in the spring of 1867 during a world tour, wrote how he had been entertained at a spa inn by geishas performing what he described as 'the classic dance of Japan!', which he called the '*chiri-fouri*' (presumably a French phonetic rendering of the Japanese *shiri-furi*, literally, 'waggling of the buttocks'). In this dance,

> [t]he dancers divide into two parties, and while dancing and throwing their hands about in time, as if to challenge, one begins a rhythmic sentence, which another continues, then a third, and so on; so that each one contributes, in her

11 Geishas dancing, late nineteenth-century hand-tinted photograph by Tamamura Kōzaburō.

12 Party entertainment – women dancing to a *shamisen*, late nineteenth-century hand-tinted photograph.

turn, an improvised song of a capricious and sportive nature, in which the wit is as lively as the gestures . . . . as soon as a dancer made a mistake in the rhythm or the time, she must . . . for a forfeit discard some part of her dress. Gradually they get more excited; the pride of each is in the game, the eyes sparkle, and all laugh wildly. First the right sleeve falls, then the left, then the scarf, then the robe, and the sash . . . .[81]

Dances of forfeit are mentioned frequently in western accounts of Japan, although visitors disagreed as to whether such dances were indicative of the loose morals of geishas, of habitués of teahouses or of foreigners who expected to see them performed. Aimé Humbert, in 1870, called this kind of dance an 'innocent prank' which the Japanese thought nothing of indulging in because its worst outcome – total nudity – was no more shameful than what they were accustomed to seeing in their bathhouses. But in 1907 Clive Holland wrote that the dance of forfeit called *chon kina* was 'performed chiefly in the Treaty Ports for the benefit of the foreigner, though sometimes referred to as a *geisha* dance'.[82] 'Chon kina' was originally a children's nonsense rhyme to which the hand-game *kitsune-ken* (one of many games similar to 'Scissors, Paper, Stone') was played. The American banker and author Walter del Mar describes five verses of the song in his 1903 account of his visit to Japan and makes it clear that the dance *chon kina*, as performed in certain teahouses, was a raucous, lewd form of entertainment.[83]

In January 1877 Beato sold his entire photographic stock to the firm of Stillfried & Andersen. Baron Raimund von Stillfried-Ratenicz was an Austrian soldier, diplomat and merchant, as well as an artist and a photographer, who had set up his own photographic business in Yokohama in 1871. Stillfried went into partnership with Hermann Andersen in 1876. The firm's work was shown at photographic exhibitions in America and Europe, but the partnership lasted only a little over two and a half years. In the summer of 1878, Andersen took over the firm, confusingly retaining the original company name. Meanwhile, Stillfried sold what stock he had in his possession to his brother Franz, crossed over to continental Asia and worked there as a photographer before returning to Vienna. In 1885 both Andersen and Baron Franz von Stillfried sold their businesses to the Italian-born American businessman Adolfo Farsari, whose firm in Yokohama published and sold guidebooks, maps and language books to visitors from abroad. Farsari & Company remained one of the best known suppliers of photographs of Japan even after Farsari's departure from the country in 1890. Because Farsari himself trained as a photographer and produced many of the images he sold through his studio, as well as acquiring Beato's, and later Stillfried's, negatives along with their businesses, it is often difficult to ascribe a particular picture precisely to one or another of them. Beato, Stillfried and Farsari all employed Japanese colourists to tint their photographs. Beato had this done to his photographs of people, though not to all. It appears that Stillfried later had colour added to Beato's landscape photographs.[84]

Stillfried took ethnographic curiosity about the Japanese a step further than Beato had ever done. In many of Stillfried's photographs, women are engaged in similar everyday activities but with their breasts exposed. They either have one shoulder out of their kimono, or their kimonos are drawn down to their obi. The Japanese custom of applying thick, white powder not only to the face but down the back of the neck served as a pretext for showing women in states of extreme undress. Beato had produced a photograph of a woman applying powder, whose kimono had slipped far down her shoulders, but he did not expose her nipples as Stillfried did. Although a few photographers did produce outright pornographic photographs showing women completely naked or with their kimonos open in front exposing their pubic area (rather reminiscent of the pose of the girl in Tissot's *Japonaise au Bain*),[85] Stillfried – and his imitators – masked the salacious nature of their topless photographs under the guise of ethnological interest, just as happened with the photographic postcards produced at the beginning of the twentieth century of naked South Sea islanders and North African women.

The photographers in Yokohama did not, by and large, attempt poses inspired by western antique statuary or European Old Master paintings, as photographers did in the west for the pornographic market, but one classically inspired theme that was repeated in many Yokohama photographs was that of the Three Graces, the three sister goddesses of ancient Greek mythology who presided over joy, charm, kindness and conviviality and were attendants (some also said daughters) of Aphrodite. They were depicted in classical statuary and in subsequent western art as three nubile women (often but not necessarily naked)[86] dancing hand in hand, or with their arms around each other or on each other's shoulders to emphasise their closeness and intimacy. Beato introduced this theme in a photograph of a group of three women; John William Murray, in his caption, wrote that while these three might lack the captivating looks suggested by the idea of the Graces, Japanese women more than made up for any physical shortcomings with their charming, delightful demeanour.[87] There were many subsequent variations on the theme of the Three Graces, all featuring a trio of women with their arms around one another or with their hands entwined. In Beato's photograph and many later ones, the women remained fully clad, but there were others in which the women were shown, awkward and gauche, with their kimono drawn down to their waist. The image of young girls embracing became a favourite among photographers producing souvenir photographs and postcards for the tourist market, even though displays of intimacy of this kind were never customary in Japan. On the surface, the image suggests the guileless, sentimental affectionateness of childhood; yet it hints at something much more physical and sexual.

While photographers such as Beato sought to record what struck them as so unfamiliar about life as it was led in this strange new country in which they found themselves, the dissemination of their images, frequently sold in albums containing 50, sometimes 100 or even 200 photographs, helped to fix the impression of alien-ness – the notion (already heavily promulgated in travel writing) that the ways in which the Japanese conducted their lives were (if picturesque at times and gratifyingly bizarre at others) perversely 'topsy-turvy', going against the grain of sane, sensible, western modes of behaviour. The restrictions on travel placed on foreigners until 1899 limited many to a narrowly circumscribed glimpse of life as it was led by the locals. Painters such as George Henry and E.A. Hornel, fellow members of a prominent Scottish group of artists known as the Glasgow Boys, who together visited Japan between 1893 and 1894, borrowed motifs for their Japanese paintings from souvenir photographs,

13 Three women holding hands, late nineteenth-century hand-tinted photograph by Baron Raimund von Stillfried-Ratenicz.

and they employed photographs (as did many other artists of the period, both painters and sculptors) in arranging the composition of their works. This, in turn, no doubt contributed to the success of Hornel's Japanese paintings, when he exhibited forty-four of them in Glasgow in the spring of 1895. The *Glasgow Evening Citizen*, reviewing the exhibition on 25 April, reported that the subject matter of these works included singing girls, dancing girls, fêtes, flower festivals, leisure boating, and the theatre, while the same body of work was described the following year in *The Studio* as a 'comprehensive pictorial record of Japanese life'. Henry and Hornel are thought to have collected around 140 souvenir photographs, or *Yokohama shashin*, during their stay in Japan.[88]

14 Three bare-chested Japanese women holding hands, late nineteenth-century hand-tinted Japanese photograph.

Souvenir photographs were such a commercial success that from 1882 onwards they appear in lists of leading Japanese exports. Kusakabe Kimbei, who had once worked for Beato hand-tinting photographs, established his own studio in 1881, and by 1892 had an inventory of around 2,000 negatives. Tamamura Kōzaburō began exporting photographs around 1881, a year before he moved his studio from Tōkyō to Yokohama; he went into business with Farsari in 1885, around the time the latter bought out Baron Franz von Stillfried and Hermann Andersen. Farsari and Kusakabe Kimbei were two of the main suppliers of souvenir photographs in Japan. After Farsari left the country in 1890, the chief producers in the business were all Japanese. Leading photographers in Yokohama included Sakurada Yasutarō, Suzuki Shin'ichi and Usui Shūzaburō, the last two having trained under Shimo'oka Renjō. Another prominent photographer of the day, Ogawa Kazumasa (also known as Isshin), who studied photography in America in the mid-1880s before setting up a studio in Tōkyō, utilised the style of the *Yokohama shashin* in some of his work, while widening his scope to record, as one of Japan's earliest photo-journalists, important events of his day, as well as the changing appearance of society.

Photographs of young women, nothing like as expensively and ostentatiously dressed as high-status courtesans of the pleasure quarters, appear to have been in much greater demand among foreign visitors than those of *oiran*. But Japanese brothel quarters, especially the Shin-yoshiwara in Tōkyō, did feature in landscape photographs. There were street scenes, as well as photographs of individual brothels, often with the inmates lined up in a row in front of the building or on the balcony. A number of photographs has survived of the 'Jinpooro' (Jinpūrō), or Brothel Number Nine, the Yokohama brothel famous among the international seafaring community. They show the brothel as it looked in several different locations, since it was rebuilt each time the city's brothel quarter was moved. There are photographs too of the Jinpūrō's other brothel, which was in the nearby town of Kanagawa.[89] Although the women in these 'Jinpooro' photographs are referred to simply as 'girls' in the English-language captions (when there is one), many wear flimsy sashes tied in a knot in front – such sashes, so unlike the heavy proper obi, are indicative of the very low status of these prostitutes. Yet photographs of these 'girls' appeared on picture postcards, and were sold in Yokohama. Photographs of prostitutes sitting behind barred windows were likewise used on souvenir postcards, produced, moreover, by Japanese firms. If there is a caption on these postcards, it is often in both English and Japanese, so it is clear that postcards of this sort were aimed at foreign tourists. Whether bought as mementos of a visit to a brothel or more generally as exotic scenes from Japanese life, such photographs helped to reinforce the association of Japan with prostitution.

15 'New No. Nine Girls Kanagawa', late nineteenth-century hand-tinted Japanese photograph.

The heyday of the souvenir photograph passed with the dawning of the new century. In 1888, George Eastman invented a camera which amateurs could operate. The British writer Douglas Sladen records using one such camera in Japan in 1889 – with near disastrous results on one occasion when the flash exploded in his hand while he was trying to photograph some geishas at a dinner being held at the Maple Club in Tōkyō.[90] However, while the demand for souvenir photographs dwindled, a new market was opening up for the commercially printed picture postcard, which, in Japan, were permitted for overseas use in 1899, and, in the following year, for domestic use. Firms such as Farsari & Company began reproducing their photographs on postcards. The development of cheaper printing processes made picture postcards much more affordable than souvenir photographs had ever been.

While many postcards again featured bare-chested women, others were more insinuating. One produced by the Yokohama studio of the American photographer Karl Lewis[91] features a serious-looking American seaman, a smirking Japanese girl, and a bottle of Kirin beer, together with the caption (borrowed from *Macbeth*), 'When shall we 3 [*sic*] meet again?' The girl has her

Yoshiwara, Tokyo.   原 吉 〔所名京東〕

16 'Yoshiwara, Tokyo', early twentieth-century hand-tinted picture postcard of a *harimise* scene.

hands clasped behind her head in a coquettish manner that draws the viewer's attention to the region of her bosom, decently enough covered, it is true, but suggestive nonetheless. The pose would have been familiar to westerners: it was used in pornography, but it was also commonly adopted in corsetry advertisements in Britain and America near the end of the nineteenth and the beginning of the twentieth centuries. While it serves the obvious function of drawing the viewer's attention to the relevant part of the model's anatomy, it hints at the woman's sexual availability and turns her into a temptress figure.[92] The Japanese girl is being presented in a way that a western viewer would register as saucy: the subliminal message is that the Japanese girl *is* saucy, but the language of gestures employed here is strictly western. Gabrielle Ray, the musical comedy actress and famed beauty, projects an air of sauciness in one of her picture postcards by assuming a similar pose in a kimono. The kimono wafts suggestions of sensuality because, on the one hand, the garment was associated with a race belonging to

17 'When Shall We 3 Meet Again?', early twentieth-century hand-tinted picture postcard.

the supposedly licentious east, and, on the other, because it had come to be adapted in the west as intimate boudoir wear, especially for women.

The idea of Japanese port life, reduced to a round of frivolous amusements, found its way to the west. It became, for instance, the subject of the musical comedy *The Geisha, a Story of a Tea House*. *The Geisha*, which opened at Daly's Theatre, London on 26 April 1896, did more to popularise the image of the Japanese geisha among the general public in Europe than any other work of mass entertainment. Sauciness, but without overt impropriety, was the flavour of musical comedies, and the subject of geishas fitted the bill perfectly. The British theatre manager George Edwardes, who produced *The Geisha*, was renowned for the musical comedies he staged at the Gaiety Theatre. He had once been Richard D'Oyly Carte's theatre manager at the Savoy Theatre. In September 1885 (and six months into *The Mikado*'s run), Edwardes left the Savoy to take up the management of the Gaiety, which had been notorious for its burlesque shows and scantily clad girls. At the Gaiety Edwardes created a new style of musical entertainment – the musical comedy – which proved phenomenally popular

18 Black and white picture postcard of Edwardian musical comedy actress Gabrielle Ray.

at least up until the outbreak of the Great War, and paved the way for the development of the West End musical in the 1920s. Musical comedy tended to be a somewhat uneasy cross between light opera and broad comedy, romance and crude slapstick, lyricism and farce. Edwardes's success lay in making burlesque's sexual provocativeness outwardly respectable. A theatre critic delivering his verdict on *Dorothy*, the Gaiety Theatre's 1886 offering, neatly summed up the appeal of Edwardes's musical comedies: 'good music, well-sung, pretty faces, pretty scenery and pretty dresses and a little broad fun and no vulgarity'.[93]

Edwardes was a master of titillation, and *The Geisha*, safely set in distant Japan, used comedy to blur the issue of prostitution, while exploiting the sexual frisson in the plot by disguising it as flirtation. It had a libretto by Owen Hall (the nom de plume of journalist and theatre critic James Davis), who had already written two highly successful musical comedies for Edwardes, *A Gaiety Girl* (1893) and *An Artist's Model* (1895). The lyricist Harry Greenbank and the composer Sidney Jones, who had teamed up for Hall's two previous shows, supplied the score. Additional songs were composed by Lionel Monckton and James Philp. Running for 760 performances, *The Geisha* was one of the most successful stage musicals to be put on in London up to 1966. It did well in the United States and in continental Europe, where its situational humour, its exoticism, farce and sexual innuendo made it more popular with audiences than Gilbert's flourishes of verbal wit in *The Mikado*. Chekhov, in his short story 'The Lady with the Dog' (1899), sets a reunion between a pair of former lovers at a provincial Russian premiere of *The Geisha*.

The Geisha featured geishas, not courtesans or prostitutes. But at the same time, geishas and courtesans historically shared a similar fate in that they were indentured into service, and the suspicion that this was actually a form of sexual slavery is exaggerated in *The Geisha* into an auction scene, in which geishas are the object of the bidding. Similarly, it is the exaggerated cavorting of an English character, Molly Seamore, pretending to be a geisha which communicates the insinuation that the much-vaunted innocence of the geisha girl might be more of an affectation than the Japanese cared to admit. Molly disguises herself in order to win back the affections of her erring fiancé, the British naval lieutenant Reginald Fairfax, who has become infatuated with O Mimosa San, a geisha at the Teahouse of Ten Thousand Joys. While she is still passing herself off as Roli-Poli, Molly gets caught up in the auction, but she dances spiritedly in front of the bidders, and sings a ditty entitled 'Chon kina', after the salacious dance known to returnees from Japan:

> I can dance to any measure that is gay,
> To and fro in dreamy fashion I can sway,
>> And if still my art entices
>> Then at extra special prices
> I can dance for you in *quite* another way.

> *Chon kina, chon kina,*
> *Chon chon, kina kina,*
> *Nagasaki, Yokohama, Hakodaté hoi!*

Walter del Mar noted in his 1903 book on Japan that the version of 'Chon Kina' from *The Geisha* had already crossed the seas to Japan, and was known as the 'new verse' to the song.[94]

Audiences, meanwhile, could feel free to enjoy the antics of the actress Letty Lind playing Molly Seamore pretending to be the geisha Roli-Poli, since this was ostensibly a satire on the Japanese. Molly alias Roli-Poli gets herself purchased for her pains by a lecherous Japanese marquis, who had forced the sale of geishas belonging to the Teahouse of Ten Thousand Joys in order to purchase Mimosa for himself, but has been outbid by the redoubtable Lady Constance Wynne, a friend of Molly's who is primarily concerned to keep Mimosa out of Fairfax's hands. The story concludes with sexual decorum re-established. Molly is reunited with the contrite Fairfax, and Mimosa is safely bestowed upon a suitably honourable fellow countryman of hers, Captain Katana. Mimosa, in gratitude to Lady Constance for keeping her out of the clutches of her unwelcome suitors, orchestrates a switch of 'brides' in order to rescue Molly from the marquis. In Molly's place Mimosa substitutes the pert, socially ambitious interpreter at the teahouse: a Frenchwoman, no less, who transgresses national identities by 'going native'. She welcomes a 'Japanese' marriage, especially if the groom is titled, and even if he happens to possess a harem already.

Edwardes's canny ability to keep just within the bounds of acceptable innuendo is reflected in the critics' general commendation of *The Geisha*. The London *Times* praised it for succeeding in being 'humorous without eternally transgressing the laws of decency' (27 April 1896). The *Stage* pointed out that the Japanese teahouse was 'according to Occidental morals . . . a place of questionable resort', but felt that this dangerous fact was 'sufficiently remote and obscure as to be beyond the cognisance of the audience' (30 April). Both the *Pall Mall Gazette* and the *Illustrated London News* (2 May) were coy about what the 'merry little pattering and laughing Japs' were supposed to get up to at their teahouses. The latter hinted that the song 'A Geisha's Life', sung by Marie Tempest in the role of Mimosa, threw a '*couleur-de-rose* air' over the realities of Japanese life. The review went on to suggest that readers who wanted to know more about the 'kind of happy-go-lucky life led by mousmees and Geisha girls, samisen-players, and tea-house idols' should consult 'that delightful story called "Madame Chrysanthème" by Pierre Loti' – which the review described as a 'delightful sunny romance'. The *Daily Telegraph* (27 April) murmured darkly of the venal soul of Japanese women who preyed upon unsuspecting European males. Such sinister truths about Japan could be found in books like *Madame Chrysanthème*, which (contrary to the view of the reviewer for the *Illustrated London News*) had to be carefully kept away from the chaste eyes of one's female kin; meanwhile, *The Geisha* provided a pleasant illusion of a happy, guileless,

19 Black and white cabinet photograph of actress Marie Tempest as O Mimosa San in the musical comedy *The Geisha* at Daly's Theatre, London, 1896.

obliging people. The reviewer for the *Telegraph* praised *The Geisha* for being a delightfully innocent diversion from reality. He felt that the show, moreover, had the additional gratifying effect of highlighting the 'commanding presence, the assertive beauty, and the proud dignity of the Anglo-Saxon race', in contrast to the 'bowing and scraping little [Japanese] dollies'.

The geisha has retained in the west the sort of popular kitsch appeal which is in evidence in a work such as *The Geisha*. She is appreciated for being supremely decorative. Strangely enough, it seems that the question of whether or not a

20 Jean Faust, *Fleurs de Japon*, late nineteenth-century, oil on canvas.

geisha is, strictly speaking, a prostitute appears not to impinge much upon this decorative appeal, even though this issue constantly crops up in western discussions of the geisha. On the other hand, because most people outside Japan remain unaware of the sartorial distinctions in the way the kimono is worn by different people, Japanese women in various types of traditional dress are easily misidentified as geishas when it suits the beholder to do so. Geishas and ordinary young Japanese women exist interchangeably in the western imagination in the twilight zone between respectability and decadence, between prudery and immodesty. This ambiguity is apparent in paintings intended to have popular appeal, such as *Fleurs de Japon* by Jean Faust, a nineteenth-century French artist. The sloe-eyed subject of the painting wears a kimono-like gown open practically to her waist. Two enormous scarlet chrysanthemums are stuck in the piled-up hair on either side of her head (bunches of flowers – usually chrysanthemums – worn like a pair of gigantic earmuffs became part of a clichéd 'Japanese' look), and she gathers more blooms to her chest, though not so close as to inadvertently conceal any of her pearly skin. The facial features of the woman are racially ambiguous, although her dark hair and eyes suggest the east. She does not alienate the viewer with shocking evidence of racial difference. Nor does she offend with explicit bawdiness. She is not specifically identified as a geisha and she exudes enough coy innocence to remain within the bounds of inoffensive prettiness. Her moral ambiguity is merely hinted at by the neckline of her pseudo-kimono, the angle at which she tilts her heavily laden head and the suggested fullness of her lips. In such a way have geishas and ordinary Japanese women merged into one another in the western imagination.

CHAPTER THREE

Madame Butterfly's Antecedents: The Women of the Ports and Japanese 'Wives'

In pronouncing the musical comedy *The Geisha* a suitable entertainment for respectable company, its London reviewers praised the production for its success in throwing a rosy veil of deception over the unsavoury reality of prostitution in Japan's international ports and cleverly creating the illusion that the Japanese were primarily a fun-loving, happy-go-lucky race. But when reviewers declared themselves relieved that *The Geisha* managed to gloss over the kinds of detail that one might find in a book such as Pierre Loti's *Madame Chrysanthème*, they were, of course, piquing the interest of those members of the public (gentlemen, it was hoped, rather than ladies) who desired a more 'accurate' account. The 'truth', it was implied, was that those entertainments in which the Japanese indulged in their teahouses were decadent rather than innocent, and that all those amiable-looking Japanese women were rather more venal at heart than magnanimous.

Two influential western narratives appeared in the last decades of the nineteenth century dealing directly with the subject of a westerner's liaison with a local girl in Nagasaki: *Madame Chrysanthème* (1887), and the novella *Madame Butterfly* (1898) by the American writer John Luther Long. Pierre Loti was the name under which the French naval officer Julien Viaud established his literary reputation as the author of a series of exotic novels with a thinly disguised, semi-autobiographical French protagonist who has a romantic relationship with a local woman in faraway settings such as Istanbul, Tahiti and Senegal. *Madame Chrysanthème*, too, was based on Loti's personal experience, in this case from the summer of 1885 when he was stationed with his ship *Triomphante* in Nagasaki. Loti kept a detailed diary of a relationship he contracted at the time with a local girl named O-Kane. In the novel, Loti refers to his narrator and alter ego Pierre's relationship with a local girl as a 'marriage'. He describes in detail the steps Pierre, a naval officer like Loti, takes to find a 'bride' through the matchmaker M. Kangourou; his encounters with Japanese officials when he formalises his relationship with his eventual choice, Madame Chrysanthème; and the daily routine into which his life quickly settles once he is installed along with Chrysanthème in the house of paper he had imagined living in while still on his ship headed for Japan. Then, after all the preparation he has gone through, Pierre discovers he finds everyday life with Chrysanthème deeply tedious. Having secured Chrysanthème by means of a monthly payment of twenty dollars to her mother, he then complains of the lack of an emotional bond between them. He blames this lack of empathy squarely on the girl: on her lack of passion for Pierre and on her abysmal failure to arouse in him any interest in or desire for her. Pierre feels duped and cheated by the idea of a Japanese 'wife', of which he has dreamt on his way to Nagasaki. It is as though Chrysanthème is a product that has been sold to him under false pretences. On top of it all, at the very end of his stay in Japan, Pierre accidentally discovers Madame Chrysanthème's true colours. He comes across her singing to herself as she tests the silver dollars, Pierre's last present to her, with a little mallet. So Madame Chrysanthème turns out to be not just shallow and boring, but venal and duplicitous to boot. Pierre goes away feeling vindicated that he had never become attached to her.

In *Madame Chrysanthème* there is hardly any sense of shame on Pierre's part for participating in this charade of a marriage, bought with money. There is no sense of wrongdoing in making the most of what opportunities are open to him. Pierre has been told by fellow naval officers that setting up house with a local young woman was the thing one did when one was in Nagasaki. So Pierre arrives in Japan with every intention of trying out the arrangement for himself. Indeed, Pierre is really more interested in the *idea* of a Japanese 'marriage' than in meeting a particular woman:

> I shall choose a little yellow-skinned woman with black hair and cat's eyes. She must be pretty. Not much bigger than a doll . . . . A little paper house, in the midst of green gardens, prettily shaded. We shall live among flowers, everything around us shall blossom, and each morning our dwelling shall be filled with nosegays, nosegays such as you have never dreamt of.[1]

John Luther Long's novella *Madame Butterfly*, which first appeared in the *Century Magazine* (New York), was in part a riposte to Loti's extremely popular novel. Long based his novella on an anecdote that had been related to him by his sister, who was a missionary in Nagasaki. It had concerned a sweet 'tea-house girl' named Chō, or Butterfly, who had been abandoned, together with her baby, by her lover from the west, a navy man, like Loti. He had promised he would come back to her one day, but he never did. The faithful girl had spent months peering down at the harbour from behind the sliding paper screens of her house, waiting for the return of his ship. Then, one day, she was gone, her house was empty, and nothing more was ever heard of the girl by the foreign community in Nagasaki.[2] Long worked his sister's account into a tale of callous selfishness on the part of the western lover and tragic misunderstanding on the part of the Japanese heroine, culminating in her attempted suicide. In 1900 it was adapted into a successful stage play by the American playwright, director and theatre producer David Belasco, working in collaboration with Long.

In contrast to Loti's collected, composed and undemonstrative Chrysanthème, John Luther Long created in his Cho-Cho-San an exuberant, effervescent chatterbox who is naïve, trusting and childishly loving. Loti's Pierre and Chrysanthème are a couple trapped in an arranged marriage in which neither party particularly cares for the other. It could have happened in Japan or indeed in France. Chrysanthème is very much like an idle, bored bourgeois nineteenth-century Parisian wife in a comfortable, arranged marriage, supported financially by her husband and with servants to take care of the housework. Long's Cho-Cho-San, on the other hand, falls passionately in love with her American 'husband' at first sight, although she had actively disliked the idea of becoming the 'wife' of an American before meeting him and had only accepted the proposition out of consideration for her family's financial situation. The beastly barbarian she had dreaded had turned out to be a god – ' "so tall an' beautiful" ',[3] she breathlessly tells the American consul. She is deliriously happy that Pinkerton pays her so much attention, not realising that he is amusing himself at her expense, treating her like a plaything and cracking cynical jokes – what Long calls Pinkerton's 'whimsy'[4] – which Cho-Cho-San naïvely takes at face value. Her depth of credulity is such that Long's Cho-Cho-San comes across as a condescending portrait of the ignorant but trusting foreign native of the kind whom well-meaning visitors from the west might make the mistake of treating as nothing more sophisticated than a prattling young child, as Pinkerton and his American wife do.

Whereas Pierre, in Loti's novel, hones his feelings of exquisite boredom by accompanying Chrysanthème on her rounds of senseless social frivolities with her friends and relations, Pinkerton, in Long's novella, bans Cho-Cho-San's relatives from their house because he finds them 'wearisome'. He has no time for their traditions or their beliefs. Unlike in Puccini's opera, in which Cio-Cio-San (as her name is rendered in Italian orthography) is rejected by her uncle, the Buddhist priest, and the rest of her family for having paid a visit to the Christian mission, in Long's novella it is Pinkerton who brings about Cho-Cho-San's estrangement from her family. He not only isolates Cho-Cho-San from her living kinsmen, but tells her she must do without her 'ancestors' as well. When Cho-Cho-San becomes alarmed at this (since, according to the novella, she believes along with all Japanese people that life in the hereafter depends upon her filial devotion to her family and her ancestors), Pinkerton suggests that from now on he will be her sole family and her religion, adding, by and by, that the west has its own methods for attaining spiritual redemption, which Cho-Cho-San, contrary to Pinkerton's intention, takes seriously, betaking herself to the mission just in case her ties to her family should become severed. This is exactly what happens: Pinkerton's rejection of her family leads to their disowning her. This pleases Pinkerton because he now has her all to himself. In cutting Cho-Cho-San off from her traditions, he amuses himself with the thought that he has brought her ' "up-to-date" ', that he has succeeded in shaping her into 'an American refinement of a Japanese product, an American improvement in [sic] a Japanese invention'.[5]

While Chrysanthème in Loti's novel remains untouched in any way by her encounter with Pierre, Cho-Cho-San is changed by her relationship with Pinkerton, although she understands him imperfectly (the difficulties of communication caused by the language barrier are suggested in Long's novella and Belasco's play by the garbled English she is given to speak) and, as for his jokes and ironically meant observations on the customs of his own country, they pass completely over her head. On one level, she discovers passion; on another, her fidelity to him is underpinned not by her Japanese habit of obedience but by love. She, in fact, turns Pinkerton's cynical take on American ways on its head: he has facetiously told her that American couples stay together because divorce proceedings take so much time to go through the courts, but she comes away with the idea that the sanctity of marriage is upheld by American law. She forsakes all others (including her custom-bound family) to cleave unto her husband, just as the Christian marriage service enjoins her to do – although Long only mentions a 'wedding' and does not go into the details of a ceremony, while Puccini's opera has the couple united by an 'Imperial Commissioner' – a wholly fictitious official. The America seen through Cho-Cho-San's innocent eyes is the promised land of liberty and freedom. Through her guileless lips, the ideals of American society are reaffirmed in all their pristine simplicity. Cho-Cho-San believes she has made an American marriage and identifies herself with America; to her misfortune, nobody else does. In *Madame Chrysanthème*, Pierre expects more from the 'marriage' than he actually finds; in the Madame Butterfly story, it is Cho-Cho-San who expects her 'marriage' to be something more than it actually is.

John Luther Long does not refer to a marriage ceremony but he does blur the distinction between formal Japanese marriages and those make-believe ones of the ports by employing Japanese terminology referring to aspects of the former in order to indicate elements of the latter. For example, he calls Goro a 'nakodo', or 'matchmaker'. The *nakōdo* is the indispensable sponsor of a legitimate (that is to say, socially recognised)[6] Japanese marriage. Long also refers to the visit Goro arranges for Prince Yamadori to make to Cho-Cho-San's house as a 'look-at meeting', presumably referring to the Japanese custom of *miai*: the formal occasion on which a prospective bride and groom, whose marriage is being arranged, meet each other for the first time. In the case of *Madame Chrysanthème*, the narrator Pierre's union with Chrysanthème is frequently referred to throughout the novel as a 'marriage', and much is made of the serious-ness with which Chrysanthème's relations take the formalisation of the match, but there is nothing about a marriage ceremony as such. The only formality the couple actually undergo is to appear together at what Pierre believes to be some kind of registry office, where their names are recorded in a register in front of Japanese officials and policemen, and Pierre is issued a permit on ricepaper allowing him to reside in his house with Chrysanthème.[7]

Puccini's opera, however, confuses matters by introducing a marriage cere-mony which is presided over by an Imperial Commissioner who gives leave for Pinkerton and Cio-Cio-San to be united in wedlock, thereby appearing to estab-lish that their union is indeed a legitimate marriage. Pinkerton boasts to the American consul Sharpless of the advantage of marrying in what he calls the Japanese way:

> Thus I am marrying according to Japanese custom
> for nine hundred and ninety-nine years.
> Every month free to go on my way.

It is not altogether clear whether the opera is suggesting that the marriage is actually a bona fide one, and that it is the fault of the laws of Japan that divorce is so easily obtainable and Pinkerton feels he can walk away from his 'wife' with such impunity (Cio-Cio-San later says that to divorce a wife, all a Japanese man has to do is turn her out of doors), or whether the opera wishes to show the wedding ceremony as a gross travesty in which the Japanese themselves are complicit, a pretence which they keep up in order to disguise the ugly truth, which is that the transaction that takes place between Pinkerton and Cio-Cio-San is essentially one of prostitution. In any case the whole wedding ceremony in *Madama Butterfly* is ahistorical: not only are the Imperial Commissioner's words based on a western, Christian conception of marriage, but there was no such official as the Imperial Commissioner in Japan. Many Japanese productions of the opera have tried to get round this problem by turning the Imperial Commissioner into a Shinto priest, but have thereby ended up creating more problems for themselves since it then makes nonsense of

Cio-Cio-San's espousal of Christianity, for which she is disowned by her uncle the Bonze and the rest of her family.

So, what was the nature of these contracted relationships between foreign men and Japanese women in Japanese port towns? Though *Madame Chrysanthème* and Long's *Madame Butterfly* both imply that what Pierre and Pinkerton were doing was merely to avail themselves of something which the Japanese were offering to them, access to women was, historically speaking, a problematic issue that cropped up from the very moment Commodore Perry's American naval squadron first appeared in the Bay of Edo in 1853. In February of the following year, when Perry returned to Japan with an even bigger fleet in order to negotiate a treaty between America and Japan, Rear Admiral George Henry Preble, who was attached to Perry's company, recorded in his journal that the 'Lieut[enant] Gov[ernor] of Uraga' had told some of his fellow officers that the Americans 'could have plenty of Japanese wives' once the treaty was signed.[8] It is paradoxical that the Japanese gained a reputation for being a sexually loose society because of the very measures the Shogunate put in place in an attempt to redirect sexual energy into channels which it could countenance. The Shogunate, as well as local officials in port towns, was anxious to strictly control the amount of contact between foreigners and ordinary Japanese, especially women.

Walter LaFeber claims in his book *The Clash: US–Japanese Relations throughout History* (1997) that even before the treaty was signed, the Shogunate 'used their women to appease and distract the powerful [i.e. the Americans]'.[9] But it was not that the Americans had women thrust upon them. Demand also came from the American side. In the spring of 1854 A.L.C. Portman, a Dutch interpreter attached to Perry's expedition, appears to have complained in a private letter to his Japanese counterpart that he had been unable to meet any local girls in the port of Shimoda because Japanese officials were keeping them exclusively for themselves.[10] Later that same year, when Portman was back in Shimoda, he made a request through a Japanese interpreter for a female attendant, a request which was later turned down by the Japanese magistrate.[11] However, the idea of employing geishas in order to appease the Americans when they were being particularly difficult over treaty negotiations does seem at one time to have been mooted at state level, although it appears the head of the *shōgun*'s Council of Elders, Abe Masahiro, rejected the proposal as being more trouble than it was worth.[12]

The issue of women, nonetheless, remained. Henry Heusken, the Dutch-born interpreter who arrived in Japan on 21 August (21 July local date) 1856,[13] accompanying Townsend Harris, the first American consul-general to Japan, stalled negotiations in the spring of the following year on the grounds that it was unfair of the Japanese to turn down the consul-general's perfectly reasonable request for a woman servant each for himself and Heusken to nurse them in times of ill health.[14] A seventeen-year-old girl named Kichi, the daughter of a ship's carpenter's widow, was appointed by Japanese officials to become Harris's companion, and a fifteen-year-old named Fuku to be Heusken's. A sum of money was paid out by the Americans as an advance to each girl, and a monthly allowance for each was also decided upon. Kichi appears to have commuted to the consulate for only three nights. From Harris's journal, it is clear he did suffer bouts of very bad health, but according to Japanese records, Kichi was specifically told to stay away from the consulate when Harris fell ill.[15] Fuku, however, was reported as having found favour with Heusken. Not only was she given an extra sum of money as a present, but she received a severance payment when the time came for the interpreter to travel to Edo with Harris that autumn. Other Japanese women (along with the sums which were fixed as their allowances) are mentioned in Japanese records as having been appointed at various times in subsequent years as attendants to either Harris or Heusken, both at the consulate in Shimoda and at Edo, where Harris moved the American diplomatic legation in the spring of 1859.

The problem of women only increased after the British, Dutch, French and Russians set up their own legations in Edo. The Japanese authorities had to contend with more requests for consent regarding the hiring of female servants. Although the Miyozaki brothel quarter in Yokohama was being set up with westerners specifically in mind, foreigners were still banned from the Shin-yoshiwara quarter in Edo. It was, however, the daughters of respectable townspeople – shopkeepers and artisans (albeit, perhaps, in financially straitened circumstances) – who gradually came to be linked in the public mind in Japan with the strangers based at the legations. Shadowy stories abounded of girls being supplied to the legations, for example, by Kobayashi Denkichi, who served as a 'boy' with the British legation and had even taken British citizenship. He had originally been a fisherman; he had been caught up in a storm at sea, rescued by an American whaler, and taken to Hawaii, where he had learned some English. In Edo he was rumoured to be in league with some of the most successful matchmakers who made a business out of supplying western clients with young mistresses, local girls who were willing to accept – or could be coerced into entering – such relationships. Among the women Denkichi recruited, there was said to have been the daughter of a *soba*-noodle restaurant owner, as well as a daughter of a Buddhist priest. In 1860, Denkichi was murdered in front of the gate of Tōzenji Temple, in which the British legation was based. This was at a time when anti-western sentiment was intensifying among samurai disaffected by the Tokugawa Shogunate's foreign policy, and violent attacks on foreigners were on the increase. In the early summer of 1861, a dozen or so rebel samurai (known as *shishi*) launched an attack on the legation. Among the British staff, Laurence Oliphant, former secretary to Lord Elgin and now first secretary to the legation, and, George S. Harrison, the British consul to Nagasaki, were seriously wounded. The bodies of two young Japanese women were said to have been discovered with sword wounds on beds in separate rooms in the temple complex.[16]

In Yokohama, almost as soon as the provisional brothel quarter opened in the summer of 1859, women were being sent to visit western clients at their lodgings. The first two were prostitutes belonging to the brothel proprietor Suzuki Zenjirō. They were hired out on a monthly basis to one of the foreign trading houses. It continued thereafter to be the practice for prostitutes to be sent over to those clients who did not care to be seen frequenting the brothel quarter. Only legitimate prostitutes and courtesans registered with a brothel in the Miyozaki quarter were allowed to become the mistresses of foreigners. In 1860, there were about thirty such women; by the following spring the number had increased to approximately eighty, and by the summer there were over a hundred. Many only visited their lovers at night, returning in the morning to their brothels. Not only did the Shogunate not recognise marriage between Japanese women and foreign men (it was not until 1873 that the new government in Japan legalised marriage between Japanese and foreign nationals), but any sexual congress between foreigners and ordinary women – that is to say, non-prostitutes – was strictly banned on pain of punishment (to be meted out to the female partner alone, however). One reason for this prohibition appears to have been the fear on the part of the Japanese authorities of even greater anti-western wrath being whipped up among the *shishi*. The Shogunate was, moreover, keen to prevent the proliferation of clandestine prostitution. But access to women was just another of those areas of daily life in which westerners felt unreasonable constraints were being imposed upon their personal freedom. In 1859, the crew of four Russian battleships anchored off Shinagawa in Edo Bay attempted unsuccessfully to force their way into several of the brothels in the Shinagawa pleasure quarter, where they were said to have met fierce resistance from the prostitutes and courtesans. A similar incident occurred in 1860, this time involving Prussian naval personnel. Foreign residents of Yokohama were not always satisfied with the choice of women available at the official brothels designated for their use.[17]

When it first started getting around the local Japanese community in Yokohama that prostitutes and courtesans of the brothel quarter were becoming the mistresses of western men, a great deal of public ire and hostility was aroused, much of it directed at the women themselves. Kichi, the girl who was appointed Townsend Harris's female attendant, had been taunted with the nickname 'Tōjin O-Kichi' – O-Kichi the Foreigner. There is an account of another woman who in the autumn of 1860 was discovered stripped naked and tied to a pine tree in Yokohama. The author of the account had no pity to spare for the woman. He reports how her gallant western rescuer was himself overcome with embarrassment and outrage at the woman's sheer indifference to the ignominious abuse she had just suffered.[18]

The mistresses of foreigners, particularly of western men, were sneeringly referred to as *rashamen* by the Japanese inhabitants of Yokohama. This insult was commonly used in Edo as well as Nagasaki (where the presence of Russian sailors may have given the term a further resonance) and, later, Kōbe. The word itself denoted 'wool sheep': the first part, *rasha*, refers to a type of thick woollen cloth, and derives from the Portuguese word *raxa*. The origins of the use of the word *rashamen* as a term of abuse are obscure. One early explanation was that Europeans were observed allowing their dogs to sleep with them in their beds, leading to the suspicion that westerners also committed bestiality with sheep (which western ships sometimes carried on board for food), and that the word for sheep was then transferred to women who became the sexual partners of foreign men.[19] Another theory relates to an incident which was supposed to have occurred early in 1859, in which three Japanese women huddling in grimy woollen blankets were said to have been discovered by a Japanese merchant aboard a British whaler he was restocking with food and fuel while it was anchored off Yokohama. The women had supposedly been rowed out secretly to the whaler by a recruiting agent working in tandem with somebody on board ship. Stories spread of other low-class, clandestine prostitutes doing the same kind of thing, and it was rumoured that these women could be identified around town by their woollen blankets, which were common enough on western ships but still a rare commodity in Japan at that time.[20] Yet another suggestion is that the term *rashamen* was used of foreigners' mistresses because the men were supposed to keep them close to their bodies like woollen blankets.

Among the Russians, who were allowed shore leave in the Inasa quarter of Nagasaki, only the officers enjoyed the privilege of possessing mistresses. One was said to have kept two sisters simultaneously, the younger of whom was still fourteen. There was also the story of the mistress who ran away complaining that she had been led to believe she would only be required to have sex once a day. The prostitutes who worked in Inasa were originally required to register with brothels in the Maruyama-Yoriai brothel quarter and were permitted to stay in Inasa only while Russian vessels were docked in Nagasaki. There was a continuing problem with clandestine prostitution, leading in 1872 to women being banned from visiting Russians at their lodgings. But before long a new type of prostitute emerged in the Inasa district. They dressed in western-style gowns, brandished western-style parasols, and went openly to see their lovers at their lodgings. The proprietress of a restaurant in the area was suspected of acting as procuress. In 1873, the Inasa pleasure quarter was granted independent status, which meant that its courtesans were from then on permitted to be based there. Until the end of the nineteenth century, the Inasa district retained a strong Russian character. The mistresses of Russian officers were locally nicknamed *kutsu-migaki* (shoe-shiner), but they were also called *karasunedōma*, from the Russian for 'red house' (*krasni dom*), because they lived in red-painted residences built in a mixture of western and Japanese styles. Examples of such dwellings are said to have survived in the area until the mid-1950s.[21]

What surprised the Japanese authorities was the willingness of ordinary young townswomen to enter into a liaison with foreign men, despite the antagonism they met with from their fellow Japanese. In Yokohama, the Shogunate intended the official Miyozaki brothel quarter to serve all western incomers as an exclusive conduit for their pent-up sexual energy. If any ordinary women wanted to enter into concubinage with a foreigner, they were required first to register with a brothel as a prostitute (and even take a professional name as a courtesan) before they could enter formally into the relationship. The allowance the girls were to receive from their lover was set in advance by the brothel quarter: there were three grades, the most expensive at 20 *ryō*, the cheapest at half that sum. Out of this monthly allowance, the girls owed their brothel proprietor a commission. They were also required to disclose all additional gifts of money they received from their lover. If a girl reneged on her payments, she could be stripped of her privilege of being a foreigner's mistress and made to work as a common prostitute in the brothel until she had paid back the full sum she owed to the proprietor. The brothel proprietor himself was only obliged to notify the local magistrate of the names of those of his girls who had become the mistresses of westerners. Mistresses were enjoined to be obedient to their foreign masters, and to avoid pregnancy at all costs. A similar system was put in operation in Nagasaki, and the former prohibition on westerners visiting the brothels of the Maruyama quarter was lifted. The British physician Dr William Willis noted in a report he compiled for the British Foreign Office in 1867 on the subject of prostitution in Japan that foreigners were obliged to pay the 'brothel authorities' for a 'licence' in order to keep a prostitute as a mistress: this fee was lower in Nagasaki than in Yokohama, where at one time it was as high as 24 *bu* (a *bu* was worth a quarter of a *ryō*) or about 32 shillings.[22]

The demand continued to increase in Yokohama for mistresses who had originally been not prostitutes but ordinary *musume*. It was not the professionals who appealed to many foreign residents. Besides, there was the lurking suspicion that the prostitutes and courtesans who were kept apart for the pleasure of foreigners in the Miyozaki brothels were considerably inferior in looks and refinement to the ones reserved exclusively for Japanese clients. Another incentive to take up with a decent *musume* was the desire to avoid venereal disease, which was rife in the brothel quarter. Dr Willis vented his exasperation in 1863 at the spread of syphilis and gonorrhoea among British troops based in Yokohama, ascribing the situation to the men's insistence on going with 'Japanese women of the lowest class, who are diseased as a rule'.[23] As a precaution against infection, women who became mistresses were warned against entertaining Japanese lovers on the sly. Often they were discouraged from even speaking to Japanese men.

As early as the summer of 1861, daughters of solid local families in Edo and Yokohama were apparently being recruited by professional matchmakers trying to supply women to foreigners who wanted a mistress. The client paid the intermediary a fee for finding a suitable girl; the girl's family also paid a fee to the intermediary for finding her a situation. It was rumoured in the Japanese community in Yokohama that foreigners generally paid a generous monthly allowance to their mistresses. In 1867, Willis estimated that of the approximately one thousand prostitutes in Yokohama, two to three hundred were being kept by westerners as mistresses. The average monthly allowance such women received was between fifteen and twenty dollars.[24] William Willis himself kept a mistress in Yokohama, and later had a Japanese 'wife', the daughter of a samurai, during his last seven years in the country (between 1870 and 1877), which he spent in the southern city of Kagoshima. Pierre Loti's reference in *Madame Chrysanthème* to the derision with which the procurer Kangourou greets the narrator's suggestion that a '*Guécha*' would serve him very well as a 'wife' shows that the perception existed in Nagasaki at least until 1885, when Loti was there, that *musume rashamen* were preferable as mistresses to professional courtesans or geishas. The narrator Pierre quickly realises that he has made a vulgar proposition by suggesting a geisha: 'one would really suppose I had talked of marrying the devil'.[25]

Early in 1862, brothel proprietors in Yokohama protested to the local magistrate about these clandestine *musume rashamen*, who were not being formally signed up with one or another of the brothels of the Miyozaki quarter before becoming mistresses. Government officials attempted to assert their authority over the situation by meting out punishment to the girls' fathers, as well as penalising the matchmaker deemed to have been the worst offender. Foreign residents in Yokohama complained, however, that the Japanese authorities were trying to interfere in their private lives, and there were protests from those who had their mistresses taken from them. The *rashamen*, for their part, protested against being registered as courtesans and having to pay commission to a brothel. There appears to have been no shortage of ordinary *musume* disposed to the idea of becoming mistresses, so long as they were not subjected to the humiliation of being formally registered as prostitutes.[26] Among the younger generations of women, the sight of westerners seems to have inspired curiosity rather than fear or revulsion or awe. There were rumours that even daughters of samurai families in Edo were involved.

Rather than running the risk of souring diplomatic relations (especially since the Tokugawa Shogunate was keen to push ahead with armament deals with western powers), the magistrate's office in Yokohama decided to turn a blind eye, if the women conducted themselves with discretion. Matchmakers were theoretically banned from pursuing their recruitment activities, but they had no scruples about flouting this order by operating very successfully in secret. Other Japanese tradesmen accustomed to doing business with westerners also began to take on commissions. Recruitment took place not only locally and in rural regions around Edo, but increasingly in the city of Edo itself. The demand for mistresses was no longer primarily in Edo (by the summer of 1863 *musume rashamen* had all but disappeared from the capital), but in Yokohama, where girls from Edo were particularly popular. The number of officially registered prostitutes engaged as mistresses in Yokohama had dropped dramatically by this time, the residual demand in this class being only for the cheapest kind. The *musume rashamen* themselves were soon being accused by their fellow Japanese of brazen behaviour. Contemporary accounts of the period compiled by their countrymen complain about these women flaunting their ostentatious finery, and accuse them bitterly of being proud and vain.

Many male visitors to Japan were attracted to the country by the prospect of easily available sex, and Japan was something of a destination for early sex tourists. Some quickly became, like Loti, disillusioned. Walter del Mar, who was in the country in 1899, reported that of his bachelor acquaintances, both residents and temporary visitors alike, all but one found Japanese women completely useless as ' "wives" ', although it was generally agreed that they made excellent 'housekeepers'. Del Mar wrote that one of these acquaintances had come all the way out to Japan with the idea of settling there because of what he had read about Japanese brothels and their inmates, only to realise within a few weeks of his arrival in the country that he had already had enough of Japanese women.[27] It appears that fantasy had inflated expectations. The Swiss envoy Aimé Humbert spelt out at some length the ghastly consequences in which an unwary foreigner was likely to find himself enmeshed once he had introduced a sweet, modest, innocent-looking Japanese 'mousmé' into his household. These girls showed their western masters such pathetic gratitude that one would think they were freed slaves. Their requirements were so simple; they took up so little space in the house; and they ate so frugally. A 'mousmé' cost so little to maintain at the beginning. Then, one day, she brings around a sister, who, it turns out, is in a precarious financial situation. Next, it is a helpless, aged parent, or a brother who was sure to become a great merchant if only somebody would lend him the money with which he could get started. Humbert provides a cautionary tale of how a 'mousmé' insinuates herself into the life of a vulnerable, lonely foreign resident in Yokohama, where most incomers were unmarried or without their spouses. The advantages to the girl are, in Humbert's eyes, obvious: a relationship that is supposed to be for only a few months' duration ends up lasting years, at the end of which the girl has amassed enough money to pay off her debts to the 'gankiro' (brothel), with a little bit extra besides, which ensures her future independence. A mistress was, in the end, a great financial drain, a source of tiresome worries, a 'hellish nightmare'.[28] Docile, unassuming, faithful and trusting, a *musume*, in the end, was really no better than a leech, sucking her lover dry of affection, patience, and cash.

Loti made his Madame Chrysanthème into a much more venal character than O-Kane, the Japanese woman he actually lived with in the summer of 1885, appears ever to have been. Nicolas Serban suggested in his 1924 study of Loti that the latter's main motive for setting up house with O-Kane had been to try to escape the tedium of hotel life. Funaoka Suetoshi, on the other hand, points to the detailed journal which Loti kept during his stay in Japan and postulates that he had entered the relationship with the intention of writing up his adventures in the form of a novel.[29] Chrysanthème – Kiku in Japanese (or Kikou as Loti spells it) – appears to have actually been the name of O-Kane's cousin, a rickshaw man, who is referred to in the novel only by the number of his vehicle. The broker who arranged Loti's 'marriage' with O-Kane was a laundryman just as he is in the novel, but by the name of Sejiu rather than Kangourou – the latter is possibly a play on the word 'kangaroo' and the name of the famous Yokohama brothel the Gankirō (Kangourou may in turn have suggested to John Luther Long the name of his marriage broker, Goro – which also happens to be a perfectly good masculine first name in Japan). Although much of *Madame Chrysanthème* closely follows Loti's journal, he did add an amount of fictional material. For example, there is no mention in the journal of an initial meeting with the matchmaker at a teahouse or of a rejected first candidate such as Mlle Jasmin, the procurer Kangourou's choice whom the narrator Pierre spurns in favour of Chrysanthème.

Also noteworthy is the absence in the journal of anything corresponding to the crucial scene towards the end of the novel which establishes Chrysanthème for good as an unsympathetic character. When Pierre surprises Chrysanthème singing insouciantly as she tests the silver coins he had given her the previous evening, he at first fails to identify the tapping noises he hears and wonders what sort of game Chrysanthème could be playing – whether it might be quoits. The implication is that for Chrysanthème her relationship with Pierre had been nothing more than a game played to a set of elaborate rules. Recovering quickly from her discomfiture at being discovered in an unguarded moment, she reverts immediately to those social rules of politeness which to Pierre are nothing more than hypocritical affectation. Pierre now smugly believes that the scorn with which he had always treated Chrysanthème in particular and Japanese *mousmés* in general is entirely justified. In his journal, however, Loti merely mentions how, on parting, O-Kane had accompanied him in silence to the outer garden gate of their residence, her eyes lowered and 'a little sad'. The journal entry dwells instead on the romanticised figure of his own self, striding away from the house without a backward glance, jaunty and carefree as if it was nothing more to him than a chance lodging where he had spent a single night. It is as though his having managed to keep his heart unensnared has been some kind of triumph.[30] By making Chrysanthème behave in the way she does in the house the couple are about to vacate, Loti makes it possible for his alter ego, his narrator Pierre, to walk away without a bad conscience.

Chrysanthème's composure seems at times to be an indication of her lack of an emotional life, at others to be a sign of her deviousness. While it is her air of detachment which attracts Pierre in the first place, it later offends him that she does not respond to him as passionately as his former Turkish lover Aziyadé, the heroine of Loti's novel of that name published in 1879, in which Aziyadé risks her life escaping from her master's harem in order to cast in her lot with Pierre's. In *Madame Chrysanthème*, Pierre lies next to the unresponsive Japanese 'wife' he has procured through a broker and for whom he feels no desire, and dreams nostalgically of the rapture to which he had once thrilled in the arms of Aziyadé in faraway Istanbul. Impulsive Aziyadé, full of fire, candour and physical bravery, is everything a Japanese woman cannot be, with all her layers of artifice. The smile of a Japanese *mousmé* is 'candidly meaningless'.[31] The idea of unmasking the Japanese – or rather, the inability to do so – is a recurring theme in Loti's novel. Pierre oscillates between his conviction that the 'almost absolute blank of the human countenance'[32] of the Japanese indicates an absence of the processes of thought, and his impression that there is 'some indescribable *Japanesery*'[33] in Chrysanthème, something akin to a soul yet 'of a different species to my own'.[34] These '*japoneries*' defy description – but not because they are too sublime to be contained within language. Both Tahiti and Istanbul, Pierre tells his readers, pierced his soul with an intensity of delight. Japan, on the other hand, evokes in him sensations which are too trite, too tedious, too inconsequential, to deserve the effort of describing them. The French language is too rich and evocative to deal with such banality: 'Here . . . words exact and truthful in themselves seem too thrilling, too great for the subject; seem to embellish it unduly'.[35] For Loti at least, oriental societies were not all alike.

Madame Chrysanthème was widely read throughout Europe. It was the best-known treatment of the theme of a westerner's temporary Japanese 'marriage' with a local girl until Puccini's opera *Madama Butterfly*. But Loti's harsh portrait of Madame Chrysanthème did draw some sentimental objections in France. Chrysanthème was transformed into a tragic heroine in André Messager's opera *Madame Chrysanthème* (1893), which Puccini's librettist Luigi Illica certainly knew. Messager's *Madame Chrysanthème* was a *comédie-lyrique* with a libretto by Georges Hartmann and André Alexandre based on Loti's novel. Whereas the chief protagonist in Loti's book is without doubt the narrator, Messager's opera centres upon its soprano role: Madame Chrysanthème herself. In Loti's novel, Pierre is unable to penetrate Chrysanthème's language, let alone fathom the meaning of her songs. Both Pierre and Chrysanthème allow language to alienate them from one another. Messager's opera quietly drops the issue of the language barrier and all the characters simply use French. Chrysanthème, moreover, is turned into a geisha, who sings for a living. She is articulate and invites the audience's sympathy.

Madame Chrysanthème in Messager's opera is only too aware of the pathos of her existence. As if her vulnerability needed further emphasis, Messager and his librettists make her an orphan.[36] This Chrysanthème's persona of the blithe, smiling *mousmé* is anything but a reflection of a shallow insincerity. It is a mask behind which she conceals a tender heart and her oriental fatalism. She is convinced of the inevitability of disaster, even as she spends her working moments helping her patrons pleasantly while away their time. On the other hand, Pierre's attitude to life, in the opera, can be summed up in the words *carpe diem*. He finds the pleasures of the moment that much more exquisitely sweet because he knows that, when the time comes for them to end, he will be able to walk away without a qualm. When Pierre facilely reassures Chrysanthème that their present happiness will never end, Chrysanthème is not deceived. Her reticence, her wariness of Pierre, her reluctance to join in completely with his more ebullient moods, are all misinterpreted by Pierre as indifference. He is aggrieved by Chrysanthème's refusal to agree that she is his, and his alone. He fantasises that she must be in love with his companion Yves instead. As the rift widens between the two of them, Chrysanthème resumes being a geisha and finds an outlet for her emotions in her singing. This only inflames Pierre's jealousy further. Messager's opera ends differently from Loti's original novel. Pierre spies a downcast Chysanthème bidding farewell to Yves, and assumes she is more saddened by Yves's departure than his own. But what Chrysanthème has been doing is giving Yves a letter to pass on to Pierre once they are out at sea. In the epilogue to the opera, Pierre reads the letter, and realises he has been wrong about Chrysanthème all along:

> You said, I was never anything to you but a puppet, a *mousmé*. . . . But, if I was able to see you leave with a smile on my lips, I want you to know when you are far, very far from me, that in Japan too there are women who love . . . and who cry.[37]

The opera concludes with Pierre and Yves agreeing in astonishment that women are alike the world over.

The French artist Félix Régamey also produced an adaptation of Loti's novel. Régamey, who had accompanied the industrialist and art collector Émile Guimet to Japan in 1876, was indignant at the cavalier manner in which Loti in his novel disparaged both Japanese women and Japanese aesthetics.[38] In 1894, Régamey published *Le Cahier rose de Mme Chrysanthème*, describing Chrysanthème's marriage to Pierre in journal form from the Japanese girl's point of view. In the preface to his book Régamey professed deep regret that Loti seemed to have been suffering from a 'painful hyperexcitability' which caused him to 'vent spleen in a British fashion' against all things cheerful and charming in Japan.[39] Régamey exonerates Japanese women from Loti's charge of mercenary ruthlessness by turning the relationship between Chrysanthème and Pierre into an ill-starred, one-sided love affair on the part of Chrysanthème. Just as in Messager's opera, Chrysanthème is turned into a tragic figure, rejected and abandoned by the man she faithfully loves. She is misunderstood because she knows only one way of making herself pleasing to a man: to smile, repress her own feelings and be submissive in all things.[40] She is unable to comprehend why she cannot make Pierre happy no matter how meekly she abases herself before him. The more dejected she feels about her inability to penetrate Pierre's deep melancholy, the greater care she takes not to let her perplexity show. She does not cajole and she is never reproachful. On the morning of their parting, she does not try to disabuse Pierre when she realises that he has misinterpreted her action of tapping the coins he had given her. In Régamey's version of the story, Chrysanthème has been striking the coins with a mallet and singing a 'famous' Japanese song warning of the evils of avarice. Once Pierre has sailed away, Régamey's Chrysanthème wraps the coins in a swathe of precious silk along with talismanic scraps of Pierre's jottings (which she is unable to read because she has very little French), and throws herself into the sea. She is, however, rescued.

Pierre Loti's own attitude to Japanese women later underwent a change. In December 1900 he was back in Nagasaki after an absence of fifteen years, this time on board the *Redoubtable* for a ten-month-long deployment in Japanese waters. No longer preoccupied with the idea of a Japanese 'marriage', he developed a rapport with a diminutive young geisha he called Pluie-d'Avril ('Miss April-Shower'), whose real geisha name was Sonotarō. He also formed a close friendship with a young woman who lived up one of the hills surrounding Nagasaki. In *La Troisième Jeunesse de Madame Prune* (1905), the novel into which Loti reworked his journal chronicling this period of his life, this '*mousmé*' is called Inamoto. It was not that the suggestion of a new Japanese 'wife' had not come up again. Loti recorded in his journal that he had run into his erstwhile '*belle-mère*' ('mother-in-law') Madame Renoncule, who informed him that 'Chrysanthème' (as Loti refers to O-Kane in his journal) was now married to a M. Pinson, a wholesale manufacturer of lanterns, and was comfortably settled in a nearby town, though childless. Mme Renoncule then asked Loti to a gathering so her family could get reacquainted with him, although Loti never saw Chrysanthème again because Madame Renoncule tactfully did not invite the Pinsons.[41] In the tenth chapter of *La Troisième Jeunesse de Madame Prune* (Madame Prune being Pierre's landlady in *Madame Chrysanthéme*, with whom the narrator also renews acquaintanceship), Mme Renoncule broaches the idea of '*une union morganatique*' between him and another of her daughters, her youngest this time, called Fleur-de-Sureau ('Mademoiselle Elderberry-Flower'). A fortnight later, she still has not given up on the idea, even though the narrator is less than enthusiastic. An indiscretion, however, committed by an attractive married cousin of 'Chrysanthème's' with regard to the narrator's attendant Osman puts a permanent freeze on his subsequent relations with his former '*belle-famille*' (in-laws).[42]

Instead of entering into another brokered relationship, Loti unexpectedly found he had developed a fascination for Pluie-d'Avril's dancing and singing. It was as if the removal of the pressures of an imposed, forced intimacy with an unfamiliar woman allowed Loti to become more responsive to the women he did meet. Pluie-d'Avril entertained him at teahouses, accompanied on the *shamisen* by her companion Matsuko, whom Loti also got to know. In *La Troisième Jeunesse*, Loti does not exaggerate the extent of his relationship with Pluie-d'Avril. He condescendingly likens the young geisha's hold over the affections of his narrator to the mysterious but powerful appeal which a beloved, playful pet cat might exert over its owner. Yet the narrator forms a genuine regard for her. At one point in the novel, he goes to Pluie-d'Avril's own house and surprises the girl stooped over a washbasin with her arms bared, wearing only a simple blue cotton kimono, very unlike the finery in which he is accustomed to see her. This glimpse into the girl's humble private life generates in the narrator strong feelings of both compassion and respect. His friendship with Pluie-d'Avril and Matsuko remains innocent, as does his relationship with Inamoto. In Inamoto, the narrator sees something very different altogether – a sincerity and frankness which make him drop that affectation he naturally assumes with more worldly ladies such as Madame Prune and Madame Renoncule. Having first come across Inamoto in the necropolis of her father's temple, high up one of the densely forested slopes above Nagasaki, the narrator starts paying regular visits to the cemetery so he might encounter her on her daily ramblings. In Inamoto he discovers a kindred spirit. Despite their limited ability to communicate with one another in each other's language, their friendship is not marred even once by 'an equivocal moment, an instant of disquiet'. Whether this relationship was based on personal experience or remained a creation of Loti's imagination, is impossible to tell from his journal. He merely records encountering an impressive funeral procession while out on a walk in the hills above Nagasaki with a woman named Inamoto. There is also a single mysterious reference to a nameless young woman with a small house up in the hills, with whom Loti appears to have been in the habit of having secret trysts – a woman, he wrote in his journal, whom he loved with all his senses, yet with something more besides.[43]

John Luther Long's Lieutenant Pinkerton, of course, has more in common with the earlier Pierre in Loti's first novel about Japan, *Madame Chrysanthème*. Pinkerton, like Pierre, is a self-satisfied character who thinks he knows the world. Long assumes a knowing, droll narrative tone of voice throughout his novella, as though he shared Pinkerton's exasperation with the naïvety of the Japanese and their topsy-turvy way of going about everything in life. This flippancy, which relegates Cho-Cho-San to the category of 'impossible little thing[s]',[44] forms the background against which her tragic tale of betrayal is told. Long's portrayal of Cho-Cho-San is a sympathetic one, even though her naïvety and the extent of her credulity concerning everything Pinkerton has told her might strike modern sensibilities as somewhat patronising. Whereas Pierre Loti's Madame Chrysanthème turns out to be no better than an unemotional, mercenary sort of woman, Cho-Cho-San proves to be a passionately devoted wife and mother.

It is an aspect of Cho-Cho-San's supposed ridiculousness – as Long's facetious Pinkerton would have it – that she, a creature whom Pinkerton cannot take seriously, should take the drastic, tragic step of trying to kill herself when she finds out that Pinkerton has an American wife and will not be returning to her. It is out of all proportion to her ingenuousness, her artlessness, that she should turn to the custom among the samurai, commiting *seppuku*, or, to use the more vulgar term, hara-kiri, in order to avoid dishonour. Such grand gestures belong to the realm of heroes. But Long's readers are told that this is how her father had died, and she seeks to emulate him. Cho-Cho-San is a modern-day Dido, transposed from Virgil's realm of gods and heroes to the seedy demi-monde of the late nineteenth-century port town of Nagasaki. She tells her maid Suzuki that she is ' "disappoint – a liddle – disappoint" ',[45] and that she is weary of life. But in John Luther Long's original novella, Cho-Cho-San does not die. Suzuki binds up her wound, and the little family disappears, just as in the account Long heard from his sister. When Mrs Pinkerton arrives at Cho-Cho-San's house the next morning to pick up the baby, everybody is gone.

It was the canny American theatre director David Belasco who changed the ending so that Cho-Cho-San dies in Pinkerton's arms. Belasco's one-act play, which he wrote in collaboration with Long, is set in Cho-Cho-San's house, and concentrates specifically on the denouement of her story: her wait (which is approaching its tragic end), her rejection of Prince Yamadori's offer of marriage, her overnight vigil on seeing Pinkerton's ship return to Nagasaki Harbour (involving a show-stopping twenty-minute sequence of lighting effects, which Puccini later transformed into his 'Humming Chorus'), Pinkerton's cowardly inability to face her (let alone ask for the baby as he has promised his wife he would), the appearance of Mrs Pinkerton (named Kate in the play rather than Adelaide as in the original novella), and finally Cho-Cho-San's suicide. In Long's story, Pinkerton is not described as coming ashore at Nagasaki again. Cho-Cho-San spots him on the deck of a ship anchored in the harbour. He has a blonde woman on his arm. It turns out later that he has gone on to Kōbe, leaving his American wife, Adelaide, behind in Nagasaki. Adelaide comes to see the American consul just as he is having a meeting with Cho-Cho-San. Not realising who the Japanese girl in the office is, Adelaide blithely tells the consul she wants him to telegram her husband to the effect that she has seen Cho-Cho-San's baby and that she wants him for herself. David Belasco, on the other hand, had Pinkerton turn up at Cho-Cho-San's house, have a look around and realise the cruelty of what he has done:

> My room . . . just as it used to look . . . my chair. Poor kid! Its toy. Poor little devil! . . . Sharpless, I thought when I left this house, the few tears, sobs, little polite regrets, would be over as I crossed the threshold. I started to come back for a minute, but I said to myself: 'Don't do it; by this time she's ringing your gold pieces to make sure they're good.' You know that class of Japanese girl. . . .[46]

Belasco's play opened at the Herald Theatre in New York City on 5 March 1900, with Blanche Bates in the title role. Within a few weeks, it was playing at the Duke of York's Theatre, London, with Evelyn Millard as Cho-Cho-San. The composer Giacomo Puccini, while in London in the spring of 1900 overseeing a Covent Garden production of *Tosca*, attended a performance. Belasco later claimed that Puccini came to the greenroom immediately after the show to seek his permission to turn the play into an opera. Puccini's *Madama Butterfly* was composed between 1901 and 1903. Its premiere was on 17 February 1904, in Milan where it met with a hostile reception. A revised version was performed in Brescia in May of that year, and Puccini revised the opera two further times, for its 1905 premiere at Covent Garden and again for its 1906 Parisian premiere at the Opéra-Comique.

Puccini's revisions to the first act of his opera consisted mainly of tempering the racial antagonisms of the marriage scene. The Paris version, which is now the version most frequently performed, no longer contains Pinkerton's insulting reference to the Japanese servants as '*musi*' (ugly mugs) and the description of Japanese food as consisting of repulsive items such as candied spiders and flies – one of

21 The English actress Evelyn Millard as Cho-Cho-San in the London staging of David Belasco's play *Madame Butterfly*, *c.*1900.

Puccini's librettists, Luigi Illica, took the idea of the perversity of Japanese cuisine from the wedding scene in Messager's opera *Madame Chrysanthème*. The boorish antics of Cio-Cio-San's drunken uncle Yakusidé are also toned down. On the Japanese side, Puccini deleted the section in which Cio-Cio-San's guests gossip among themselves about whether or not they would have turned Pinkerton down if he had been offered to them first. Most significantly, he also took out Cio-Cio-San's shy confession to Pinkerton (derived from Long's novella) that she had initially been vehemently opposed to the idea of having to take Pinkerton as a 'husband' because she had been prejudiced against Americans. She had imagined he must be 'A savage! A wasp!' But by doing away with Cio-Cio-San's admission of her initial disgust at the idea of a relationship with Pinkerton, Puccini made it less clear why she should be so amazed, as she declares to Pinkerton she is, that he now seems to her to be 'heaven's bright eye'.[47]

In the latter half of the opera, Puccini's changes to his first version include alterations to the scene in which Pinkerton makes a brief appearance back at Cio-Cio-San's house, as well as to Kate Pinkerton's role in the action. In Belasco's play, Pinkerton arrives at Cho-Cho-San's house with the intention of carrying out his wife's request that he should ask Cho-Cho-San for the baby. But at Cho-Cho-San's approach, Pinkerton loses his nerve and runs away. Kate Pinkerton enters asking for her husband, and Cho-Cho-San realises who she is. Kate, for her part, realises Pinkerton has not managed to do what he was supposed to, and proceeds to ask Cho-Cho-San for the baby herself. 'Let us think first of the child. For his good . . . let me take him home to my country . . . I will do all I would do for my own,' she cajoles, and when the Japanese woman hesitates at the idea that her own baby would grow up never knowing the woman who had given birth to him, Kate coaxes, 'It's hard, very hard, I know, but isn't it best?' Puccini's first version of his opera had Pinkerton make an equally rapid and cowardly exit after giving the American consul Sharpless some money to pass on to Cio-Cio-San. Kate then enters with Suzuki, Cio-Cio-San's maid, and speaks directly to Cio-Cio-San. After the Milan premiere, Puccini decided to extend Pinkerton's declaration of remorse, and gave him the aria '*Addio, fiorito asil*' (Good-bye, flowery retreat). Sharpless then hastens him on his way, and when Kate enters behind Suzuki, Sharpless speaks on her behalf to Cio-Cio-San. It is Sharpless who is first to ask Cio-Cio-San to forgive Kate; it is he who tells Cio-Cio-San to have courage and to make the sacrifice for the sake of her son.

The other major change Puccini introduced to the second half of his opera had the effect of shifting the opera's emphasis away from Cio-Cio-San's mother-love and towards the sense of her own personal dishonour. Having just revealed her blond-haired, blue-eyed son to Sharpless, Cio-Cio-San sings of the pathos of the alternative she would face if Pinkerton did not come back: that she might have to go out in the rain to wander the streets with her boy in her arms, singing for their supper. In the original version of *Madama Butterfly*, Puccini took from Long's novella the scene in which Cho-Cho-San in high spirits describes to Suzuki her fantasy about her son being spotted by the emperor of Japan and raised to the rank of prince. Puccini turned this into Cio-Cio-San's heart-rending vision of her beloved son's triumph at the moment of their greatest despair, raised from the condition of outcast to the noblest position in the land by none other than the Mikado himself. For Paris, however, Puccini rewrote Cio-Cio-San's aria as an outpouring of anguish and grief at her own fate, concluding it with her declaration that she would rather kill herself than resume the dishonourable life of a geisha:

No, no, not this!
Not the profession that leads to dishonour!
Death! Never more will I dance!
I would rather cut short my life!

This change also adds some confusion to the question of why Cio-Cio-San feels impelled to take her life. In her final scene in the opera, Cio-Cio-San declares she is going to die in order to free her son for his new life in America. She will excise herself from his life. He will never know she existed and he will never have to torment himself with the thought that his own mother rejected and deserted him and continues to live somewhere contentedly without him. On the other hand, there is the dagger which Cio-Cio-San has inherited from her father – the dagger inscribed '*Con onor muore chi non può serbar vita con onore*', or in Long's words, 'To die with Honour/ When one can no longer live with Honour'. This is the dagger the Mikado had presented to Cio-Cio-San's father with which he might expiate his dishonour. Long's novella implies that this disgrace proceeded from a defeat in a battle during the Satsuma Rebellion, in which Cho-Cho-San's father is supposed to have fought on the imperial side. But because the term 'honour' has connotations of female chastity, there remains the lingering suggestion that Cho-Cho-San/Cio-Cio-San takes her own life because she has lost her good name now that she has been abandoned by her lover. Osman Edwards in *Japanese Plays and Playfellows* (1901) certainly felt that this was the implication: commenting on Belasco's play, he argued that a Japanese girl in Cho-Cho-San's situation would not feel that 'she had suffered a dishonour expiable only by death'. 'The infidelity of her partner might wound her heart', he wrote, '[but] it could not strike her conscience'.[48] But the seriousness with which Cho-Cho-San/Cio-Cio-San takes her 'marriage' suggests that were she to yield to the financial exigency of entering a new liaison with another man, such as Prince Yamadori (as the matchmaker Goro and the American consul Sharpless both urge her to do), she would in her own mind be, for ever and irreversibly, an inconstant, unfaithful woman. Puccini's revisions of his opera for Paris, which link the profession of geisha to the condition of being a fallen woman, introduces a further twist: that Cio-Cio-San would consider having to return to being a geisha an intolerable disgrace after having been the wife of an American.

Cio-Cio-San has had a brief tantalising glimpse of a better world, which she is now told is not for her. Understanding that that world belongs to Pinkerton, his American wife and her own blond-haired, blue-eyed son, Cio-Cio-San gives them her blessing to go and be happy. She tells Kate Pinkerton

> Under the great bridge of heaven there is no lady happier than you.
> Remain happy always, and don't grieve on my account.

Cio-Cio-San then obligingly does away with herself, availing herself of the one thing her own culture does provide her with – a method of quitting this existence without being branded a coward. While opera audiences are invited to feel pity for Cio-Cio-San for being so cruelly denied the better life she dreams of with Pinkerton and their son in Pinkerton's own country, there is nevertheless the disquieting sense that order is restored in the end (as in, for example, the musical comedy *The Geisha*) with Pinkerton married to a woman of his own nationality and race, while Cio-Cio-San returns to her Japanese roots, following in the footsteps of her father. The threat posed by miscegenation is defused.

Cho-Cho-San/Cio-Cio-San sacrifices herself on the altar of a superior, western concept of love as an indissoluble union of two souls and two bodies (as represented by the state of marriage), but it is her Japanese heritage that gives her the courage to carry her bloody purpose to its bitter conclusion. John Luther Long and David Belasco shared a nostalgia for a chivalric world which they projected on to a romanticised image of a Japan that was supposed to be rapidly disappearing. In the actual Satsuma Rebellion of 1877 (otherwise known as the Seinan War) in which Cho-Cho-San's father is supposed to have participated, it was the forces of the new government fighting in the name of the emperor which crushed a group of former samurai who had rebelled against the government for implementing modernising reforms which they feared were whittling away their old privileges.[49] In Long's novella and Belasco's play, however, as well as in Puccini's opera, the Japanese emperor functions as a symbol of those ancient Japanese values associated by western enthusiasts for the 'old' Japan with the samurai. Long's romanticisation of Japanese traditions makes him link the emperor with feudal customs associated with samurai culture, which was in any case becoming rapidly anachronistic in Japan by the late nineteenth century. This sentimentalising of a more heroic past is the major theme of Belasco's other Japanese play, *The Darling of the Gods* (1902), on which he also collaborated with John Luther Long. Its high-born heroine Yo-San (played on Broadway by Blanche Bates, who created the role of Cho-Cho-San) falls in love with a samurai opposed to the westernisation of Japan. She has, however, been imbibing ideas about love from books imported from the west, and what she yearns for, above all else, is personal happiness for herself and her lover. To achieve this end, she acts in a foolish and selfish manner which leads to her lover being ensnared in a trap set by his enemies. Faced with inevitable defeat, he commits *seppuku*, and she pays for her sins with her own courageous suicide. Critics of *The Darling of the Gods* scathingly pointed out similarities with the plot of Sardou's 1887 play *La Tosca* (on which Puccini based his opera). Tosca (first played by the French actress Sarah Bernhardt) allows her jealousy to betray the whereabouts of her lover to his enemy, the chief of police. Although she plots desperately to save her lover, she ultimately fails and, when she realises all is lost, flings herself to her death from the battlements of the Castel Sant'Angelo in Rome.

Cho-Cho-San/Cio-Cio-San, on the other hand, is exemplary in her observance of the traditional Japanese virtue of self-abnegation. She first sacrifices her good name by becoming a geisha in order to provide for her mother and grandmother, who have been left destitute by the suicide of her father. Then, for Pinkerton's sake, she willingly forgoes her family, who, for their part, have disowned her. Subsequently, she sacrifices her chance of financial security with a new lover by remaining loyal to the absconding Pinkerton. Finally, she sacrifices her very life for the future happiness of her son. Cho-Cho-San/Cio-Cio-San is cast in the mould of the noble savage: innocent, artless, trusting and full of the desire to drink from the well of western knowledge, yet capable of brutal acts of courage driven by an exacting sense of honour. Modern commercialised Japan, in contrast, is represented by the obsequious, grubby matchmaker Goro, modelled on Loti's M. Kangourou. M. Kangourou makes his first appearance in *Madame Chrysanthème* clad in a suit of grey, with a bowler hat – and white silk gloves.[50] The British diplomat and author A.B. Mitford lamented in 1870 that westerners, wherever they went, managed to have a corrupting effect on the natives.[51] It was not very long after Japan had opened her ports to foreign shipping that the Japanese were being denigrated as servile imitators of the west, an aspersion which has continued to be cast upon the Japanese ever since.[52] Would-be Japanese gentlemen in ill-fitting western-style coats, to say nothing of their graceless wives swaddled in dresses imported from the west, were the subject of derisive mockery in countless travel books and newspaper articles on Japan of the period. For the Puccini scholar Michele Giraldi, *Madama Butterfly* illustrates just how far apart western and eastern ways are: Goro is representative of the corruption spawned when east and west intermingle. Giraldi's repugnance towards this 'contaminazione' is felt in the distaste with which he describes the odious Goro sporting a bowler hat.[53]

By choosing to die, Cho-Cho-San/Cio-Cio-San returns to her cultural roots. Long suggests that at the moment when she is about to take her own life, she turns back to her gods of old: 'She had not forgotten the missionary's religion; but on the dark road from death to Meido [the Buddhist afterworld] it seemed best now to trust herself to the compassionate augustnesses, who had always been true'.[54] By seeking to unite herself with Pinkerton, she had become unclassifiable. Disowned by her Japanese relations and discarded by her American lover, she is no longer fully Japanese, yet she was never going to become American no matter how ardently she desired it. Belasco, and Puccini following him, supplies Cho-Cho-San's story with an even more satisfying closure than even Long himself – by allowing her to die. With her death, Cio-Cio-San comes full circle: to the satisfaction of a western audience, her identity as a Japanese is safely re-established. Catherine Clément, in her classic study *L'Opéra, ou La défaite des femmes* (1979), translated into English in 1988 as *Opera, or the Undoing of Women*, objected to Cio-Cio-San being made to die this 'death of a Japanese woman', accompanied by the sound of 'a distinct and ritual rhythm'. 'Mystical harmonies' and 'resonant gongs' signal the rekindling of Butterfly's 'ancestral religion' in her house, and in this atmosphere of revived Japanese-ness Cio-Cio-San remembers what she now has to do.[55] Japan's native patriarchal culture provides Puccini and his librettists with yet another novel way of enacting the oppression of woman and, in the process, making an exotic spectacle out of it. Cio-Cio-San must die because she is Japanese and because she is a woman.

Cio-Cio-San's suicide provided an opportunity for a Grand Guignol ending, as David Belasco very well realised. Nineteenth-century theatregoers in Europe and America had a taste for death scenes, just as did Japanese audiences, with their kabuki traditions. In Puccini's opera as well as Belasco's play, Cio-Cio-San's death is turned into a voyeuristic spectacle: sexual climax perpetrated by a phallic dagger. Pinkerton had awakened her to the knowledge of carnal joy; now that he is taking that joy away from her for ever, she cannot continue to live. As she plunges her sword into herself, what the French call *le petit mort* becomes one with her physical death. Cio-Cio-San's transformation in her death scene from an artless adolescent into a woman with nerves of steel who deliberately – rather than impulsively – kills herself makes one think of Pierre Loti's remark about the sudden flashes of 'Japanesery' his narrator (and alter ego) Pierre notices in Madame Chysanthème – something alien and savage and not at all western. Cio-Cio-San is at her most Japanese when she destroys herself. The most Japanese thing a Japanese person can do in the Madame Butterfly story is to kill herself. Japanese culture is presented as one of self-annihilation. There does not seem to be much point in the west subduing Japan, crushing it or transforming it. Left to itself, Japanese society seems ready to self-destruct.

Seppuku, or hara-kiri as it was more commonly known outside Japan, was an aspect of Japanese culture that was long a subject of gruesome fascination in the west. The London *Times*, reviewing *Manners and Customs of the Japanese* on 31 July 1841, picked out the custom for mention, referring to it as the 'happy despatch'. The British diplomat A.B. Mitford, who was in Japan between 1866 and 1870 serving as second secretary to the British legation, incorporated many references to hara-kiri in his book *Tales of Old Japan* (1871), including an account of his own attendance at the *seppuku* of Taki Zenzaburō in early 1868. Taki had been in charge of a Japanese patrol which fired on British and French nationals in the foreign settlement at Hyōgo (now Kōbe), and his *seppuku* was ordered by Emperor Meiji's nascent government, before it had even moved to Tōkyō.

Mitford's description of Taki Zenzaburō's ritual suicide was extensively quoted by the Japanese educator Nitobe Inazō in *Bushido, the Soul of Japan*, his noted exposition of the samurai way of life, which was originally written in English for a western readership and first published in 1900. Although Nitobe was a devout Christian (he was baptised in Japan by an American Methodist missionary, but in the mid-1880s became a Quaker while studying at Johns

Hopkins University in Baltimore), his interpretation of the samurai ethos was heavily influenced by Confucian morality. Just as the Catholic Church frowned on those who hastened or invited their own martyrdom (for that would be to commit the sin of pride), Nitobe Inazō attempted to distinguish true *seppuku* from mundane suicide that resulted from vanity or plain despair. *Seppuku*, in his view, was not to be used as a way out of suffering.[56]

Seppuku was the ancient prerogative of the warrior, the last and desperate means by which he could avoid the shame of being captured in battle. Originally, it consisted of two incisions cut into the abdomen in the shape of a cross (called the 'figure-of-ten' since the cross is the Chinese ideogram for the word 'ten'). A single horizontal incision in the abdomen rarely proved immediately fatal and usually necessitated another, mortal blow, most commonly to the windpipe. If this was still insufficient, a companion would swiftly cut off the suicide's head with a sword. Away from the heat of war, especially during the two centuries of peace under the Tokugawa Shogunate, *seppuku* became increasingly ritualised, and customarily involved the assistance of a second person.[57] It became an accepted method by which men of the samurai class (the *bushi*) could demonstrate their innocence when an accusation was made against them, atone for an offence committed, or avoid incurring a stain on their reputation. During the long reign of the Tokugawa dynasty, there certainly was a rash of suicides by samurai. But just because a samurai committed suicide, it did not mean he had necessarily undertaken it in the correct spirit of *seppuku*. Men died like summer insects plunging into an open flame, wrote Nitobe in *Bushido*.[58] That is to say, in Nitobe's view, samurai were killing themselves out of petulance, or for reasons unworthy of the supreme sacrifice of death.

Nitobe Inazō also took up the subject of female *seppuku* in his study. According to Nitobe, a woman of the samurai class took her own life in order to preserve the honour of her family. If she died to preserve her chastity, it was so that her family's honour should not be tarnished. It was also important that she should not ignore decorum in death or fail to maintain her modesty. To this end, she bound her thighs together before she knelt on the floor so as to prevent her body from collapsing in an unseemly manner in death. A member of the samurai class, whether male or female, was required to exercise composure in the face of death.[59] A good, composed *seppuku* required freedom from longing and regret. A clinging attachment to the things of this world was a sign of weakness. The Japanese word for lingering regret, *miren*, has negative connotations suggestive of cowardice, indecisiveness, meanness, unmanliness. The Japanese cult of suicide provided John Luther Long with the opportunity to give Cho-Cho-San's attempt on her own life a particularly Japanese twist. But however high the suicide rate has been among the Japanese and however much suicide has been aestheticised in

Japanese culture (when performed under specific circumstances), not every Japanese suicide involving a blade is a *seppuku*. Cho-Cho-San/Cio-Cio-San's is, in the end, a pathetic, rather sordid, domestic suicide.

The Japanese possessed their own sentimental legends about pitiable courtesans who, in the early days of the reopening of Japan to the west, paid with their lives for the intrusion of lustful western men into their world. One of the more famous of these legends involved a celebrated *yūjo* named Kiyū, who was said to have belonged to the Gankirō brothel in Yokohama in the days when the Tokugawa Shogunate still ruled Japan. Her misfortune was to have caught the attention of an American merchant, when she was one of those courtesans who only saw Japanese clients. He demanded the same right to buy her favours as her Japanese patrons. She was supposed to have committed *seppuku* with a dagger on the night the American was due to pay her his first visit. There is a poem attributed to Kiyū, purportedly composed just before her death: 'A *yūjo* I may be, but like the *ominaeshi* flower of Japan that scorns even to be brushed with drops of dew, I will not wet my sleeve in falling American rain'. At least two *ukiyoe* prints exist depicting the courtesan in her last moments as she prepares to take her own life: *Kokon meifu kagami Shōgi Kiyū* by Adachi Ginkō, and the triptych *Shōgi Kiyū no wasetsu* (1878) by Yamazaki Toshinobu. She was believed to have been the daughter of a doctor in Edo, although there is not much in the way of historical documentation to back up the legend that grew up around Kiyū's life and death.

The story is related in Nakazato Kian's study of *rashamen*, published in 1931, at a time when anti-western sentiment was again running high in Japan and the military was tightening its stranglehold on the running of the country. Indeed, the book itself is dedicated to the memory of Kiyū. Nakazato made Kiyū's father into a nationalistic patriot, portraying him as a doctor who fell on difficult times after he had had his licence suspended for treating a wounded *shishi*, a samurai with anti-western leanings. In Nakazato's version of the story, the despised suitor is not an American merchant but a French arms dealer operating incognito in Yokohama disguised as an American trader. Nakazato shows him taking advantage of his position to lean on the Tokugawa Shogunate, which was eager to procure western armaments, to get the proprietor of the Gankirō to force an unwilling Kiyū to agree to an assignation.[60] Kiyū is portrayed as a filial daughter who willingly sells herself to a brothel in order to support her ailing father, but refuses to demean herself by becoming the plaything of a western barbarian. Her conduct is presented not only as a salutary contrast to the selfish behaviour of the *musume rashamen* who appear in the rest of Nakazato's book – ordinary girls who thought nothing of becoming the mistresses of foreign strangers merely for the sake of money and gifts – but as an admonition to all those Japanese women who might be tempted to put greed, vanity or their own personal happiness before patriotism in consorting with the enemy in times of national peril.

Kiyū's tragedy is supposed to have unfolded in the last years of the Tokugawa Shogunate. *Seppuku* was an act performed under a feudal system of social obligation and duty. Although the phenomenon of Japanese soldiers committing suicide as a gesture of military defiance, in order to avoid surrender or capture in wartime, did not disappear, such suicides are generally referred to as *jiketsu*. The joint suicides, by blade, of General Nogi Maresuke, a veteran of the Russo-Japanese War, and his wife on 13 September 1912, just as a volley of cannon fire signalled the departure of Emperor Meiji's funeral cortège from the Imperial Palace in Tōkyō, was a demonstration of feudalistic allegiance. Japanese newspapers described their deaths as *junshi*, a suicide following the death of one's master. The Tokugawa Shogunate had tried to put an end to the custom of *junshi* as early as 1663, though it was not until 1668 that the practice began to disappear. Although Nogi's action was hailed as an example of extraordinary devotion, his suicide was, nonetheless, a deeply anachronistic one. It harked back to a bygone era.[61]

Cio-Cio-San's death scene thus flouts many of the resonances – moral and aesthetic – with which the ritual of *seppuku* has been overlaid in Japan, by history as well as by the ways it has been represented in Japanese art and literature. Not least, there is the way in which Cio-Cio-San re-emerges, after plunging her dagger into herself, as a frightful ghoulish spectacle with a gory scarf wrapped around her neck, but with just enough life left to drag herself across the floor and clasp her (no doubt terrified, albeit blindfolded) toddler to her dying bosom. A Japanese audience might be appalled by the sheer un-Japanese nature of the scene at the moment when she is being presented in the story as being at her most Japanese, but David Belasco, after all, designed his play as a sensationalist, melodramatic stage spectacle, and Puccini's opera inherits much of that aspect of Belasco's piece. Cio-Cio-San's death scene successfully serves up the exotic heroine as victim, and her prolonged death agonies, expressive of her unbreakable, yearning love for her son, are undoubtedly effective in reducing an audience to tears. The boy, meanwhile, carries the promise of the future with him away from his mother's land to the bright shores of the United States. His blond hair and azure eyes will presumably help him to merge with his father's people better than if he had taken after Cio-Cio-San.

Children born to foreign men and their Japanese mistresses were all too poignant a reality in Japanese treaty ports. The American physician Albert Leffingwell, writing in the early 1890s under the nom de plume Albert Tracy, reported being told by a long-time western resident of Yokohama that 'in every one of the new treaty ports a new race is growing up, corresponding with the Eurasian of British India.'[62] The question of who should care for the children born of temporary liaisons between Japanese women and foreign nationals had always been a fraught one, involving as it did the willingness or unwillingness of the father to acknowledge a child as his own, the acceptance or rejection of the child by the mother, the desire on the part of the earlier Shogunate government to restrict the amount of communication that took place between foreigners and Japanese, and the resentment felt by the foreign community in Japan at what it took to be interference in private affairs by Japanese officialdom. Feelings of paternal responsibility had not been totally absent from those employees of the Dutch East India Company who had children with Japanese mistresses. Cornelis van Nieuwenrode, *opperhoofd* from 1623 to 1633 (with a brief hiatus in 1631), had two daughters by different local women. When he fell seriously ill while still in Hirado, Van Nieuwenrode made a will providing for both his daughters and their mothers. After his death, the children were entrusted to a VOC employee and in 1637 taken to Batavia (modern-day Jakarta), the Company's administrative centre in Asia. The elder daughter Hester married a British army officer in Batavia in 1644, and the younger, Cornelia, a merchant with the VOC in 1652. A family portrait from 1665 by J.J. Coeman survives of Cornelia van Nieuwenrode with her husband Pieter Cnoll and two daughters.[63] François Caron, who arrived at Hirado as ship's scullery boy, became fluent in Japanese, and rose to become *opperhoofd* of the trading post between 1639 and 1641, took his mistress and their children to Batavia with him when the time came for him to leave Japan. Two years later, he petitioned Dutch officials for his surviving children – three sons and two daughters – to be declared legitimate. He had been in no hurry to marry his mistress, however, who in any case died soon after the move to Batavia.[64]

As the Tokugawa Shogunate started to accelerate its plans to eradicate Catholic influence from Japanese territory, 287 Portuguese nationals, Spaniards and persons born to Japanese mothers and either Portuguese or Spanish fathers were deported to Macao in 1636. Once Japan entered its period of international isolation, during which only the Dutch East India Company and Chinese merchants were allowed to maintain a presence in the country, foreigners were not permitted to take their children (or the children's mothers) with them when they left the country. This was formally laid out in a set of regulations issued in 1715 by the local magistrate of Nagasaki (on behalf of the Shogunate) regarding the conduct of courtesans apropos of Chinese and Dutch merchants.[65] The German botanist Philipp von Siebold, who arrived in Nagasaki in 1823 in the capacity of doctor in the employ of the VOC, had a beloved daughter, Ine, by his

Japanese mistress, a courtesan known as Sono Ōgi, born Kusumoto Taki. When Siebold was expelled from Japan towards the end of 1829 for having tried to take maps and other items banned for export out of the country the previous year, Ine was still only two and a half years old. The portraits on Japanese lacquer of the mother and the daughter are preserved in the National Ethnographic Museum, Leiden. Siebold also kept clippings of their hair. He made financial provisions for Taki and Ine, but after his return to Europe he married the daughter of a German nobleman. Taki, for her part, later married a fellow countryman. Ine was educated by her father's former Japanese students, and grew up to become Japan's first female obstetrician working according to western medical principles. When Siebold returned to Japan in 1859, accompanied by his thirteen-year-old eldest son Alexander, he is said to have been reunited with Ine and Taki, who in the meantime had been widowed.[66]

When the Dutch were negotiating a new commercial treaty with the Tokugawa Shogunate in 1858, the Dutch negotiator appears to have requested the lifting of the ban on Dutch nationals taking their children with them when the time came for them to leave Japan. But no reference to this survived in the final version of the treaty. The Shogunate, however, was forced to acknowledge that some foreigners wished to assume custody of their half-Japanese children. It was becoming increasingly difficult for the Japanese authorities to insist on banning this, especially when the mother was willing to release the child to the care of the father. Besides, it was and continued to be a common practice throughout Japan for mothers to be expected to give up a child (regardless of their personal wishes) if the family situation demanded it, whether because of poverty or because the child was needed to carry on a family line to which the mother herself had never or no longer belonged. In 1862, the Shogunate instructed local magistrates in Nagasaki, Kanagawa (Yokohama) and Hakodate that children born to foreigners and Japanese courtesans should be considered as belonging to the father, and notified foreign consulates that such children would henceforth take the nationality of the paternal parent. This, however, met with heated opposition from foreign consuls.[67]

There were many more men who did not want anything to do with the children born as a result of their liaisons. Brothel proprietors were warned by their foreign clients that they rejected in advance responsibility for any children who might be born. Any extra allowance paid to a pregnant mistress was not to be taken as an admission of paternity. Brothels warned their women to take precautions against pregnancy. Professional prostitutes and courtesans had their methods of contraception, which included douches, as well as wads of strong Japanese paper chewed until soft and inserted as a barrier inside the vagina. But non-professional *musume rashamen* were often less careful. Children were generally unwelcome to their mothers. There was much prejudice against having half-caste children. Some pregnant *rashamen* were said to have hanged themselves or thrown themselves into rivers or the sea. Others sought abortionists. From the seventeenth century until around the end of the nineteenth, there were doctors in Japan referred to as *chūjōryū* who specialised in abortions, mostly using drugs. They were predominantly to be found in Edo, but some abortionists appear to have been working in Yokohama, several of them frauds who dispensed extremely poisonous substances. Other women abandoned their babies. There was even one barbarous story of a mother who stuffed her newborn into a wooden box and sent it to the ship on which the unfortunate child's father was serving. Many respectable members of the foreign community in Yokohama were horrified to hear of such acts of violence being perpetrated by young women on their babies, their foetuses, and on themselves. One matron took in abandoned children born to foreigners and their Japanese lovers. Principal Brown of the Ichimei Eigakusho English School wrote in dismay to the local Japanese magistrate, insisting that something had to be done about the proliferation of both mistresses and abortionists, and that immediate action was necessary to ameliorate the suffering of the mothers and their offspring.

In 1873, the Meiji government decided that natural children born to Japanese women and foreign nationals should be registered as the mother's illegitimate issue and take Japanese nationality. Paternity was to be recognised only in cases in which the father specifically chose to acknowledge the child as his own.[68] Some men salved their conscience by making some kind of financial arrangement for their lovers and their children before returning to the west. Others did not wish to be parted from their children and took them away with them, leaving the mother behind. The French caricaturist Georges Bigot, who was reputed to have had relationships with several Japanese women during his stay in the country from 1882 to around 1899, had with him his son Gaston Maurice (who, incidentally, possessed French nationality) on his return to France. Bigot was said to have formally married the boy's mother, Sano Masu, in 1894, but divorced her before his departure from the country; she remained behind in Japan.[69]

William Seward, an American tourist who, in the course of a round-the-world trip taken for the sake of his health, passed briefly through Japan in the autumn of 1870, encountered a German merchant and his half-Japanese child, 'a pretty brunette boy, two years old', on board the ship he was taking out of Nagasaki:

> The father brings him to us to be caressed. We ask, 'Where is the Japanese mother?' 'I have left her behind; she would not be fit to bring up the boy, or to be seen herself in a European country.'[70]

The boy is another of the tidy profits the merchant has accrued during his short but lucrative stay in Yokohama. The Japanese woman who had carried the child was now redundant, an embarrassment, even, that had been jettisoned. The German is quite unsentimental and pragmatic about it. But he is clearly very fond of his son. Considering the reluctance of many former mistresses (to say nothing of their families) to raise the half-caste children born as a consequence of a transient, often – though not always – financially motivated relationship, this child was, perhaps, fortunate to have at least one parent who wanted him.

A novelist of the period who wrote sympathetically (if sentimentally) of children of mixed Caucasian–Japanese background was Winnifred Eaton, who was born in 1875 in Montreal. She was the eighth of fourteen children born to a Chinese mother and English father. Her eldest sister Edith also became a writer, publishing under the name Sui Sin Far. Sui Sin Far's modest body of work constitutes some of the very first articles and short stories to appear in North America dealing with the hardships and prejudice faced by Chinese immigrants. Winnifred Eaton, on the other hand, assumed a Japanese persona and found literary success writing under the name Onoto Watanna. Her first novel *Miss Numè of Japan* (1899) concerned two mixed-race relationships: one (unsuccessful) between a Japanese youth who has been educated at Harvard and a charming but flirtatious American girl; the other (successful) between the American girl's erstwhile American fiancé and the Japanese girl to whom the Harvard-educated Japanese youth had been betrothed by his family in childhood. *A Japanese Nightingale* (1901), Watanna's second novel and the one for which she was best known,[71] took up the popular subject of Japanese wives-for-money, giving it the unusual twist of making the heroine Yuki a Eurasian, the daughter of a well-born but impoverished Japanese woman and a Japanophile Englishman who had adopted his wife's country and nationality. Brought up in Japan by her mother, with her father long dead, Yuki has a tradition-ally Japanese attitude to family duties. Unbeknownst to her brother Taro, she has been struggling to support his studies in the United States by working as a geisha. She enters into a temporary marriage with an American in order to earn the extra money needed to bring her brother back home now he has finished university. With her blue eyes and red-black hair, she has attracted the attention of Jack Bigelow. But Bigelow just happens to be Taro's college chum, who has preceded his friend to the Far East. Taro, who has warned Jack off the idea of forming a relation-ship with a local Japanese girl, is bitterly opposed to matches between westerners and Japanese women because he is, as Watanna puts it, 'Westernized enough to appreciate how lightly such marriages were held by the foreigners'.[72]

Jack, in the meantime, has fallen in love with the geisha Yuki, having no idea she is Taro's own sister. He first sees her at a teahouse dancing. Then a matchmaker brings Yuki to him, and she begs Jack to 'marry' her. Jack is reluctant, knowing he will only be in Japan for a little while, and would prefer being just 'friends'. But Yuki is not interested in this, though Jack senses she is attracted to him. Afraid that he will lose her to some other westerner, he finally agrees to 'marry' her. Yuki is charming, but to Jack's distress she keeps using blatant ploys to get as much money out of him as she can. She is, moreover, very secretive about what she wants all the money for. Jack oscillates between his suspicion that he has 'married' an adventuress and his belief that Yuki truly loves him. But when she begins to drop hints that they will soon have to go their separate ways, Jack tells himself that she must be a heartless trollop after all. He then receives news that Taro has arrived in Japan. Jack confesses to Taro his involvement with a Japanese girl, noting that, in any case, the girl is preparing to desert him. He brings Taro home to meet her.

Of course, Taro and Yuki recognise one another immediately. Shocked that her secret has been discovered by her brother, Yuki runs off and disappears. Taro's mother admits to her son that she had persuaded a reluctant Yuki to enter into a temporary 'marriage' with a rich foreigner so they would have enough money to send him for his passage home. Taro is horrified to learn he has been living off his sister's self-sacrifice. He is also tormented by the thought that his sister's life has been ruined by his own friend. His anguish is such that he succumbs to a fatal attack of brain fever. Jack vows to his dying friend that he will find Yuki and make her his proper wife. After more than a year of wandering the globe, Yuki, who has been in love with Jack all along, returns to the house she used to share with him. There, she is miraculously reunited with Jack, who has also been drawn back to the house by his memories. Taro's distrust of western men is proved to have been misguided, Jack's mistrust of Yuki is shown to be unfounded, and Yuki is absolved, through her suffering, of her guilt in having exploited the man she loved for money.

Whilst the plots of Watanna's novels remained fairly conventional, Watanna was original in employing characters of mixed Caucasian and Japanese parentage and in delving into issues relating to their cultural and personal identity. Unfortunately, she was let down by her limited knowledge of Japan; she had no first-hand experience of the Far East and derived all she knew of the country from her reading of books and articles about Japan and its people. Her characterisation of Japanese culture tends towards stereotypes: women are self-abnegating, men are obsessed by honour, the faceless peasantry are superstition-bound. What she had insight into, however, was the feeling of not belonging. In 1898 Watanna published an article entitled 'The Half-Caste', in which she described how children of mixed Caucasian and Japanese parentage (she had already begun to present herself as a Japanese woman) were forced to learn to protect themselves from the hostility and condescending pity they received. They had to build around them, according to Watanna, a wall of proud disengagement and coldness. Watanna ascribed such feelings to a hypothetical half-Japanese girl of twelve:

It made her angry to find people patriotic, because patriotism seemed to her so selfish – an exalted sort of conceit. This is how patriotism appeared to a little girl who had no real country to be proud of. Perhaps both of the countries she might have called home, had bruised her so that in the midst of her yearning and love for them, she resented the fact that she herself belonged to neither of them, inasmuch as she was an alien on both soils – entirely different from those about her.[73]

The Heart of Hyacinth (1903) is the most remarkable of all of Watanna's Japanese novels for its depiction of the clash that can occur between cultural and racial identities. The eponymous heroine is a Caucasian girl who has been raised since birth by a Japanese lady, and has grown up never doubting she is anything but Japanese. Hyacinth has been brought up by the widow Madame Aoi, who happens to have a half-English son, Komazawa. Everybody naturally thinks Hyacinth is Komazawa's sister. Komazawa has been raised without his English father, who died in his son's infancy. The new Christian missionary to the area is appalled when he learns this and insists that Komazawa is sent immediately to England to learn about his paternal heritage and take possession of the family estate that has been left to him. The Reverend Mr Blount firmly believes Komazawa to be ' "one of us" '. Komazawa, he declares, ' "has the physical appearance . . . and, let us hope, the natural instincts of the Caucasian," ' and in Mr Blount's view, therefore, it would be ' "not only ludicrous but wicked for him to continue here [in Japan] . . . where he is, may we say, an alien" '.[74]

Hyacinth, on the other hand, demonstrates the effect of nurture over blood. Hyacinth is the daughter of an American woman who had run away from her philandering English husband and had been found by Madame Aoi ill, destitute and on the verge of giving birth. Enjoined by the dying mother never to give up the baby to its father, Madame Aoi has raised Hyacinth as her own. But whereas she has done her best to inculcate in her own son an awareness of his English background, she has never attempted anything similar with the girl. Once Komazawa has left for Britain, Aoi increasingly reverts to her old Japanese ways. Hyacinth enters the local school and grows up alongside the other children, from whom she learns to call all westerners 'barbarians'. Meanwhile, the derogatory remarks the other girls make about her grey-blue eyes and white complexion fail to dent either her self-esteem or her confidence in her own beauty. Being taunted for looking different from her companions does not in itself distress Hyacinth. She seems to possess a sense of absolute beauty, impervious to the opinions of the people around her.

One day, Hyacinth discovers that her natural father, having been apprised of her existence, has sent his attorney to find her. Hyacinth is distraught and insists that Japan is her home. Her father's lawyer maintains that because she is still a minor her father is entitled to have custody of her, whether she likes it or not. ' "You belong to his home",' he declares. ' "It is some fatal and horrible miscarriage of fate that has cast your destiny among this alien people." ' Hyacinth fiercely argues that the Japanese are her people. The lawyer is aghast that Hyacinth seems to be ' "more Japanese than anything else" '. His companion, a young man from the American consulate, finds the situation ' "grotesque, impossible, horrible" '.[75] Meanwhile, Hyacinth, who is betrothed to the son of a rich local merchant, finds out that her prospective in-laws, who had been willing to countenance the idea of a match if she had at least one Japanese parent, no longer want anything to do with her now they have learned that she has no Japanese blood at all. To add to Hyacinth's unhappiness, her father Richard Lorrimer turns up in person, with his second wife in tow. The second Mrs Lorrimer, who happens to have been the mistress who had caused so much misery to Hyacinth's mother, is horrified not just at how Japanese Hyacinth looks but by the Japanese manner in which she behaves. Mrs Lorrimer decides a white girl who looks and acts Japanese is simply ' "unnatural" '.[76] Lorrimer suggests, without much hope, that in time Hyacinth might eventually be civilised and modernised. Far from being uncertain about her own identity, Hyacinth knows what she is. She is adamant that she is Japanese, and just as the second Mrs Lorrimer rejects the idea of her as a stepdaughter, she rejects the idea of Mrs Lorrimer becoming her mother.

Hyacinth is rescued from her predicament by Komazawa, who arrives back from England and promptly falls in love with her – rather incestuously, it has to be admitted, but then they are not related by blood after all. Komazawa is torn between desire for her and his belief that it would be best for Hyacinth if she were to go with her father, broaden her horizons and step into that position in the world which belongs to her by right of birth. This being a novel by Onoto Watanna, love triumphs in the end. Hyacinth realises that it had only been out of vanity that she had accepted the proposal of marriage from the son of the wealthy Japanese merchant. Komazawa vows to be Hyacinth's guide and protector when the time comes for her to travel to the west. Who but Komazawa, with a mother in Japan and a large estate to maintain in Cheshire, could understand the situation of a girl who has a foothold in two separate worlds without really belonging to either?

Watanna's Caucasian–Japanese heroines became blonder with every novel, and increasingly alienated from their Japanese surroundings. In *Tama* (1910) the eponymous heroine is golden-haired, fair-complexioned, and the object of the entire local community's superstitious hatred. They call her the fox-woman, a being with the body of a human and the soul of a fox. Her parents, a Japanese temple priestess of noble blood and a foreign sailor with whom the priestess had fallen in love, have been slaughtered by a mob of religious fanatics. Tama is blind, but she is also a true child of nature, more so than any of the other Japanese characters in the novel. She is befriended by an American, referred to throughout the novel only as the Tojin (*tōjin*), in other words, the 'Foreigner', who has been employed as a teacher by the local lord (or *daimyō*). The Tojin recognises that Tama is not very Japanese, while Tama associates the Tojin with her dead father. Tama and the Tojin are drawn to each other as fellow outcasts – as spiritually enlightened, morally superior westerners adrift in a hostile eastern world of superstitious intolerance. In the temporary absence of the *daimyō* from his demesne, the locals rise against the Tojin and Tama. The two flee together into the mountains. They are only saved from the same fate as Tama's parents by the intervention of the *daimyō*, who, like a *deus ex machina*, suddenly returns, restores order and punishes the evil ringleaders. As for the common people, who are unable to think for themselves and can only follow the example of those who seek to manipulate them, they blithely welcome the Tojin back, as though they had never turned against him for having taken pity on the fox-woman they feared and hated so much.

Watanna's last novel on a Japanese theme, *Sunny-San* (1922), takes its eponymous mixed-race heroine out of Japan and into American society. Sunny-San is the daughter of an American and a geisha, herself the child of a Japanese mother and a Russian father. Sunny-San has been brought up in Japan and is indentured to an unscrupulous teahouse owner, from whom she is rescued by a group of rich young American men on a tour of the Far East. They buy her her freedom. Although Sunny-San describes herself as ' "white on my face and my honorable body, but . . . Japanese on my honorable insides" ',[77] the novel makes it clear that she belongs in America. Once she is there, Sunny-San instinctively knows how to make maximum use of her radiant beauty and charm to get on in the world. The same physical attributes – the white complexion, the golden hair – which made Tama an object of fear among the Japanese win Sunny-San admiration in American society and facilitate her integration into it. By the end of the novel, she is restored to her long-lost, wealthy and socially prominent American father, and is engaged to the most gallant of the young men who had originally rescued her. In the end, Sunny-San's Japanese 'insides' do not count for very much. Besides, she is ready to cast off her Japanese ways rather than allow them to impede her progress up the ladder of American society. Onoto Watanna, the Chinese-Canadian writer who originally launched her career by moving to America and, taking advantage of the contemporary vogue for Japonaiserie, publicised herself as being Japanese, concluded her series of Japanese novels with a fantasy of a mixed-race woman like herself who succeeds in blending into the American establishment.

The Madame Butterfly story employs the east-meets-west framework to retell the paradigmatic tale of the innocent girl who is destroyed by the betrayal of her callous worldly lover. For Onoto Watanna, herself caught between two racial iden-tities, the subject of interracial relationships allowed her, in her novels, to enter into various issues regarding an individual's sense of racial and cultural affiliation. The Japanese, for their part, found a favourite tragic heroine of their own in the figure of O-Kichi, the woman who was appointed as an attendant to the first American consul to Japan, Townsend Harris. O-Kichi exemplified the tragic consequences of becoming the object of a foreigner's desire. But she was not portrayed solely as the victim of a westerner's caprices. A great deal of her suffering was ascribed to her treatment at the hands of her fellow Japanese, including government officials and fellow villagers, as well as members of her own family. She has served in some degree as a focus for contrition for the general bigotry that used to be directed at Japanese women who associated with foreigners.

O-Kichi's life was fertile ground for the cultivation of legends. Whereas the first mistress of Harris's interpreter Henry Heusken appears to have later married and lived out a quiet and blameless life in the village of Shimoda, O-Kichi's life after her brief spell as Harris's attendant was by all accounts an extremely unsettled one. Heusken's Japanese manservant Sukezō relates in his memoirs how O-Kichi was reviled by her fellow villagers as Tōjin O-Kichi, O-Kichi the Foreigner. By 1868 she was in Yokohama, living with a Japanese lover. Three years later she was back in Shimoda working as a hairdresser, but this did not last very long and she moved away. She had returned to Shimoda again by 1882, and was running a small tavern with no great success. She is reported to have become a very heavy drinker. Her health deteriorated and in the spring of 1890 she drowned in the River Inōzawa outside Shimoda. It was never ascertained whether she had accidentally fallen in or had committed suicide. She was fifty years old.[78]

Three novels by the writer Jūichiya Gisaburō, based on the researches of Muramatsu Shunsui, a Shimoda doctor with an interest in local history,[79] brought the legend of O-Kichi to national prominence in the late 1920s. The first, *Tōjin O-Kichi* (O-Kichi the Foreigner) was published in 1928; the second, *Toki no haisha Tōjin O-Kichi* (Defeated by history: O-Kichi the Foreigner) appeared a year later, and its sequel, in turn, in 1930.[80] Jūichiya Gisaburō follows the tradition that O-Kichi was already established as a popular geisha in the village of Shimoda when she was appointed to attend on Harris.[81] He portrays her as a woman who is treated cruelly by men – all men – both Japanese and

American. The Japanese authorities use her as a pawn in placating a difficult diplomatic adversary. She is betrayed by the local man to whom she is already engaged, who succumbs to the bribe of a position in Edo in exchange for giving her up. She suffers abuse at the hands of local villagers, her fellow countrymen on whose behalf she has sacrificed her personal happiness. Her loyalty is taken for granted by the homesick, elderly American consul Harris, who, in moments of intense loneliness, makes her promises he has no intention of honouring, and who casts her off once he is back in the company of fellow Americans.

Much of the force of Jūichiya Gisaburō's vision of O-Kichi as a tragic figure comes from the way in which, in his second novel, he depicts her life after Harris. She drifts back to being a geisha, and for a while she is in demand as a curiosity. Her patrons find her misanthropy amusing, until they begin to get frightened of the pitiless excoriations she relentlessly directs at herself. Indifferent to the exigencies of everyday life, yet refusing to be seduced by death, she remains fearless and defiant. She will not endure her unhappiness meekly, and savagely scorns being turned into the object of pity and charity. She will not forget or bury the past. She, who – despite everything – had always been decent to Harris, receives anything but decent treatment from all those around her. She is ferocious in her despair, rails against the hardness of fate, and is magnificently rude in her drunkenness, overthrowing all the rules of Japanese female decorum.

Jūichiya Gisaburō's version of O-Kichi's life was immediately adapted for the screen. Mizoguchi Kenji's motion picture was one of two films about O-Kichi which appeared in 1930, and another four films were made before the end of the decade. Her legend was dramatised by Mayama Seika in 1929. Even more famous was Yamamoto Yūzō's four-act play *Nyo'nin aishi* (1931), which is still frequently revived. In this play, O-Kichi becomes enmeshed in a web of diplomatic machinations between the Americans and the Japanese. The Japanese offer O-Kichi to Harris in order to appease him, but it has not occurred to them to get her consent first. When she baulks, the Americans insist that the Japanese keep their promise to deliver her to Harris: they consider the inviolability of contracts more important than the personal happiness of an individual woman. Meanwhile, O-Kichi is unable to forget the unfaithfulness of her Japanese lover who deserts her for the promise of an appointment to a post in Edo. Even when they later find each other again and try to forge a life together after all their tribulations, O-Kichi cannot forget his former betrayal and she turns her back for good on domesticity and respectability.

Although O-Kichi was portrayed in these popular works by Jūichiya Gisaburō and Yamamoto Yūzō as a victim of general masculine – rather than specifically American – egotism, the Japanese historian Yoshida Tsunekichi relates that in the early days of the Allied occupation of Japan after the Second World War, he received a visit from an American official attached to the Civil Information and Education Section of the occupation forces' General Headquarters in Tōkyō, who complained that interest among the Japanese public in the legend of O-Kichi tended to peak at times when political relations between Japan and the United States were at their nadir.[82] There had been, however, an attempt in the years leading up to the outbreak of the war in the Pacific to turn the story into an opera which celebrated peace and international understanding. The initial idea was that this new piece should be performed at the Century of Progress International Exposition, which was to open in Chicago in 1933. The libretto was commissioned by the Chicago Grand Opera from Percy Noel, a Japanophile journalist with the Associated Press agency. Noel approached his friend the Japanese composer Yamada Kōsaku to compose the music. *Kurobune* (Black Ship) was Yamada Kōsaku's third operatic work, but it is the first truly Japanese opera to experiment with Japanese musical idioms within the context of the western musical format of the grand opera. The overture was completed by 1929, but the proposed Chicago premiere fell through when the opera company unexpectedly folded. The composer then translated and reworked the libretto himself into Japanese. He renamed the opera *Yoake*, or 'Dawn', although it is now generally referred to by its original title. In the spring of 1939 Yamada was still hopeful that the work could be taken on tour to the United States. The proposal that it should be premiered as part of the celebrations which were planned for 1940 to mark the 2,600th year of the Japanese imperial family's reign attracted criticism from ultra-nationalists, as well as from self-appointed custodians of high culture, who were offended that the composer had stuck with a subject that had initially been chosen by a westerner, one, moreover, which they considered to be degrading and humiliating to the Japanese. *Yoake* was finally performed on 28 November 1940, at the Tōkyō Takarazuka Theatre.

The opera was an expression of the optimism shared by Percy Noel and Yamada Kōsaku that amity, symbolised by the love shared by O-Kichi and the American consul, could and should exist between Japan and the United States. The action revolves around a fictitious anti-western, anti-Shogunate samurai named Yoshida, who attempts to persuade O-Kichi to act in the service of her country by assassinating Harris. O-Kichi, who on meeting Harris for the first time is struck by his air of authority, his magnanimity and his goodness, cannot believe that the American consul could really be so devious as to be plotting the overthrow of Japan's rulers. She questions whether it is justified for her to take Harris's life that peace might be restored among her own countrymen. She feels it cannot be right that Harris should be so hated by her fellow Japanese.

The consul demonstrates his selflessness by risking his own life rescuing O-Kichi when they are caught in a violent storm at sea. Just as they are proclaiming their love for one another, they receive the long-awaited news that the *shōgun* will receive Harris at Edo. Their moment of exultation, however, is interrupted by the rebel samurai Yoshida, who lunges at Harris with a drawn sword, ready to sacrifice his own life in this daring attempt. Yoshida sincerely believes that the assassination of the American consul would awaken his countrymen to the danger which the presence of foreigners posed to Japan's independence. Harris is deeply moved by Yoshida's selfless love for his country, even as his own life rests on a knife-edge. Empathising with the samurai's sentiments, he warns him that although he personally does not fear death, his murder is certain to herald the horrors of war rather than the benefits of peace. At this crucial moment, a missive arrives for Yoshida from the 'Taikun' in Kyōto. *Taikun* was the title by which foreigners referred to the *shōgun*, but here it is employed in a wider sense to signify the emperor, to whom Yoshida has pledged undying allegiance. The 'Taikun' informs Yoshida that it is his desire that Harris should not be slain in his name. Yoshida commits *seppuku* to atone for his failure to anticipate the emperor's will, and dies with the hope for peace on his lips. Harris laments the self-sacrifice of such a noble samurai and hopes his death will seal a dawning age of peace between Japan and the United States.[83]

In the triangular relationship between the three characters Harris, O-Kichi and Yoshida, it is female intuition and love which open the eyes of the Japanese woman to the virtues of the American. It is empathy with masculine sentiments such as noble patriotism and self-sacrifice that allows the American to understand the Japanese samurai and the motives which drive him to accomplish that deed which O-Kichi cannot bring herself to perform. Still, at least one appreciative music critic who attended the premiere in 1940, Yamane Ginji, was genuinely baffled by Yoshida's sudden suicide. He felt that the suicide had been included only to satisfy the originally intended western audience's desire for a display of exotic spectacle, rather than for a genuine psychological or dramatic reason. In any case, Japan's mounting military aggression on the Asian continent and worsening relations with the United States put an end to any vague ideas of the work being taken on an American tour. The composer himself swung rapidly to the right of the political spectrum, and was soon composing songs celebrating Japanese militarism.

After the Second World War, Hollywood had its turn at transforming the fleeting historical encounter between Harris and O-Kichi into a symbol of a symbiotic relationship between the United States and post-war Japan. *The Barbarian and the Geisha*, which starred John Wayne woefully miscast as the American consul Townsend Harris and Eiko Ando in her only film role as O-Kichi, was released by 20th Century-Fox in 1958. The film attempts to redress the negative image of the rapacious American projected by the character of Pinkerton in the Madame Butterfly story. It was not, alas, one of the director John Huston's better efforts. Townsend Harris is portrayed descending upon Japan as a bringer of peace and progress, somewhat in the style of General Douglas MacArthur, commander of the Allied occupation forces in Japan after the Second World War. This Harris is the archetypical American man of action, a benefactor to an obstinate race which could at times be as infuriating as a wayward child. O-Kichi, in this film, is sent by Tamura, the fictitious governor of Shimoda, to insinuate herself into Harris's confidence and spy on him. But she is quickly won over by the American's chivalrousness as much as by his manliness. Tamura has had O-Kichi trained as a geisha at his expense, and expects her to act as his tool. As O-Kichi explains in a voiceover, 'I was a geisha; I knew men. I was to please Harris-*san* in every way, and watch his every move.' The film would, perhaps, have been more suspenseful if, at the outset, O-Kichi harboured at least some animus towards the Americans and their forceful ways. In the event, she has nothing but deferential respect for the dynamism of the heroic Harris. It would have enlivened the film, moreover, if O-Kichi had been allowed to be even slightly seductive – enough to pose a threat to the noble American consul's virtue. But the potential danger to American masculinity which her foreign sexuality represents is carefully underplayed. The film uses the cover of propriety to shun the attempt to suggest what the geisha's much-vaunted special skills in pleasing men might consist of. The most O-Kichi is allowed to do is to sway her hips as she slinks along swathed in her tight-fitting kimono. Otherwise she arranges the occasional flower, deftly pours *sake* for Harris and looks engagingly baffled by the consul's inane magic tricks at the dining table.

The locals, who are initially hostile to the stranger, come before long to share O-Kichi's humble admiration for the American consul, when Harris single-handedly eradicates cholera from the village by burning down all their houses in the name of sanitation (the disease is brought to Shimoda in the first place by an American ship which the consul, earlier in the film, insists should be allowed into the port). Even Tamura feels deeply indebted to Harris for this service and facilitates the consul's reception at Edo. The villagers are so grateful to their benefactor that they form a procession to take Harris to Edo, and dance all the way to the *shōgun*'s capital. The *shōgun*'s ministers are also favourably impressed by Harris, and despite a momentary setback when one of Harris's chief supporters at Edo is fatally shot with an arrow during an archery demonstration, they vote in favour of the trade treaty with the United States.

The one discordant note in the general chorus of acclaim for Harris is provided by Tamura, whose personality oscillates between, on the one hand, high-minded patriotism combined with an acute sense of honour and, on the other, low cunning and deviousness. Tamura's family is convinced of the necessity of silencing Harris if Japan is to remain free of foreign interference. Tamura is chosen to assassinate the consul. He, in turn, orders O-Kichi to assist him. She is told to place a red handkerchief in the door to Harris's bed chamber so that Tamura can find it and kill the consul in his sleep. O-Kichi, however, directs Tamura to her own room instead. Just as he is about to strike with his sword, Tamura realises it is O-Kichi under the bedclothes, not Harris.[84] O-Kichi is ready to die in Harris's place, but Tamura does not have the heart to put her to death. Nor has he the spirit left to take a swing at Harris when he encounters the startled consul in the corridor. Conceding that he has failed in his sacred mission, Tamura dashes outside and commits *seppuku*. The last embodiment of feudal opposition to Harris self-destructs.

As for O-Kichi, she too feels she has failed her people. Harris tells her he has to return briefly to the United States (the treaty was signed in 1858, and Harris did not in fact leave Japan until 1862), but promises to come back to her, so that they might live out their lives together in a mountain idyll in some remote part of Japan. Faced with a choice between the American and her own people, O-Kichi decides she must return to the ways of her ancestors. She goes away, leaving behind for the consul the present of a broken comb and a mirror. Heusken is called in to interpret these symbolic gifts: the first, he says, represents their permanent parting, the latter, O-Kichi's soul. She has left her soul with Harris, Heusken tells him, but she has left him for her own mysterious Japanese reasons and Harris will never find her again. Harris is thus disburdened of the two Japanese who have had the greatest hold over his destiny in this film. Without having to behave like a Pinkerton, Harris (played as a man in his full-blooded prime by John Wayne rather than as the elderly man he actually was) is released from his commitment to O-Kichi and is free once more to pursue those great acts which American heroes are supposed to perform on the world's stage. O-Kichi relinquishes her claim upon him without shedding her own blood. She will continue to worship him from afar. In the last scene of the film, O-Kichi is seen reverently joining a crowd of natives who are cheering on Harris as a procession carries him triumphantly to the signing of the treaty between the two countries.[85]

The activities in the last years of the Tokugawa Shogunate of the *shishi*, those samurai opposed to western interference in Japanese affairs, on the one hand, and the *musume rashamen*, on the other, provided a convenient binary dramatic framework for representing Japanese responses to the west: male hostility and rejection, represented by the sword-wielding samurai, and female appreciation and acceptance, represented by geishas. In *The Barbarian and the Geisha*, John Wayne basically reprises his familiar screen role of frontiersman. Instead of opening up the American West to settlers keen to make their fortunes, here he prises open Japanese ports to American commercial enterprise. The sexual over-tone of the idea of forcible entry sets up an equation of Japan with the feminine, although the image that is being implied is closer to that of a blushing bride than a rape victim. But the film pulls back from the inference of miscegenation. Its simplistic attitude to cultural pluralism – allow the natives to carry on with their picturesque customs so long as they do not interfere with those fields of activity in which Americans stand to profit – reflects the paternalistic side of American cultural imperialism. The Madame Butterfly story admonishes its American characters for their failure to fulfil their paternal duty to peoples of non-western lands, to those 'people accustomed to small, simple and quiet things', as it pleases Cio-Cio-San to describe her countrymen to Pinkerton, and to care for and protect them with 'a little love, the love of a child'. The matchmaker Goro in the Madame Butterfly story symbolises the corruption which contact with westerners spawns, when the latter fail to set the right example. Given the hostile press Japanese businesses were to receive later in the twentieth century, partic-ularly in North America, it is ironic that one of the first memorable cultural representations in the west of the international businessman of Japan was the odious, unctuous character of Goro, the broker in female flesh.

CHAPTER FOUR

Hara-Kiri! Sadayakko and Madame Hanako on the Western Stage

Around the time, in February 1900, that David Belasco was preparing his *Madame Butterfly* for the New York stage, a troupe of Japanese actors arrived in the city, fresh from performing in front of the American President in Washington, DC. They had spent the last eight and a half months crossing the continental United States and had built up a considerable reputation for their extravagant stage spectacles. At the centre of the troupe was a slim, demure, melancholy-faced actress named Kawakami Sadayakko (or Sada Yacco, as her name was frequently spelt in the west), whose most celebrated role was that of Katsuragi in the play *The Geisha and the Knight*, a coolly elegant courtesan who becomes maddened with jealousy, bludgeons to death her rival in love, and finally expires in her lover's arms from the sheer violence of her emotions. During the course of the troupe's tour of the United States, Sadayakko had become its undisputed star, as her husband Kawakami Otojirō, the leader of the company, wryly admitted on their return to Japan. By the time the troupe reached Paris in the summer of 1900, via a run in London, Sadayakko was being trumpeted as the Ellen Terry – the Eleonora Duse – of Japan, and was also being compared favourably to Sarah Bernhardt. Sadayakko certainly shattered any preconception the western public might have had of Japanese women as simpering ingénues. When Gilbert and Sullivan's *The Mikado* was in rehearsal, W.S. Gilbert had employed a male dancer and a teahouse girl from a Japanese exhibition that was being held at Knightsbridge in London to coach his cast on Japanese deportment. Sadayakko, on the other hand, provided an opportunity for American and European audiences to see a Japanese actress portraying a Japanese character, and her most famous role, that of the wrathful courtesan Katsuragi, was no Yum-Yum from *The Mikado* or Mimosa-San from *The Geisha*. Sadayakko thrilled and terrified audiences with her character's violent, unexpected turns of passion. The theatre reviewer for the London *Times* shivered at her sudden transformation from the 'dancing doll with the impassive face and fixed smile' into 'a Japanese Clytemnestra, a pallid, haggard, dishevelled figure of vengeance' (24 May 1900). Sadayakko's many admirers in Europe's artistic and literary circles, from up-and-coming artists such as Picasso to Jean Cocteau, still a youth of eleven, wondered at her physical refinement, and her ability at the same time to unleash the soul's primal, amoral energy.

The Geisha and the Knight, which was devised by Sadayakko's husband Otojirō as a two-act play tenuously held together by a discontinuous plot,[1] serves as an interesting contrast to the Madame Butterfly story, since its heroine Katsuragi, the geisha referred to in the title (though she is not actually a geisha but a high-status courtesan, or *oiran*), is rejected by her lover, like Madame Butterfly, in favour of a more socially acceptable choice of wife. But unlike Cho-Cho-San, Katsuragi refuses to relinquish her claim on her lover's affections. Cho-Cho-San, a passive victim of her lover's cruelty, turns her dagger on herself, but Katsuragi allows the blind impulses of rage and jealousy to turn her into a perpetrator of brutal acts. Pursuing her lover Nagoya and his betrothed Orihime to the Buddhist temple where they have taken refuge, Katsuragi attempts to inveigle her way into the temple precincts under the pretext that she has come to dance in honour of the installation of the temple's new bell. The monks, tempted by the idea of seeing her dance, trick her into performing for them by hinting that they might allow her to enter if first she gives them a demonstration of her abilities. Hoping to bend the monks to her will, Katsuragi proceeds to execute several exquisite dances. But the monks, once they have had the pleasure of watching her dance, continue to bar her way into the temple. When Katsuragi realises they have taken advantage of her, she makes one last desperate plea to be allowed in. The monks still refuse. All at once, Katsuragi breaks into a frenzy of rage. She rampages through the gates and dashes off in search of her rival Orihime. At this point, Sadayakko, as Katsuragi, rushed off stage and stormed back moments later, rendered unrecognisable by a rapid costume change which transformed her in a *coup de théâtre* into a demonic-looking madwoman with dishevelled hair standing on end, like Medusa's crop of snakes. Driving the unfortunate Orihime before her, Katsuragi batters her to death with a bell hammer. Her former lover Nagoya arrives on the scene as she is battling with a temple guard. He comes to her defence, and just as he takes her into his arms, Katsuragi briefly comes to her senses and recognises him before she draws her last, agonised breath.

Readers of books and articles published in the west about Japan would have been familiar with the idea of the long-suffering, uncomplaining, forgiving Japanese woman who happily sacrifices herself for the benefit of her father or her husband or her son, as the case may be. Cho-Cho-San is cast in this mould. But most of Sadayakko's American and European audiences would have been unaware that Japanese legend and literature possessed a long tradition of recognising the dark savagery of human emotions – the anguish of the human soul goaded by the barbs of thwarted desire and driven blind by rage. There was a superstition in Japan from ancient times that a hostile, vindictive spirit – whether of a person already dead or of one still alive – could visit grievous harm, in the form of dire illness and even death, upon the object of its hatred. One of the most famous literary manifestations of such a figure appears in *The Tale of Genji*: Rokujō-miyasundokoro, a former lover of Prince Genji, whose spirit leaves her body in her sleep and bludgeons Genji's first wife, Aoi-no-ue, to death. Even after Rokujō's own death, her tormented spirit continues to persecute other women who subsequently enter Genji's life. Similarly, the legend upon which Sadayakko's husband Otojirō based the second act of *The Geisha and the Knight* involves thwarted love, wounded pride, foiled hopes and the lust for revenge. In this legend, a woman develops a violent passion for a monk and falls under the misapprehension that he reciprocates her love. The hapless monk, for whom nothing could be further from the truth, runs away to seek sanctuary from her importunity in the temple Dōjōji. She pursues him there, turns herself into a gigantic serpent and, coiling her body around the temple bell under which the monk has hidden, she roasts him to death. The story served as the basis of a noh play as well as several kabuki dances, one of which – the *Musume Dōjōji*, dating from 1753 – was in Sadayakko's repertoire. She frequently performed it in America, during the first leg of the Kawakami troupe's visit to the west. She would wear a silvery kimono which she had brought with her from Japan: its scale-like pattern suggested the snake theme of the original legend. However, when Otojirō came to refashion the legend for his own play, he left out the supernatural elements so characteristic of early Japanese legends and moral tales influenced by Buddhism, and kept his protagonist Katsuragi human to the end.

The publicity which was produced about Sadayakko both in America and in Europe made much of her supposed legitimacy as an actress back in Japan. The *Grand Rapids Herald*, for instance, informed its readers how Sadayakko's spirited attempt to become 'the first woman to ever appear on the stage of a Tokio theater in a performance in which the opposite sex participated' had generated 'a storm of protest from the old conservative element', which included thinly veiled threats to disrupt the show, as well as threats to her person. Violence, according to the article, had been averted only by the presence on the night of no less a figure than the 'Mikado' himself, who, by attending the performance, was supposed to have extended his encouragement to the courageous new actress. The *Boston Post* explained that the Japanese emperor had personally granted Sadayakko permission to perform alongside the male members of her husband's company on stage back in her native country.[2] When Sadayakko and the rest of her husband's troupe were in London in the early summer of 1900, the playbill advertising their appearance at the Coronet Theatre in Notting Hill Gate referred to them as the 'celebrated Japanese Court Company, from Tokio'. Sadayakko's husband was described as 'Japan's most Distinguished Actor'.

It was all a fiction. Sadayakko had never aspired to become a professional actress. She had never fought to overthrow the male domination of mainstream Japanese theatre, let alone been supported in the endeavour by such an exalted personage as the emperor of Japan himself. It was not even true that she was the first woman to appear on stage in Tōkyō alongside male actors. Nor had Otojirō ever belonged to any of the tight-knit circles of acting families that passed on from generation to generation the jealously guarded traditions of kabuki theatre. Otojirō had fallen rather accidentally into acting. With his less than impeccable stage credentials, he made it his lifelong ambition to champion a new type of drama in Japan, one that was less stylised than kabuki and flexible enough to show emotion with greater realism. But he was essentially an outsider in his own country – an innovator to some, a charlatan to others.

There was a significant difference between Sadayakko and Otojirō, however. Sadayakko had closer links to mainstream kabuki than her husband did. She had been brought up from childhood to become a geisha. This meant that from a young age she was rigorously trained in the disciplines of music and dance, many important styles of which had evolved over the previous three centuries in close conjunction with kabuki. In her professional capacity as a geisha, Sadayakko met many top-class kabuki actors; she was even engaged to one for a time. Having always been a keen participant in amateur dramatics, she appeared alongside her fellow geishas in the benefit performances which geishas were called upon to take part in from time to time. On such occasions, she was able to draw upon her highly placed contacts in professional kabuki for advice and coaching. Sadayakko, incidentally, preferred to take leading male roles, rather than play female characters.[3]

What was never widely publicised in the west was that, in her own country, Sadayakko had been, not a professional actress, but one of the most sought-after geishas in Tōkyō, who had enjoyed the patronage of high-ranking politicians as well as important figures in the world of industry and commerce. An exception was the French writer Judith Gautier, daughter of the writer Théophile Gautier and herself a highly acclaimed expert of the day on the Far East (even though she had never travelled there), who, in an article for the journal *Femina* in 1901, during Sadayakko's second tour to Europe, made a point of mentioning that Sadayakko was known in her own country foremost as a celebrated, highly accomplished geisha, for Judith Gautier's contention was that the geisha was the utterly chaste epitome of artistic finesse, elegance and beauty.[4] Nonetheless, it was not generally realised by those who flocked to see Sadayakko perform in *The Geisha and the Knight* that they were in fact watching a former geisha enact the role of a geisha/courtesan.

Sadayakko and Otojirō met in 1891 when she was still a geisha and he was just beginning to win some notoriety in Tōkyō for his stage appearances. Sadayakko was born Koyama Sada in downtown Tōkyō in 1871, the fourth year into the new imperial regime which supplanted the old Tokugawa Shogunate. As a very young child she was adopted (apparently not against her will) by Hamada Kame (Kamekichi), the proprietress of a geisha house called the Hamadaya in the Yoshichō district of Tōkyō. Sadayakko always said that Kamekichi had not adopted her with the intention of making money out of her, either as a geisha or by establishing her as some rich man's mistress.[5] Yoshichō was not one of the most prestigious or exclusive of the many pleasure quarters in the Japanese capital, but Sadayakko's adoptive mother had a reputation as a fine singer and she knew influential politicians.[6] At the age of twelve Sada began accompanying her older sister-geishas to their engagements, and assumed Koyakko as her first professional name. Two years later she fell in love with a student who rescued her from a bolting horse (she was a keen horsewoman, something still quite unusual at that time). But this romance was cut short when the young man was chosen by his mentor, the prominent Japanese intellectual Fukuzawa Yukichi, to be the future husband of his second daughter and sent off to study in the United States. In 1887, at the age of sixteen, Koyakko became a fully fledged geisha. She dropped the 'ko' (which means 'little' in Japanese) from her professional name and became known thereafter simply as Yakko. The man who performed her *mizuage* – the man, that is, who took her virginity – was widely reputed to have been Itō Hirobumi, who had become Japan's first prime minister at the end of December 1885. Though he does not appear to have been her lover for long, he continued to look out for her interests to the end of his days.

Kawakami Otojirō had been born Kawakami Otokichi in 1864 in the port city of Hakata in the north of the western Japanese island of Kyūshū. The son of a well-off shipping agent, he ran away from home at the age of fourteen, and eventually ended up in Tōkyō. In his late teens he was caught up in a nascent populist movement which was agitating for democratic reform. This movement was patriotic and anti-establishment, and it rapidly attracted adherents, some of whom were sober political theorists, but many more were predominantly interested in direct confrontation with the authorities. The central government attempted to suppress it by force, and the harder the authorities tried to do this, the more radicalised the movement became, splintering before long into factions which were as violently opposed to each other as they were to the government. On the outer fringes of these groups there was a fair number of hooligans, as well as extremists who were hostile to the ruling political oligarchy. Political gatherings often descended into rowdy affairs, with ruffians hired by opposing camps to disrupt proceedings. *Sōshi*, the term originally used of activists pressing for democratic rights, also came to refer to such thugs. Otojirō became a public speaker, flitting between the cities of Nagoya, Kyōto and Ōsaka. Inevitably he became the subject of gagging orders.

It was as a way of evading government restrictions on political speeches that Otojirō switched ostensibly to various forms of traditional storytelling such as *kōdan*, which featured tales of heroic deeds from the past, and *rakugo*, which took its subject matter from everyday life. *Rakugo* in particular, which used humour and sharp wordplay, appealed to Otojirō's love of satire and hyperbole.[7] There is not much to suggest that Otojirō was ever actually motivated by specific political principles or that he advocated any concrete policies for political reform.[8] He was essentially a showman, and he relished public exposure. In 1887, he briefly joined a troupe of kabuki actors in Kyōto, but he was so inept in his first role that he was not offered another part. He went back to *rakugo* and in 1888 had his first major success with an interval act, a satirical song entitled 'Oppekepē'. Set to the tune of a well-known comic song, the lyrics by Wakamiya Manjirō satirised the self-satisfaction of Japan's autocratic politicians and their pretensions to western culture.[9]

In the same year, 1888, an amateur actor by the name of Sudō Sadanori – who had previously been a political activist, or *sōshi*, like Otojirō – formed a troupe of actors in Ōsaka. Otojirō himself became interested in the idea of performing satirical skits with a political edge. In February 1891, he launched his own troupe of predominantly untrained actors.[10] His objective was to put on original plays on topics of contemporary interest, mostly to do with acts of heroism, valour and patriotism. Many members of his troupe were former *sōshi* like himself. This type of theatre, presented by actors who had not undergone rigorous training in the traditions of kabuki, was known as *sōshi shibai* or *shosei shibai*. It advocated greater realism on the stage, especially in the depiction of emotion, but in reality this often boiled down to brawls on stage in place of kabuki's highly choreographed and stylised fight scenes. Roughhousing, nevertheless, proved a definite crowd-puller. After an initially difficult launch of his troupe, Otojirō succeeded in securing an engagement at the Nakamuraza, one of the three prestigious kabuki theatres in Tōkyō, through a contact of his, a *sōshi* who happened to have been born into the professional theatre world. The run, in June 1891, was an instant sell-out.[11] On the back of this success, Otojirō's troupe was booked for two further runs later the same year.

Yakko went to see Otojirō perform, and before long she was committing herself deeply to this still unproven but nonetheless audacious young actor, who had plenty of admirers among the geishas of Tōkyō. She sank her own money into the running of his troupe, money which she was earning as a successful geisha. The couple were married in 1894. Sada then formally withdrew from being a geisha, gave up her professional name Yakko, and reverted to her own given name. She was twenty-three; Otojirō thirty.

Otojirō was ambitious, opportunistic and impulsive. In January 1893, he went off by himself to France, where he spent a month attending the theatre. The trip inspired him to produce a type of drama new to Japanese theatre: the crime thriller, featuring larceny and murder in a contemporary setting. When, at the beginning of August 1894, the First Sino-Japanese War erupted over control of Korea, Otojirō immediately staged a battlefield play with pyrotechnics for theatrical effect. This too was an instant success. He then hit upon the idea of going to the war zone himself to experience the war at first hand. Towards the end of October, he crossed over to the Korean Peninsula, spent a month there, and by December was ready to put on a jingoistic war play based loosely on what he had seen.[12]

Although an overseas tour was something Otojirō had always vaguely dreamt of, the proposal to take a company of actors to America came up quite fortuitously, in 1899. The previous couple of years had been difficult for Otojirō and Sada. Otojirō had borrowed heavily in order to build a modern theatre of his own in Tōkyō. He also ran unsuccessfully for a seat in the lower house of the Japanese Diet in the two snap elections which were held in 1898, the first in March and the second in August. The theatre faltered, and was repossessed by its creditors. His troupe was disbanded. In September 1898, Otojirō bought a boat just four metres long and open to the elements, and with Sada at the rudder, a thirteen-year-old niece of his and a dog named Fuku, he set sail for the open seas.[13]

He later maintained that their idea had been to cross the Korean Strait and head for the Chinese coast.[14] What they actually managed to do was to follow the coast around the main Japanese island of Honshū. They reached the port of Kōbe in January. While recuperating there, Otojirō and Sada were approached by a local impresario Satō Yūtarō with the idea of taking a group of actors over to San Francisco. A troupe was hastily assembled, and performances were quickly put on in Kōbe, Kyōto and Ōsaka to raise money for the journey. It was during these fund-raisers that Sada first appeared on stage as a member of her husband's troupe. Professional kabuki forbade female players, and Otojirō too had always employed *onnagata*, male actors who took female roles. The troupe he took to San Francisco included two, both of whom died while the troupe was playing in Boston: Maruyama Kurando, still in his early twenties, who succumbed to lead poisoning resulting from his long-term use of heavy white face make-up, and Mikami Shigeru, who developed a brain disease. After the two deaths, the wig master Taka'i Hanjirō took their place as the troupe's *onnagata*. Otojirō later recalled with amusement how Hanjirō, with his height and deep-set eyes, proved popular with western audiences, despite the fact that he did nothing to disguise the mannish pitch and tone of his voice.[15]

Many years later, when she was back in Japan, Sadayakko insisted that she had not gone abroad with the aim of launching herself as an actress. She had accompanied her husband, she said, only to look after him. There are indications, however, that well before they set off on their journey to the United States, Otojirō was contemplating putting his wife on stage once they got there. As Sadayakko would have it, her picture was already on posters when the troupe reached San Francisco, so she had been unable to refuse to join the rest of the actors on stage. Besides, she said, their promoters in America had been adamant that in America a man in drag just would not be an adequate alternative to an actress. Otojirō, of course, was well aware that American audiences were unfamiliar with male actors taking female roles – and knew instinctively that a beautiful woman would be a good draw. On the other hand, employing women in a mixed company of players was a new challenge in Japanese terms, and what better place to engage in the experiment than the United States, where actresses were taken for granted? It was convenient that Sada had happened to pack her costume for the kabuki dance *Musume Dōjōji* in her luggage. As for her stage name Sadayakko (which combined her personal name and her professional name as a geisha), she later explained that an acquaintance had come up with it in San Francisco, but it has been pointed out that a theatre programme for the Nakaza in Ōsaka, where the troupe put on a pre-voyage, fund-raising performance, already refers to her by it.[16]

Otojirō's company of nineteen individuals set sail from Kōbe on 30 April 1899, and reached San Francisco on 23 May. There were ten actors including Otojirō himself, along with two child actors (Otojirō's sixteen-year-old brother and an eleven-year-old niece), a singer and a *shamisen* player to provide the musical accompaniment traditional in Japanese drama, a wardrobe manager (one of Sada's older brothers), a wig master, a property master, a clerk, and, of course, Otojirō's wife Sada. All but Sada and Otojirō's niece Tsuru were male. They had a successful few days playing San Francisco before they discovered that their Japanese tour manager (to whom they had been turned over on arrival in the city) had absconded with most of their recent earnings. Never one to beat a retreat, Otojirō managed to dissuade his troupe from boarding ship straight for home. He let the clerk go, found a situation locally for his brother, and had his niece adopted by a local Japanese artist Aoki Toshio (Tsuru grew up to become an actress and married Sessue Hayakawa, who went on himself to become a Hollywood star). The troupe proceeded north along the western seaboard, playing principally to Japanese immigrants and expatriates.

They found themselves welcomed and spurned in equal measure by their fellow Japanese. Many considered them no better than vagabonds, a potential source of disgrace to the nascent communities the Japanese were struggling to establish in a new, often unfriendly country. Besides, acting (not excepting kabuki) had traditionally been disparaged in Japan as an ignoble profession. For predominantly Japanese-speaking audiences, Otojirō's troupe put on his trademark contemporary battlefield plays. But in Seattle they staged for the first time a version of what was to become their signature piece, *The Geisha and the Knight*. This play was specifically aimed at western audiences.

Otojirō freely acknowledged afterwards that, from the Japanese point of view, the plot of this play was an outrageous hotchpotch. He had, after all, cobbled together two separate, well-known kabuki plots. But Otojirō defended his methods on the grounds of practicality: he was putting on Japanese plays for audiences who were ignorant not merely of Japanese theatrical conventions but of the language itself. Lots of stage business and picturesque costumes had been absolutely essential to keep the audience's attention, and the tempo of the performance had had to be considerably speeded up.[17] For western audiences Otojirō concentrated on stories from Japanese legend and history. He appreciated the fact that the main attraction of his troupe was most likely to be its exoticism, but to avoid alienating the public, he cut back the dialogue, and even kept the musical accompaniment to a minimum in deference to western tastes (on the ship bound for San Francisco, he had carefully observed the bemused reaction of many westerners to the music which members of his troupe performed as onboard entertainment).[18] This meant his plays relied heavily on vigorous action and dance. Thus the reviewer for the London *Times* was left baffled as to how he was to read for nuances of emotions, but found he could nonetheless enjoy the actors' exhibition of their sheer physical prowess:

> The players . . . all have the appearance to a Western eye of grotesque mechanical toys. None of their movements resemble ours, their faces seem *bizarre* masks. . . . The question whether they are expressing joy or sorrow, fear or exultation, is for the audience often the merest guesswork. There are, however, two things which can be understood at sight all the world over – fighting and dancing – and, fortunately, these are the chief ingredients of the plays presented.[19]

In mid-October 1899, Otojirō, Sadayakko and their actors arrived in Chicago practically destitute. It was in this city, however, that they finally had their much-awaited big break. After a great deal of hardship, Otojirō managed to secure a Sunday matinee slot at the Lyric Theatre. This led to sporadic follow-up engagements, and Otojirō came up with the idea of drumming up publicity by having his actors parade through the streets of Chicago dressed in their outlandish stage costumes, banging on drums and blowing conch-shell horns. They were earning so little money that they hardly had enough to eat. By their own account they collapsed on stage from hunger during one performance. Afterwards they claimed that the reversal in their fortunes came about when their audience mistook their very real physical exhaustion for vivid acting, and gave them a rousing ovation. In any case, the complimentary reviews they received in local newspapers (some of which mentioned that audiences would be able to see 'real geisha dances') led to the acquisition of their first American manager.[20]

The tour thereafter continued to gain momentum. Travelling steadily east and playing in towns and cities along the way, the troupe reached Boston on 3 December. The programme they offered there included *Kesa, the Faithful Wife*, the heroine of which offers up her life in order to save her husband's; *The Geisha and the Knight*; *The Royalist (Kojima Takanori)*, a reworking of a legend ascribed to the eponymous twelfth-century warrior who was famous in Japanese tradition for his loyalty to his emperor; *Soga Brothers*, in which the brothers seek retribution for the murder of their father; *Zingoro*, a Pygmalion story with dancing by Sadayakko; and *Sakurada chizome no yuki* (Blood-stained Snow on the Field of Cherries), a dramatisation of the arrival of Commodore Perry in Japan and the assassination in 1860 of the *shōgun*'s chief minister Ii Naosuke near the Sakurada ('Field of Cherries') Gate of Edo Castle. Otojirō discovered that Sir Henry Irving and Ellen Terry were in town, offering *Robespierre*, *The Bells* and *The Merchant of Venice*. Nothing if not a consummate showman, Otojirō produced on the spot his own Japanised version of Shakespeare's play, focusing primarily on the trial scene. He set his adaptation in a fishing village near the northern Japanese port of Hakodate and turned Shylock into Sairoku, a crabbed, old, avaricious fisherman, a former samurai-turned-miser, whose only joy is hoarding the money he is given by the occasional grateful seaman who, because of Sairoku's hearth fire, had managed to avoid running his ship aground on the desolate shore. Sadayakko took the role of Portia, or O-Sode as Otojirō renamed her.[21]

Irving came to see the Japanese troupe perform. He suggested to the Kawakamis that they should take their plays to London, and generously wrote an introduction for them to present to the manager of the Coronet Theatre.[22] But before crossing the Atlantic, the troupe went to Washington, DC and then on to New York City. In Washington, they were invited by the Japanese minister to the United States to perform at a reception at the Japanese legation. This was held on the nights of 6 and 7 February 1900, and the guest list for the second evening included the President, William McKinley, and senior members of his administration. Otojirō's troupe presented three pieces on this occasion: two plays featuring samurai and sword-play while the third piece was the kabuki dance *Musume Dōjōji* performed by Sadayakko.[23]

In New York, where the troupe arrived on 8 February, Otojirō once again demonstrated his knack for taking advantage of an unexpected opportunity. The theatregoing public in the city was in an uproar over a stage adaptation by Clyde Fitch of Alphonse Daudet's 1884 novel *Sapho*. Playing to sell-out audiences at Wallack's Theatre on Broadway, it had already toured several American cities, generating plenty of furore over one particular scene, in which the heroine (a *grande horizontale*, or courtesan) seduces a young man with whom she is in love and is carried in his arms up a flight of stairs to his bedroom – and, presumably, to his bed. The play was closed down on 5 March, and its British star Olga Nethersole was arrested on charges of offending public decency, although she was later acquitted at her trial in early April and *Sapho* reopened for another run.[24] Otojirō, whose troupe transferred from the Berkeley Lyceum to the Bijou Theatre on Broadway in the middle of March, decided to put on his own, cleaned-up version of the seduction scene, substituting for the smouldering sexual confrontation between the two lovers several demure Japanese-style love scenes in which the couple (who are brought together by chance during an innocent frolic with friends in the Mukōjima district of Tōkyō during cherry-blossom time) signal their mutual attraction with nothing much more than bashful glances and the slightest touching of hands.[25] Otojirō disapproved of western theatre's preoccupation with love and romance, and what he considered to be its lenient attitude to displays of promiscuity – by which he meant the kissing, embracing and fondling, of which he thought there was far too much. He later boasted that he had told this to the Secretary of State John Hay, when the latter had asked him at the reception at the Japanese legation (and in the presence of the President) what he thought of western drama.[26] In any case, *Sapho: A Japanese Idea* met with the approval of even the most fanatical among the self-appointed champions of public morality – especially the indomitable society ladies of New York. Although the general public must have found the Kawakamis' version less titillating than the original play featuring the delectable Olga Nethersole, novelty value nonetheless led to respectable audience numbers.

On 28 April the troupe embarked on their sea journey to England. They docked at Liverpool on 8 May at six in the morning, caught the eight o'clock train and were in London by noon.[27] They found the Coronet Theatre fully booked for the next fortnight, and it was not until 22 May that they were able to open. They succeeded, however, in attracting good enough audiences for their run to be extended three times.[28] The Coronet's playbills show that the repertory was initially made up of the three plays: *Zingoro (An Earnest Statue Carver)*, *The Loyalist* (as *The Royalist* was now called)[29] and *The Geisha and the Knight*. Later on, they substituted *Kesa* for *The Geisha and the Knight* for their matinee performances, but they brought back the latter for the final few days of their engagement. On 27 June, they performed *The Loyalist* and *The Geisha and the*

Knight before the Prince of Wales at a reception held by the banker Henri Louis Bischoffsheim and his wife at their Mayfair mansion, Bute House, in the garden of which a temporary stage for the evening's entertainment had been erected.[30] While the Kawakamis were still in London, the fashionable American dancer Loie Fuller came over from Paris to sign them up for her theatre at the Exposition Universelle, which was being held in the French capital that year. Fuller had learned about the Kawakami troupe from a former manager of hers, Edward A. Stevens, who had attended their performances back in New York.[31]

In Paris the troupe appeared from 4 July to 3 November 1900, at the Théâtre de la Loïe Fuller. Initially, they performed *Zingoro* and *The Loyalist*, as well as *The Geisha and the Knight*. Eventually, however, they came to concentrate on just two of their plays, *Kesa* along with *The Geisha and the Knight*, giving daily performances of each, the former as a matinee and the latter as the evening show. On Fridays they gave three performances, sometimes even four, and Fuller charged higher ticket prices. Sadayakko became one of the prime attractions of the entire Exposition Universelle. On 19 August, Sadayakko and Otojirō attended an Elysée Palace garden party at the invitation of Émile Loubet, the French President. Before finally leaving Europe for Japan, the Kawakamis signed another contract with Loie Fuller, this time for a tour around Europe lasting a year. After a brief visit to Brussels, they boarded their ship home at Liverpool on 9 November, and arrived in Kōbe on the evening of New Year's Day 1901.[32] They returned to Europe later that same year to fulfil their new contract with Fuller.

Kesa, in which Sadayakko played the eponymous tragic heroine Kesa Gozen, was another example of Otojirō rewriting the plot of a well-known Japanese story to suit western tastes. The point of the original legend surrounding Kesa was to explain how the samurai Endō Moritō was awakened to the teachings of Buddha and became the monk Mongaku. Moritō, who conceives a lustful passion for Kesa Gozen, the wife of Watanabe Wataru, tries to have his way with her by threatening to harm her mother. Kesa, in desperation, pretends to accept his advances and suggests to him that he should murder her husband while he is asleep in bed. But on the prearranged night, she substitutes herself for her husband and Moritō ends up killing her, only realising his mistake when it is too late. He repents and in atonement enters the religious life, as do Kesa's husband and mother.[33]

In the first act of the Kawakami version, however, Kesa is abducted by bandits and is forced against her will to entertain them with dancing. This provided an opportunity to introduce dances by Sadayakko into the play: how ironic that, as a former geisha, Sadayakko should now find herself an actress, perforce in her husband's troupe, acting out in *Kesa* the shame of being made to dance under the gaze of strangers. Kesa is then rescued by Moritō, to whom she becomes betrothed. But Moritō sets off on a long journey in search of adventure and, during his absence, Kesa is married to Watanabe Wataru. Moritō returns and discovers Kesa is now the faithful wife of another man. In his rage, he plots to kill the husband, for whose sake Kesa sacrifices her own life.[34]

Kesa shows up the contradictions between the many things Otojirō was trying to achieve in theatre. On the one hand, he was earnest about the reforms he felt Japanese drama needed to undergo in order to regain the elasticity that would enable it to take on subject matter derived from the modern world. On the other, he remained deeply conservative about the message he wanted his work to convey. Back in Japan, his jingoistic fervour had found an outlet in flag-waving plays about contemporary wars in which Japan was embroiled abroad. In America and Europe, he chose historical settings in which to illustrate traditional values drawn from the samurai's code of conduct. Otojirō never doubted that the moral of his plays was perfectly intelligible to western audiences. He did, however, believe he detected subtle differences in taste from country to country. The Parisians, in Otojirō's view, had a particular liking for tragedy, for cruelty and gore on stage – although London audiences appear not to have been immune to the excitement of grisly scenes, seeing that the reviewer for the London *Times* described with relish how a 'thrill of horror ran through the house' when Otojirō, in the role of the murderous Moritō in *Kesa*, 'wiped his hands and reeking knife' after his awful deed (13 June 1900). Otojirō attributed the Parisian taste to their historical experiences during the Reign of Terror. It was ironic that in satisfying this penchant which he thought he perceived in the French, Otojirō reinforced western prejudices about the grotesqueness, brutality and sheer bloodthirstiness of the Japanese.[35]

In Paris, Otojirō was asked by Loie Fuller to rewrite the ending of *Kesa* so it concluded with Moritō committing hara-kiri. Fuller was not the first to ask Otojirō for a hara-kiri scene. Back in Washington, he had been informed that one of the guests who had been invited to the reception at the Japanese legation was keen to see how a *seppuku* was performed, and he had obligingly changed the ending to the *Soga Brothers* (whose tale was one of the most famous of all historical legends in Japan), making both brothers commit suicide after they had avenged the murder of their father.[36] Fuller told Otojirō that Parisians had been curious to see how hara-kiri was done ever since news got back to France of the incident which occurred in March (February, local date) 1868, when twenty samurai and foot soldiers were ordered to commit *seppuku* after a skirmish with French naval personnel (who had landed in the port city of Sakai without giving proper notification to Japanese authorities) ended in the deaths of eleven French sailors.[37] Besides, Fuller declared herself outraged at the notion that the killer of an innocent woman should be allowed to go unpunished. Otojirō later insisted in his memoirs that he had vigorously tried to defend the original ending:

everybody in Japan, after all, knew that Moritō lived on to become the monk Mongaku, for the whole point of the story was to explain the transformation of a worldly sinner into a holy man. According to Otojirō's account of events, the Japanese minister to Paris had had to be called in to mediate. In any case, Otojirō eventually acquiesced to Fuller's demand. On a subsequent occasion, Fuller advertised that both Otojirō *and* Sadayakko were to perform hara-kiri on stage that evening.

The western taste for an anachronistic Japan is reflected in Henry Fouquier's review of Sadayakko's performance, published in the journal *Le Théâtre*:

> The Japan, which Madame Sada Yacco has brought us, happily is not modern Japan. . . . The Japan at the Exposition is a Japan somewhat of the past, exquisitely out of date, a Japan still feudal, simple and violent, where there are knights and holy courtesans, where one cuts open one's stomach on a point of honour with swords with engraved hilts . . . .[38]

Although he could not know this, Fouquier instinctively picked up many of those aspects of Otojirō's staging which the latter had adopted with the aim of making his plays more acceptable to an audience which did not understand the Japanese language. Fouquier noted that the plots were perfunctory and naïve, only really sufficient in the west for a pantomime or ballet. He remarked on how brief, curt and broken up the dialogue tended to be, and how the plays' psychological insight was limited to strong, simple emotions. Based on his own observations of the performances, Fouquier jumped to conclusions about the general nature of Japanese theatre. A Japanese dramatist, he explained to his readers, was neither expansive in developing his plot nor prodigal in his use of words. Fouquier decided that gesture ('*la mimique*') was the primary method by which Japanese actors conveyed emotion. It was in the physical representation of such visceral sensations as fear, for instance, and sensual pleasure that Fouquier felt both Sadayakko and Otojirō excelled, and he did not consider Otojirō's power of expression in any way inferior to his wife's. Fouquier was particularly impressed by the mobility of their facial expressions, their ability to capture the most subtle nuances and variations on the basic types of human emotion. It was their ability to portray extremes, from acute terror to the voluptuous languor of post-coital gratification, which interested him most – emotions which civilisation had taught the peoples of the west to disguise for the sake of public decorum. Referring to the rumour that Sadayakko had wept when she heard that a French comedienne had called her 'a pretty little animal', Fouquier, in his article, reassured the Japanese actress that this was far from an insult, but instead a term of praise when applied to her, since Japanese art was 'an art of exquisite naturalism'.

It was for her portrayal of the courtesan Katsuragi's death at the end of *The Geisha and the Knight* that Sadayakko was acclaimed as a great actress by critics on both sides of Atlantic. Even the influential poet and literary critic Arthur Symons, author of *The Symbolist Movement in Literature*, who found the troupe's performances on the whole to be rather contemptible ('it is difficult not to laugh', he wrote dismissively, 'at some cat-like or ape-like trick of these painted puppets . . . swathed like barbaric idols, in splendid robes without grace'), applauded Sadayakko as a 'great artist' for her death scene. He confessed its effect was 'overwhelming' because Sadayakko succeeded in showing 'the whole woman' die. He found her compelling in a way even Sarah Bernhardt could not better.[39] Audiences marvelled at Sadayakko's abrupt leaps from aloof serenity to tormented rage to loving sorrow. The journalist and critic Lady Colin Campbell gave a breathless account of the denouement of the play:

> Her face has completely changed; all the serene, mask-like impassivity of expression has gone, and the lovely doll is now indeed alive, an outraged and passionate woman . . . . Katsuragi is transformed into a Maenad. . . . She is the incarnation of fury – speechless, gasping – athirst for the blood of those who have wronged her. All her sufferings have reached their climax . . . she has but one desire – to kill, and to die killing. If such a scene were to be attempted by a European actress, it would be ridiculous; acted by this little Japanese doll, it grips you as a most extraordinary revelation of primeval passion. In rushes Nagoya and takes her in his arms. In her blind frenzy she turns to strike him. . . . At his voice her passion breaks down, and she turns to him with the movement of an awakened child. She tries to hold him to her, but the fury of revenge has been too much for her delicate and overwrought frame. . . . One can see the life ebbing, ebbing out of her, the eyes glazing and turning up as if to see the approach of Death . . . and, like a puppet whose strings are snapped, she slips through the arms of the man who has broken her heart, and dies at his feet . . . .[40]

The redoubtable French actor Jean Mounet-Sully, renowned for his portrayal of Oedipus in Jules Lacroix's French translation of Sophocles' tragedy, praised Sadayakko highly for her climactic rage scene. Louis Fournier admiringly noted how Sadayakko portrayed the imminent arrival of death 'with every muscle of her face wrenched with pain – all the agonies of death so terribly, and yet so truly depicted'. The French tragedienne Sarah Bernhardt 'has died in all possible ways, screaming, moaning, coughing, smiling – but has ever one of them proved so enthralling as that of Sada Yacco?' he asked pointedly (Bernhardt's own response when asked by Fournier for her opinion of the Japanese actors was '*Atroce! abominable! horrible!* – a pack of monkeys, my friend, a pack of monkeys!'). For André Gide, the supreme moment was Sadayakko's final cry:

22 Sadayakko as Katsuragi in the play *The Geisha and the Knight,* coloured illustration from the cover of *Le Théâtre.*

23 Sadayakko as the maddened Katsuragi in the play *The Geisha and the Knight,* coloured cartoon by Leonetto Cappiello.

when she finally realises that it is he [Nagoya] who holds her in his arms, whilst death is already parting them, she gives a great cry of loving surprise. . . . It is actually the only cry that escapes her in the entire piece; and even this supreme cry of love is tempered; it wonderfully and simply satisfies an expectation, an expectation that has been well prepared.[41]

Fouquier admired Sadayakko and Otojirō's portrayal of emotion for possessing a non-verbal – practically pre-verbal – immediacy. But other reviewers, particularly in Britain, were more doubtful about the artistic merit of a style of acting that seemed to appeal for a visceral response from the audience. The influential British critic William Archer was put off by the literalness of Sadayakko's death scenes: he recollected Kesa's twitching legs with particular distaste.[42] The critic for the *Stage* who reviewed *Kesa* during Sadayakko and Otojirō's second tour to London in 1901 was certain that Otojirō and Sadayakko demonstrated 'Japanese art at its best', only he found it rather shocking that this 'best' was 'a rather crude and unpleasant, though certainly powerful, realism' – a consequence, this critic concluded, of the Japanese not possessing 'the art which conceals art'.[43] Some critics thought that the gesticulations of the Japanese actors signified nothing more sophisticated than a basic physical response to stimuli, with consciousness – or indeed the conscience – playing little part. To Arthur Symons this suggested the absence of the mediating agency of intellect. 'It is the emotion of children,' he decided, 'naked sensation, not yet clothed by civilisation.' Symons, like Fouquier, evoked the image of animals when describing Sadayakko, but in his case, the comparison was not particularly complimentary. What she demonstrated to Symons's mind was how much the human body remained at the mercy of the 'animal force of its instincts'. The relative absence of dialogue in the troupe's plays made Arthur Symons think of human beings stuck at a primitive stage of development, one characterised by a lack of advancement in that skill of communication which distinguished humankind from beasts – language. 'Men spit and sneeze and snuffle', he wrote, 'without consciousness of dignity or hardly of humanity, under the influence of fear, anger or astonishment.' This did not mean that the performance necessarily lacked energy. Indeed, without the restraining influence of mind, there could be rather too much of it.[44] The reviewer for the London *Times* refused to recognise the passion portrayed by Sadayakko as anything akin to the sublime sentiment of love as he felt it was properly understood in the west. Love as represented by Sadayakko was nothing more than the 'the dumb affection of some domestic animal, the purring and sidling of a kitten'. Her jealousy was but 'a natural force let loose' (19 June 1901).

William Archer characterised Sadayakko's performance as a 'muscular accomplishment, like that power of wagging the left ear'. What she proved was that she possessed physical dexterity rather than true imagination, the 'source of all truly artistic effects'. The convulsions in her death scenes were mechanical, and in this respect not much different from the writhing of puppets, and therefore Archer found the effect more comic than tragic.[45] The stereotype of the Japanese woman as an impersonal doll, bobbing and swaying and gesticulating in her stiff kimono, led naturally to the image of puppets and marionettes. (The British artist Charles Ricketts described in his journal the beguilingly mixed nature of Sadayakko's performance, at times so 'curiously natural in her acting', at other times lapsing into 'marionette actions of the arms'.)[46] This was a reflection of the prejudice that the Japanese were propelled by the external agencies of habit and custom rather than the internal propulsion of individual thought, in behaving in the elaborately cere-monious way they did towards one another. Arthur Symons's remark about the actors' 'ape-like trick[s]'[47] implied that they were merely aping – that is to say, mechanically reproducing – the outward manifestations of grief or anger. The image of monkeys, no less than that of dolls and puppets, suggested that the actors were soulless, but also that they were clever mimics, proficient in imitating gestures with no insight into the motivations which underlie them. William Archer, like Symons, reached the conclusion that the acting style of the Japanese troupe resem-bled the unselfconscious behaviour of children. They were like 'a company of very clever and highly-trained children' merely playing at acting, who are able to pull off a superficially brilliant spectacle, but one lacking in depth or insight. Still, at their best, they could be entertaining for all that: as Archer put it, 'one enters with gusto, and even, it may be, with a sense of refreshment, into the spirit, the cleverness, the innocence of the game.'[48]

It was not that Archer found Sadayakko disagreeable or boring. On the contrary, he conceded that she did have a 'considerable gift of emotional expression'. But in the death scene of her eponymous character in *Kesa*, Archer felt there was very little evidence of an 'impersonative imagination' at work.[49] In this regard, the Paris corre-spondent for the *New York Times*, reporting on Sadayakko's appearances at the Exposition Universelle, was of a similar opinion. He declined to agree with those of his fellow critics who praised Sadayakko's death scenes as excelling those of Sarah Bernhardt. Sarah Bernhardt was 'an actress purely', declared this correspondent; Bernhardt 'personifie[d] and incarnate[d]' her stage character with an art that derived its power from the 'closest study of nature in direct action'. Sadayakko, on the other hand, merely produced poses, however rhythmically and gracefully she moved on stage. The *New York Times* correspondent claimed Sadayakko had confessed to him in person that she had never seen anybody die. How then could she portray death with realistic conviction? She was not basing her performance on observation and direct study of life; rather, according to the correspondent, she was following what she had been taught to do by her husband.[50]

William Archer felt that the manner in which the Japanese actors depicted emotion remained 'primitive' and 'crude'. 'Japanese realism' failed to impress him. For Archer it was above all the actors' monotonous tone (or so it sounded to him) of delivery which betrayed their art's lack of sophistication, although for Henry Fouquier, the very suppression of inflection (on top of the absence of introspective monologues and flashes of eloquence) seemed to approximate the supposed use of monotonic chanting (*la mélopée*) in classical Greek theatre. When it came to the contest between greater realism and greater abstraction, it is not surprising to find Archer criticising the Japanese troupe for exaggerating stage conventions instead of striving for an illusion of reality. He was, after all, an influential advocate of the work of Henrik Ibsen, whose plays he translated for the stage. Archer readily conceded that a lack of knowledge of the Japanese language hampered his understanding of the Japanese plays. But he felt justified in passing judgement on the troupe's acting style, even though – or rather, precisely because – he did not comprehend what was being spoken.[51]

The troupe's plays were, in effect, being treated as pantomimes, but it had become a commonplace in the west to describe Japanese dance as pantomimic. John L. Stoddard, in the popular series of lectures based on his travels abroad which he toured to various American cities in the last decades of the nineteenth century, described Japanese dancers as 'merely represent[ing] in graceful pantomime some song or story, flitting about like pretty butterflies, or swaying back and forth like flowers in a summer breeze'.[52] The same basic idea (apart from Stoddard's association of Japanese dance with non-human elements of the natural world) was reiterated by Marcelle A. Hincks in 1910 in her monograph on Japanese dance:

> Whereas our dance consists almost entirely of rhythmical gymnastic with no set purpose but that of striking graceful attitudes, the Japanese dance, like the ancient Greek dance, is entirely of a pantomimic nature, and strives to represent in gesture an historical incident, some mythical legend, or a scene from folklore. . . . The Japanese have extraordinary mimetic gifts which they have cultivated to such an extent, that it is doubtful whether any other people has ever developed such a wide and expressive art of gesture.[53]

Every movement, from a subtle twist of the neck to sleeve-waving and the stamping of feet, had an emotional connotation, Hincks explained. The novelist Félicien Champsaur took this idea to its extreme, fantasising in his scabrous novel *Poupée japonaise* (1900) a mime performed by a trio of Yoshiwara *oiran* – for the delectation of a pair of British naval officers – representing activities typical of a day in the life of a courtesan, culminating in three simultaneous simulations of explicit love-making (with invisible partners) and three finely synchronised orgasms. Hincks, however, did not take such a literal approach. She pointed out that the gestural language used in Japanese dance was not universally comprehensible. Quite the contrary: she thought there was nothing more different to 'the natural and spontaneous gestures wherewith we should express similar emotions'.[54]

In *The Geisha and the Knight*, Sadayakko performed a sequence of dances in front of the monks guarding the temple into which her character Katsuragi seeks entry. Some of these were more overtly pantomimic than others; none was especially erotic or sexual in nature. Lady Colin Campbell, who attended a performance of the play in June 1900, described what she saw in some detail: after a hieratic noh dance, the Geisha persuaded the monks to throw stones at some cherry trees to bring down imaginary clusters of flowers, which she then mimed weaving into a ball. This was followed by a dance with fans decorated with cherry blossoms, and then the ' "Kappore", or dance of the rice-harvest'. At this point, the monks joined in with their own 'water-wheel' dance using blue-and-white umbrellas. Lastly, the Geisha gave 'the curious, most ancient, and weird "Fox Dance" ', accompanying herself on a tambour. Judith Gautier recorded a slightly different list of dances for the troupe's appearances at the Exposition Universelle in Paris. The noh dance, executed to the tolling of the temple bell, was followed as in London by the dance with the imaginary ball of flower blossoms. The monks then performed a comic dance of their own, miming the frolicking of small fish known in Japan as *dojō* (Gautier spells it *'dodjio'*). The Geisha then gave a dance with a hat decorated with flowers. After the monks performed the dance of the umbrellas, the Geisha danced with a tambour.[55]

At least one London critic felt these dances held up the narrative drive. The *Illustrated London News*, reviewing Sadayakko and Otojirō's performances in London in 1901, did not know what to make of the actors' jarring hotchpotch of 'quaint gesture, naïve pantomime, grotesque realism, a baffling insertion of dance and farce into would-be romance' (22 June). This oscillation of tone made the task of trying to understand the characters' emotional development all the more baffling. Sadayakko's swings between blank inscrutability and wild frenzy did not seem quite human at times. Far from agreeing with Henry Fouquier that the gestures of the actors were naturalistic expressions of sentiment which were imme-diately comprehensible to a universal audience, the critic for the London *Times*, echoing Pierre Loti, decided 'What their souls are like . . . it is quite beyond us to conjecture'. He was only confirmed in his prejudice that the oriental mind was inscrutable, a closed book to the probing western intellect. He suspected that the book very likely had but few inscriptions:

What is the *état d'âme* of a Sada Yacco? There is no speculation in those eyes that she doth glare with. One conjectures the existence of a quite infantile mind behind that set white mask. (19 June 1901)

Other critics likewise were less convinced than Fouquier about the decipherability of the Japanese actors' gestures and expressions. During the troupe's first appearance in London, the reviewer for *The Times* observed that their performances – while preserving the 'rudimentary simplicity' of fable – were 'not always comprehensible . . . as interpretations of emotion' (24 May). Max Beerbohm, in the *Saturday Review*, reflected how alien Japanese expressions of feeling appeared to a British audience: 'So differently are the emotions expressed in Japan', he marvelled, 'that illusion is completely merged for us in curiosity.'[56] Beerbohm found it peculiar that in situations in which – on the western stage, as in real life – one might expect human beings to make use of language as the most direct (though by no means exclusive) means of articulating thoughts and feelings, the Japanese actors merely snarled, snorted or rolled their eyes. These physical responses were often unexpected ones, moreover, and seemed very odd to Beerbohm's mind. When a woman is threatened by imminent death by a sword-wielding villain, Beerbohm mused, she might be expected to scream, to collapse or to attempt to run away. But Koromogawa, Kesa's mother, merely stood still, rolling her eyes and grunting. Beerbohm found that this sense of strangeness kept his emotions from becoming engaged and left his sympathies unaroused. Nevertheless, he was happy to concede that visually, at least, Sadayakko's movements and gestures were exceedingly fascinating. It was just that he realised he did not care in the least what happened to her character.[57]

Fouquier may have found the Japanese actors' faces mobile and expressive, but Sadayakko's traditional thick white make-up had an alienating effect on many members of the audience. It appears that back in San Francisco Sadayakko had started out making up in the manner of the traditional kabuki *onnagata*, using very thick white paint to conceal her eyebrows and then drawing in new brows higher up the forehead. The reaction of local Americans was that her face looked corpse-like. She took care thereafter to use less white powder and to leave her brows natural. She also made a conscious effort to smile as she danced, something strictly frowned upon in Japan, but Otojirō felt it was expected of dancers in America.[58] Even so, audiences continued to carry away a strong impression of a blankness of expression. Arthur Symons referred to her disquieting 'geometrical symbol of a face': 'the scarcely human oval which represents a woman's face, with the help of a few thin curves for eyelids and mouth'.[59] Max Beerbohm too found Sadayakko remote from most familiar points of reference: 'her face is a mere inscrutable oval, and her gestures have for me no meaning, and to her gait I know no parallel'.[60] William Archer agreed with the opinion expressed by the actress Helen Faucit regarding the heavy use of cosmetics on the French stage: ' "When the skin is covered with what is, in effect, a painted mask, the colour, which under strong emotion would come and go, is hidden under it, and the natural expression of the countenance destroyed." '[61]

The American critic Katherine Metcalf Roof, on the other hand, wrote more appreciatively of the imperturbable mask-like quality of Sadayakko's face: '[I]t is only by an uneasy movement of the eyes – the slightest, almost imperceptible change about the tilted eyelids – that we are made to realize the tragedy taking place within the woman's soul; but it is enough. A more accented expression would have been untrue art.'[62] Masks, of course, were known to have been used in Roman theatre as well as in ancient Greek drama. The poet Percy Bysshe Shelley suggested in his *Defence of Poetry* that the use of masks was a method by which human passions might be depersonalised, the one unchanging expression of the mask subsuming all the changes of emotion that a dramatic character undergoes in the course of a play. Shelley felt that without such a device, an actor was forced to turn himself into a mimic, forever chasing the illusion of ever greater realism by attempting to capture every shifting shade of emotion. W.B. Yeats, in later experimental plays such as *At the Hawk's Well* (first performed in 1916), turned to the Japanese tradition of noh and its use of masks, music and stylised movement in order to achieve a vision of beauty that stimulated the intellect and imagination of his audiences by avoiding literalness. While Shelley felt that the mask was able to represent some universal idea of humanity, Yeats employed them to heighten the mystery, the strangeness, of his characters. For him, the mask was an alienation technique, while in itself being an object of supreme beauty that drew the audience's attention to it.

Both conceptions of the mask are relevant to their use in noh plays. Actors in both noh and kabuki are exclusively male, but it is only in the former that masks are used to portray women of all stages of life (as well as supernatural female beings such as spirits and ghosts). Kabuki sought its ideal female beauty in the mire of the secular world; noh found this beauty in the stillness of eternity that encompasses the pains and sorrows of the mundane world. But the technique in both has been to pare away at the particular and the incidental until an archetypal image of womanhood is achieved. Movement became stylised, its purpose no longer to preserve the illusion of realism. The individualisation of characters by the actor was not the objective of either kabuki or noh.

Still, Osman Edwards, who in 1901 published one of the first studies produced in the west on Japanese theatre, considered kabuki's attitude to characterisation a weakness rather than a strength. He felt that not enough of the action in kabuki was adequately connected to the sentiments of individual characters. Poses and facial expressions were intended to appeal primarily to the eye, rather than to the intellect.[63] Actors striking dramatic poses in character had always been a popular subject in *ukiyoe*, and inasmuch as this was the case, many critics, including Beerbohm, were not far from the mark when, in describing the appeal of Sadayakko and Otojirō, they turned to Japanese woodblock prints as their point of reference, despite this being rather an obvious cliché. 'Straight from the prints and drawings of Utamaro and Hokusai these creatures have come to us,' wrote Beerbohm. He went on to compare the experience of watching the troupe's performance to flicking rapidly through a series of prints:

> Nothing is blurred by mobility. Nothing escapes us. It is as though one were not seeing actual life in unrest, but inspecting at leisure a whole series of those instantaneous plates which are contained in a cinematograph. . . .[64]

He thought Sadayakko's gestures and poses beautiful, attractive and decorous, because he could appreciate that they adhered to some intricate aesthetic code, alien though it was to an uninitiated European. It did not matter to him that he remained emotionally detached from what was taking place on stage. 'To watch the Japanese players was a delight,' he recollected in a review of a troupe of Sicilian actors in 1908, 'because their every movement and posture was learnedly contrived in accordance to certain elaborate traditions of beauty.'[65] For Arthur Symons, the Japanese actors were fascinating simply because they were so unfamiliar, so strange, so alien, possessing 'the charm of something which seems to us capricious, almost outside Nature'. Far from being exquisite naturalistic reflections of human nature, or the embodiment of natural forces, the Japanese were, in Symons's regard, unnatural, inhuman and irrational.[66]

Characterisation was not what particularly interested André Gide, who saw *The Geisha and the Knight* six times. What captivated him was the sense of rhythm that seemed to him to pervade the movements of each of the actors, and the way they interacted with each other. Each gesture seemed to him to flow into the next, and the motions of each character were, to his eye, perfectly assimilated into the measured effect of the whole ensemble. This effect, for Gide, was a sense of intense lyricism. He praised Sadayakko for her control and restraint. Even the way she expressed rage possessed a rhythm that made it akin to the 'sacred emotion of the great plays of antiquity'. As Gide saw it, this supreme restraint could not be exercised unless the artist embraced a higher concept of ideal beauty. Only when realism was made to submit to the artist's preconceived ideal concept of beauty did Gide consider a work of true art a possibility.[67] And Sadayakko was always serenely beautiful, a cumulative impression which became stronger as the performance unfolded.

Sadayakko's emotionally expressive yet dispassionate dancing caught the imagination of three important contemporary western dancers: Loie Fuller, Isadora Duncan and Ruth St Denis. All three were innovators who created new styles of expressive dance which broke free of the conventions of traditional ballet. Loie Fuller, who took on the management of Sadayakko and Otojirō's troupe,[68] started out on her stage career as an ambitious, if somewhat mediocre, actress, but it was for her dance spectacles, in which she glided and whirled while deftly manipulating swirling yards of diaphanous cloth (held up from inside her costumes by means of long rods) that she became a celebrity in Paris during the 1890s. She created an uncanny, ethereal effect out of a play of fluid motion and perpetually shifting shapes, an effect enhanced by her clever use of electric lighting and rapid changes of coloured lights to accentuate ripples of light and shadow. Her famous dances, such as *The Butterfly, La Danse du feu* and *La Danse du lys*, were in accord with the aesthetics of the art nouveau movement in the visual arts, which drew inspiration from the ways in which living forms were depicted in Japanese decorative arts. Fuller, who was adroit at taking advantage of current cultural trends, professed a fascination with all things Japanese. However deep her actual interest in Japanese culture went, her style of dance reflected the artistic imagination of the *fin-de-siècle* period.

Isadora Duncan and Ruth St Denis both saw Sadayakko dance in Paris in 1900. Duncan was twenty-three, and had just arrived from London, where she had begun to establish herself as a dancer under the patronage of a circle of painters chiefly associated with the New Gallery in Regent Street, many of whom, like Lawrence Alma-Tadema, had striven to reinterpret on canvas the flavour of life in the classical world, a fascination with which Duncan shared and from which she drew a great deal of her inspiration. Not long after arriving in Paris, Duncan was being invited to dance at the best salons in the city. In January 1902, just as Fuller was about to set off from Paris for a continental tour with Sadayakko, Otojirō and their troupe, she offered to take Duncan under her wing. Duncan was pleased to accept, and caught up with Fuller and the Japanese actors in Berlin. But in Vienna, the insubstantial costumes in which she danced caused a public outcry, and her insouciant attitude to the distinguished guests to whom Fuller wanted to show her off signalled her growing disdain for her would-be mentor's desire for control. Duncan abruptiy turned her back on Fuller and struck off on her own for a triumphant appearance in Budapest.

While Fuller and Duncan found their creative home in Europe, Ruth St Denis helped create a fertile ground for the development of modern dance back in America. Not only did she herself tour extensively around the United States, but together with her husband Ted Shawn she founded the influential dance company Denishawn, which nurtured such young talent as Martha Graham. Born Ruthie

Dennis, St Denis began her dancing career at the age of fifteen in vaudeville and variety. In the spring of 1900, when she was twenty-one, she landed a small role in David Belasco's hit play *Zaza* and joined the cast for their tour to London. It was Belasco who afterwards gave St Denis her stage name. Already attracted to the exoticism of the Far East and the elements of mysticism in its religions, St Denis approached Belasco in London with the idea of performing a Japanese dance of her own composition between the acts of *Zaza*. Belasco, who had brought his *Madame Butterfly* along with *Zaza* to London, responded favourably to the suggestion, although in the end St Denis's plans seem never to have been realised.[69] It was after the London run of *Zaza* had finished that St Denis went on to Paris to visit the Exposition, where she saw Sadayakko.

Isadora Duncan, as well as Ruth St Denis, sought to reconnect the outward motions of dance with the dancer's inner state of being or awareness. Both dancers rebelled against nineteenth-century ballet's emphasis on physical virtuosity and technical perfection. The dance to Duncan was an outward manifestation of the dancer's soul when it was attuned to the natural world's cosmic rhythms.[70] It was a reflection of the dynamism of life, and the beauty and sacred mystery of nature. For Duncan, waves exemplified both nature's harmonious rhythm and its transformative power:

> The [dancer's] movements should follow the rhythm of the waves: the rhythm that rises, penetrates, holding in itself the impulse and the after-movement; call and response, bound endlessly in one cadence.[71]

Like André Gide, Duncan stressed the importance of restraint, especially in the expression of violence: 'Even violence is the greater when it is restrained: one gesture that has grown slowly out of that reserve is worth many thousands that struggle and cut each other off.'[72] Duncan's emphasis on rhythm connects with Gide's admiration for the rhythmic harmony that he felt wove Sadayakko's movements and those of her fellow Japanese actors into a single entity. The British artist and theatre designer Charles Ricketts also saw Sadayakko as an avatar of nature's non-human kinetic energy. In his journal, he wrote admiringly of the 'wild "electric" grace' of her dancing, and comparing Sadayakko to an *ukiyoe* print, he drew upon the image of a 'wave or a tiger by Hokusai'.[73]

Ruth St Denis too felt that a dancer's movements should reflect the fluidity of natural phenomena. She once wrote, 'Take the invisible motions of the clouds at sunset; one form melts into another, while one is almost unconscious of a change. No motion should be sharply abrupt. There must be no angles.'[74] St Denis attempted through her dances to explore the tribulations of the soul exposed to the temptations of the senses and, strongly drawn to spiritualism and eastern

mysticism as she was, she strove to communicate states of spiritual enlightenment. After the brief tour to London with *Zaza*, St Denis continued to work for
Belasco for another five years. In the late autumn of 1905, she had her first opportunity to present her Indian fantasy *Radha: The Mystic Dance of the Five Senses.*

Dance, for Duncan as for St Denis, was a non-verbal means of expressing
metaphysical or spiritual truth. Duncan resisted the notion that dance had to
have recourse to pantomime in order to express ideas:

> The pantomimists pretend to speak with gestures; they try to imitate language.
> Art is more natural; it does not imitate, it does not seek out equivalents, it does
> not pretend to speak – it has its own language.[75]

Such art applied not only to dancers, but to actors as well. In a short essay entitled
'Dancing in Relation to Religion and Love' (1927), Duncan expressed her admiration for Eleonora Duse's non-verbal powers of expression. She recounted the
first occasion she saw Duse perform. This was in 1899 when Duse was appearing
in London in Arthur Wing Pinero's *The Second Mrs Tanqueray*. Duncan found the
first two acts banal and utterly unworthy of an actress of Duse's calibre. But in
the third act, in which Duse's character Mrs Tanqueray unflinchingly faced the
inevitability of her fate, Duse, Duncan wrote, stood very still, and seemed 'to grow
and grow until her head appeared to touch the roof of the theatre'. In Duse's stillness Duncan saw motion: the expansion of the spirit in its awareness that it was
one with the universe, that its fate was being driven by the same inexorable energy
that propelled the celestial spheres in the heavens.[76]

Another profound admirer of Duse, the Austrian poet and playwright Hugo von
Hofmannsthal, who is also remembered as one of Richard Strauss's most important librettists, drew a parallel between St Denis and Sadayakko. Hofmannsthal
may have attended a performance by Sadayakko in 1900 while he was in Paris;
he certainly knew of the actress, who was hailed as the 'Japanese Duse' by the
Viennese public when she appeared in the Austrian capital in February 1902. For
Hofmannsthal, Duse's genius lay in her ability to assume a role with her entire
body – to his mind, a form of communication superior to the mere delivery of lines.
The consummate actor, like Duse, was one who had the power to convey the
complexity of a character through a single significant gesture. Ruth St Denis
performing her Indian-inspired mystical dance *Radha* reminded Hofmannsthal of
Duse's gestures. As the new century unfolded, Hofmannsthal became increasingly
interested in modern dance, and he formed a strong friendship with St Denis,
whom he first met in the late autumn of 1906 in Berlin. He thought more highly of
her dancing than he did of Duncan's, feeling St Denis's style to be much closer in
spirit to the Greek ideal of freedom from sentimentality. He admired the way in

which St Denis wove each one of her gestures into a seamless continuum. In an essay of 1911, 'Über die Pantomine', Hofmannsthal mentions Sadayakko alongside St Denis and Nijinsky as examples of dancers who are able to turn their simplest gestures into ceremony, by giving to their movements a profound significance that satisfies the human need for spiritual or religious enlightenment.[77]

Hofmannsthal's deepening fascination with non-verbal communication was shared by the German poet and literary critic Julius Hart, who believed that the Japanese actors had given him a glimpse of the future of western theatre, when drama would finally be freed both from the tyranny of language and the conceptual worlds constructed upon words. Actors would no longer be subservient to the playwright, but would wield for themselves their unique medium of communication, the body. In his review of the Japanese actors which appeared in the Berlin newspaper *Der Tag* on 12 December 1901, Hart acknowledged that the language problem precluded any understanding of the poetic meaning of the Japanese plays, but by privileging gesture and movement over words he put aside the issue of a non-European language which he did not comprehend. Sadayakko's body was so eloquent, Hart rhapsodised, she had no need for a poet to give her any lines. This universal language of the body addressed itself to the senses, and its main purpose was to convey delight.[78]

Max Beerbohm, one of those inclined to question the scope of this supposedly universal language of the body, declined to add his voice to the virtually universal acclamation of Eleonora Duse's artistry. Yet Beerbohm could not help but admire Sadayakko for those very qualities he deplored in Duse. In a review of Duse's appearance at the Lyceum Theatre, London, in May 1900, Beerbohm professed that he did not care much for Duse's non-verbal conceptions of her roles, complaining that '[s]he treats them [her roles] as so many large vehicles for expression of absolute self'. In contrast to Hofmannsthal, who felt that Duse's body spoke a completely different language with every role she assumed, Beerbohm saw the same Duse – her ego – appear over and over again in every play in which she featured. He felt cheated by her adamant refusal to 'impersonate'. Beerbohm considered an overriding egotism of this sort objectionable in actresses, although cheerfully admitting he admired a forceful personality in male actors. He refused to succumb to Duse's mystique, however, and he did not discern in her acting a revelation of some deeper universal truth about human existence.[79]

A year later, Beerbohm was acknowledging that the very thing that put him off Duse – the forcefulness of a great actor's exceptional personality, which resists being subsumed into whichever role the player happens to be playing, but on the contrary imprints the role with its own distinctive character – was what thrilled him about the actresses Sarah Bernhardt, Réjane and, above all, Sadayakko. 'The great actors', he concluded, 'are never the good actors.' And in the contest of personalities of these three contemporary tragediennes, Beerbohm gave the crown to Sadayakko. Her technique being totally unfamiliar to westerners, Sadayakko's gestures, movements, even her facial expressions were just as enigmatic to Beerbohm as was her language. Yet he found her the most fascinating because she remained the most inscrutable of them all, with an aura of the numinous about her. Through her, the audience caught a glimpse of the ineffable mystery of existence and of human destiny.[80]

Loie Fuller complained in her memoirs that the extensive tour around Europe on which she took Sadayakko and Otojirō between 1901 and 1902 lost her money, mainly because of the exorbitant expense and bother to which the Kawakamis' entourage put her.[81] It was during this later tour that Puccini was drawn by Sadayakko's fame to see her perform in Milan. He borrowed a motif from the Japanese tune 'Echigo Jishi,' which Sadayakko played on the thirteen-stringed *koto* in the play *Kesa*, and used it in the musical passage that announces Cio-Cio-San's entrance in the first act of *Madama Butterfly*.[82] Loie Fuller was canny enough to see that the European public had not yet had its fill of graphic Japanese-style death scenes, particularly when executed by an entrancingly delicate Japanese actress who possessed the aloofness of a goddess combined with the vehemence of a Fury. In 1905 she decided to take another group of Japanese players under her management. Among them she had spotted a diminutive woman who was 'refined, graceful, queer, and so individual as to stand out, even among those of her own race'. When she was acting, she performed her role 'very intelligently, and with the oddest mimicry'.[83] Fuller decided that she would be her new Sadayakko.

This actress was Ōta Hisa, known in the west by her stage name Madame Hanako. Like Sadayakko, she had been a geisha back in Japan, although not one as eminently placed in society. A string of chance events landed her amidst a company of Japanese actors travelling around Europe. Hisa was born in 1868, the eldest child of an affluent farming family which also ran a shop in Nagoya selling the cloth which the women of the family produced. When she was still a toddler, her grandfather sent her to live above the family shop in the city with the nursemaid, with whom the child's father was rumoured to be having an affair. In Nagoya, Hisa became the object of the doting affection of a childless neighbourhood greengrocer and his wife, who begged to be allowed to adopt her. The inhabitants of Nagoya were well known for their enthusiasm for such genteel accomplishments as music and dance, and Hisa's new adoptive parents, who were prosperous, were keen for the little girl to possess all the necessary cultural refinements. She began learning dance at the age of five, and started on the *shamisen* not long after that.

The greengrocer, however, allowed his all-consuming love of sumo to ruin him. He lavished money on his favourite wrestlers, accumulated debts and neglected his business. Finally he vanished, abandoning his wife and Hisa in Nagoya. Mother and daughter moved to a poorer area of the city, where one of their neighbours happened to be Nakamura Kōkichi, the leader of a troupe of travelling female kabuki players.[84] There were several successful female acting troupes based in Nagoya. The Tokugawa Shogunate had banned women in 1629 from participating in public performances of dance, narrative songs (*jōruri*) and kabuki. Nonetheless, female stage performers did not totally disappear. Regional lords (*daimyō*), for example, often retained companies of female players to entertain them in the privacy of their palaces. In their style of performance, women generally conformed to the artistic standards set by their male counterparts. This meant that female performers of kabuki, even when playing characters of their own sex, adhered to the dramatic conventions of mainstream kabuki established by a long succession of male actors. Although the prohibition on all-female performances of kabuki officially remained in effect in Tōkyō, Kyōto and Ōsaka even after the new Meiji regime assumed power in 1868, the popularity of female acting troupes did not diminish. It was in 1877 that a company of female players was for the first time granted a permit to perform in a theatre in Tōkyō. By that time the ban had ceased to apply in most other regions of Japan, including Nagoya.[85]

One time when Nakamura Kōkichi's company found itself short of a child actor, Kōkichi asked for the loan of Hisa, who she knew was already a competent dancer. Hisa was then about ten years of age. She accompanied the troupe on an arduous year-long tour around the mountainous region in the heart of central Japan. Later she worked with other notable female players such as Bandō Rikie, Nakamura Taikichi, and the blind Nakamura Tamakichi. At the age of twelve, she was back in Nagoya, where she discovered that her adoptive mother now wanted to sell her to an *okiya*, or geisha house. She protested and, as a compromise, was allowed to join a group of child players. But this was not for long, and she was indentured as an apprentice geisha, or *maiko*, to a geisha house in the Nagoya pleasure quarter of Shinchi. She became a geisha at the age of sixteen. Her birth parents were no longer in a financial position to be able to rescue her from her fate.[86]

Hisa was sent to work in a different pleasure district after she fell in love with a young patron of the Shinchi quarter. She then met a prosperous building contractor, twenty years her senior, who offered to marry her. Hisa accepted his proposal, but unfortunately (for both parties) she had no personal liking for the man. She nevertheless remained with him for ten years, during which time she was serially unfaithful. Her husband continued to take her back uncomplainingly, even paying off the debts she accumulated with one of her lovers. He steadfastly refused to consent to a divorce until 1898, when Hisa ran off with a young pawnbroker from Kyōto whom her husband had asked to mediate between himself and his wife on a previous occasion when she had tried to leave home. Hisa married her lover, and they went to Yokohama, where they used up all the money they had with them. The pawnbroker returned to Kyōto to see his parents about some more funds, but he never came back. Their divorce was finalised in 1901.[87]

In Yokohama, Hisa began to work as a geisha again, but she was no longer in the first flush of youth and it was difficult to establish herself in a new town. Then she heard that a Danish trader based in Japan was looking for some Japanese dancers to appear at a Japanese exhibition he was planning to put on at the zoo in Copenhagen. This trader was assembling a variety of performance artists – illusionists, acrobats, sumo wrestlers and the like – as well as artisans such as painters and fan-makers to demonstrate their skills in front of the paying public. He was also intending to make use of the occasion to sell his stock of Japanese artworks and antiques. According to Hisa, she was one of five dancers who were picked for the venture, three of whom were granted permits by the Japanese government to travel abroad. They left Japan at the end of May 1902. Hisa was thirty-four years old.[88]

The Copenhagen engagement lasted three months. After it was over, Hisa, unlike her homesick compatriots, opted not to return immediately to Japan. She remained behind in Antwerp, where her erstwhile colleagues boarded ship for home. Antwerp, a busy international port, already had a small, flourishing community of Japanese expatriates. Hisa found work at a Japanese restaurant, and dreamt about putting together a small group of dancers to take around Europe. In 1904 she was approached by an elderly German impresario and a Japanese entrepreneur to join a group of actors they were hastily assembling for an appearance in Düsseldorf as a replacement for a troupe of talented illusionists from Japan, whose star, Shōkyokusai Tenkatsu, was ill with appendicitis. The majority of the actors had already been hired in London, but the only woman they had with them was half-German and unable to deliver her lines competently in Japanese.

With Hisa the troupe ultimately came to sixteen players. The play they gave in Düsseldorf was sweepingly entitled *Bushido* (The Way of the Warrior); its plot, however, was very basic. A quarrel breaks out in the brothel quarter among some dissolute samurai; a sword fight ensues; the loser commits hara-kiri. The troupe, nevertheless, succeeded in attracting full houses. When their initial engagement finished after five months, the German impresario approached them for a further year-long tour through Germany.[89] The troupe eventually took *Bushido* as far east as Istanbul. The tour was a great success, helped in no small degree by the interest in the Japanese generated by Japan's unexpected routing of Russia in the recent Russo-Japanese War.

The troupe's success encouraged its members to consider dispensing with the services of a manager, and they pooled their money to have costumes and props sent over from Japan. When their term with the German impresario ended, they turned down his offer of a further year under his management and decided to try their luck in Britain.[90] They toured to Bristol, Birmingham, Liverpool and Manchester, but they suffered from their lack of managerial experience. Despite attracting good audiences, they discovered that most of their earnings was going towards paying the theatres their cut of the profits, or simply being swallowed up in costs. By the time they reached York, they were penniless. They were befriended by leading society ladies of the city, who gave them financial assistance and counselled them to seek professional advice. The troupe turned to a Japanese acrobat-cum-theatrical-agent named Oto, who was married to an Englishwoman and had settled in London. Oto's opinion was that they should abandon the idea of performing tragedy in England and put on comedies instead – he believed that comedy was definitely more to the English taste. Hisa, moreover, had a flair for drollery that the more sombre Sadayakko lacked. The troupe devised a loosely knit play in which a variety of people travelling along a public highway (among them a geisha named Akoya) try to wheedle their way past the guardian of a check-point (a samurai named Kagekiyo) by amusing him with their music-making and dancing. With this new play the troupe resumed its tour of the north of England, and under Oto's guidance the actors finally began to earn money. Then they succeeded in booking an engagement at the Savoy Theatre, London.[91]

It was while they were at the Savoy that Loie Fuller either went to see them perform or, as she claimed in her autobiography, they came to see her. Fuller's autobiography, however, makes no mention of the troupe's appearance at the Savoy. According to her, the troupe had been unable to secure an engagement in London and she found them an impresario who took them to Copenhagen, where she had later met up with them and discovered Hisa's potential as a tragedienne. Fuller also maintained that she had renamed Hisa 'Hanako' in Copenhagen. But Hisa is already referred to as Miss Hanako in a Savoy Theatre playbill advertising that, from 2 October 1905, the troupe would be appearing in a play called *Hara-Kiri*, which was to be given as the curtain-raiser to the main show *What the Butler Saw*. Although the troupe itself is still identified by its original name, Arayama's Company of Japanese Artistes, it is probable that Loie Fuller had already started to exert her influence.[92]

In any case, Fuller demanded complete artistic control as a condition of taking charge of the company, and installed Hisa as the star. She decided on the repertory, bringing in dramatic material similar to that which she had seen Kawakami Otojirō and Sadayakko stage to such good effect. If there was one thing she wanted above all else, it was a dramatic female death scene. In her auto-biography, she describes how she had Hanako die at the end of one of the plays:

> With little movements like those of a frightened child, with sighs, with cries as of a wounded bird, she rolled herself into a ball, seeming to reduce her thin body to a mere nothing so that it was lost in the folds of her heavy embroidered Japanese robe. Her face became immovable, as if petrified, but her eyes continued to reveal intense animation. Then some little hiccoughs convulsed her, she made a little outcry and then another one, so faint that it was hardly more than a sigh. Finally with great wide-open eyes she surveyed death, which had just overtaken her.[93]

After Hanako became famous, Fuller appears to have tried to claim a great deal of the credit, casting herself in the role of Hanako's creator. On one occasion, when Auguste Rodin's secretary René Chéruy expressed his admiration for one of Hanako's death scenes, in which she chattered guilelessly away as her jealous lover stepped up behind her and strangled her with a scarf, Fuller told him she had been the one who had taught Hanako how to realise that scene.[94]

Hanako took *Hara-Kiri* to Copenhagen along with two other plays: *Galatea* and *La Revanche d'une geisha*. *Hara-Kiri*, which retained the characters Akoya the geisha and the samurai Kagekiyo from the troupe's earlier play, now featured a *seppuku*, as its title suggested, though not of Hanako's character as in some of her later plays.[95] *Galatea*, like Sadayakko and Otojirō's play *Zingoro*, was a fantasy about Hidari Jingorō, a famous sculptor of Japanese legend. The troupe proceeded to tour Scandinavia and northern Germany. They were already having problems with Fuller not paying them as agreed (Sadayakko and Otojirō had similar trouble with Fuller's cavalier business practices and her unreliability when it came to payment), but they continued anyway with a tour of Germany, Austria, Belgium and the south of France, where Fuller arranged for them to appear at the Exposition Coloniale which was being held in Marseilles in 1906. It was here that Rodin saw Hanako perform for the first time. A great friend of Loie Fuller, he had attended Sadayakko's performances back in 1900. He appears to have asked Sadayakko to model for him but was turned down. In the summer of 1906, Rodin became interested in a troupe of Cambodian court dancers who were appearing at the Exposition Coloniale. Rodin, however, saw them first in Paris on the occasion of a royal visit by the King of Cambodia. When the dancers returned to the Exposition, Rodin followed them to Marseilles. There he saw Hanako in *La Revanche d'une geisha*.

La Revanche d'une geisha had an extravagant, overblown plot consisting of one sword fight after another, culminating in a death scene by Hanako. Hanako again played a geisha, this time one named O-Sode. O-Sode is the beloved of Chokichi, the son of Kampei, a wealthy merchant. When Kampei's servant fights a duel with Washizuka, a samurai, and loses, Kampei decides to avenge the disgrace by challenging Washizuka to another duel. This time Washizuka loses. Incensed at his defeat, he ambushes Kampei as the merchant is making his way home. Kampei's lifeless body is discovered by Chokichi and O-Sode, who have come out to see why it is taking Kampei so long to return. Washizuka flees the scene of the murder. In the second act, Chokichi and O-Sode, who are in pursuit of Washizuka, enter a teahouse which happens to be Washizuka's hideout. Washizuka catches a glimpse of O-Sode and immediately conceives a passionate desire for her. The mistress of the teahouse puts poison in Chokichi's drink, and when he collapses she whisks O-Sode away with her. At the beginning of the third and last act, Washizuka, maddened by O-Sode's obstinate refusal to marry him, is about to kill her with his sword when Chokichi (who has been revived by his servant) rushes in to her rescue. But in the process of saving her, he is fatally wounded. O-Sode then avenges the deaths of Chokichi and his father by plunging a dagger into Washizuka. As for the manner of O-Sode's own death, with which the play concluded, there are several different accounts. The synopsis provided for Danish audiences and later at the Exposition Coloniale merely mentions that O-Sode collapses dead on top of her lover's lifeless body. But many years later, Hanako described in an interview with a Japanese journalist how Rodin had wanted to model her expression in her death scene in *La Revanche*, explaining to her interviewer that her character was killed by a brigand under blossoming cherry trees. On the other hand, Sukenobu Isao, who has published a study of Hanako, believes her character committed suicide in the manner of a *seppuku*, by putting a dagger to her throat. Like Kawakami Otojirō, Hanako used a red liquid to simulate blood in her hara-kiri scenes. The liquid was hidden in the hilt of her stage dagger and released as the blade was retracted.[96]

Rodin went to see Hanako in her dressing room after the show. He expressed his admiration for her performance and invited her to come and see him when she was in Paris. The opportunity, however, did not arise for some time. The troupe quarrelled with Fuller over pay, and in protest they split up. On the subject of this break-up, Fuller merely observed in her autobiography that the company had come to the end of their contract. Hanako went back to Antwerp with several of her fellow actors. Fuller later claimed that Hanako wrote to her from Antwerp asking for financial help. In Hanako's own account of her life, published in Japan in a magazine in January 1917, she described how she encountered, one evening, a heavily veiled lady who turned out to be Fuller's secretary, by whom she was secretly whisked back to Paris that very night by automobile, together with another Japanese woman, O-Toku, with whom Hanako had become friendly in Marseilles. (According to Hanako, O-Toku was a nanny who had been brought from Yokohama to Europe by her French employer, with whom she had subsequently fallen out.) In the car, Hanako found a former colleague from her troupe, Yoshikawa Kaoru. Yoshikawa had once attended an American university and could speak some English, French and German. He had been the troupe's spokesperson and interpreter, as well as being an actor. Once Hanako was back in Paris, they were married. In her autobiographical article, Hanako is reticent as to whether her marriage was a love match. She merely mentions that Loie Fuller acted as matchmaker.[97]

Fuller, in her autobiography, recounts how she had to come up with a play in a hurry in order to secure Hanako an engagement at the Théâtre Moderne on the Boulevard des Italiens in Paris. The ensuing piece, *The Martyr*, was a reworking of *La Revanche* using the same three principal characters, O-Sode, Chokichi and Washizuka. According to Fuller, she had only four Japanese actors at her disposal: Hanako, her husband, her 'maid' (that is, her friend O-Toku), and one other actor, who had been engaged in London through an agent. Hanako herself mentions two actors from London. In any case it was a small company of players, and in October 1906 they began their run at the Théâtre Moderne, playing for three consecutive months. *The Martyr* served as a vehicle for another hara-kiri scene by Hanako. It had a ridiculous plot involving a young woman (O-Sode) who substitutes a life-size doll of herself in her place to see what her suitor's reaction to it will be. Her suitor, unable to tell the difference, declares his love to the doll. As it remains stolidly impassive, he takes this for a rebuff, and out of outraged pride is about to rush upon it with his sword when O-Sode's brother Washizuka dashes into the room, convinced that O-Sode's suitor is about to kill her. The two men fight, and O-Sode, who has been watching the proceedings from a secret hiding place, jumps into the fray to separate them. But she is too late: her suitor Chokichi is mortally wounded. Only then does her brother realise that the figure he had taken for his sister had been nothing but a doll all along. Horrified at what he has done to Chokichi, he tries to commit hara-kiri on the spot, but O-Sode persuades him that the tragedy was entirely of her own making and commits hara-kiri herself. *The Martyr* was well attended and attracted much publicity in the press, especially on the occasion when Hanako's stage blood splattered on to the immaculate white waistcoat of a gentleman in evening dress sitting in the front row. Hanako wrote later that she had been embarrassed by the play on account of the many Japanese students and scholars who were in Paris. She said she had protested to Fuller about the plot, but in vain since the play was already attracting full houses. Fuller recollected that she followed up *The Martyr* with another tragedy, this time entitled *A Drama at Yoshiwara*.[98]

It was during this period that Hanako formed an odd but lasting friendship with Rodin and his long-suffering companion Rose Beuret, who were settled in a villa near the town of Meudon on the outskirts of Paris. Rodin was intensely drawn to Hanako's way of realising the emotions of her characters. As Hanako remembered it, she first modelled for Rodin in September 1906, but he had not liked the results and had asked her back again the following year.[99] Between 1907 and 1912, Rodin produced up to sixty representations of her face in the form of mask, head and (very rarely) bust, and in various media including terracotta, plaster, *pâte de verre* and bronze. Yet Hanako and Rodin hardly shared a language and, verbally at least, could barely communicate with each other. René Chéruy, who was Rodin's confidential secretary between 1902 and 1908, remembered how difficult it had been for any of them to make themselves understood to Hanako. They had found Hanako's male companion – presumably her husband Yoshikawa Kaoru – not much help either. Neither his French, nor his English for that matter, had been at all adequate.[100]

The language barrier prevented Hanako from ever becoming Rodin's confidante in the way that some of Rodin's other female muses, such as the sensitive and cultured Helene von Nostitz, were able to. There is no indication that Hanako ever came to feel possessive towards him, as many other women did – Loie Fuller, for example, as well as the artist Gwen John, sister of Augustus John and one of Rodin's former models, and the American-born marchioness (and later self-styled duchess) Claire de Choiseul. Nonetheless, Hanako always sent Rodin and Rose postcards from wherever she found herself on tour. They were mostly written in either French or English, although several in German have also survived. Hanako continued to tour intensively, mostly through Europe, right up to the outbreak of the First World War. She took her troupe to America twice, first in 1907 and then again in 1909, though this time less successfully. She also undertook three tours to Russia. The first was in the winter of 1909–10, during which she was forced to leave her husband, who was gravely ill with advanced tuberculosis, behind in a hospital in Berlin. When she returned, he had died. Hanako went to Russia again in the autumn of 1911, and her third tour to Russia lasted from the autumn of 1912 to the end of the summer of 1913.

When Hanako was in Paris, she went to stay with the Rodins at the Villa des Brillants, their residence near Meudon, where a cottage in the grounds was put at her disposal. Neighbours gossiped about seeing her taking a stroll around the garden with her host but Hanako always denied she had ever been Rodin's lover. She continued to model for him whenever her work brought her back to Paris. None of the pieces Rodin did of Hanako were commissions. He executed them for his own artistic satisfaction, and it was not until three years after Hanako had first started modelling for him that Rodin was ready to exhibit publicly any of his studies of her. The pieces remained in his possession during his lifetime and eventually passed to the French state along with the rest of Rodin's work, his papers, and his sculpture and photographic collections. Most of the Hanako works are still in the Musée Rodin, which houses the Rodin collections at two sites, both former Rodin residences – the Hôtel Biron, in Paris, and the Villa des Brillants, which Hanako had so frequently visited.

Rodin had a deep fascination with dancers, especially those who were experimenting with new styles of expression. He had admired Loie Fuller's dances ever since she rose to prominence in Paris with her 'Serpentine Dance', her earliest experiment in transforming the saucy vaudeville skirt dance into an airy, fantastical spectacle of floating, diaphanous fabrics and coloured lights. He met Isadora Duncan in 1900, after she attended a retrospective of his work which was being held concurrently with the Exposition Universelle in Paris. Duncan was so moved by what she saw that she subsequently sought him out at one of his Parisian ateliers and invited him back to her own studio, where she danced for him. Rodin appears to have responded in a characteristically sensual and physical manner to her brilliance. Duncan recollected how he had come up to her with 'blazing' eyes, running his hands over her neck, breast and hips, her bare legs and feet. 'He began to knead my whole body as if it were clay', she wrote in her memoirs. Frightened, Duncan asked him to leave, but she later said she regretted not having taken the opportunity of offering up her virginity to a man of such genius. Rodin and Duncan met again in 1902, and became close friends. Ruth St Denis had a similar experience to Duncan when she modelled for Rodin in 1906. But unlike Duncan, St Denis was left profoundly disillusioned. A great artist she admired had turned out to be 'only an ordinary French sensualist', she wrote in her autobiography.[101]

Enthralled as he was by the pliancy and elasticity of the human body, as well as its strength, Rodin's interest in dancers was not surprising. He was likewise intrigued by the expressiveness of the human body when engaged in mundane everyday activities. The American music and art critic James Huneker considered Rodin's sketches of men and women in their unselfconscious moments to be as vivid as those by Hokusai.[102] Rodin, after all, was a collector of Japanese woodblock prints and illustrated books,[103] and he shared with artists such as Hokusai a fascination with the human body's limitless range of expression. In the last decades of his life Rodin produced drawing after drawing in pencil and in watercolour of female nudes. These works are characterised by a fluid use of contours that releases the human form not only from the artistic strictures of classical and academic nudes, but more generally from socially imposed inhibitions based on notions of decorum.[104]

Hanako posed for Rodin in the nude on at least one occasion, if not more, although nude modelling, traditionally unheard of in Japan, was still a matter of some controversy in her home country. Perhaps Rodin enlisted the help of Rose in persuading her to agree to it.[105] Many of these rapidly executed drawings of

Hanako catch her in motion. Rodin captures her exquisite sense of balance and the muscular control which her training in Japanese dance had honed in her. Other sketches show Hanako lolling in a carefree manner on the floor: in one, she casually lies on her stomach, waggling one foot in the air, while in another, she reclines on her back, her hands coupled in a tomboyish manner under her head, her right leg carelessly resting on her left.[106]

Rodin discovered beauty in the naked Japanese body in a way Pierre Loti could not or would not. The dancer Ruth St Denis, who actually took lessons in Japanese dance from a former geisha who had emigrated to California, once commented on the discipline which was required: 'The trend of concentration is toward contraction. . . . Study the posture of the geisha. Her shoulders are drawn back, perhaps her face upturned in the similitude of trust, . . . but her muscles are taut as the rope that holds a straining ocean-liner at anchor.'[107] It was not an inane marionette that Rodin discovered under the folds of the kimono, but a strong, lithe athlete – beautiful despite the differences between her physique and typical western ones. He told Paul Gsell:

> Her muscles stand out as prominently as those of a fox terrier; her sinews are so developed that the joints to which they are attached have a thickness equal to the members themselves. She is so strong that she can rest as long as she pleases on one leg, the other raised at right angles in front of her. She looks as if rooted in the ground, like a tree. Her anatomy is quite different from that of a European, but, nevertheless, very beautiful in its singular power.[108]

Rodin saw beauty in taut muscles poised with purpose and direction. Physical movement was beautiful to him in that it was an expression of the stirring of the spirit within. For Rodin, it was this purposeful energy he discovered in the natural world around him which he then strove to capture in his own work. ' "In short," ' Gsell quotes Rodin saying on a different occasion, ' "the purest master-pieces are those in which one finds no inexpressive waste of forms, lines, and colours, but where all, absolutely all, expresses thought and soul." '[109]

But it was Hanako's expressive face which Rodin found engrossing above all else. He was intrigued by the ways in which her face managed to convey her stage character's complex emotions at the moment of death. His friend Judith Cladel was struck by Hanako's ability to hold a single grimace 'for hours'. To Cladel this knack suggested something eerie, unnatural and inhuman even, as though it were characteristic of the tenacity, as well as the ferocity, of the oriental person:

> Hanako did not pose like other people. Her features were contracted in an expression of cold, terrible rage. She had the look of a tiger, an expression

thoroughly foreign to our Occidental countenances. . . . It cried out revenge without mercy, the thirst for blood. A baffling contrast this – the spirit of a wild beast appearing on the human countenance.[110]

Rodin worked obsessively on a very small number of Hanako's typical expressions. The Musée Rodin has grouped Rodin's masks and heads of Hanako into seven general categories according to their predominant expression. Five of the seven take as subject matter Hanako's own representation of her stage persona at the moment of committing hara-kiri. Beginning with a study of shattered innocence and an accompanying wakening of inner strength (the face known as Type A), Rodin concentrated ever more on capturing the tension in Hanako's countenance, every muscle taut with anguish, bitterness, resentment, regret and fierce resolve. This strength of concentration and stark acceptance of fate are represented in the masks of the Type B group by Hanako's inward-looking eyes and parted lips. Like these pieces, many of the Type C masks retain a rough, lumpy surface, as though this unfinished, unpolished quality reflected not only the clash of

24 Auguste Rodin, *Hanako* (head, Type A), plaster, 17.6 × 12.5 × 11.2 cm, photographed by Adam Rzepka.

emotions raging within, but the fury with which Rodin's own imagination has been at work. The head known as *La Tête d'angoisse de la mort* (Type D) shows Hanako's face frozen in a contorted glare, her brows knitted together in a ferocious sidelong squint, her lips drawn tightly over her mouth, a corner of which is wrenched downwards, exposing a glimpse of clenched teeth. In an astonishing vision of an emotional intensity that, to Rodin's mind, united two very different artists, Rodin contemplated using this head of Hanako as the basis of a bust of Beethoven.[111]

Another of Rodin's earliest images of Hanako is a haunting one. Known as Type E, this countenance shows Hanako's lips hanging open; her eyelids droop heavily and her eyes are glazed over, unseeingly directed towards some distant and unfathomable void. A stillness hangs over this face, as though all agony, all horror, had in mid-gasp come to a sudden end. In 1910 the French government bought a bronze version of this face for the Musée du Luxembourg. In the following year Rodin was approached by the artist Jean Clos with the idea of reproducing some of his work in *pâte de verre*, a composition of opaque, coloured glass, the use of

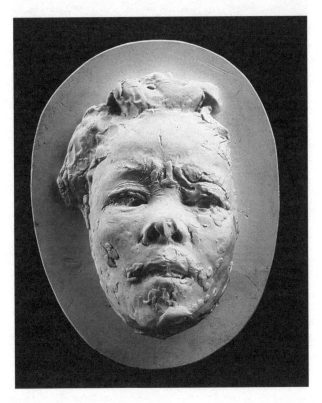

25 Auguste Rodin, *Hanako* (mask, Type C), plaster, 26 × 20 × 12.4 cm, photographed by Adam Rzepka.

which Clos's father Henri had been instrumental in reviving.[112] Perhaps the most eerie and disquieting versions of the Type E mask are those in this material, four of which survive. Albert Harlingue produced a photograph of one of them nestled deep in a cushion, looking like, if anything, a carefully composed decapitated head.[113] Of Hanako's mask in *pâte de verre* Judith Cladel wrote:

> One might call it a condemned person, a being so terrified by the approach of death that all the blood has rushed to the heart. It is a spirit frozen with fear, the eyes looking toward the unknown, the large nostrils scenting death. . . . Obstinate, although conquered, it will draw its last breath without a cry.

However, it seemed to Cladel that the deep shadows cast by the light of a candle softened the face and made its expression more sympathetic, more akin to human emotions:

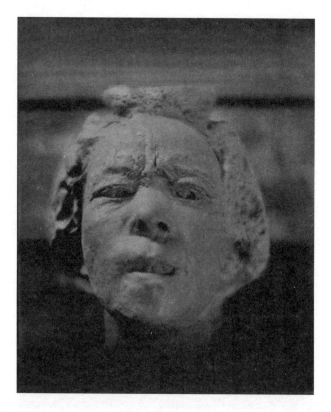

26 Edward Steichen, *Mask of Hanako in the Dépot des marbres atelier,* undated photograph of Rodin's mask of Hanako (Type D, known as *La Tête d'angoisse de la mort), tirage au charbon,* 24.4 x 20 cm (Paris, Musée Rodin, Ph 675).

How gentle and touching it seems now! It is no longer bloodthirsty and savage; that exotic expression which repelled me has quite disappeared. These features, expressing the innermost self under a stress of emotions, reveal a poor creature that has loved and suffered. It is a pitiable face that has been molded by life. I have seen that same sad, tired expression of anguish in one whose whole strength is gone, but who still makes an effort to understand misfortune in order to strive against it. I have seen it on my mother's face when one of us was ill.[114]

Rodin revelled in the calm beauty of other women who sat for him. In his busts of such society women as Luisa Morla Vicuña, Eve Fairfax and Kate Simpson he caught their loveliness, poise and gentle grace. He told the poet Countess Anne de Noailles that what fascinated him about her face was her 'expression of contemplative sensuality'.[115] Judith Cladel (herself not a beauty) felt that the play of light and shadow 'harmonize[d] best with the softness and delicacy of the feminine flesh': its effect was to evoke 'the mystery of an inner life

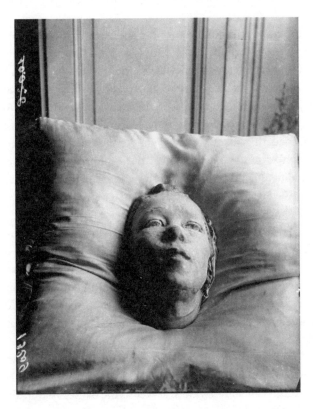

27 Albert Harlingue, *Mask of Hanako*, undated photograph of Rodin's mask of Hanako (Type E in *pâte de verre*), aristotype, 13 x 18 cm (Paris, Musée Rodin, Ph 1992).

more secret, more intimate than that of man'.[116] But Hanako gave Rodin an insight into the soul's innermost torment – the agitation, the bewilderment, the haunting sadness that he had striven earlier to capture in the figures of the damned for his never-completed *Gates of Hell*, the bronze doors he had been commissioned in 1880 to produce for the yet-to-be-built Musée des Arts Décoratifs. Although one stereotypical western view of the Japanese was that their faces were inscrutable, Hanako's face, as far as Rodin was concerned, was the opposite of expressionless.

Hanako's portrayal of her character's emotions depended more on the idea of distinct situations rather than on a concept of her character's cumulative growth through the course of a play. The plays which Hanako and her troupe performed were never much more than coarse and crude cannibalisations of material derived from popular Japanese history and legend. Indeed, what Hanako seemed to require was not so much a play involving character development as a sequence of sensational situations which called for her to employ her repertoire of emotional expressions.

Hanako performed many of these for her audience on the occasion, in January 1913, when she was invited to the Moscow Art Theatre's Studio for young actors to demonstrate the ways in which emotion was expressed in Japanese theatre. The event was attended by the theatre director Konstantin Stanislavsky, his students, and actors and actresses affiliated to the Moscow Art Theatre. Stanislavsky, one of the founders of the Moscow Art Theatre, was then in the midst of consolidating his acting system. At the Studio, Hanako performed a series of short scenes to illustrate her style of acting. She demonstrated, for example, the different way an older woman might show grief compared to a younger one. She enacted both a youthful and a more mature woman committing suicide to show how differently each might face death. Recollecting the occasion much later, Hanako wrote that she had dwelt not so much on the act of suicide itself as on such emotions as might flood into the mind at the approach of death – emotions that needed to be conveyed with the most subtle movements of the eyes and mouth. Hanako attributed her method of acting to the training she had received as a child working with actresses who had adopted their style from the most admired (male) stars of mainstream kabuki. Unlike either Otojirō or Sadayakko, Hanako did not see herself as attempting anything revolutionary. As far as she was concerned, she was part of a long, unbroken tradition.[117]

In Moscow Hanako met Olga Knipper-Chekhova, a star of the Moscow Art Theatre and Anton Chekhov's widow, as well as the dancer Isadora Duncan, with whom Stanislavsky had a close artistic bond.[118] In *My Life in Art* Stanislavsky described the experience of watching Duncan dance: 'her developing emotion would first change the expression of her face,' he recounted, 'and with shining eyes she would pass to the display of what was born in her soul.'[119] Just as Duncan felt that truly creative dancers did not merely try to reproduce the physical manifestations of an emotion recollected from memory, but spontaneously danced the music they heard in their souls, so Stanislavsky believed that the actor needed to feel sincerely the truth of the emotions he was portraying. 'For this', he wrote, 'it is necessary for the actor to develop to the highest degree his imagination, a childlike naïveté and trustfulness'. Only when the actor himself was faithful to his feeling for the truth was he justified in the way he played his role on stage.[120] Stanislavsky considered Hanako to be truly creative. In his eyes, she was not simply reproducing conventional gestures which belonged to the theatrical traditions of her country. On the contrary, she demonstrated how exquisitely she had tuned her creative powers so as to be able instinctively and spontaneously to transform herself into whatever character she was asked to portray.

For the critic Mikhail Bonch-Tomashevsky, who also attended Hanako's demonstration at the Studio, it was her comic acting which confirmed to him that she was a true artist. Bonch-Tomashevsky appears to have had enough knowledge of the traditions of kabuki to be able to inform readers of his essay on Hanako that the actress was no more representative of authentic Japanese theatre than Sadayakko. Nonetheless, he emphatically declared Hanako to be a consummate artist, with perfect mastery – honed since childhood – of the disciplines of traditional dance and music. This absolute command of her body and voice was the foundation of her expressive acting. She had a gift, Bonch-Tomashevsky felt, for making her audiences see the world through her character's eyes, whether it was a servant girl peeking into her mistress's room, a cowardly man attempting *seppuku*, or students engaged in horseplay in a classroom. For him the uproarious laughter she generated was Homeric, and he found it both wholesome and cathartic.[121]

Hanako's aptitude for both comedy and tragedy is reflected in the alternative endings to her dramatic vehicle *Otake*, which, like *The Martyr*, was a play about mistaken identity. In *Otake*, Hanako played the eponymous lead, a lady's maid who surreptitiously dresses up in finery belonging to her mistress and finds herself mistaken for her by her mistress's noble lover. Unwilling to betray herself, O-Take continues to pretend to be her mistress, but refuses to speak a word to the ardent suitor, who jumps to the conclusion that his beloved no longer cares for him. Enraged, he tries to strike O-Take down. Hanako performed *Otake* (along with a scene from *Hara-Kiri*) before the Austrian emperor Franz Joseph at the spa resort of Karlsbad in 1909. Reminiscing about this occasion in her 1917 autobiographical magazine article, Hanako refers to *Otake* as a comedy. The synopsis of the play in the programme which accompanied Hanako's performance of *Otake* at the

Ambassador Theatre, London, in January 1915, gives its comic ending: O-Take deftly evades the frenzied nobleman's sword thrust just as her mistress makes a timely entrance accompanied by her manservant Gonsuke, who happens to be O-Take's true love. O-Take throws herself into Gonsuke's arms with a peal of laughter, the noble lover is overcome with confusion and relief, and all misunderstandings are pleasantly resolved.[122]

The play's darker ending is described in an article eulogising Hanako written by the Russian theatre director Nikolai Evreinov, who saw her in *Otake* during Hanako's first tour of Russia in 1909. Evreinov was enchanted by Hanako's evocation of the mischievousness and exuberant good humour of an innocent, naïve young girl, who does not have the slightest notion of the deadly passions she has stirred up in the heart of her mistress's proud samurai lover. The nobleman is on the point of drawing his sword, but O-Take remains oblivious to her imminent danger. When he presses her for a final answer, O-Take trembles and demurs, but still in the spirit of fun. All of a sudden the nobleman stabs her. Evreinov thought Hanako's death scene was superb. Taken completely by surprise, O-Take murmured silently 'like a wounded bird' (in Evreinov's words), breathed in deeply, and shot a glance 'with childlike eyes' upon the world she was about to bid farewell – a look which asked reproachfully, 'Why?'[123] This ability of Hanako's to switch abruptly from gleeful, carefree joy to the deepest horror, pain and death likewise left an impression on the seminal twentieth-century linguistic theorist and thinker Roman Jakobson, who remembered going in his youth to see a performance by the actress in Moscow. In a letter to Sawada Suketarō, Hanako's biographer and kinsman, Jakobson remarked on the naked violence of the moment of change – a violence presented without sentimentality or affectation.[124]

Audiences found Hanako's portrayal of the moment of death compelling in its detail. V. Yur'ev, reviewing *Otake* in 1913, recounted Hanako's 'brief struggle with death, a shudder at the final end – a death portrayed with unbelievable, incomparable realism, and yet with simplicity, without a sound, with no superfluous gestures'. Yur'ev praised Hanako for her unromanticised portrayal of 'how life departs from the body, how a lifeless body falls to the ground'.[125] At the same time, Hanako's performances appealed equally strongly to those who belonged to a different school of dramatic theory from that of theatrical realism. Vsevolod Meierkhol'd (Meyerhold), who began his career as a stage director in the Symbolist theatre and derived inspiration from the traditions of the *commedia dell'arte* as well as the circus, went on to develop his own theory of acting which concentrated on movement and gesture as the primary way into a character's psychology. He felt that it was in her dancing that Hanako found her means of expressing the soul in ecstasy. It was therefore through dance (such as her gleeful frolic in *Otake*) that Meierkhol'd believed she succeeded in most profoundly affecting her audiences.[126]

Notwithstanding all the favourable critical reception Hanako received during her stay in Moscow in January 1913, there was one admirer of Stanislavsky's work who failed to share his enthusiasm for the Japanese actress. This was the earnest young Japanese theatre director and playwright Osanai Kaoru, who became a leading proponent in Japan of a new style of theatre, one which incorporated western acting methods. During the winter of 1912–13 Osanai was in Moscow to observe Stanislavsky's work, after having spent some time in Berlin studying the technique of the Austrian theatre director Max Reinhardt. In his memoirs of his European trip, Osanai recollected how he had been invited to a New Year's Eve party at the Stanislavsky household only to be asked by the great man himself what he, Osanai, thought of Sadayakko, whom Stanislavsky had not managed to see perform. The interest Stanislavasky showed in Sadayakko left Osanai dumbfounded. He recollected blurting out that Sadayakko was not an artist. Stanislavsky had then asked him why not, to which, to his great discomfiture, he had been unable to give an answer. Next, Stanislavsky asked him about Hanako. This was even worse for Osanai, since he had never even heard of Hanako, which was not surprising from the Japanese point of view, but Stanislavsky had appeared incredulous when he told him he had never come across her in Japan. Osanai was mortified to learn that Sadayakko and Hanako were being taken seriously as Japanese actresses. In his eyes, they were nothing more than charlatans and great embarrassments to their fellow countrymen. There is no indication that Osanai went to see Hanako for himself during her month-long run at the Miniature Theatre in Moscow.[127]

It was for different reasons, however, that the avant-garde British actor, theatre producer, stage designer and drama theorist Edward Gordon Craig (one of whose major successes was a *Hamlet* he designed for Stanislavsky at the Moscow Art Theatre in 1912) was dismissive of Sadayakko and Hanako. He actively disliked their naturalistic approach to the portrayal of death. The son of the actress Ellen Terry and the architect and designer Edward William Godwin, Craig drew considerable inspiration from Japanese art, but he held a particular theory about it: that it was 'contrary to realism'. Of Hanako he commented in 1914 that she was a 'remarkable actress', but not an 'artist'. 'Hokusai would have hated Hanako,' he wrote. Indeed, in Craig's view the whole idea of Japanese actresses sharing the stage with their male counterparts was a retrograde step. In 1910, he suggested in an article on Sadayakko that Japanese theatre, in managing to keep women off the stage, had succeeded in achieving art by eschewing the pursuit of realism. Despite having designed productions for his mother early in his career, Craig signalled he was in agreement with practitioners in eastern theatre that 'only the masculine mind was fit for stage performances'.[128]

The outbreak of the First World War heralded the beginning of the end of Hanako's stage career. Together with her company of actors, she took refuge in London, where she presented *Otake* along with another hara-kiri piece *Ki-musume*, as well as a one-act farcical curtain-raiser entitled *Oya, Oya!*[129] She also appeared in a gala benefit performance put on in aid of wounded servicemen (Japan fought on the side of the Allies in the First World War), and in a revue along with other popular actresses of the day. But attendance at theatres was declining, and in the autumn of 1916 Hanako set off on her first trip back to Japan in order to hand-pick female dancers for a stage extravaganza in London which she hoped would draw back big audiences. Although she returned to Britain in 1917 with four promising young dancers, she never did launch the intended show. Instead, she opened a Japanese restaurant, the Kogetsu, in Dorset Square. Fitted out with authentic Japanese furnishings, the restaurant became a favourite gathering place for Japanese expatriates. Meanwhile, Hanako learned of the deaths of Rose Beuret and then of Rodin. Both died in 1917, Rose in February and Rodin in November. Hanako began to contemplate the idea of retiring and returning to Japan for good. She finally took the step in December 1921, handing over her restaurant to her secretary. She took back to Japan two works Rodin had made of her: a bronze version of the mask which had made Judith Cladel think of her own mother, and a version in terracotta of *La Tête d'angoisse de la mort*. Hanako went to live with a sister who was running a geisha house in the town of Gifu, located to the north of Nagoya. She died in 1945.[130]

Hanako never appeared as an actress in Japan. Sadayakko, on the other hand, did go on to make a professional reputation for herself back home, although it seems to have been with some reluctance that she first decided to appear on stage in front of a Japanese audience.[131] After Sadayakko and Otojirō returned to Japan in 1902 on the conclusion of their second European tour, Otojirō conceived the idea of re-branding his style of theatre as *seigeki* ('legitimate theatre') by putting on Japanese adaptations of Shakespearean plays. He began with *Othello*, which he set in Taiwan, a contemporary Japanese counterpart to Shakespeare's Venetian-occupied Cyprus, as Taiwan had been annexed to Japan following the First Sino-Japanese War. The role of Desdemona (renamed Tomone) was assigned provisionally to an *onnagata*. Sadayakko may have had some reservations about the fortuitous manner in which she had become an actress, or else she may have been uncertain as to whether or not she had come to full maturity as an actress. There may have been some unwillingness on her part to be made to appear presumptuous; on the other hand, her hesitancy may have been a demonstration of wifely deference to her husband lest she inadvertently steal the limelight away from him.[132] In any case, Otojirō was insistent that he needed an actress. *Othello* opened in February 1903, with Otojirō in the title role and Sadayakko as Tomone. It was followed the same year with the court scene from *The Merchant of Venice*, translated from Shakespeare, and an adaptation of *Hamlet.*

Sadayakko was not the first actress to perform professionally in a Japanese theatre in the modern period. In Tōkyō the first play to have a mixed cast (which included among its female players a geisha who, like Sadayakko, hailed from the Yoshichō district of the capital) was staged as early as 1891. But the climate of opinion differed from region to region, and it was not until Otojirō and Sadayakko took their *Othello* to Nagoya in 1905 that mixed casts were permitted by public authorities in that city. Critics were divided over the question of whether the presence of actresses added anything to a theatrical performance. Some argued that Japanese theatre owed its unique characteristics – its tasteful sense of decorum and delicacy of sentiment – to the fact that female roles were traditionally taken by *onnagata* instead of real women.[133] On the other hand, a new movement was afoot to present western plays not in the form of adaptations such as Otojirō's, but in scholarly, yet at the same time performable, Japanese translations. This *shingeki* movement soon had its own leading female star in the charismatic actress Matsui Sumako. The proponents of *shingeki* aimed to raise drama from the level of popular entertainment to that of high art (one of its first and most important theatre directors was Osanai Kaoru). Matsui Sumako – unlike Sadayakko – was trained for the stage, and specifically in *shingeki*'s style of acting. She was cast as Ophelia in 1911, and later that same year she made *A Doll's House* an important critical success with her portrayal of Nora.

Sadayakko and Otojirō's experiments in mixing Japanese styles of theatre with contemporary subject matter were left uneasily trapped between the traditionalists championing the aesthetics of kabuki theatre and the advocates of western methods of acting. At Otojirō's side, Sadayakko was always the loyal, supportive wife, so much so that it is almost impossible to distinguish how and to what extent she helped shape the direction in which Otojirō's ideas about theatre developed. Sadayakko refused, however, to retire meekly into the discreet shadows of widowhood after Otojirō died of complications arising from peritonitis on 11 November 1911. Sadayakko assumed leadership of his company of actors, and despite calls from certain quarters of the press for her to retire, she carried on with an active stage career. She was now a celebrity in her own country, and people continued to flock to see her, if only out of curiosity. She worked alongside actors of a wide range of traditions, from mainstream kabuki to *shingeki*.

She no longer had Otojirō to deflect criticism from her. Critics struggled to make sense of her, now she had finally emerged from behind her husband's larger-than-life presence. In 1913, two years after his death, Sadayakko wrote of her resolve to open a new chapter in her career,[134] but the prevailing view of her post-Otojirō years came to be that she had ceased to develop as an artist. Some critics thought she had taken to acting mechanically, that she had become repetitive and complacent, happy to bask in the glory of the past. One of her most thoughtful critics, the playwright and novelist Hasegawa Shigure, also made what is possibly the most damning of criticisms that can be aimed at any actor. Sadayakko, she said, possessed no creativity: Sadayakko had been unable to progress with the times and had been left behind; she had contented herself with earning the money with which to pay off her husband's debts and to erect a statue in his memory; she had not, in the end, struggled enough with her art.[135] Even so, Hasegawa Shigure believed that Sadayakko at least possessed a scintillating, beguiling quality of beauty. Sadayakko was vibrant, she thought, when she played western women such as Ophelia, Desdemona and Tosca. Other critics, however, disagreed. Some declared that Sadayakko strangely lacked allure, that she failed to draw her audiences to her.

Sadayakko attracted widely divergent evaluations of her artistry. One Japanese critic, who saw her as Tosca, considered her superior to her much-admired rival Matsui Sumako when it came to mastery of expression. He wrote how the entire audience on the night he attended Sadayakko's performance had been mesmerised by the way the actress had been able to plumb the depths of passion, rage and hatred. On the other hand, a different critic accused her of not being rigorous enough in her study of character. This critic pointed out that what a traditional kabuki *onnagata* was unable to do was to convey in a naturalistic manner a real woman's raw and naked emotions. Actresses, on the other hand, had a privileged insight into these emotions, and the unique contribution they had to make to theatre was to express them. Sadayakko just managed to get away with it when she played a foreign woman, such as Marguerite in *La Dame aux camélias* or Tosca. But, the critic felt, her vacuity became painfully apparent whenever she attempted to play Japanese women. Ironically, he thought she failed particularly badly in the role of geishas. Hasegawa Shigure too wondered why Sadayakko was unable to bring that radiance and energy she possessed when playing western women to her roles as Japanese characters.[136] The actress who captured the imagination of western audiences with her frenzied portrayal of an exotic Japanese geisha was appreciated best in Japan for her passionate portrayal of exotic western women.

In the autumn of 1917 Sadayakko announced her retirement and in October gave her last series of performances in Tōkyō. One of the roles in which she appeared on that occasion was Aida, in a play adapted from Verdi's opera. She then went on a farewell tour around Kyūshū, and, lastly, appeared in Ōsaka in November 1918. She had not yet given up entirely on the idea of a tour to the United States, but this fell through on account of worsening diplomatic relations between America and Japan. Since Otojirō's death she had contemplated the idea of a tour abroad on four other occasions, but none of the proposals had ever come to anything.[137] Putting her acting career behind her, she reverted to her real name Kawakami Sada and settled down as the mistress of the man with whom she had first fallen in love at the age of fourteen when he rescued her from her bolting horse. She ran his household in Nagoya for six years, and helped entertain his numerous important business associates. When he returned to Tōkyō in 1924, Sada started a children's musical drama academy in the capital. She continued to be involved with it intermittently until it folded in 1932. She remained with her lover until the beginning of 1933, when, with his health deteriorating, they decided they should separate and he should return to his family. He died five years later. Sada began writing her memoirs, but most of her manuscript was lost when her house in Tōkyō was destroyed in an air raid in 1945. She died of cancer in the following year at the age of seventy-five.[138]

Sadayakko does not appear to have had Hanako's gleefulness or her earthy bond with both life's laughter and pain. Instead, Sadayakko possessed that forbidding remoteness that Puccini was later to encapsulate in the character of Turandot.[139] Hanako's role in all her plays was that of the victim, either mercilessly murdered or forced into committing hara-kiri in order to preserve her reputation. Sadayakko's most famous character Katsuragi, on the other hand, lashed out at all around her in her thirst for vengeance – as does Turandot, who punishes her suitors for the degradation an imperial ancestress of hers had once suffered at the hands of a man. Puccini's Cio-Cio-San compares herself to a moon goddess who descends to earth at night and enraptures human hearts; Turandot, princess of China, is also associated with the moon. But the chilly and remote moon to which the people of Peking offer up their supplications is likened to a severed head, bloodless and silent, the image of the heads of Turandot's unsuccessful lovers who have been beheaded for their presumption in seeking her hand and their failure to answer her three Sphinx-like questions. Turandot, the castrating, unobtainable dragon lady of the east, is a manifestation of the image of the cruel oriental woman, haughty and beyond reach, which surfaces time and again in the western imagination and serves as a paradigm for defiant female sexuality that challenges men to tame it. The decadent, 'oriental' image of Salome, dancing provocatively before her stepfather for the head of John the Baptist, had cast a long shadow over the *fin de siècle* and the first decades of the twentieth century. Sarah Bernhardt was originally to play Salome in Oscar Wilde's drama, which was later turned into an opera by Richard Strauss.[140] Dancers from Loie Fuller to Ruth St Denis, Maud Allan (who became a sensation in London in 1908 for her erotic Salome), the spy Mata Hari, the actress Gertrude Hoffman and a host of lesser lights appearing in vaudeville and variety assumed the persona of the Hebrew princess. Like Salome, Sadayakko's Katsuragi in *The Geisha and the Knight* seemed to epitomise the frightening irrationality of womanhood in the throes of passion – the object of masculine fear and fascination. The misogyny is present already, of course, in the primary source for the play, the Japanese, Buddhist legend of Dōjōji. The French critic Arsène Alexandre characterised Katsuragi as a woman destroyed by the ferocity of her own passions as much as by the mistreatment she has received at the hands of men.[141]

Charles Ricketts, who was impressed by the energy of Sadayakko's dancing, expressed in his journal his wish to see her in the role of Salome.[142] Sadayakko in fact did play Salome, although much later in Japan in 1915. The regal manner in which Sadayakko portrayed her was widely praised, but the novelist, play-wright and theatre critic Okada Yachiyo (sister of the theatre director Osanai Kaoru) complained that, beautiful and elegant as Sadayakko always looked, her Salome was not terrifying enough. She thought Sadayakko failed to convey any sense of Salome's superhuman and amoral will or her overpowering sensuality. On the other hand, the *shingeki* star Matsui Sumako, who had played Salome the year before Sadayakko, had not been, in Okada Yachiyo's view, as refined as a princess might be expected to be, but she had possessed a brutality, an animal-istic edge, which Sadayakko lacked.[143] Sadayakko's carefully controlled, stylised movements, the unfamiliarity of which seemed to her western audiences to make her portrayal of female passion all the more fearsome, was already starting to look stiff, formal and old-fashioned back home.

Hanako does not appear in the annals of modern Japanese theatre, and even Sadayakko has tended to be marginalised, as though her brand of hybrid theatre were something of an embarrassment not to be mistaken for serious art, a bastardised form of kabuki laced with sentiments superficially borrowed from western theatre to appeal to the public's appetite for novelty. But what has seemed in Japan to be their weakness – their lack of credentials as actresses – was also their strength, for they had the flexibility to adapt to the unusual circumstances in which they found themselves. It is ironic that the two actresses were acclaimed in the west for the manner in which their on-stage characters embraced death, for in life both Kawakami Sada and Ōta Hisa were remarkable survivors.

CHAPTER FIVE

From Foe to Friend: Geishas in Anglo-American Popular Culture before and after the Second World War

In his novel *Madame Chrysanthème* Pierre Loti stressed the lack, as he perceived it, of any commonality between the Japanese and people of the west. In his view, the Japanese were aliens with whom 'we have absolutely nothing in common'. Pierre, the author's alter ego and his narrator in *Madame Chrysanthème*, feels his 'wife' Chrysanthème possesses a soul 'of a different species' to his own.[1] Loti's polarisation of the Japanese and the peoples of the west is reflected in John Paris's first and most notorious novel *Kimono* (1921), the product of a time when tensions between Japan and western nations were intensifying. Captain the Honourable Geoffrey Barrington, who belongs to an ancient, aristocratic, but now impoverished, British family, unsuspectingly weds a charming Japanese heiress named Asako Fujinami, an orphan of mysterious origins who has had, to all appearances, a respectable upbringing in a French convent. Only later, when the honeymooning couple are in Japan on a visit, does Geoffrey discover – from a sexually predatory woman of Scottish and Japanese parentage, who becomes hell-bent on humiliating him after he rejects her advances – that his bride's wealth derives from the brothels of the Yoshiwara. Meanwhile, Asako's new-found Japanese relations scheme to separate her from her husband and seize control of both her person and her share of the family wealth. The author John Paris overloads the slight framework of a conventional melodramatic romance with his contentious cultural critique of the Japanese. The Yoshiwara functions as a symbol for all the dirty proclivities which the novel implies lie behind the meticulous façade of Japanese respectability: their rapaciousness, their ambitiousness, their furtiveness – and their superstitiousness, by which means they attempt to ward off the pangs of their guilty consciences.

28 Dust jacket design by 'Givo' for *Kimono,* by John Paris.

Passages from some of the more sensational reviews of the novel were reprinted on the flyleaf of the first American edition, including one from the *Nation and Athenaeum*, a British weekly journal with a Liberal-Labour leaning:

> Mr. Paris shows the Japanese to be institutional and racial fanatics, darkly conservative of their customs and religion, and of the special form of Oriental living and thinking which is their nature and inheritance; that they loathe and use us, that they will not and can not assimilate the good in our civilisation, and that they cling stubbornly to the good and the bad in their own.

The novelist Rose Macaulay's comments, originally published in the *London Daily News*, were also quoted:

> If Mr. John Paris has succeeded in ever so slightly damming the flood of pretty books about Japanese life by his story of that life as actually lived, he deserves our thanks. What is remarkable . . . is the careful study of a little-known people, at home, its habits and outlook. A repellent people, obviously, and not good to marry into. . . .

John Paris's portrayal of the Japanese as a cunning, duplicitous and, above all, ruthless race is worth noting, not only because the novel was much read, but because of the author's background. John Paris was the nom de plume of Frank Ashton-Gwatkin, a young up and coming British diplomat who specialised in Japan. In 1921, the same year as the publication of *Kimono*, Ashton-Gwatkin produced a confidential British Foreign Office memorandum entitled 'Racial Discrimination and Immigration', which acknowledged Japan to be 'the only non-white first-class Power' in the world, but declared nonetheless that

> however powerful Japan may eventually become, the white races will never be able to admit her equality. If she can enforce her claim she will become our superior; if she cannot enforce it she remains our inferior; but equal she can never be.[2]

In Ashton-Gwatkin's view the east was too different from the west for there not to be a titanic clash of fundamental moral and religious principles. The 'white and the coloured races cannot and will not amalgamate', Ashton-Gwatkin wrote in his memorandum. Subjugation was inevitable: 'one or the other must be the ruling caste'.[3]

Ashton-Gwatkin's first appointment on joining the British consular service had been to Yokohama as a student interpreter. In 1918 he had been posted to Singapore as an attaché with responsibility for Japanese affairs, after which he spent a couple of years in the Foreign Office's political intelligence department. He was attached to the entourage of Japan's Crown Prince Hirohito during his visit to Britain in May 1921. In the same year, Ashton-Gwatkin transferred permanently to the Foreign Office, where he served for nine years as a Japan specialist. He was a junior member of the British delegation to the Washington Conference of 1921–22, convened to negotiate a reduction of the naval strength of the US, Britain, Japan, France and Italy. One of the aims of the conference was to put the brakes on Japanese expansionist activity in the Far East. Ashton-Gwatkin was mistrustful of Japan's territorial ambitions in east Asia.[4]

Japan was an anomaly: a non-white empire-builder. Back in the middle of the nineteenth century, in an age of aggressive colonial rivalries between western powers, Japan had managed to survive a revolution in its system of government with its independence intact. But no sooner had the country emerged from its self-imposed isolation of more than two centuries than its new leaders were reigniting the country's age-old ambition of subjugating the Korean Peninsula. In the summer of 1894, Japan clashed with China over control of Korea. Japan's ensuing victories over Chinese forces both on land and at sea during the First Sino-Japanese War (1894–95) signalled the arrival of a new expansionist force on the Asian continent that was in competition with western imperialist powers for supremacy in vast swathes of Chinese territory.

This triggered fears of the 'yellow peril' in countries such as France and Germany, which had colonial interests of their own in China. In the United States, there was rising opposition to immigration from Japan, particularly in California.[5] The Immigration Act passed by the US Congress in 1924 did not just impose immigration quotas that heavily discriminated against Italians and eastern Europeans, especially Jews; it barred immigration altogether by 'aliens ineligible for citizenship', by which Asians were meant. The legislation was brought into effect by President Calvin Coolidge, who had authored, when Warren Harding's vice-president, an essay claiming the superiority of 'Nordic' blood and the degeneracy that would ensue from intermarriage between Caucasians and non-Caucasians.[6]

Britain, on the other hand, had been keen to contain Russia's encroaching influence in the north-eastern region of China, and to this end had entered into an alliance with Japan in 1902. The fact that Japan was an ally of Britain against Russia was reflected in the way the Russo-Japanese War of 1904–5 was reported in the British press. On 6 February 1904, just as hostilities were breaking out in the Far East, an article in the London *Times* put Japan, rather than Russia, on the side of modernity. *The Times* thought that the Asiatic component in the Russian national character, more so than in the Japanese, had a stronger tendency towards the tyranny and despotism which Europe had always associated with the

Orient. As another example of Japan's modernity, *The Times*, on 24 September 1904, praised Japan's efforts to administer its newly acquired colony Taiwan: there was enough evidence 'to convince even the most sceptical that Japan is not only an able colonizer but possesses quite exceptional aptitude for colonization'. But by the beginning of the 1920s, distrust of Japan was growing within the British Foreign Office. A consequence of the Washington Conference was the dissolution of the Anglo-Japanese Alliance, the advisability of continuing with which Ashton-Gwatkin too had privately questioned.[7]

Within the narrow novelistic scope of *Kimono*, Frank Ashton-Gwatkin, alias John Paris, reiterates his warning about getting into bed with unknown bedfellows. Asako Fujinami, the Japanese bride in the novel, is suspect from the outset not just because her wealth derives from a yet unidentified source. As a Japanese who has been uprooted from her native soil in earliest infancy and transplanted to France, she is problematical because she is Japanese by blood and western by upbringing. An orphan, she has no more knowledge of her origins than her not particularly erudite English husband.[8] The question the novel poses is whether nurture can totally suppress nature. The suggestion is that it cannot. However much Asako's European education has given her a veneer of western urbanity, her eyes remain those of 'the Oriental girl, a creature closer to the animals than we are, lit by instinct more often than by reason'.[9]

In practical terms, her hybrid nature means that her allegiance wavers at crucial moments. Before the idea of extending their honeymoon to include a stay in Japan comes up, Asako identifies herself completely with her western upbringing. She tells Geoffrey she would really rather be English or French than Japanese: ' "I don't want to be a Jap. I don't like them. They're ugly and spiteful. Why can't we choose what we are?" '[10] Once they get to Japan, however, and Asako meets her own kinsmen for the first time in her life, she starts to see herself as Japanese. Her new-found relations encourage Asako in this self-deception, while mocking her western ways behind her back. They are pleased to see how this begins to drive a wedge between Asako and her husband. Meanwhile, Asako predictably is unable to perceive the moral turpitude that lies hidden beneath the picturesque charm of the country.

In Japan Geoffrey too awakens to his wife's racial affiliation. Back in Britain, Asako had seemed merely exotic. Now he becomes aware of her as a member of an inferior race. When he overhears two western merchants who have obviously spent a long time in Japan making derogatory remarks about westerners who marry Japanese women, Geoffrey is assailed with doubts. He is reminded of those promising white officers in India who had ruined their careers by 'pawn[ing] their lives to yellow girls'. Was he not likewise marked out as a failure now by having become the 'husband of a coloured woman'?[11]

Geoffrey's ambivalent feelings towards Asako are never satisfactorily resolved. When he learns that her family make their money from brothels in the Yoshiwara quarter, his instinct is to take Asako back with him to England immediately and have nothing more to do with her accursed clan. But he is too late. Asako's relations have already poisoned her mind against him. They have been feeding her with anti-western invectives, disparaging all westerners for being 'notoriously treacherous to women' and caring only about 'money and material things'. They ridicule Asako for believing that Geoffrey could really have been in love with a woman of a different race to his own, and they denounce mixed marriages as 'an offence against nature'.[12] As the proverb says, it takes one to know one. John Paris implies that all the nasty accusations which Asako's spiteful relatives use to malign Geoffrey could equally be levelled against them. Asako meanwhile consoles herself with the thought that at least 'she was among her father's people who loved her and understood her'.[13] Her one desire now is to transform herself completely into a Japanese person. Geoffrey decides she has indeed succeeded: Asako has become 'a person absolutely different from himself, a visitant from another sphere'.[14] He agrees to an annulment of their marriage and returns to England alone.

At this point, the focus of the novel switches to Asako. Inevitably her touching, naïve faith in her Japanese family is betrayed. Once they have her in their grasp, they reveal their true colours. Asako is robbed of her independence and her privacy. She is subsumed into the intricate network of Japanese social and family life. She is made to assume chores which reinforce her junior status in the family hierarchy – tasks, like scrubbing Mrs Fujinami's back in the bath, which one suspects readers of the novel are expected to feel are demeaning to a person such as Asako, brought up in the west with a proper awareness of her own dignity. Asako loses control over her possessions, and her male relations scheme to marry her off advantageously so that her share of the Fujinami fortune will remain in the family. The women of the household sneer at her and call her a *rashamen*, saying 'she smelt like a European.'[15]

Rabid as the anti-western prejudices of the Japanese characters are in *Kimono*, the language used to critique Japanese culture is also extreme – although, in the latter case, the author does not doubt that such harshness is justified. A worldly British character in the novel explains to his fellow countrywoman that a Japanese man did not bother indulging in the fantasy that he might find love in the Yoshiwara quarter, but bought a woman to satisfy his lust in the matter-of-fact way a farmer in other countries might purchase a cow.[16] Elsewhere in the novel, the author John Paris uses as his mouthpiece Asako's deceased father, who is supposed to have written an inflammatory polemic castigating the Japanese for deluding themselves into believing they had joined the advanced races of the world when they were in fact still wallowing in barbarism. According to Asako's father, the Japanese had to 'denounce the slavery of ancestor-worship, and escape from the rule of the dead', if they were to escape their savage condition.[17] There was no contest when it came to the superiority of the enlightened idealism of the west over the benighted, befuddled thinking of the Japanese and the little niceties of Japanese etiquette which for them passed as civilisation. The Japanese lacked principles to guide their conduct in both public and private affairs. According to Asako's father, it was time for the Japanese, for their own sake, to acknowledge their immaturity and humbly espouse the transcendental truths that had been revealed to humankind by the most sublime philosophers and poets of the west.[18]

Asako is converted by her father's book to his way of thinking, although – simpleton that she is – there remains more than a little suspicion that this is the result not so much of rational reflection on her part as of her sentimental attachment to the father who had died while she was still an infant. In any case, Asako becomes rapidly disaffected with her Japanese relations. This signals the beginning of her rehabilitation. At least in Asako's case, there is still the possibility of change. But, in John Paris's view, a person born of parents belonging to two different races cannot ever understand the concept of loyalty. Products of 'the blasphemy of mixed marriages' do not, nor can they ever, belong anywhere. They do not respect anybody's traditions. They inhabit a twilight realm which does not have 'an acre of dry ground for its heritage or any concrete symbol of its soul'.[19] Yaé Smith, who precipitates the crisis in the Barringtons' marriage by trying to seduce Geoffrey and then giving away the secret about the Fujinami clan's fortune, is representative of this class. She is totally narcissistic, self-centred and irresponsible.

Asako falls deeper into trouble the further she is sucked into Japanese society. The Fujinami family lawyer tries to take advantage of her vulnerability. When he is found murdered, Asako is arrested as the prime suspect and maltreated by the brutal Japanese police. She is only rescued from her dire predicament by the intervention of her highly placed friends – the wife of the British ambassador to Japan and Countess Saito, the wife of the former Japanese ambassador to Britain. Geoffrey writes through intermediaries that he would like Asako to return to him. Now that Asako has learnt her lesson the hard way, he is presumably able to take her back. The Japanese diplomat Count Saito, on the other hand, kindly though he is to Asako in person, sees her as a potential propaganda tool. He tries to persuade her that even when she is back in Britain, her loyalty must remain with Japan. It is the urbane Count Saito who articulates Japan's aspirations to world power, the threat Frank Ashton-Gwatkin believed Japan posed to western nations. ' "Japan is proud to be England's younger brother",' he tells Asako, 'but the elder brother must not take all the inheritance. He must be content to share. For perhaps he will not always be the strong one. . . . Already the people of Asia are saying, Why should these white men rule over us? They cannot rule themselves; . . . their time is over and past. Then, when the white rulers are pushed out of Asia, Japan will become very strong indeed.'[20]

Asako, however, has had enough of being Japanese. She declares she ' "could never like Japan" ' now. 'Never' is a word that recurs over and over again in *Kimono*: the rejection of the other must be absolute and final. At the point when Asako and Geoffrey become most estranged from one another, she tells Geoffrey, ' "I am Japanese. You are English. You can never really love me." '[21] When Asako begins to develop doubts whether she could – or ought to – embrace the Japanese way of life, her kinswoman Sadako snaps back at her that she had already made her choice: ' "You can never be English again." '[22] Now, at the end of the novel, Asako informs Count Saito that her aversion to anything Japanese is absolute.

In 1946 *Kimono* was reissued as a paperback in Britain and the United States. In the intervening quarter of a century since the novel's initial publication, the savagery of Japan's invasion of China, followed by the ferocity of the Pacific War, cast the preoccupations of Paris's novel into the shade. Still, the racial antagonism depicted in *Kimono* was an element in the conflict between Japan and western forces. The intense enmity of the Allied powers and Japan throughout the Pacific War was coloured by virulent racism that denied the notion of a common humanity and led each side to vilify the enemy as less than human. Assumptions of racial superiority were also behind much of Japan's attitude to the Asian countries it overran. The concept of the Greater East Asia Co-prosperity Sphere (*Dai-tōa-kyōei-ken*), which appears to have crystallised in the minds of Japan's wartime ministers in the late 1930s, trumpeted an idealistic pan-Asian community of countries liberated by Japan from the yoke of western imperialism and now united by common aims, but in reality it served as a smoke-screen to disguise the arrogance and brutality of Japanese conduct towards the peoples of east and south-east Asia.[23]

Japanese propaganda characterised Americans and the British as 'savages' – the term *kichiku* was comprised of the Chinese ideographs signifying 'ogre' (*oni*) and 'beast' (*chikushō*). On the Allied side, Pearl Harbor etched the association of the Japanese with treachery into the American psyche. The bitter fighting that took place, island by island through the Pacific, was bloody, and the Japanese treatment of prisoners, whether military or civilian, was frequently vicious. News of atrocities perpetrated against captured Allied soldiers was widely reported in the west, reinforcing traditional western prejudices about the inherent barbarity, sadism, cruelty and deviousness of the eastern races – prejudices which had once been applied equally to the Chinese and Japanese but were now focused mainly on the latter. As animosity towards the Japanese increased in the United States, so did sympathy for the Chinese. With Franklin D. Roosevelt's administration backing up the Nationalist government of Chaing Kai-shek in China, the official American position was that the Chinese people stood shoulder to shoulder with Americans against Japanese tyranny. The Chinese were depicted as a courteous and civilised race of independent people who upheld liberty and all other democratic principles sacred to American hearts.[24]

There was a marked difference in the United States in the way the Japanese were perceived compared to the populace of the two other Axis countries. Whereas the American media tended to identify the enemy in Europe as the 'Nazis', rather than the German people in general, no such distinction was made when it came to the enemy in the Pacific. Hollywood films were willing to contemplate the idea of the 'good German', but the term 'Japs' suggested that the entire Japanese race was America's enemy. The old western prejudice that individuality was absent among the Japanese race – that not only were they barely distinguishable from each other in appearance, but that they acted as one according to some kind of herd instinct – contributed to this sentiment.[25] In the United States and Canada, this guilt-by-race stigmatisation was one of the factors which led to citizens of Japanese descent being marked out as potential enemies of the state and incarcerated in internment camps.

In the intolerable conditions of the tropical jungle, it was even easier to depersonalise – to dehumanise – the enemy. When the legendary American war correspondent Ernie Pyle was transferred in February 1945 from Europe to the Pacific theatre of war, he wrote back home:

> In Europe we felt that our enemies, horrible and deadly as they were, were still people. But out here I soon gathered that the Japanese were looked upon as something subhuman or repulsive; the way some people feel about cockroaches or mice.[26]

The portrayal of the Japanese as yellow monkeys, apes and gorillas was widespread in the American and British press. It was also the standard way in which the Japanese were caricatured by frontline troops. Vermin imagery (rats, especially) aided in the rhetoric of annihilation. It was applied not merely to Japanese combat troops, but eventually to the civilian population of Japanese cities, which became the targets of American fire-bombing.[27] The well-publicised tendency of Japanese soldiers to fight to the death was labelled fanatical, but neither were Allied officers inclined to take many Japanese prisoners of war. The blanket slaughter of Japanese combatants seemed no more than just retribution for the horrors inflicted on Allied servicemen by the Japanese.[28]

In the light of the bitter racist rhetoric which was exchanged by both sides during the Second World War, it was perhaps surprising that the post-war occupation of Japan by Allied forces, led by the Americans, turned out to be as free of violence and rancour as it was. The historian John Dower has suggested that a reinterpretation by both Americans and the Japanese of old stereotypes of the 'other' under new peacetime conditions may have aided this easing of racial tensions. The American image of the Japanese as monkeys, children or madmen was readily modifiable to embrace the notion that they could be tamed, taught and treated. Meanwhile, the traditional Japanese idea of hierarchy helped the country's post-war leaders to accept the reality of America's dominant position in the world.[29] Be that as it may, after years of food shortages and with most major cities (with the exception of Kyōto) now reduced to cinders by Allied bombing, the general populace of Japan was too exhausted and hungry – too stunned by the shattering of the illusion of a divinely led empire which they had been fed for decades by their political and military rulers – to be in a mood to express active resentment of the forces of occupation.

The days which preceded the arrival of the first American occupation troops, which took place on 26 August 1945, were, nonetheless, a period of great uncertainty for the Japanese. The chief concern of Japan's immediate post-war cabinet was the preservation of the national polity (*kokutai*) as embodied specifically in the Imperial Throne and, in order that this might be achieved, the emperor's ministers were willing to co-operate with the occupation. On the other hand, Japanese officials who had inside knowledge of the atrocities committed by their soldiers abroad feared that Japan's civilian population now faced a similar fate. Rape was a particular worry, not just on account of the threat it posed to the safety of individual women, but (perhaps more importantly to government ministers) because there was apprehension that rumours of Japanese women being raped by occupation soldiers might antagonise volatile sections of the population (especially former Japanese military officers and demobbed servicemen) and stir up hostility to the presence of foreign troops in the country. The Japanese public had, after all, been taught for years to expect nothing but savagery from American and British soldiers. The initial reaction of the governor of the prefecture of Kanagawa, where Yokohama and the important naval port of Yokosuka are located, was to advise all female local government employees to leave the cities and seek refuge in the countryside. This sort of alarmist talk sparked off a great deal of panic, and several communities within the prefecture ordered the evacuation of their womenfolk.[30]

The response of the new prime minister Prince Higashikuni Naruhiko's cabinet was led by the Minister of State Prince Konoe Fumimarō (himself a former prime minister): this was to agree that prostitutes were to become the first line of defence in the safeguarding of the virtue of respectable women and girls. As early as 18 August 1945, three days after the Shōwa Emperor (Hirohito) announced in a public broadcast to the Japanese people that Japan was accepting the Potsdam Agreement of 2 July 1945, effectively surrendering to the Allied forces, the Japanese Home Ministry issued instructions to prefectural governors to begin putting into place plans for 'recreational facilities' or 'comfort stations' (*ian shisetsu*) in locations where occupation troops were likely to be posted. The primary function of these facilities was to provide prostitutes for the use of the soldiers. The prostitutes were to be recruited from among the legion of women who already belonged to this underclass: geishas, licensed and unlicensed prostitutes, waitresses and female bar workers.[31]

The exploitation of women in the name of patriotism was nothing new. Since the 1930s, the Japanese military had supplied prostitutes (called *ianfu*, or 'comfort women') to its forces out in its theatres of battle. The practice had intensified after the horrific Japanese attack on Nanking (Nanjing) in 1937. Geishas and prostitutes were shipped out from Japan, ostensibly to prevent the further brutalisation of local populations, although there is no indication that this was the actual effect. Fukuda Toshiko, a Shin-yoshiwara restaurateur, remembered that when the quarter was instructed in 1941 to supply its quota of prospective 'comfort women', some prostitutes were enticed into volunteering by the promise that the debts they owed to the proprietor of their brothel would be cancelled.[32] Only around 10 per cent of all 'comfort women' attached to the Japanese military during the war were actually Japanese, however. The rest were nationals of subjugated countries. Sexually inexperienced women, thought to be least likely to have been in contact with venereal disease, were forced into this form of sexual slavery. Most were Koreans, but a proportion was made up of Chinese, Burmese, Vietnamese and Dutch women, as well as Filipinas, Indonesians, Malayans and Formosans. Thousands of these comfort women were also sent to Japanese military camps on home territory, for example on the island of Okinawa.[33]

The difficulties of life in post-war Japan, particularly in urban areas, meant that the prospect of free food and shelter was enough to lure many destitute women to work in brothels. In Tōkyō, the Metropolitan Police liaised with the city's restaurateurs' association, as well as with guilds and associations variously representing proprietors of geisha houses, *machiai* teahouses, *kashizashiki*, and different types of brothels, both licensed and unlicensed. On 23 August 1945, a new association was set up to provide 'special recreational facilities' for occupation troops. It was soon renamed the Recreation and Amusement Association, known by its acronym RAA. Because the ostensible purpose of the new recreational facilities was not to make money but to provide frontline defence of a sexual kind to protect the virtue of the rest of Japanese womanhood, the prostitutes were promised a bigger cut of takings than had hitherto been the norm in the city's pleasure districts. It was common practice for brothel propri-etors to appropriate three-quarters of a woman's earnings, on top of which they demanded payment for lodging, board, clothes and other necessities. The RAA advocated a 50:50 split instead. This was a slightly more advantageous arrange-ment for the women, but there still remained room for abuse inasmuch as clients did not pay the women directly for their services (supposedly so that the women would not feel they had been turned into some kind of commodity) but bought tickets instead, which they handed in to the prostitutes, who were later paid by office staff according to the number of tickets they had amassed.[34]

Although the first women recruited by the RAA were professional sex workers, by the end of September – with the burgeoning of brothels, dance halls and beer halls catering to occupation servicemen (as well as a couple of exclu-sive restaurants intended for the use of high-ranking officers) – an increasing number of ordinary women were swelling the ranks of the staff at these estab-lishments. Some privately run places were extorting more and more money from their prostitutes supposedly for rent, food, clothes, cosmetics, and necessary medicines. Women begged chocolates, food rations, cigarettes and other goods from GIs, and sold them on the black market to supplement their income.[35]

The first RAA establishment was Babe's Garden, known in Japanese as the Komachi'en, a former restaurant located in the Ōmori Kaigan district, an area straddling the boroughs of Shinagawa and Ōta in the southern part of the city of Tōkyō, on the main route between the capital and the ports of Yokohama and Yokosuka. It was already prepared for business when the first advance troops of the occupation arrived in Japan on 28 August 1945. Within two months, nine more 'recreational facilities' had sprung up in its vicinity. The joints clustered in the area known as 'Riverside' were also popular among GIs. This had formerly been the old pleasure district of Mukōjima, on the opposite bank of the Sumida River from Asakusa, with its famous temple and sprawling entertainment quarter. Some of Mukōjima's geishas appear to have been unwilling to appear in front of foreigners. When *machiai* teahouses, geisha houses and bars – all of which had been ordered to suspend business during the last years of the war – were permitted by the Metropolitan Police in October 1945 to reopen, they were told to supply geishas regardless of the nationality of the men who asked for them. As it happened, many former legalised pleasure quarters, the Shin-yoshiwara and Shinagawa for example, as well as unofficial pleasure districts such as Kameido and Fukagawa, were restricted to foreign servicemen anyway. The Shin-yoshiwara had only seven buildings left standing. The air raid on Tōkyō which took place on the night of 9–10 March 1945 had destroyed a total of 280 businesses in the quarter. Of the seven surviving buildings, four were briefly reopened as brothels during August, only to shut once the end of the war was declared. With the start of the occupation, all seven buildings were turned into 'recreation facilities' for occupation troops. One was designated for the use of black servicemen; another for whites; while yet another was exclusively reserved for the use of officers.

Whilst the sort of widespread rape and pillage which Japanese authorities had feared at the start of the occupation did not materialise, there were, nonetheless, a substantial number of crimes committed by members of the occupation forces against local people, among them violence towards women. According to Fukuda Toshiko, the proprietress of a Shin-yoshiwara teahouse, rape was committed by American GIs in that district. Japanese news media were banned from reporting such incidents. When the American press suggested that persistent stories of occupation servicemen committing violent crimes were being served up by the Japanese as anti-American propaganda, an American serviceman stationed in Japan wrote in anonymously to *Time* magazine swearing that such crimes as rape did take place, since American soldiers barely considered the Japanese to be fellow human beings (12 November 1945). Rape continued to be a problem around US military bases throughout the occupation, and still remains a contentious issue between US troops stationed at bases in Japan (especially on Okinawa) and local inhabitants.[36]

Commanding officers with the American troops were not particularly opposed to their men using RAA brothels. Lieutenant General Walter Krueger, commander of the Sixth Army, which had fought its way up the Philippines, told Colonel Crawford F. Sams, Chief of the Public Health and Welfare Section of the occupation's General Headquarters in Tōkyō, that he was not going to stand in the way of his boys celebrating their victory with a bit of fun after all they had been through in the mosquito-ridden jungles of south-east Asia. The women in the brothels were referred to in English as 'serving ladies' or 'organised prostitutes', to distinguish them from unregistered prostitutes and streetwalkers. American military police were called out to maintain order among servicemen waiting their turn at these establishments. When it came to prostitution and the welfare of American soldiers, Crawford Sams's chief worry was not the state of his men's morals, but (as it had been in the nineteenth century) venereal disease. Men were required to cleanse themselves after sex at so-called 'prophylactic stations', which were set up near the brothels – Fukuda Toshiko remembered the Nissen hut which had been constructed for this purpose in the Shin-yoshiwara quarter. Men were also issued with sanitation kits. It was only when a particular brothel began showing signs of a high rate of transmission of venereal disease that it would be declared off limits to US military personnel.[37]

There was a good deal of tacit collusion between General Headquarters and Japanese authorities in relation to prostitution. Although the occupation's broad objectives were the dismantling of the Japanese empire, the demilitarisation of its institutions and the introduction of democratic reforms, the policy of GHQ was to implement changes not by means of direct military rule, but indirectly through guidance and instructions issued to Japan's civil administration. But GHQ also had to be mindful of public opinion back in America. There was the need to keep grand-standing politicians and policymakers in Washington at bay. Japan's notorious system of licensed prostitution was one of those aspects of the country's social life which most Americans back home found objectionable, not least because thousands of their menfolk were now serving in Japan. In January 1946, GHQ sent a memorandum to the Japanese government calling for the abolition of all laws and regulations related to legal prostitution, on the grounds that they were contrary to the principles of democracy. The government obliged, and on 20 February scrapped all legislation governing the practice of licensed prostitution. This move, however, did not lead to a decrease in prostitution in the country. Prostitution was still allowed if it was a woman's only means of support and so long as she was not being coerced into it. Besides, proprietors of former brothels and similar establish-ments were unofficially informed as early as January of the impending changes, and told to reopen their businesses as *settaisho*, or reception halls. They were allowed to continue employing women, who were now to be known as 'reception women' (*settaifu*); they were still, de facto, prostitutes.[38]

The rate of infection with venereal disease among American servicemen did not decrease. Meanwhile, chaplains attached to occupation troops complained that not enough was being done to safeguard the morals of the men. Finally, in March, all brothels and 'comfort stations' were declared off limits to occupation personnel. The Shin-yoshiwara, along with the other former pleasure quarters which had been turned over to the exclusive use of occupation servicemen, was now permitted to receive Japanese clients. All twenty-one RAA establishments closed on 27 March 1946, although as an organisation the RAA survived until 1949. The 55,000 women employed by the RAA (at the height of its popularity it was employing up to 70,000 women) were thrown out of work. Many became streetwalkers, vying with each other for the custom of foreigners.[39]

Streetwalkers had been a visible presence from the very beginning of the occupation. They were derogatorily called *pan-pan* girls by their fellow

Japanese. The term *pan-pan* was sometimes applied to prostitutes in general, a distinction being made between the *yōpan*, who went with westerners, and the *wapan*, who only saw Japanese men. Women who went with only one man were called *onrī* in Japanese from the English word 'only'. There are several theories about the derivation of the term *pan-pan*, some tracing its origins to Japanese army slang brought back from south-east Asia. But it seems more likely that *pan-pan* was a Japanese rendition of the English 'pompom' or 'pompon'. Harold S. Williams, the author of numerous books and articles on the history and experience of foreigners living in Japan, thought it had been American GIs who had come up with the term early on in the occupation to refer to Japanese street-walkers.[40] What is less certain is whether 'pom-pom', as a commonly used onomatopoeic rendition of the sound of automatic gunfire, referred to the use to which these women were put, or it was the women's breasts which were being likened to the cheerleader's pair of tufted accessories – or whether there was some residual western cultural memory at work of the large pompon-like bunches of chrysanthemums Japanese women were supposed to wear on either side of their heads according to the popular western stereotype.

Pan-pan girls were heavily stigmatised by their fellow Japanese. They were despised for going about openly with foreign servicemen. They were reviled for the way they dressed in swanky western clothes and for wearing heavy western-style make-up. They were scorned for their hedonistic attitude to life, and secretly envied for the covetable American goods they carried about with them. They were hated for their desperate self-reliance, for their rejection of the defeated, emasculated Japanese male, for their defiance of the conventions of a social order now reduced to a state of total disarray. The post-war period saw the emergence of strong, independent women. It is a sad irony that prostitution was one of those areas in which they were most in evidence. If there was one area of reform General Douglas MacArthur, Supreme Commander for the Allied Powers in Japan, was particularly proud of having introduced to Japan, it was the contribution he felt he was making to the emancipation of Japanese women from the fetters of feudalism. For the first time in the history of Japan, women were given both the right to run for public office and the right to vote in elections. When the first post-war election to the House of Representatives, the lower house of the Japanese Diet, was held on 10 April 1946, 39 out of a total of 466 seats went to women. But it was above all else the hardships of wartime and of the immediate post-war period which gave women their strength. Innumerable families were left without their men, and it was often the women who had to shoulder the responsibility of supporting their more vulnerable relations at a time when there was severe economic disruption and very few opportunities for work. On 19 December 1946, the first union of female workers was formed in the Shin-yoshiwara quarter to protect the health and welfare of its members. Among streetwalkers, organised gangs were beginning to emerge, headed by one of their own, offering in exchange for protection money some defence against male racketeers – as well as scaring off other women trying to encroach upon their patch.[41]

New contradictions began to appear in GHQ's policy on prostitution. Having ordered the abolition of Japan's system of licensed prostitution, the US military authorities remained fearful of the spread of venereal disease among their men. To combat the threat, they now implemented round-ups of streetwalkers, who were sent on the spot to VD hospitals for genital examinations. These draconian measures unfortunately violated the civil liberties not only of the prostitutes but of ordinary women as well. Often caught up by mistake in these seizures, they too were forced to undergo the horrors of an examination. The round-ups were conducted by American military police until September 1949, after which Japanese authorities took over full responsibility for them. They occurred not just in Tōkyō but across the country.[42]

The need was felt at GHQ for further discouragement of openly promiscuous behaviour between occupation personnel and local women. In March 1946 an anti-fraternisation order was issued to the men attached to the US Eighth Army based in Yokohama. They were forbidden to kiss Japanese women in public, to take them to restaurants, or to allow them to ride in US military vehicles. Yet no prohibition was put on seeing women in the privacy of their homes, and violations of the off-limits rule itself were also often condoned, so long as there was no substantial rise in the number of cases of VD.[43]

Along with venereal disease, the aspect of organised prostitution which had concerned GHQ the most was the Japanese practice of tying prostitutes to their brothels with crippling loans. With post-war inflation spiralling out of control and the difficulty of procuring food in city districts, women and girls were still being sold into prostitution in exchange for loans (boys were being sold as labourers); although the burden of debt which prostitutes were being made to carry was not quite as heavy as it had been in the days before the war. A split was becoming evident within GHQ, however, between the reformists, on the one hand, whose goal remained the comprehensive transformation of Japanese institutions, society and culture, and military pragmatists, on the other, who were willing to see old Japanese customs remain in place if this served the purpose of quickly building up Japan as an effective bulwark against the new perceived international enemy – communism. GHQ became increasingly preoccupied with the threat of communism after the Communists finally succeeded in wresting control of China away from the Kuomingtang (Nationalist) Party, establishing the People's Republic in 1949. Apart from the geopolitical situation, prostitution continued to satisfy a need among occupation servicemen.

Brothel owners understood that the Americans were primarily concerned about the coercion to which the women were subjected. They found it in their own interest not to transgress too blatantly on such issues. The practice of forced indentured labour did not, however, disappear. Several notorious cases involving young women came to light in the mid-1950s, contributing to a growing revulsion among the Japanese public against organised prostitution. But the Japanese police continued to favour the idea of having approved districts in which prostitution could operate. For one thing, this made it easier for authorities to test prostitutes for disease, as GHQ demanded. Former brothels and *kashizashiki* which had turned into *settaisho* were re-designated as 'special restaurants' (*tokushu inshokuten*) in September 1946.[44] They were required to have a bar or a couple of tables for the look of the thing, and the prostitutes were now officially classified as restaurant employees. They were not to be forced into working for one particular establishment, or tied down by means of a loan of money. In November, zoning was introduced: the areas in which these 'special restaurants' were clustered (and prostitution tacitly tolerated) were marked out in red on police maps and became known as *akasen chitai* (red-line zones). By 1950, there were seventeen of these zones in Tōkyō. They tended to overlap with the old familiar pleasure quarters and districts around the capital. In distinction to the 'red-line zones', the term *aosen chitai* (blue-line zones) was applied to locations where there was a concentration of inns and cheap eateries operating illegally as brothels. Places where streetwalkers congregated were called *shirosen chitai* (white-line zones), but many people used *aosen chitai* to refer generally to areas where all kinds of unauthorised prostitution were to be found.[45]

The 1950s saw little decrease in the numbers of women involved in prostitution, whether they were plying their trade to foreigners or to fellow Japanese. As the economy of the country underwent cycles of upheaval and restructuring during the late 1940s and into the 1950s, women often had to bear the brunt of financial hardship. Women migrated from depressed agricultural and fishing communities seeking jobs in factories in towns and cities, but as working-class women could already attest, female employees were heavily discriminated against, and rarely treated in parity with their male co-workers, even when they were chief breadwinner of the family. Many women who felt they had no other option but to resort to prostitution in order to make ends meet preferred to work legally in the red-line zones, and they opposed the anti-prostitution measures which were being proposed by female Diet members in the years between 1953 and 1956. They were dismayed that politicians had so little understanding of the precariousness of their existence. They objected to being penalised by legislation ostensibly aimed at eradicating institutions which fostered prostitution and they dreaded the probability that the closure of tolerated 'special restaurants' would put them at the mercy of the vicious pimps and gangsters who operated in the blue-line and white-line zones. The Anti-Prostitution Act nonetheless became law on 24 May 1956, without adequate provisions to protect former prostitutes. It came into force a year later, but only when infringements of the new law became a prosecutable offence in the spring of 1958 (six years after the end of the occupation) did the *akasen chitai* – the red-line zones – disappear for good.[46]

Elliott Chaze's *The Stainless Steel Kimono*, published two years after the end of the war, captures the awkwardness of relations between victors and vanquished in the early months of the occupation. A reporter with the Associated Press before the war, Chaze was a member of a paratroop division posted to a camp near the city of Sendai in the north-eastern prefecture of Miyagi in 1945. Chaze does not pretend to feel any empathy for these people who had until so recently been the enemy, and were now a burdensome responsibility that kept US troops from being able to return to their civilian lives back home. Chaze's contempt for the Japanese is reflected in the first paragraph of his foreword to the book:

> I believe the reaction of most occupation troops in Japan is that of a person suddenly handed a brimming bedpan and told to guard its contents carefully. . . . His initial impulse is to remain as aloof from the Japanese as possible. But as time and circumstance prove this unworkable, the occupation troops devise their own methods for forgetting that the thing entrusted to them seems hardly worth the trouble.[47]

Chaze's resentment at being stuck in Japan makes him irritated by all that is foreign about the country – the sheer Japanese-ness of everything. He finds the apathy of Japanese men maddening. Stupefied by the collapse of their world and by their hunger, they stand silently outside the GIs' mess-hall window, 'mak[ing] weak embarrassed faces, silently apologizing for the discomfort they cause the eaters within, unable to look away from the food and ashamed of their weakness.'[48] The women are unappealing, and they are everywhere the Americans are: in the nightclubs, even at the ski lodge the Americans have taken over as a leisure facility for themselves. The girls at the ski lodge call themselves 'room girls', and two 'fat-eyed' specimens of the type give the narrator's pal Cole a 'Jap rubdown', giggling as they slap and punch his naked flesh. The narrator finds more 'room girls' in the communal bath and the communal lavatory. ' "[T]here's no false modesty about sex in Japan",' says a lieutenant who acts as though he is totally au fait with the customs of the natives. But the narrator is unsure, despite the lieutenant's hearty reassurances. ' "There doesn't seem to be any kind of modesty",' he mutters back.[49] Yet he is in no personal danger of succumbing to lusty impulses, for Japanese women do not arouse any in him. In his eyes Japanese women are simply not attractive, nor does their forwardness – their lack of 'false modesty' – have any charm. Elsewhere in the book, Cole complains that you just cannot get rid of a Japanese woman. He relates how he had once 'exchanged chocolate and chewing gum for the intimate affections of a Japanese girl'. But when he stopped visiting her, she kept coming over to his barracks to see him. Cole would hear her wooden *geta* clip-clopping down the asphalt-floored corridor, sounding 'like a herd of peg-legged horses'. If he threw her out of his sleeping bag, she would sit all night on the cold floor next to his cot, and he would have to lie in the sleeping bag listening to the rattling of her little gold teeth.[50] The horrible teeth of Japanese women keep reappearing throughout Chaze's book like the theme of a continuing nightmare: the 'monkey-like dame' in the Japanese nightclub has four stainless steel ones, in each of which the narrator can see the reflection of her match whenever she lights up a cigarette. This post-war Japan is a world of shifting, unreal images that multiply ad nauseam leaving the narrator feeling queasy and wanting to retch.[51]

The paratroopers in Chaze's stories act as they think victors should, swaggering, treating the locals with high-handed condescension mixed with contempt. They go and have a look at one of those brothels intended for the Americans, where kimono-clad girls sit in a 'glass cage' in full view of the GIs outside. The men have an altercation there with another group of American servicemen. Fists and furniture are thrown around, and the interior of the house gets smashed up. On another occasion, the narrator and his chums swindle a bunch of unsuspecting Japanese – the locals seem fair game for extortion to them. One of them approaches a potential victim and offers to sell him his army-issue comforter. It is a bitterly cold winter, and the victim usually cannot resist the temptation of a quilted bedcover. Once the transaction has been made, the seller disappears and the other two Americans turn up, pretending to be military police. They accuse the terrified purchaser of being in unlawful possession of US army goods and get the comforter back, along with a little 'protection bonus' for promising not to report the incident. This ruse is repeated five times before they run into a real MP, whose clutches they escape by rapid flight. The experience makes the narrator aware of his mixed feelings towards the people the Allies had just defeated. 'It would be dishonest to say that we didn't get a certain satisfaction from cheating the Japanese,' he confesses. After all, they had been trained to kill Japanese, and they had been, as the narrator puts it, 'shampooed regularly with anti-Jap propaganda'. But he knows that by treating the Japanese like scum, they were acting like scum themselves.[52]

Then the impossible happens, and another of the narrator's buddies, Wagman this time, falls in love with one of these Japs. She is only a third-rate singer hired as Saturday night entertainment to perform in the company recreation room. Wagman arranges with her father to pay 1,500 yen a month to live with her on weekends and any other time he can get away from camp. When he is with her, he treats her brusquely and is constantly finding fault with her. She, in turn, is always asking him ' "You pistoff?" ' These appear to be the only English words she knows. She seems to need to check regularly that she has not offended him somehow. It is as though she expects to be discarded at a moment's notice. She is aware, the narrator notes, that she is 'something to be apologized for'. She is always apologising. When Wagman talks about having to return eventually to the United States, she cries and clings to him. Wagman discovers he enjoys this: it makes him feel good to be wanted.

It is impossible to tell what the woman's true feelings really are – whether her affections are sincere or whether she just needs the money. The only thing that is clear is that she is willing to risk quite a lot in terms of her own personal safety by doing the things she does. A friend of hers has had her head and face beaten to a pulp and her breasts burnt with matches for sleeping with Americans. As for Wagman, he actually feels quite tenderly towards his Japanese girl, only he is ashamed of this and acts tough to cover it up. But when she is attacked by some Japanese men, the best thing he can think of doing, to shield her from further violence, is not to fight back, not to use the pistol he flourishes in front of the narrator in a show of bravado, but to leave her. It is a lopsided relationship from the start, tainted by the fact that it is a commercial transaction: Wagman feels obliged to act the part of the indifferent purchaser; the girl is obliged as her end of the bargain to make sure he is not unhappy. Her own happiness does not come into the transaction, yet Wagman does do the honourable thing by her. The irony is that the best thing he can think of doing for her is the one thing that is going to make her deeply unhappy.[53]

Elliott Chaze's book reflects the ambivalent attitude of the occupation troops towards the people who had until so recently been the hated, barely human enemy but had now turned into America's ward. The very docility of the Japanese seems almost an affront, as though it puts the onus of behaving in a civilised manner upon the Americans, forcing them to contain their feelings of animosity, anger and desire for revenge instead of being free to act the part of the victors and treat the Japanese with the roughness that a defeated enemy deserves. In contrast to Chaze's *The Stainless Steel Kimono*, the hugely successful Broadway play *The Teahouse of the August Moon* served up a much rosier picture of the relationship between occupier and occupied. The play, for which the playwright John Patrick won the 1954 Pulitzer Prize for Drama, was based on a 1951 novel of the same title by Vern Sneider. The play ran from October 1953 to March 1956, garnering the 1954 Antoinette Perry (Tony) Award for best actor (David Wayne in the role of the Okinawan interpreter Sakini), best play, and best scenic design. It also won the 1953–54 New York Drama Critics' Circle Award for Best American Play of the Year. In 1956 Patrick adapted his play for the screen, with Marlon Brando in yellow-face taking over the role of Sakini, which on Broadway had been played by David Wayne, Burgess Meredith and Eli Wallach.

In *The Teahouse of the August Moon*, set on the southern island of Okinawa, the relationship between the occupation forces and the locals is smooth. Ironically, this relationship, in reality, was even more one-sided on Okinawa than in Japan itself. After the Second World War, Okinawa – one of the main islands comprising the Ryūkyū Islands (administratively known as the Nansei Shotō), the archipelago that stretches between Taiwan and the southern tip of the western Japanese island of Kyūshū – was under the direct control of an American military government (which, incidentally, the author of the original novel, Vern Sneider, worked for).[54] The island was invaded by American forces towards the end of the war. The assault on Okinawa was launched on 1 April 1945, and the battle for the island lasted until 23 June, when the main body of the Japanese military resistance on Okinawa finally crumbled with the suicide of the commander of the Japanese forces there, Ushijima Mitsuru.

The Americans are just the latest in a long line of invaders of the island, as Sakini, the Okinawan interpreter, notes in his prologue which opens John Patrick's play. Among these conquerors, Sakini lists fourteenth-century Chinese pirates and eighteenth-century Japanese warlords.[55] Historically, the Ryūkyū Islands had paid tribute to the imperial courts of China since the middle of the fourteenth century. In 1609 – rather than in the eighteenth century – the islands were conquered by the lord (*daimyō*) of the powerful Japanese province of Satsuma on the island of Kyūshū. Thereafter, the Ryūkyū Islands were considered part of the domain of Satsuma, although the islands' king continued to pay tribute to China. After the Meiji Reformation, the new central government of Japan unilaterally abolished the kingdom in 1872, designated the islands a separate province, and terminated their ancient diplomatic relations with China. Strong local resistance to these changes was put down by force, and in the spring of 1879 the prefecture of Okinawa was formally declared. The Americans in *The Teahouse of the August Moon* pride themselves on being the liberators of the islands and the bringers of democracy. But their methods are those of men who wield military might. The Americans think in terms of imposing democracy on the locals. As Colonel Wainright Purdy III, commander of Camp Team C–147 of the Military Government, memorably says in Patrick's play: 'my job is to teach these natives the meaning of democracy, and they're going to learn democracy if I have to shoot every one of them.'[56]

Okinawa as portrayed in *The Teahouse* barely shows any scars of the ferocious fighting that claimed the lives of so many locals. Of the 500,000 inhabitants of the island, only around 80,000 had been evacuated before the battle for the island commenced. The rest were caught between the invading Americans and the Japanese Imperial Army, the bulk of which was holding out in the south of the island. By the time the fighting finally ended, more than 120,000 islanders were dead, including approximately 13,000 of the 25,000 men and youths mobilised by the Imperial Army to defend the island. Of the 2,000 high school students, both male and female, who had been sent into battle, 1,100 perished. Thousands of civilians who were not killed in artillery fire succumbed to starvation and disease. Many hundreds of non-combatant islanders died at the hands of the Japanese army itself: some were executed on the charge of being spies for the Americans or on suspicion of contemplating surrender; others were killed for their unwillingness to give up to Japanese soldiers their shelter or their precious stores of food, or even for making a sound while hiding from the invading enemy; still more people were goaded into taking their own lives rather than surrender.[57]

Civilians upon capture or surrender were interned by the Americans in detention camps, rudimentary compounds surrounded by barbed wire fences within which perimeters the detainees huddled in improvised tents and makeshift huts. There were ultimately twelve of these camps dotted around the island, as well as separate prison camps for military captives and Korean forced labourers who had been attached to the Japanese army. Sanitary conditions were bad, and people were dependent on American handouts of food, in exchange for which they were required to provide labour. Islanders were not able to begin returning to their former villages until October 1945. But Okinawa had been comprehensively devastated by war. Cities and towns, down to the tiniest hamlets, had been razed, and the ground was cratered and scorched from the ferocity of the bombardment the Americans had rained upon the island. Large areas of land were now cordoned off, moreover, by the American army for its own military use. This meant that whilst many islanders were back in their former villages by the middle of 1946, some communities did not get resettled until the second half of 1947.

In *The Teahouse*, however, the Japanese (or the Okinawans, who stand in for them) have somehow managed to revert from ferocious subhuman wartime killing machines to amenable, if childlike, students of the democratic way of life as well as of laissez-faire economics. The islanders are already back in their villages, indolently spending their days chasing after their errant goats and pigs. (According to the memoirs of Uehara Eiko, a former Okinawan courtesan, livestock did not reappear on Okinawa until late 1947 when the islanders began receiving pigs, goats and cattle donated by Okinawans living in Hawaii and by American Christian groups.)[58] Captain Jeff Fisby, who has been posted to the remote village of Tobiki, can barely get his villagers to look after their own sweet-potato fields. Meanwhile, his chief, Colonel Purdy, has an elaborate education programme which he expects Fisby to implement in his village. In both Sneider's original novel and Patrick's play, Fisby finds it impossible to impose an alien system on the indigenous culture. Not having been endowed with a particularly domineering personality, Fisby is led around by the nose by the locals, headed by the wily interpreter Sakini. But while Fisby gives in to the villagers' insistence that what the village of Tobiki needs is a teahouse rather than a schoolhouse, he is shown making use of this project to inject a spirit of American enterprise and initiative into the locals. In Sneider's novel, he single-handedly lifts Tokibi out of its subsistence-farming culture and propels it into a mercantile one. With the wholehearted support of the men of the village behind him, Fisby is able to encourage them to build up their island-wide bartering network, by which means they are able to procure the materials they need for the construction of the teahouse. When he realises that just a single loom for the weaving of *tatami*-mats was hardly going to be enough to keep up with the demand for the villagers' products, he figures out by himself how to build some more, first by dismantling the existing loom (to the horror of the villagers, who are slow to realise what Fisby is up to) and working out how to create parts for new looms out of scrap from the army salvage dump. The extensive bartering network encourages industry in Tobiki village: the villagers make *geta* (wooden pattens), salt, *tatami*-mats and lacquerware, which they swap for goods from other villages, as well as from the American Officers' Club. They supply souvenirs for the American PX to sell. There appears to be no shortage of raw materials or foodstuff. The villagers are issued rations by the Americans, but they seem nonetheless able to rustle up a sukiyaki to celebrate the opening of their teahouse. When the geisha First Flower decides she has had enough of sweet potatoes, she directs villagers to take nets down to the sea and catch some fish; they immediately have a surplus which they are able to trade for other island commodities. First Flower also knows where the Japanese army had hidden secret stashes of food during the war, including rice. This means that they can have sushi at the teahouse. A supply of a more varied range of vegetables is made possible by the green-fingered Doc McLean, who joins Fisby in Tobiki. Originally sent by Colonel Purdy to keep Fisby under observation, the Doc becomes fired up with enthusiasm at the chance to realise his lifelong dream of setting up a farm on the latest scientific principles.

The village's biggest success with their American customers turns out to be alcohol: their 'brandy', or *shōchū*, a distilled liquor made from sweet potato (Uehara Eiko remembered that her fellow inmates in the detention camp actually made an ad hoc liquor, not out of something as precious as sweet potatoes, but out of leftover rice from the Americans' mess halls and kitchens – a vinegary potion which became something of a hit among the GIs).[59] Once the new teahouse in Tobiki is up and running, the realisation strikes Fisby that it cannot continue providing meals and entertainment for free. The use of currency, which had been suspended by the Military Government at the start of the occupation, was resumed in reality in March 1946, with a mixture of American B-yen military scrip and the new Japanese yen.[60] In Vern Sneider's novel, Fisby single-handedly reinstates currency economics in Tobiki when he decides that the time has come for certain forms of labour to be recompensed with money. Liquor becomes a main source of earning occupation currency from the Americans. By the end of the novel, Fisby has re-established old trade links with Chinese villages across the South China Sea. Without any directives issued by Colonel Purdy, let alone the Military Government on Okinawa, Fisby demonstrates the American pioneer spirit and creates a thriving community of hard-working inhabitants, with local shops and a flourishing cultural life.

The flow of cultural transmission is not presented as entirely one-way, however. Fisby, for his part, is shown to have things to learn from the islanders. For instance, he grows – in a rather William Morris sort of way – to appreciate craftsmanship in the place of American-style assembly-line mass production. One of the earliest indications of Fisby 'going native' is his doffing of his regulation uniform and adopting 'native' clothes instead: first, *geta*, instead of army boots, and then, as a substitute for an authentic kimono, his bathrobe. The latter is approved of by the villagers – apparently the locals find a striped American bathrobe a perfectly adequate alternative to a formal kimono. But Fisby's lessons mostly involve learning to stop rushing about. He is taught by First Flower to sit quietly out on the veranda of the teahouse and listen to the wind blowing through the pines across the lotus pond. If he is abstracted in business matters all the time, how can he fully appreciate the flavour of the pickles that are being served at the teahouse? In John Patrick's play, Fisby initially has a great deal of difficulty overcoming his inhibitions to the extent that he can start to accept the ministrations of the geisha Lotus Blossom. He is partly the chivalrous western male whose self-perception as the protector of women is threatened by an inkling that he might actually enjoy being waited on by a woman; partly the indignant, morally upstanding westerner, horrified at the pollution represented by the eastern whore; and, at the same time, the fractious little boy trying to escape his mother's firm guiding hand. Lotus Blossom has to manhandle him into submitting to her attentions

The whole matter of the teahouse rises in the first place because Fisby is given some geishas as a 'souvenir'. Whenever the good-natured Okinawans want to get on the good side of Fisby, they bring him presents. In the novel, Fisby is given two girls: First Flower, a 'geisha girl first class', and Lotus Blossom, a geisha of the second class who, according to Sakini, is ' "study[ing] real hard to pass her first-class exams." '[61] The play and subsequent movie reduce the number of geishas to just one, retaining the name Lotus Blossom. In any case, Fisby is dismayed. 'I know what she's trained to do,' he snaps in Patrick's play when Sakini tries to tell him that Lotus Blossom is 'trained to please you, boss.'[62] Later, he demands of Sakini: 'What do you mean, geisha girls aren't prostitutes? Everybody knows what they do' (the explicit word 'prostitutes' was deleted in the film, and the question is allowed to hang in mid-air). Sakini explains then what geishas are really paid for:

Poor man like to feel rich. Rich man like to feel wise. Sad man like to feel happy. All go to geisha house and tell troubles to geisha girl. She listen politely and say, 'Oh, that's too bad.' She very pretty. She make tea, she sing, she dance, and pretty soon troubles go away. Is not worth something, boss?[63]

In Sneider's novel, Sakini goes on to explain that Naha, the prefectural capital of Okinawa, formerly had three hundred geishas, among whom First Flower had been – of course – the most famous. She used to dance for the governor at his big banquets. Political bigwigs, Sakini explains, often went to the Tsuji, Naha's pleasure quarter, to 'have a cup of tea' and talk things over whenever they had some big issue to resolve. Sometimes, they would even ask the geisha girls to help them solve their problem.[64] Of course, Sakini himself had never been able to afford anything more than a cup of tea and a bowl of noodles during his annual or, at the most, twice yearly visits to the Tsuji quarter, when he went to Naha to sell his crop of sweet potatoes. He delicately explains to Fisby that the geisha's relationship with the geisha-house proprietor was basically a financial arrange-ment. The proprietor buys six- or seven-year-old girls from their impoverished parents, and sends them to school to learn good manners, flower arranging, tea drinking and the proper way to talk to gentlemen 'to make them feel good inside'. They are taught to sing and dance and play the *jabisen*, the Okinawan three-stringed, snakeskin banjo out of which the Japanese *shamisen* evolved. The 'geisha owner' then buys the geisha 'nice kimonos and stuff', and 'set[s] her up in business'. Fisby thinks he understands the arrangement: ' "So then the girls have to pay him back for the money he spent, plus interest, of course?" ' Sakini confirms that this is the case – only sometimes the girls are never able fully to recompense their owner because the owner keeps on remembering ' "something else they owe him for" '.[65] The picture Sakini paints is an intentionally naïve and idyllic one, intended to persuade Fisby of the innocuousness of the geisha business. Fisby, ever gullible, accepts it and agrees to the construction of a teahouse in Tobiki, in which direction Sakini had been deftly manoeuvring him all along.[66]

It is, in the end, the geisha who teaches Fisby the virtues of the island's slower pace of life. From First Flower he absorbs the local sense of time, and he learns to appreciate the phases of the day and the changing of the seasons. Fisby, in turn, introduces democratic changes to the geisha's life. First Flower cannot believe that Fisby does not want even the 50 per cent cut of each day's profit that the most generous of geisha owners usually demanded.[67] Fisby flatters himself he has won the esteem and admiration of First Flower, this famous geisha who had formerly danced only for the most powerful men on the island. But in Sneider's novel, any hint of a possible romance between the American captain and First Flower is quickly quashed. It is made clear that First Flower's heart already belongs to some-body else, the artist Seiko, a fellow Okinawan and a former habitué of the pleasure quarter. First Flower and Seiko spend much of the novel assiduously ignoring each other and surreptitiously seeing how the other is taking the cold-shoulder treat-ment. Fisby ends up acting as a go-between to bring the warring couple together. Besides, First Flower likes to work, and she decides she wants to keep working after she is married, although she concedes that she cannot continue as a geisha. She is going to teach instead. She will offer instruction in the tea ceremony and flower arranging. She also dreams of opening a school for aspiring geishas. She sees this as an opportunity to introduce radical reforms to the geisha business. Traditional operators will be banned from the village. A guild, into which prac-tising geishas would pay their dues, would then provide loans to fledgling geishas to enable them to purchase the expensive kimonos they need to set up in business. First Flower's dreams keep expanding: she is going to start a school for men who want to learn garden design, and organise a troupe of kabuki actors to perform in the village.[68]

In John Patrick's play, however, Lotus Blossom and Fisby's relationship is different. The geisha falls in love with the American officer. She finds him attrac-tive; besides, she has been deeply moved by his generosity in refusing to put her to work for his own personal monetary gain. In the last scene of the play, disaster strikes the village: the whole teahouse project is plunged into peril, and it looks as though everybody will have to go their separate ways. Lotus Blossom asks Fisby to marry her. She does not have any English, and needs Sakini to act as her interpreter. In both the play and the motion picture, all her lines are in Japanese (in Sneider's novel, on the other hand, the native characters are described as talking in the local Ryūkyū island dialect). Nonetheless, she insists she loves Fisby, and tells him (through Sakini) that she wants to go to America with him. Fisby, however, gently turns her down. In the play, even more so than in the novel, Fisby is sensitive to the fragile beauty of the local culture. He worries that now that the war is over, American activity on the island might indelibly change the character of the local society. He asks Sakini to tell Lotus Blossom 'that I am clumsy, that I seem to have a gift for destruction. That I'd disillusion her as I have disillusioned her people.' His further explanation – '[T]ell her that I love what she is, and that it would be wrong to change that. To impose my way of life on her' – was left out of the film. In the play, Fisby's disinclination to impose occidental ways on Lotus Blossom extends to his unwillingness to see her dressed in an American-style sweater and sport shoes: she would look like 'an American looking like an Oriental'. He wants to preserve difference, yet he also observes that – despite America's much-vaunted claim to democratic values – such difference would not be appreciated on the streets of a little American town, such as the one he himself comes from.[69]

Compared with the novel, which ends with Fisby showing an impressed Colonel Purdy around the new Tobiki, a model village that mixes exotic oriental charm with bustling American-style commercial activity based on the small-town ideal, there is a stronger sense in the play, though rather watered down in the film, of an opposition between the local way of life and the American way. At the end of the play, Colonel Purdy – rather than sampling the culinary delights of the teahouse – orders its immediate destruction along with all the spirit stills in Tobiki. He blames Fisby for encouraging lewdness and drunkenness in the 'ignorant people' of the village, as he puts it, and of making money out of 'the white slave trade' and the liquor business. He even suggests that Fisby is sowing the seeds of communism, by depositing the proceeds in a bank in Seattle in the name of the Tobiki Cooperative in which all the villagers are equal partners.[70] At the very last moment, however, a reversal of fortunes takes place, and Purdy comes rushing back on scene with the news that some senators in Washington have decided that what has been taking place in Tobiki is a prime 'example of American "get-up-and-go" in the recovery program'. A Congressional Committee is on its way to see the village for itself, and Purdy needs the teahouse and the stills back up and running. While he despairs at the destruction he himself had ordered, Sakini admits slyly that what had been destroyed had been nothing more than several water butts. The real stills have been safely hidden away, ready for an immediate resumption of production. Purdy welcomes the news with elation, declaring Sakini to be 'really an American. He has get-up-and-go.' As for the teahouse (presumably because all Japanese buildings are nothing more than flimsy paper structures), it is promptly resurrected in the blink of an eye. Purdy declares, 'Fisby, this is a land of adventure. . . . It's the mystery of the Orient.'[71] Okinawa is thus an enchanted ancient land where things are evanescent, easy to pull down, and easy to reconstruct. One does not have to worry about the fate of the natives because they presumably know how to take care of themselves: they are delightful, merry tricksters who have, over the course of centuries, mastered the skill of manipulating whoever happens to be their present master. The scars of war are erased equally from the landscape of Okinawa and from the bodies and psyche of the island's inhabitants. The teahouse represents pleasure, and the enjoyment of life is presented as the lesson the ambition-driven Americans need to learn.

In many ways, *The Teahouse of the August Moon* was as much a satire on American occupation policy (or lack thereof) on Okinawa as Gilbert and Sullivan's *Mikado* was of British bureaucracy. In reality, there was no co-ordinated policy on the part of the American military on Okinawa in the immediate post-war years. Little effort was made to restore the island's destroyed services, such as electricity and running water. Military chiefs were no more concerned about the dissemination of 'American values': whatever effort was made on this front was undertaken by Christian missionaries and chaplains.[72] It was the effect of the devastation war had wreaked on the island that the fabric of its society fell apart.

Okinawan society had not regressed to some imagined state of primitive, tropical stupor. Life had always been difficult on the Ryūkyū Islands, which never had much arable land, but the savage battle of Okinawa reduced cities and towns to rubble, and completely wiped out the island's infrastructure. In the immediate aftermath of the battle, the surviving islanders were dazed and apathetic about the future. Their lethargy was not constitutional, but a direct result of the psychological and physical trauma of war. Old customs no longer possessed much meaning for the younger people. In the harsh conditions under which people had to begin rebuilding their lives, many were driven by motives of self-interest rather than the spirit of co-operation. Unscrupulous commercial dealings became rife. Pilfering of food and other daily necessities from American military supplies was endemic.[73] Prices on the black market, which was often the only place people could find what they required, were extortionate.

The sympathetic attitude to Japanese culture observable in both Sneider's novel and Patrick's play of *The Teahouse* was a reflection of how US policy in the Far East was changing in the light of what Washington, DC viewed as the new international threat, communism. This appreciation of generalised Japanese culture disguises, however, the fact that Okinawan culture was significantly different from that of mainland Japan. Both Vern Sneider and John Patrick exploit stereotypes of supposed Japanese national characteristics for laughs. While the novel and the play urge the importance of respecting local ways, stereotypical Japanese culture is transposed on to Okinawan society. The point is made that Okinawans are not really Japanese, but were in fact subjugated by them. Yet there is disregard – or, at any rate, ignorance – of the distinctiveness of Okinawan culture. This is particularly the case when it comes to the whole subject of geishas and teahouses, the very themes around which the plot of *The Teahouse of the August Moon* revolves. Local Okinawan courtesans were not known as geishas, and they did not entertain in teahouses.

The Tsuji pleasure quarter in the Okinawan capital Naha had unique traditions. Its courtesans were called *juri*. Unlike geishas in the rest of Japan, *juri* usually did not entertain their clients in teahouses or restaurants. The brothels in the Tsuji quarter were all run by women. These proprietresses, known as *anmā*, were themselves senior *juri* of the community, usually those who had a single powerful protector or financial backer. *Anmā* bought young girls and women from indigent families in exchange for a sum of money, which had to be repaid in regular instalments by the girls once they became fully fledged *juri*. A *juri* was allocated a room or a suite of rooms in her *anmā*'s brothel. This would be where she both lived and entertained her small number of established patrons. The official distinction between geishas and prostitutes, which applied in the rest of Japan, was not made in the Tsuji quarter. Only after a man had been selected to be a patron of a *juri* could he sleep with her. A *juri* not only performed Okinawan dances and songs to entertain her patron; she personally prepared his meals. If he wanted to hold a banquet to entertain his own guests, his *juri* would act as both hostess and cook. She could usually rely on her fellow *juri* in her brothel for help in the kitchen and as extra hands to serve food and drink to the diners. Banquets held in the Tsuji quarter constituted an important part of the social life of the men who ran Okinawa before the war: politicians, businessmen and military officials.[74]

Naha did also have a few exclusive Japanese-style restaurants (teahouses) which employed Japanese-style geishas. These women, who dressed in the manner of geishas on mainland Japan, performed Japanese dances and songs. They belonged, as in other parts of Japan, to *geishaya*, and these geisha houses, as well as the restaurants, were as likely to be run by men as by women in accordance with the system of organisation found in other Japanese pleasure quarters. The Okinawan *juri*, on the other hand, had a unique look in the pre-war days. She swept her long lustrous tresses up into an elaborate bun on top of her head and wore a highly polished silver hairpin called a *jīfuwā*. Different kinds of cloth characteristic of the islands of the Ryūkyū archipelago were used for kimonos, such as the pale brownish-yellow *bashōfu*, made of fibre spun from the *bashō*, the Japanese banana plant. Traditional Okinawan society was very hierarchical, with strict restrictions on the types of cloth and accessories members of each class were allowed to wear, but such conventions did not apply to *juri*, who were considered to be outside society, and they were able to wear fabrics usually reserved for the exclusive use of the aristocracy: expensive silks, as well as fabrics printed with exquisite patterns made up of flower, foliage and bird motifs rendered in shades of indigo blue and red in a style particular to Okinawa. The way in which kimonos were worn was subtly different from the manner usual throughout the rest of Japan. On the Ryūkyū Islands, kimonos were worn more loosely over the undergarments. A light summer garment called *ushinchī* was worn over white underclothing held in place with a single girdle of a bright crimson hue. Rather than using an obi, the *juri* gathered her *ushinchī* around the middle and tucked it in her girdle. When she did use an obi, the *juri* usually tied it in front. Unlike ordinary island women, *juri* were allowed to use cosmetics – powder and rouge. They also had a method for staining their fingernails a delicate pink shade.[75]

The Tsuji quarter was destroyed in the Allied air raid on Naha on 10 October 1944, and was never resurrected in its previous form again. Legalised prostitution as it used to be known on Okinawa came to an abrupt end. But prostitution itself remained rife throughout the period the Ryūkyū Islands were under American control, although in the immediate post-war period, a non-fraternisation regulation officially banned American servicemen from visiting local prostitutes. Rape was also a major problem.[76] The chaste parting between Fisby and Lotus Blossom at the end of John Patrick's play – with Lotus Blossom resignedly accepting the attentions of the local boy Seiko – neatly skirted the contentious issue of the sexual conduct of American servicemen in occupied Japan. At the same time, it has to be said that Patrick's play avoided portraying Japanese women as predatory gold-diggers. The engagingly innocent picture painted in *The Teahouse* is, however, a far cry from the frank and honest – yet not bitter – account which Uehara Eiko has written of her own experiences during the difficult years following the end of the Second World War. Raised in the Tsuji quarter of Naha since being sold there at the age of four, she survived the bombardment of Okinawa and was held in an American-run detention camp for local inhabitants. While working in a laundry detail, she endured rape at the hands of American GIs.[77] The work she found as housemaid in the household of US army officers did not bring in enough money for her to support her dependants (who included her former *anmā*), since many essential supplies were available only at extortionate prices on the black market. Uehara became the mistress of at least five Americans at different times. Whenever a lover of hers, in a mood to romance her, bought her a present – usually an item of clothing – she sold it for cash.[78] Some of her lovers were indulgent, and helped her with her English. Another employed brute force and money in alternation to get her to do as he wanted. Still another made her his mistress at the same time as telling her that prostitution was immoral.[79] One commanding officer, who was expecting his wife and daughter to join him imminently from the States, made promises to Uehara to help her return eventually to Naha if she stayed on for the time being as his wife's housemaid.[80] Ironically, Uehara got on well with this officer's matronly wife, and learned how to keep house and cook in the American way. She later put her new catering skills to practical use and set up a coffee shop in the building which housed the Military Government. In the spring of 1952, she married an American employee of the US Civil Administration of the Ryūkyū Islands, and in the December of that same year opened her own restaurant, the first to be built in the old Tsuji district of Naha. On the suggestion of an American friend, she gave her restaurant the English name 'Tea House August Moon' after the Sneider novel and Patrick play; it was known in Japanese as Matsu-no-shita. Sadly, the time and energy she poured into her business gradually alienated her husband from her and they separated.

In 1953 Uehara helped organise a local amateur production of *The Teahouse of the August Moon* at Fort Buckner as a goodwill event between the American military and local Okinawans. The cast was made up of staff from her restaurant. Uehara thought of the play as an innocuous comic romp, but she recalled that some local people were offended by the suggestion that Okinawans would put building a teahouse before a school. In response to this objection, the US military commented that the playwright was not denigrating Okinawans but satirising the ineptitude of the American administration on the island. Uehara later saw the Broadway production of *The Teahouse of the August Moon* in New York in 1954, with Burgess Meredith in the role of Sakini. She met Barbara Luna, who played Lotus Blossom (the role was originally taken by Mariko Niki), and showed her how to play the *jabisen*. In her memoirs, Uehara wrote that she had not really been surprised that the Broadway show failed to convey any idea of the distinctiveness of Okinawan culture, but reproduced instead the stereotypical western image of the Japanese-style geisha dressed in a long-sleeved *furisode* kimono with a bunch of chrysanthemums – pompons – on either side of her head.[81] The 1956 film version of *The Teahouse* did introduce some Okinawa-style dancing in the teahouse scene, but Lotus Blossom, playfully portrayed by the Japanese actress Kyō Machiko, was represented again as an essentially Japanese geisha.[82]

The Americans in *The Teahouse of the August Moon* think of themselves as liberators of Okinawa, but American military control of the three island groups which had made up the former prefecture of Okinawa continued until May 1972.[83] In the meantime, the Allied occupation of Japan ended when the San Francisco Peace Treaty, which was signed on 8 September 1951, came into effect on 28 April the following year. Japan was rehabilitated as an ally of America in the battle against the forces of communism. The outbreak of war on the Korean Peninsula ignited

Japan's post-war economic revival, as the country became a vital supply link for American troops fighting in Korea. Liberated from Japanese domination on 15 August 1945, the Korean Peninsula had been divided at the 38th parallel between a Soviet area of occupation to the north and the American sphere of control to the south.[84] On 25 June 1950, North Korean troops invaded the South. United Nations Command forces, comprised of military personnel sent by sixteen nations and led by the Americans, were deployed to defend South Korea, and fierce fighting swept up and down the peninsula for the next nine months, with China sending in its People's Volunteer Army in October to fight on the side of the North Koreans. Hostilities did not finally cease until the summer of 1953, when the United States, North Korea and China signed an armistice on 27 July restoring the original border between North and South Korea.

US servicemen and military personnel from other nations making up the UN Command forces were sent from the Korean Peninsula to Japan for rest and recuperation. The American writer James A. Michener in his Korean War novel *The Bridges at Toko-Ri* (1953) paints a picture of the pretty, young Japanese flirt of that period, decked in a snappy western outfit bought for her by one of her numerous love-struck American admirers. In the early 1950s, the ports of Yokohama and Yokosuka teemed with such girls, happy to spread their favours around American servicemen off the troop ships. The US *Navy Times (Pacific)* ran a series of cartoons by Bill Hume featuring the character 'Babysan', described as a typical example of these 'fascinating, fun-loving Japanese girls'.[85] The introduction to a 1953 collection of these cartoons cheekily suggests that these women were once the cute little local girls to whom Americans had given candy back in the early days of the occupation. Now grown up and heavily influenced by American customs, they were 'trying their best to become Westernized':

> She looks Japanese. She looks American. Nice, you think. Incongruous, you think. Sexy, you think. You don't need that next drink to understand that Babysan is a fascinating, delightful creature.
>
> Of course, so is the girl back home. But Babysan is here![86]

They emphatically were *not* geishas:

> She is not the tourist's idea of the Japanese girl and she is not exactly what the American serviceman expected. They [*sic*] had seen many misleading Hollywood versions of the 'Madame Butterfly' type. . . . They undoubtedly visualized the colorful kimono, the hair piled and planted with combs, and the timid eye peeking from behind a fluttering fan. This sort of girl still inhabits Japan, of course, but she is not usually found clinging to a serviceman's arms. In GI circles, Babysan has edged her out of the scene.[87]

"You think Japanese girls look like this?"

29 'You think Japanese girls look like this?', Bill Hume cartoon in *Babysan* (1953).

'Babysan' is sexually uninhibited and unashamedly greedy. This sort of girl wants to be wooed with classy presents and gifts of money. She does not expect her GI boyfriend to take her with him back to the United States once his tour of duty is over. She is quite candid about her lack of constancy:

> A carefree and charming girl, Babysan never forgot the acts of kindness on the part of the American. She decided, in fact, to devote herself to the cause of the American serviceman in Japan. She would make his stay in the land of the cherry blossoms a pleasant one, and – well, the way she figured it – the more GI's the merrier. There wasn't much sense in restricting her charms to one.[88]

'Babysan' was the very opposite of the Madame Butterfly stereotype, and American servicemen, it seems, loved her for it.

In the early 1950s, James A. Michener, who already had bestsellers such as *Tales of the South Pacific* (1947) to his name, published articles on Japan in popular magazines including the *Reader's Digest*, the *Ladies' Home Journal* and *LIFE*, publications which helped to generate a growing interest among the American middle class in Asia and other Third World regions around the globe, at a time when the international scene seemed to be polarising between the free world and the communist bloc.[89] Journals such as these fostered an attitude of

"Can I help if guys have a yen for me?"

30 'Can I help if guys have a yen for me?', Bill Hume cartoon in *Babysan* (1953).

tolerance of, even a certain respect for, foreign cultures, and sought common ground that allowed international co-operation between Americans and peoples of the non-white world to take place. Michener's next Korean War novel, *Sayonara* (1954), hit out hard against racist tendencies in the US military.

Set in Japan in 1952, *Sayonara* revolves around a love affair between the novel's narrator, top US Air Force pilot Major Lloyd 'Ace' Gruver, and a Japanese stage actress, Hana-ogi. Gruver belongs by birth and achievement at the heart of the American military establishment. A graduate of West Point, he is the son and grandson of generals. He has, moreover, proven his own personal courage by shooting down seven enemy fighter jets over Korea. But active duty in Korea has caused him to burn out, so he is sent to Kōbe in Japan to recover.

An easy desk job has been arranged for him by General Webster, the father of his fiancée Eileen. Eileen has been summoned to Kōbe by the general and his wife so that Gruver can marry her without further ado. Eileen is the type of girl Gruver believes in his head he should marry. She comes from a good family, they share a common background, and she understands what is expected of a wife of an officer in the US military. Gruver knows of two types of officer's wife. His mother, herself the daughter of a general, has kept out of his father's life. General Webster's wife, on the contrary, has single-handedly orchestrated her husband's rise up the military hierarchy. She is boundlessly energetic and domineering. Eileen looks like becoming a replica of this mother of hers. She is adamant that she will not allow herself to be pushed to the sidelines of her husband's life. Gruver, in truth, finds Eileen's earnestness rather irksome, and Eileen for her part worries whether he truly cares about her. It is at this crucial juncture in Gruver and Eileen's relationship that he spots Hana-ogi for the first time.

Unlike Eileen, Hana-ogi has a professional career. She is a well-established star performer with the all-female Takarazuka theatre company. She is not only a highly accomplished actress, but a distinguished dancer and singer as well. As her name suggests, she is the modern counterpart of the traditional Japanese courtesan: Hana-ogi has been given as her stage name the appellation of a famous eighteenth-century *oiran*. Her entire identity is subsumed into her existence as a Takarazuka performer. She angrily repels Gruver's attempt to find out her real name. She is as committed to the theatre company she works for as Gruver is to the US military. Her calling, moreover, requires as much self-discipline and dedication as his does.

The Takarazuka Shōjo Kagekidan (known in English as the Takarazuka Revue Company) is real and a very famous institution in Japan. Founded in 1914, it was conceived from the start as a conservatoire for unmarried young women. It provided rigorous training in dance and singing, and all members of the company were referred to as '*seito*' (students). The ethos of the company emphasised strict modesty and decorum. In contrast to traditional geishas and stage actresses, company members, or 'students', were expected to be above any suspicion of sexual laxity. Once they married, they were obliged to retire from the company.[90]

In Michener's novel, the US military and the Takarazuka company share significant characteristics. Each is as rigidly run and inflexible as the other. Public image is important to both, and the two organisations are equally keen to stifle any hint of scandal among their number. They both call upon loyalty in order to make their subordinates toe the line. The head of the Takarazuka company is as determined as the US military brass to prevent Hana-ogi and Gruver from being together.

General Webster's wife firmly believes that conquerors should not mingle with the conquered, and her husband fires off directives forbidding American officers to fraternise with Japanese women. General Webster, however, has one stubborn rebel on his hands in the person of Private Joe Kelly, an airman from Gruver's squadron back in Korea. Kelly is headstrong; he has both a temper and a reputation for being a troublemaker. He has come to Kōbe to marry his Japanese sweetheart, Katsumi. The US authorities do not have a co-ordinated policy regarding marriages between American servicemen and Japanese women. On the one hand, the US government permits them, but on the other, the US military forbids its men to bring their Japanese wives back home with them to America. Kelly's superiors in Korea have been doing everything in their power to stop him from marrying Katsumi and his colonel has refused to give him permission to marry her. The squadron chaplain, convinced that he has to save Kelly from himself, asks Gruver to remind Kelly how wholesome and desirable American women, women of his own race, are. But Kelly comes from the very periphery of American society in the first place. Of Irish descent, he is the product of a rough neighbourhood in Chicago, and since childhood he has been shunted between orphanages, foster homes and reform school. In Katsumi Kelly sees for the first time the promise of a family he has never had.

Undeterred by the threat of a court-martial for having demanded to be sent back to Japan from Korea so he can marry Katsumi, Kelly has written to his congressman back home to intercede on his behalf. The State Department, meanwhile, tries to make American servicemen give up the idea of marrying Japanese women by setting up one humiliating obstacle after another in the application process. The American consul who finally marries Kelly and Katsumi does so grudgingly. Still, Kelly is so much in love with Katsumi that he admits frankly to Gruver that he would happily give up his American citizenship for her. This strikes Gruver as the ultimate betrayal of uniform and country – until he falls in love with a Japanese woman himself.

Unlike Hana-ogi, Katsumi is ordinary, plain and rather dumpy. She is not very different from a million other Japanese girls. She has raw, chapped knuckles. But this does not matter. The secret of Katsumi's success with her American beau is not sexual seductiveness. She is able to make him feel like a million dollars. Joe Kelly tells Gruver, ' "Men with wives back in the States talk about Junior's braces and country-club dances and what kind of car their wife bought. But the men with Japanese wives tell you one thing only. What wonderful wives they have." '[91] Mike Bailey, a Marine lieutenant who becomes friendly with Gruver, is as appreciative of Japanese women as Kelly is. He puts it to Gruver: ' "Can you imagine Eileen Webster scrubbing your back?" '[92] No amount of practical intervention in a man's life, of the kind Mrs Webster, for example, has exercised in her husband's in order to make him a general, could compensate for a woman's inability to make her man feel good about himself. An American secretary at the US consulate confides to Gruver that her husband tells her she is never going to be half the wife the Japanese girl he had once loved would have been – but he had allowed himself to be persuaded that a Japanese wife would not be compatible with life back in Denver, and she had committed suicide.[93] Gruver gradually comes to understand for himself why Japanese women make such terrific wives: they do not set about demonstrating their love for a man by trying to turn him into a somebody, but by making him feel special just as he is, by washing his back and cooking his dinner. This was a lot better for many American GIs than any amount of good looks and curves. But Gruver of course gets himself the woman who happens to be the star of the most popular all-female revue in Japan – who turns out to be as eager to have sex with Gruver as he is with her.

At the beginning, though, she is distant and unapproachable. Her unavailability is symbolised by her professional status as an actress who has made a name for herself playing male roles. It is a fact that the top stars in the Takarazuka company since the 1930s have been the glamorous actresses, known as *otokoyaku*, who play male roles. One of the roles Hana-ogi is supposed to be famous for in *Sayonara* is that of Pinkerton in a fictional production called *Swing Butterfly*, a burlesque revue version of Puccini's opera. Hana-ogi, it seems, is no demure little Butterfly. She plays Pinkerton as an 'arrogant, ignorant, and ill-mannered' swaggerer. 'She was all Japanese women making fun of all American men,' Gruver thinks, feeling affronted.[94] Off stage, Hana-ogi continues to exude authority, wrapping herself up in a mantle of cold hauteur. She dresses mannishly in slacks, sweater and beret. Her attitude to Americans is brusque and unfriendly: Gruver eventually learns that this is because her father had been killed in an air raid during the war and her brother hanged as a war criminal. Gruver sees Hana-ogi as an adversary, but the more aloof she remains, the more desirable she becomes in his eyes.

Gruver wears down Hana-ogi's resistance with his sheer American audacity, tenacity and persistence, and to him alone she finally reveals the thoroughly domesticated, womanly side of herself. It turns out that she has only needed the right man to liberate the feminine in her. They take a little house in a ramshackle, overcrowded district in the heart of Ōsaka, near Kelly and Katsumi's own modest dwelling. Hana-ogi and Gruver share moments of domestic bliss whenever Hana-ogi manages to sneak away from her Takarazuka dormitory. She begins to wear kimonos when she is with him. She shops, sweeps the house and polishes Gruver's shoes. She hovers over simmering pots and pans conspiratorially together with Katsumi. Solicitously she cools Gruver's head when he is having a sleepless night. She is the epitome of the Japanese woman: 'the patient accepter, the tender companion, the rich lover'. Her nerves of steel help maintain domestic calm whenever Gruver has an attack of panic over the probable consequences of their actions. Gruver is in awe of what Japanese women have had to endure for generations: 'there had . . . been endlessly . . . this necessity to be firm, not to cry, not to show pain. . . . they had to bear cruel privations, yet they remained the most feminine women in the world.' Gruver applauds Japanese women for their capacity for 'unremitting work, endless suffering and boundless warmth'.[95] He discovers that Hana-ogi has suffered even more than he had ever imagined. Born into grinding poverty, she had been sold to a brothel, just like her eighteenth-century namesake. She had been bought out of her servitude by a famous aristocrat, presumably to become his mistress.

Katsumi too is brave, but in a quiet, unassuming sort of way. She lives contentedly each day at a time. On one occasion, she and Hana-ogi take their men to see a *bunraku* puppet play, Chikamatsu Monzaemon's classic *Shinjū ten no Amijima* (The Love Suicides at Amijima, 1721), which ends with the double suicide of a pair of lovers, a married Ōsaka paper merchant and a courtesan. In the actual play the lovers eventually choose suicide, not because they are driven to it by an unsympathetic society which seeks to persecute them for their love, but because the debt of gratitude they owe to those around them becomes so heavy they are unable to go on living without shame. But in Michener's novel, the outcome of the play – the double suicide – presages Kelly and Katsumi's choice of death over being forced by the US military to part. Both Katsumi and Hana-ogi find the play's outcome emotionally satisfying, to Kelly and Gruver's mystification. ' "The lovers",' Katsumi explains to her husband. ' "At last they found happiness." ' Joe Kelly points out, ' "They're dead." ' Hana-ogi adds by way of further explanation, ' "To have courage. To have honor. Is very beautiful." '[96]

Joe Kelly has been given orders to return to the States, in accordance with a directive which has been circulated advising that all US military personnel married to Japanese nationals would be ' "rotated home immediately lest their allegiance to the United States be eroded." '[97] Every appeal Kelly has made to have his case reconsidered (for Katsumi is now pregnant) falls on the deaf ears of a malicious, bigoted colonel. It is supposed to be, perhaps, an indication of how 'native' he has gone that Kelly, in the end, takes his own life. The military police find their bodies heaped together, Katsumi's collapsed over Kelly's. She has (like Madame Butterfly) pierced her throat. However in place of an exquisitely crafted dagger, she has used a kitchen knife. Whether Kelly's death can be seen as a desertion of Katsumi or not, she does not have any hesitation in choosing her own course of action.

It is left to Kelly and Katsumi, both without family, connections or any special talent, to demonstrate the way to die beautifully and heroically. A different fate awaits Gruver and Hana-ogi. Gruver assumes Hana-ogi will marry him if he proposes. He sincerely believes he has every intention of taking her to America with him, even if it means having to give up the Air Force. Hana-ogi, however, refuses him. Gruver is bewildered; he cannot understand why 'any Japanese girl, living in that cramped little land with no conveniences and no future' would turn down the opportunity of starting a new life in America. But Hana-ogi tells him she is Japanese. She is not going to be happy anywhere but in Japan.[98]

Then comes the news that Gruver is to be transferred back to the United States. As for Hana-ogi, she is ordered by her company to go to Tōkyō. General Webster believes he and the head of the Takarazuka company have together managed successfully to engineer the forcible separation of the lovers. But, in truth, Hana-ogi determines her course of action for herself. Unlike Katsumi, she chooses life over death. She chooses Japan over America and her own professional career over marriage to Lloyd Gruver. Her choices are the reverse of Madame Butterfly's. There is nothing left for Gruver to do but go back to the United States. A promotion to the rank of lieutenant-colonel is waiting for him there. General Webster and his wife still have not given up on the idea that eventually he will marry their daughter. It does not seem likely that, after this episode of rebellion, Gruver will be able to resist for much longer the life his seniors in the military have in store for him.

Michener's Hana-ogi repudiates the old mould of the submissive housewife. Hana-ogi does not need a husband to support her. Here is the new modern Japanese woman General MacArthur envisaged, an individual who is highly accomplished in her field and is widely admired and respected. Hana-ogi has been recognised by the Takarazuka company for her achievements, and has been picked to become a teacher at the conservatoire once her days on stage are over. At the same time, her very stage name and her own past history connect her to those professional women of the past, the courtesans of the pleasure quarters. The trajectory of her life closely follows that of the courtesan Hana Ōgi, as it is related by the twentieth-century Hana-ogi to Gruver. The historical courtesan of the Ōgiya brothel in the Shin-yoshiwara quarter (to be more precise, the fourth Hana Ōgi) was said to have run away from her brothel with a client of hers in 1794, although she was later found and brought back to the Shin-yoshiwara. Hana-ogi embellishes the story by having Hana Ōgi mysteriously return of her own accord to her brothel to resume her reign as the most celebrated beauty in the quarter. The courtesan Hana Ōgi's principal virtue, as her twentieth-century namesake describes her, is her uncomplaining patience: she does not reproach her mother for having sold her to the brothel, but continues sending her money; she never complains about how her lover had treated her, but keeps silent about her reasons for having left him, although people gossip behind her back that, like most Japanese men, the courtesan's lover must finally have got tired of her and begun to mistreat her.

Nevertheless, Japan's crowded cities, the tightly knit organisation of the Takarazuka company, Hana-ogi's family background, her own past, even her professional status as an actress who takes male roles and receives the adulation of female fans – all these factors seem to Gruver to be only so many bars that pen Hana-ogi inside a prison, keeping her from realising her potential as an individual and as a heterosexual woman. In 1957 *Sayonara* was made into a film, winning Red Buttons, who played the role of Joe Kelly, and Miyoshi Umeki, who took the role of Katsumi, Oscars for best supporting actor and best supporting actress respectively. Crucially, it diverges from Michener's novel in its ending. Whereas in the novel Gruver and Hana-ogi go their separate ways (thereby justifying the novel's title, which, of course, means 'goodbye' in Japanese), the film ends with Gruver successfully persuading Hana-ogi of the rightness of marriage, despite her insistence that they belong to two separate worlds and two separate races. Gruver (Marlon Brando) tells Hana-ogi (Miiko Taka) he does not mind that the children they will have will be 'yellow'. While by the end of Michener's novel, Hana-ogi has grown and matured as an artist through having been awakened to love, both emotional and physical, by Gruver, Hana-ogi towards the end of the motion picture version becomes increasingly dissatisfied with her professional calling, admitting to Gruver that the life has gone out of her work. Her path to self-fulfilment, it is made clear, now lies in marriage.

Hana-ogi and Gruver's union in the film symbolises the coming together of the exotic east and the manly west and is presented as a challenge to the xenophobic tendencies in the Japanese as well the Americans. But even more importantly, the film – unlike the original novel – carries a clear, conservative message to American women, who were becoming more and more independent-minded, particularly since the Second World War, when they had gone into the factories to keep wartime production lines going. Hana-ogi chooses marriage and home life over a professional career. Even as she is struggling to decide what she should do, she asks Gruver, 'Do you think I want to become a lonely old woman who teaches dancing, now that I have known you?' Why should her profession hold any attraction for her, now that she realises that with Gruver she could 'become a woman and a mother'? The only reason she initially privileges her career over the prospect of marriage is because she harbours a strong sense of gratitude and obligation to the theatre company. Once she makes up her mind to marry Gruver, she announces happily to the world that she will still be teaching dance – not to the budding stage stars of the future, however, but to the daughters she will have with Gruver.

The film shows Gruver being given a crash course in Japanese culture. Hana-ogi takes him to a tea ceremony and a performance of noh. Gruver declares he is developing a taste for these things. They visit the 'Meoto iwa', the sacred 'wedded rocks', a holy Shinto site off the coast of Ise, where a famous pair of stone outcrops are connected with a thick woven rope of rice straw. The film *Sayonara* is a paean to interracial acceptance, but it draws on images of family and marriage from Japanese culture to suggest that Hana-ogi is capable of becoming an ideal American wife and mother. The burden of carrying on the traditions of Japanese stage art is transferred to a totally new character created just for the film: a top kabuki actor (who, in a reversal of Hana-ogi's area of specialisation, plays female characters). This kabuki actor, Nakamura, inducts Gruver's American financée Eileen into the mysteries of Japanese art, and the film implies that he becomes the object of Eileen's romantic interest – only the film shies away from casting a Japanese actor in the role of Nakamura, giving it instead to the Mexican actor Ricardo Montalban, escaping briefly from his usual 'Latin lover' type roles but showing off his taut muscular torso nonetheless in a lingering camera shot during a scene in which Nakamura changes costumes in his greenroom.

The actresses who appeared in *Sayonara* as Hana-ogi and Katsumi were reunited in the 1961 film version of *Cry for Happy*, an adaptation of retired US naval officer George Campbell's bitter-sweet comic novel first published in 1958. Miiko Taka again played the more socially sophisticated of the two lead female characters, with Miyoshi Umeki in the role of the ingénue. *Cry for Happy* had the same producer as *Sayonara*, and the male lead was taken by Glenn Ford, who had played the bumbling but sincere Captain Fisby in the film version of *The Teahouse of the August Moon*. A magazine advertisement for *Cry for Happy* capitalised on these shared elements: 'Those yum-yummy girls from "Sayonara" are back . . . in a new hit from the same producer . . . with the comedy star of "Teahouse of the August Moon"!' The theme of *Cry for Happy* is geisha girls: 'You'll cry for happy, happy, happy when FOUR U.S. SAILORS TAKE OVER A GEISHA HOUSE . . . geisha girls and all!' screamed the advertisement. But for all the innuendo of the publicity material, the message the film itself conveyed was the idea that Japanese women have a lot to teach their American counterparts about being a good wife. 'Making a man happy isn't a business with you,' declares one of the Americans with some awe at one point in the motion picture, 'it's an art!'

The original book, on the other hand, was blunt about the commercial aspects of the geisha business. Andy Cyphers, chief photographer's mate, is in charge of the Pacific Fleet Combat Camera Unit, which is responsible for recording the Korean War on camera. He is a shrewd, hard-drinking schemer who likes nothing better than working out ways of circumventing well-intentioned but cumbersome military regulations. When his men are banned from the enlisted men's club for getting involved in a fist fight, Cyphers looks around for an alternative means of amusing them. Japanese bars and clubs are off-limits to American military personnel so Cyphers calls in a favour from a Japanese film-maker Yendo (spelt in the movie credits as Endo) to whom he has been surreptitiously loaning camera equipment. Yendo finds Cyphers a geisha house run by an attractive woman named Chiyoko.

Chiyoko's group of geishas are as professional an outfit as Cyphers's camera unit. Chiyoko looks after her women as Cyphers does his men. A very practical business manager, she collects her geishas' fees from the restaurants to which they have been hired out. Out of this money, she pays her establishment's household expenses, subtracts her share of the profits, and pays her girls with what is left. But requests for geishas have been intermittent recently, so Chiyoko is in the frame of mind to consider what the Americans have to offer. The relationship the men enter into with the women begins as a convenient business arrangement. After a two-week trial period to see whether the set-up is satisfactory to all concerned, Cyphers and his men agree to pay the girls what they had previously been earning from their engagements at restaurants and teahouses. In return, they get the exclusive right to enjoy the company of these women. ' "This is quite a deal",' Andy says to Yendo. ' "I'll bet this is the first package deal for a geisha house ever worked in the whole of Japan." ' [99]

The one Japanese-American member of Cyphers's outfit, George Suzuki, explains what geishas are to his comrades. The men want to know whether geishas are virgins or not. George explains that when an apprentice geisha becomes a fully qualified geisha at the age of eighteen, she takes a lover, who, as her patron, foots all her bills. George outlines the various grades of geisha, from the lowest class (those who engage in prostitution), to those with whom it is possible to arrange a discreet rendezvous, and finally to the highest rank, the women who reserve their affections for men of substantial wealth and good social standing, and are also learned and highly cultured. According to Cyphers, none of Chiyoko's girls are ' "whores" ': a couple are virginal apprentices and the rest ' "look to be the kind [who] . . . might arrange things if a fellow ain't cheap and doesn't try to rush 'em." ' [100] All of Chiyoko's geishas are bonded to indentured service with her, and Chiyoko is firm about the rules of the trade not allowing her to cancel a girl's debt, even though she is personally sympathetic towards her apprentice geisha Harue's desire to be released from her bond so she can marry one of Cyphers's men, Joe Kirk.

Red tape looks pretty much the same to Cyphers whether it is American or Japanese: in the end, it is just another obstacle between his men and their happiness, and a challenge that exercises Cyphers's ingenuity. When Joe's brother refuses to lend any money to Joe on learning that Joe wants it to marry a Japanese woman, Cyphers gets the men in his unit to pool their meagre resources to come up with the $500 necessary to buy Harue her freedom so that the lovebirds can be together. When Cyphers finds out that Harue's father is a crusty former naval officer who is opposed to an American for a son-in law, Cyphers's strategy for getting round the brittle old man is to treat him with respect. With his sense of dignity restored, the father warms to the Americans. After all, as Joe Kirk recognises, ' "captains are the same, no matter what Navy they come from" '.[101] But even Cyphers is at a loss what to do when Harue begins to attend the 'Brides' School' run by the wives of American officers for Japanese women who are about to marry US servicemen, and comes back from classes primed with newly acquired American attitudes. Views regarding the question of US military personnel marrying Japanese women have progressed so dramatically since the days of Mrs Webster in James A. Michener's novel *Sayonara* that officers' wives are now organising classes to instruct local girls how to deal firmly with their husbands in the American way. One of the ideas Harue comes away with is that husbands ought to help their wives around the house.

In any case, Chiyoko's girls become infatuated with everything American. They covet the dresses and high-heeled shoes which are for sale at the PX. They become more assertive, and they tell the men straight out that they no longer want to wear kimonos because they are uncomfortable. Besides, Harue has learned at the Brides' School that married women in America do not wear kimonos. Cyphers's men, however, no more want to be weighed down with the Eileen Websters of this world than Lloyd Gruver did in *Sayonara*. Cyphers tells the geishas, ' "You've been bamboozled into thinking that everything with a Western-style tag on it is wonderful. Well, it just ain't so. Japan has a lot of things that are just as fine." '[102] But he only manages to head off rebellion by taking the measure of peremptorily ordering the women about. After all, Japanese women, unlike American ones, have been programmed to respond to being told who's boss, and the status quo is finally restored.

In the film version of *Cry for Happy*, however, the geishas do not harbour any aspirations to Americanise themselves. It is in their very Japanese-ness that they are shown to be ideal wife material. The film reinvents Joe Kirk, George Campbell's navy photographer who marries the apprentice geisha Harue, as Murray Prince (Donald O'Connor), the breezy archetypal kind of sailor who is supposed to have a sweetheart in every port, and who persuades Cyphers that they should take a chance and stay at Chiyoko's geisha house. Murray Prince is the character in the film who has all the western preconceptions about geishas. He expects some fun – but contrary to his expectations, the women of the geisha house insist that their relationships with the Americans have to remain chaste. Prince complains that Harue (Miyoshi Umeki) is a fraud, not because Harue, as a geisha, is a loose woman masquerading as a lady of refinement, but because he had been led to believe that geishas were women of the world when they were in fact squeaky clean. Harue is on hand to lead Prince gently down the path of righteousness. Of course she has never been in love before (just as Hana-ogi confesses to Gruver in the film version of *Sayonara*) – she is the pure, innocent virgin waiting for her prince – but she already has an unshakeable belief in the importance of love and it is she who teaches the American about commitment. The tragedy of Madame Butterfly is thus avoided, and the geisha blissfully pins down her American sailor.

Cry for Happy, the motion picture, sets out to make the Japanese palatable to Americans in other obvious ways. For instance, Prince and Cyphers (Glenn Ford) find out that Harue is about to marry a rich man in exchange for a farm for her father. When they storm in on her father to protest, the father firmly informs them he is not about to sell his daughter: 'we are not barbarians', he tells the Americans. The plan turns out to have been Harue's own all long. The film also takes the novel's idea of camaraderie between navy men the world over one (implausible) step forward, by having Harue's father adopted by the US Navy as a sort of adviser. Cyphers presents the idea to his admiral as an exercise in building goodwill, so that the Japanese will feel like they are 'team mates' of the Americans instead of vanquished losers. Harue's father, a former Japanese naval officer, is piped on to an American battleship, where he makes a speech expressing his gratitude and praising the genuineness of American friendship. The didactic slant of the film is a reflection of the era in which it was made. The emphasis on military co-operation is interesting in the context of the signing of a new security treaty between Japan and the United States in 1960, six months before the cinematic version of *Cry for Happy* was released. This treaty, which committed Japan to a close military alliance with the United States, proved a much less contentious issue in America than in Japan itself, where it sparked off mass protests led by the political left, but which also drew in a significant propor-tion of the general public, from academics to mothers' associations, encom-passing protesters opposed to the remilitarisation of Japan, anti-nuclear activists and campaigners against the presence of US military bases on Japanese soil.

The film version of Campbell's novel does not just deflate the fiendish image of the Japanese officer from the Second World War. It emasculates the Japanese male in general by making Endo, the filmmaker, into a fool, a caricature Japanese who manages to be unctuous and pushy at the same time, while being locked inside his own ignorance. He only manages to be less repulsive than Goro in *Madama Butterfly* by being more inept at what he does. Endo is ridiculed for his ham-fisted attempt to transpose the traditions of the American cowboy movie lock, stock and barrel into a Japanese setting.

While Endo is made into a figure of fun for his ignorance of the most basic of American social conventions, he is also mocked for his simple-minded effort to import American culture wholesale into an alien setting obviously not ready for it. Despite the film's overall genial attitude to the Japanese, it nonetheless pokes fun at those who aspire to imitate Americans too closely. The geishas in the film do not attempt to cross the cultural boundary between east and west. There is no danger of them trying to pass themselves off as modern American women. Praise for the distinctive beauty of Japanese women when they are clothed in their unique native costume masks a warning to them not to compete with American women on the latter's own ground.

The geishas in the film *Cry for Happy* represent Japanese womanhood at its most traditional. So long as they remain in kimonos they are safely contained within the western fantasy of eastern femininity, pleasing, compliant and undemanding. The film has the obligatory bath scene in which Caucasian men are washed and pampered by youthful Japanese women. No doubt the main appeal of such scenes is supposed to be their sexual undertones, but some Japanese female commentators have caustically observed that the erotic pleasure suggested by these scenes appears to be of a more infantile kind, in which the man is allowed to regress to his babyhood and become the passive recipient of

31 An American serviceman with two *maiko* at a US forces social event in occupied Japan, 1949, black and white photograph.

the pampering ministrations of a mother figure.[103] Walter del Mar's suggestion back at the beginning of the century that Japanese women excelled at being not 'wives' per se but 'housekeepers' can be modified to 'nursemaids'.

Films such as *The Teahouse of the August Moon, Sayonara* and *Cry for Happy* served up a non-threatening image of Japan to the American public. They reflected the temperature of relations between the west and Japan, just as much as John Paris's novel *Kimono* had done in the past. But the suspiciousness of Japanese customs that characterised *Kimono* had gone. Far from being critical of Japanese traditions as having been contributory factors in the development of Fascism in the country, the films of the 1950s revel in their picturesque quaintness. But whereas John Paris warned that Japan and the west could not 'amalgamate', these motion pictures suggest rather that it was undesirable that they should. Behind the positive attitude in these American films to 'native' Japanese traditions there is an underlying resistance to the idea of Japan emulating the United States. The portrayal of Japanese women as supportive and compliant helpers to their American men, who in turn assume the role of protector, suggests a model for the relationship between Japan and the United States in the emerging world order of the late 1950s: like the dutiful housewife, Japan is not to aspire again to equal status with her lord and master.

CHAPTER SIX

Bunny-boiler or Like a Virgin: Images of the Geisha in Late Twentieth-century America

Even as geishas during the last four decades of the twentieth century were turning into anachronistic rarities in their own country, abroad they have retained their prominence as popular icons of native – that is to say, non-westernised – Japanese culture. Their exotic appeal, however, has not been the sole reason they have lived on in the western cultural consciousness. As women in western industrialised nations have advanced into the workplace and into public life, the geisha has continued to represent a more traditional role for woman as companions to men, as their helpmeets and as objects of their admiring eye or their desire. Geishas remain in the paradoxical position of being working women whose purported selling points consist of those qualities which belonged to an old-fashioned western model of the ideal wife – attentiveness, patience and loyalty, mixed with plenty of sex appeal.

In 1962 the Hollywood star Shirley MacLaine appeared in a Paramount Pictures film produced by her husband Steve Parker entitled *My Geisha*, in which she played a film star, Lucy Dell, who jeopardises her marriage to a motion-picture director by masquerading as a Japanese geisha and tricking him into casting her as Cio-Cio-San in his pet project, a film version of Puccini's opera. Lucy's husband Paul Robaix (played by Yves Montand) already resents being chiefly known as the director of the film comedies which have made Lucy famous. His cinematic version of *Madama Butterfly* is his bid to re-establish himself as a serious film director. Paul's approach to the project is to strive for authenticity. He tells Lucy he is not going to cast her as Cio-Cio-San, because he wants this film to be 'not just an opera, but *real*'. He flies out to Japan to shoot his film there (notwithstanding his purported desire for authenticity however, he does not set his film exclusively in Nagasaki, where the opera is supposed to take place, but chooses famous picturesque landmarks all over Japan against which to shoot various scenes). Above all, he wants a Japanese actress for the title role. But the Japanese actresses who come to audition for him are all anxious to demonstrate just how up to date and westernised they are. So Paul decides that what he needs is not an actress but a real-life geisha, one who is 'a plain old-fashioned real Japanese girl who doesn't sing rock and roll', and acts convincingly like a geisha because she actually doesn't know any other way to behave. He already has a certain geisha in mind. On the previous night he had been out to dinner with colleagues at a traditional-style restaurant, where their party had been attended by a bevy of geishas, one of whom had made a special impression on him. He had failed to realise that this geisha – Yoko Mori – was really his wife in disguise. Lucy had impetuously followed Paul to Japan, had turned up at the restaurant unannounced, and observing him enjoying himself in the company of geishas, she had come up with the idea of dressing herself as one of them to see whether or not she could trick Paul into believing she was Japanese and a real geisha to boot. Paul, who has no notion Lucy is in Japan, is totally fooled. Once Lucy realises that Paul is interested in auditioning her alter ego 'Yoko' for the role of Cio-Cio-San, she

32   Lucy Dell (Shirley MacLaine) successfully fools her husband Paul Robaix (Yves Montand) into believing she is a real geisha, still from the Paramount Pictures film *My Geisha* (1962) directed by Jack Cardiff.

decides to carry on with the deception. Paul's producer on the project Sam Lewis (played by Edward G. Robinson) is Lucy's personal friend and in on her secret. He decides that invaluable publicity could be generated for the movie if, at its premiere, 'Yoko' were to be dramatically revealed to the world's press as none other than Lucy Dell herself.

Paul finds 'Yoko' is perfect for his picture – until one day, towards the end of filming, he is examining the film negatives of a scene involving 'Yoko' and suddenly recognises Lucy. He concludes that his wife is a selfish, conniving vixen out to steal his project from under his very nose. Furious, he resolves to revenge himself on her and make her suffer. Well aware that Lucy is of a jealous disposition, he decides to strike where she is most vulnerable, so he propositions 'Yoko', pretending he has not seen through Lucy's ruse. The tables are turned on Lucy, and this time it is she who is completely taken in. She believes Paul is contemplating cheating on her with 'Yoko' and is utterly heartbroken. She is thoroughly humbled. Furthermore, Lucy has a lecture on how to be a good wife from Kazumi, a genuine geisha Lucy has hired to coach her on deportment. Kazumi (played by Yoko Tani) hammers home the message that a true wife puts her husband's needs before her own. Meanwhile, Lucy's new-found under-standing of the miseries of rejection adds an extra poignancy to her performance in Cio-Cio-San's suicide scene. Paul punishes Lucy for her effrontery, and at the same time gets the performance of her life out of her. His finished film turns out to be a triumph. At the premiere, a contrite Lucy yields the limelight to her husband. She refrains from revealing to the public who 'Yoko' really is, telling them instead that 'Yoko' has retreated to a Buddhist convent and will never emerge from it again. Paul is mollified by Lucy's act of self-abnegation, and condescendingly reveals to her that he had been well aware of her deception when he had pretended to seduce 'Yoko'. Paul basks in the professional glory of being the director of a critical success, while Lucy sacrifices the accolades she might have expected for her own work. Lucy is rewarded for her repentance by being told that she is still the sole object of her husband's love.

My Geisha engages in questions about authenticity. Paul shoots his film in Japan and desires an authentic geisha to play the role of Cio-Cio-San because he wants his film to be '*real*'. He casts Lucy because, as 'Yoko', she fits his precon-ception of the authentic geisha. Lucy gives Paul what she senses he is looking for. Summoned to a screen test and asked about her childhood, Lucy as 'Yoko' concocts a clichéd story sure to pique Paul's sympathy, involving an impover-ished childhood with numerous siblings, dead parents and destitute grandpar-ents, who were forced to sell her – so 'Yoko' tells Paul – at the age of five to a man who trained up young girls to become geishas. She recreates for Paul's benefit the very image of the patient, long-suffering, uncomplaining Japanese woman, confiding to him how fortunate she had been to be among the lucky few selected by the 'honourable gentleman' from among all of his young trainees to actually become a fully fledged geisha, and how happy she is to have been able to pay him back her purchase price. All of this agrees with Paul's own idea about what the geisha is. He heaps praise on 'Yoko', moreover, for being so 'natural' in front of the camera, never guessing that this is because 'Yoko' is, in fact, the accomplished actress Lucy Dell. Later in the film, Lucy – as 'Yoko' – reinforces Paul's prejudices about the sexual laxity of geishas. She tells Paul she would make love to any man who was 'entitled' to her attentions, even if she did not actually love him. This includes her 'patron' (who, she explains, 'lends her money'), as well as his 'friends'. It would be 'impolite', she declares, to turn down her patron's friends. 'Yoko' then teases Paul by flirting with him, telling him that she finds him very 'sympathy to me'. Paul is, of course, scandalised and is persuaded that a profound cultural gulf does exist between western morality and morality in Japan.

In the end, Paul is proven wrong in his belief that he needed an authentic geisha to make his movie convincing. Kazumi demonstrates to Lucy how a geisha moves and behaves, and Lucy picks up these airs and graces very quickly. Yet *My Geisha* still makes claims for the primacy of authentic experience. Lucy is convincing in Cio-Cio-San's death scene because of her own genuine unhappiness at the thought of having been rejected by her husband. *My Geisha* also suggests that she is equally convincing in the earlier scenes in her husband's film because she, like Cio-Cio-San, is deeply in love. The inference is that Lucy's ability to play the role depends less on her creative talents than on her direct experiences of the same sorts of emotion as those which Cio-Cio-San undergoes.

Lucy is spared Cio-Cio-San's ultimate fate and gets her husband back by listening to Kazumi's advice. Far from being the kind of promiscuous flirt which Lucy portrays geishas to be in front of Paul, Kazumi turns out to be a fount of wisdom when it comes to relationships between men and women. Kazumi is introduced to Lucy as one of the most extraordinary geishas in Japan. Kazumi's mentor, a venerable old man who is supposed to be a 'geisha teacher', explains to Lucy that geishas are 'bred to please and represent a flawless combination of womanly graces and skills'. He disapproves of the western practice of expecting a wife to assume the responsibilities both of child-rearing and of social entertaining. The latter, he asserts, is best left to professionals, as it is in Japan, because it entails a great deal of work and attention to detail which are beyond the capabilities of a busy housewife and mother. Kazumi, he points out, is one of the best examples of the geisha, for she is able to talk knowledgeably and tactfully about anything a gentleman might be interested in. She excels not only in traditional Japanese dance but in the tango as well. She plays golf and tennis, on top of which she is a champion skier. She speaks French, English and Chinese, and is always up to date on the latest prices on stock markets across the globe.

Kazumi's mentor informs Lucy that the art of being a geisha could not possibly be taught in a couple of days, but he agrees that she could probably pick up enough from Kazumi to 'look like a geisha'. With his blessing, Kazumi becomes Lucy's adviser. Despite his insistence that a woman cannot be instantaneously turned into a geisha, he declares what an 'honour' it would be 'to see a geisha truly portrayed on the screen'. Shirley MacLaine herself had a similar crash course in geisha etiquette. From the light-hearted article, with photographs, which *LIFE* magazine ran in its 17 Februrary 1961 issue, describing a flying visit the actress made to the Gion quarter in Kyōto in the winter of 1960–61, it is difficult to get any idea of what is supposed to be so exceptional about a geisha's accomplishments. The article reveals that MacLaine was shown how to master chopsticks, to use a toothpick Japanese-style, to strum on a *shamisen*, and to serve gentlemen 'hot towels and sake cups'. Other skills she was taught by the geishas included games such as 'pick-up-the-buttons-with-chopsticks'. She learned how to 'walk like a bird', to 'mince' around a room in a kimono, and to strike a pose with a fan. MacLaine is quoted explaining that a geisha is a ' "cultivated woman" ' who can sing, dance and discuss politics, and yet remain tactful enough to put men totally at their ease (presumably by not threatening their masculinity), and all the while remaining, magnificently, ' "a woman" '. ' "It wouldn't be a bad idea",' MacLaine exhorts her readers, ' "if more women tried it." '[1] In *My Geisha*, being 'a woman' involves more than just being socially adept. Kazumi's message to Lucy, the archetypal self-absorbed, ambitious and insecure American woman, is a very conservative one: if Lucy wants to keep her husband, she needs to make him happy, and the best way of making him happy is to set her own ego to one side and put him first. This has not, of course, worked for Cio-Cio-San, but Paul is presumably a better man than Pinkerton and he demonstrates that men are capable of honouring their commitments to a woman.

The conservative message of *My Geisha* is that a woman, no matter how successful in her professional career, would be rendered as desperately miserable as Madame Butterfly were she to be so unfortunate as to lose her husband's love. Cio-Cio-San serves as a model of womanly fidelity. The 1987 film *Fatal Attraction*, however, overturned this usual perception of the Cio-Cio-San character. It picks up on Cio-Cio-San's stubborn refusal to acknowledge what everybody else in her circle, as well as Pinkerton, knows full well: that her 'marriage' to Pinkerton is a charade. The female protagonist in *Fatal Attraction*, Alex Forrest (Glenn Close), enters into a relationship which her lover Dan Gallagher (Michael Douglas) believes they both understand perfectly will be nothing more than a brief sexual liaison. But to his horror, she moves the goalposts. She makes it out to be something much more serious. Alex, moreover, has an unhealthy obsession with Puccini's opera, and in her self-perception as the wronged woman, she identifies herself with Cio-Cio-San. Alex shares with Puccini's heroine a desire to make believe that she can have a happy family life with her lover. Like Cio-Cio-San, she projects this fantasy upon an unsuitable candidate: Alex knows before she initiates her relationship with Dan that he is already happily married. Although Alex presents herself on the surface as a successful career woman, holding down a responsible editorial position at a New York publishing house and leading an outwardly enviable independent, freewheeling lifestyle, it is as though her family instincts, having been stifled and thwarted, find their vent in the form of a pathological fixation on Dan and his family, whom she relentlessly hounds – at one point, notoriously boiling the family pet rabbit in a pot on the cooker.

The original ending to *Fatal Attraction* followed through with Alex's obsession with Puccini's *Madama Butterfly*. Alex imitates Cio-Cio-San by cutting her own throat – albeit with a kitchen knife on the bathroom floor – to the soundtrack of the aria '*Un bel dì*' ('One fine day'). Alex commits suicide in a final bid to portray herself as the victim of masculine cruelty. The knife handle has Dan's fingerprints on it, and by taking her own life with this knife, Alex (whether knowingly or not) implicates him in her death. Dan is arrested for her murder. Unfortunately, as a culmination of the acts of persecution which Alex has inflicted on Dan and his family, this last twist of the plot fails to hold much suspense, as the crisis is immediately resolved: Dan's wife Beth (Anne Archer) rushes to his desk to find his attorney's contact number and discovers the cassette tape Alex had sent Dan in which she threatens suicide.

The ending to *Fatal Attraction* was re-shot after preview audiences indicated that they wanted a different ending, one in which Beth is allowed to punish Alex. The new Grand Guignol of an ending turned away from the film's theme of Alex's narcissism, her self-absorption. Instead, Alex becomes a straight-forward blood-lusting villain. She now directs her knife, not at herself as in the original ending, but at Beth. The film implies that it is up to Dan and Beth to protect themselves: the police are portrayed as utterly ineffectual, their hands tied by bureaucracy. Dan and Beth cannot be rid of this nightmare until Alex is dead, and Beth finally triumphs over Alex by shooting and killing her. *Fatal Attraction*'s original ending made the film a study of one woman's obsessive perception of herself as a victim of exploitation, and her emotional manipulation of the object of her obsessive love. The sensational second ending transformed it into a lurid horror film, with Alex as a deranged knife-attacker who can only be stopped by a bullet to the chest. In either case, the portrayal of Alex as a psychotic evades the genuine issue – which is also present in the opera *Madama Butterfly* – of two lovers who have differing perceptions of the nature of their relationship.

The blindness of obsession is also the theme of David Henry Hwang's play *M. Butterfly*, which premiered at the National Theatre, Washington, DC, on 10 February 1988, transferring a month later to Broadway, where it ran for 777 performances at the Eugene O'Neill Theater. Hwang's play was inspired by the extraordinary case of Bernard Boursicot, a French diplomat who was arrested in 1983 for spying for the Chinese and who claimed at his trial that he had never realised throughout an affair spanning nearly two decades that his Chinese contact, his lover, was actually a man. Hwang's play also explores with savage humour western preconceptions about people of the Far East. The play's chief protagonist Rene Gallimard can only see Song Liling, the Peking Opera singer to whom he is attracted and whom he mistakes for a woman, through the spectacles of his expectations. Gallimard falls in love with the power he believes he wields over the person he takes to be the epitome of the fragile oriental woman; he glories in the idea that it lies entirely with him whether to treat this person as callously as Pinkerton or to be graciously magnanimous instead. Gallimard decides he will be magnanimous. He falls in love with his self-image as the protector of the weak oriental woman. Ironically, every concession he believes he is making to Song's innate oriental fragility, timidity, fearfulness and shyness – for he never seeks to force his will upon her – allows Song to keep up his pretence that he is a woman. Song, knowing how firmly Gallimard is in the grip of his fantasy of the meek oriental woman who is dependent on the charity of the strong occidental male, never fears that Gallimard will try to strip him/her naked. Song proceeds to exploit Gallimard's credulity in order to extract diplomatic information from him. Hwang brutally explodes the colonialist paradigm of the white man as exploiter and the Asian as the victim of exploitation.

Even when Gallimard is finally confronted by incontrovertible evidence that Song is a man – Song flaunts his masculinity in front of Gallimard – Gallimard chooses fantasy over reality, denying Song his ultimate satisfaction of getting the Frenchman to acknowledge the hold that Song has over him. In the concluding scene of *M. Butterfly*, Gallimard himself metamorphoses into Madame Butterfly – into, that is, a grotesque parody of his own fantasy of the desirable, pure and helpless woman whose ideal of love is betrayed by a worthless foreigner. Up to this moment, each character in the play maintains a wry, detached view of his identity, but in the shocking denouement, Gallimard now identifies totally with his fantasy and cuts his own throat. In Hwang's play, the white man becomes the victim of his fantasy of the victimised oriental woman. Indeed, Gallimard embraces his own victimisation. He dies for his fantasy, since, to Gallimard, to do so is to legitimise it. David Cronenberg's 1993 film version of *M. Butterfly*, however, interestingly leaves out Hwang's subversive irony. Here Song is made to suffer for his deception when Gallimard rejects him once he finds out Song is a man. Cronenberg turns the story into a tragedy of betrayed ideals: the oriental falls short of the western man's exalted vision of the ideal object of love.

In America, 'yellow fever' has been used as a term to describe the phenomenon of western men falling in love with a stereotypical image of oriental women. At the same time as such doll-like attributes as 'daintiness', when applied to Japanese women, help make them appear less threatening to western women as potential sexual rivals, the linking of Asian women with ideas of docility or vulnerability or less-than-aggressive sexuality (either pubescent or even boyish) makes them attractive to some men. Asians are thus desired not so much for themselves, as for not possessing characteristics associated with independent, self-assertive western women. The equation of the Asian with the more passive role in a sexual relationship is reflected also in many male homosexual relationships between Caucasians and Asians.[2] This sort of attention may not initially seem as offensive as outright racial abuse; it may appear flattering even, disguising the racism implicit in such attitudes. The American cultural anthropologist Karen Kelsky in her book *Women on the Verge: Japanese Women, Western Dreams* (2001) and the writer and journalist Sheridan Prasso in *The Asian Mystique: Dragon Ladies, Geisha Girls, and our Fantasies of the Exotic Orient* (2005) both give examples of Asian women who express satisfaction with, and even pride in, the idea that Asians are preferred by some white men to women of their own race as potential wife material. There is an old joke which has had some currency in America, Britain and parts of the Far East, the gist of which is that a happy man is the one who commands an American-size salary, reigns over an English stately home, has his meals prepared by a Chinese cook and enjoys the ministrations of a Japanese wife.[3] Indeed, the sympathetic portrayal of Cio-Cio-San in Long's novella as well as in Puccini's opera was possible because the desirability of Japanese women as wives was a well-established commonplace fantasy, one which it can be argued Pierre Loti was actually reacting against in writing *Madame Chrysanthème*. Pinkerton, from this point of view, is a fool to give up Cio-Cio-San for a self-assertive American version.

For Pinkerton's American wife will have things her way. In all three versions of the Madame Butterfly story, Long's novella, Belasco's play and Puccini's opera, Mrs Pinkerton is the one who decides she and her husband should have Butterfly's baby. Belasco made Kate Pinkerton into an even more forceful character than Adelaide in Long's story, by having Kate turn up at Cho-Cho-San's house and confront the mother directly with the proposition that the infant should be given up into her care. Whereas in Long's story there is more than a hint of frivolous whimsy about Adelaide's desire to adopt Cho-Cho-San's baby (she asks the American consul to telegram Pinkerton with the message: 'Just saw the baby and his nurse. Can't we have him at once? He is lovely'),[4] Belasco (followed by Puccini and his librettists) ratchets up the heartache by making Kate appeal so effectively to any mother's desire that her child should have the best possible chances in life, by arguing that it would be much more advantageous for the boy if he were to be brought up by the Pinkertons in the United States rather than by a penniless geisha in Nagasaki.

The characters of Kate Pinkerton and Cho-Cho-San constitute a classic juxtaposition of two female stereotypes: the active, plain-spoken, strong-willed American woman and the self-sacrificing Japanese woman. Kate steps in to negotiate for the child with its mother when her husband, guilt-stricken and too cowardly to face Cho-Cho-San, runs off. The flipside to 'yellow fever' has, since the nineteenth century, been a prejudice against western women as being too self-oriented, too independent or too aggressive – that is to say, too masculine. The persistence of these twinned prejudices can be seen, for example, in an article entitled 'Pretty Ethnics: The Death of the White Woman' by the columnist Tony Parsons which appeared in the spring 1991 issue of the British men's magazine *Arena*. In this article, Parsons, who, whatever else might be said of him, could never be accused of kowtowing to the dictates of political correctness, pits white women, whom he characterises as 'big brood mares with dyed hair and sagging tits', against the 'Pretty Ethnic', a term he describes as one he had first come across in the United States, and into this category he lumps Naomi Campbell together with Benazir Bhutto and the '*oh-eru*' of Japan – female office workers who, according to Parsons, are typically 'loaded down with Louis Vuitton bags and three kilos of waist-length hair'. He presents a preference for the latter as an argument for interracial harmony. But it is not merely a question of looks. Race (or non-whiteness) stands for a certain manner of behaviour, and what Parsons dislikes almost as much as big, drooping breasts is the 'complaining, big-boned, post-fem ballsy chick' – the argumentative, western, (white) career woman who is supposedly too vocal about her own feelings, too absorbed in her own wants, and too insecure about her choices to pay much attention to the needs of her man. Lest his readers mistake the reputed passivity of oriental women for feebleness, Parsons warns that one of these 'creature[s] of infinite beauty and grace', if treated badly, would not hesitate to 'spit in your eye as she walks down the aisle with another guy'.[5] It is fine that she exhibits a bit of robust, animal spirit, just so long as she does not start berating her current lover with her grievances.

Parsons's attitude reflects a late twentieth-century reaction against a perceived feminist tendency to label traditional expressions of femininity as indicative of socially imposed behaviour the purpose of which has been to reinforce women's inferior and dependent position in society. Since the 1990s some women have themselves sought to embrace sexual difference, not as a capitulation to the ideology of male hegemony, but as a positive step in defining their own individual identity. The cultural theorist Camille Paglia has, for example, extolled the pop superstar Madonna as a symbol of the modern, empowered woman, who is able to be both seductive and in control. Madonna has always revelled in transforming her stage persona, and it is not surprising that she was attracted to the idea of the geisha following the phenomenal success of the novel *Memoirs of a Geisha* (1997) by the American writer Arthur Golden. In adopting this persona, Madonna characteristically refashioned the geisha in her own image. Hers is a karate-kicking one, dressed in a low-cut John Paul Gaultier-designed mini-kimono, matching shorts, a figure-hugging leather obi and knee-high platform boots. The highly camp geisha image Madonna created for herself is sexy at the same time as it bristles with in-your-face attitude.

Madonna publicised her new interest in geishas with an interview and photo spread in the Februrary 1999 issue of *Harper's Bazaar*. Describing her fascination with Golden's *Memoirs of a Geisha*, she told the interviewer Daisann McLane that she felt that her profession made her just like ' "a modern-day geisha" '. Geishas were ' "trapped" ' by their circumstances, she explained, implying that the constraints put upon her freedom by the pressures of the contemporary music business and modern celebrity were nearly as onerous as those imposed on old-time geishas by poverty and indentured labour. There were compensations, however, according to Madonna: geishas formed a sisterhood of educated and cultured women (although in Golden's novel the women are hardly supportive of each other, as if Golden wanted to explode as a myth the whole idea that geishas might have respected the bonds of sisterhood they entered into with each other), and, above all, had the chance to associate with ' "some pretty amazing, powerful people" '.[6]

Madonna employed her geisha persona in the music video for 'Nothing Really Matters', a single from her 1998 album *Ray of Light*, and replicated her 'geisha' look for her appearance at the Grammy Awards on 24 February 1999. A couple of years later, she developed the geisha theme for a segment in her 'Drowned World' concert, which she took on tour around North America and Europe in the summer and early autumn of 2001.

Madonna's re-creation of the Japanese geisha was mirrored in her costume designers' adaptation of the kimono. In one of her outfits for the photo spread in *Harper's Bazaar*, the kimono is transformed into a black leather top and pants combination with detached sleeves fitting her lower arms and featuring long rectangular swathes of cloth, the iconic characteristic associated with the

33 Madonna performing at the 41st Annual Grammy Awards held at the Shrine Auditorium, Los Angeles, 24 February 1999.

kimono. Her white face make-up, red lips and straightened black hair are evocative of Morticia Addams, the deathly beautiful, seductive, black-draped matriarch of Charles Addams's cartoon Addams family (an earlier association between Morticia and Japanese women was made in the 1960s' US television series *The Addams Family*, in which Morticia twangs the *shamisen* and shrills '*Sashimi!*' and '*Sayonara!*'). The merging of Madonna's geisha image with her taste in the Gothic is evident in the way the swirling black gown the singer wore in her video for her single 'Frozen' (with a nod towards eastern mysticism represented by her hennaed hands) became a black 'kimono', designed by Gaultier, with sweeping sleeves (which extended bat-like for most of the length of the stage and had to be supported by dancers), when she performed the same song during the Drowned World tour. Madonna conflates the image of the geisha with that other western stereotype of the oriental woman: the dragon lady. In keeping with her image of the geisha, Madonna revealed in interviews that of all the characters in *Memoirs of a Geisha*, the one she felt the most affinity with was the hot-tempered, imperious, capricious star geisha Hatsumomo, the chief persecutor of Golden's heroine Sayuri.

In John Paul Gaultier's hands, the obi became a tight, figure-shaping corset, one of the most representative items of all fetishised western female clothing. Gaultier's thigh-length 'kimono' and 'obi' which Madonna wears in her

'Nothing Really Matters' video accentuate the cleavage and the breasts in a way the traditional Japanese versions of the garments do not. Gaultier had, of course, previously designed Madonna's iconic pink bustier with conical breasts for the singer's Blond Ambition tour in 1990. Gaultier ridiculed the hypocrisy of prudery by turning his corsets, bustiers and garters into outer garments that openly flaunted their function as apparatuses for forcibly moulding a woman's body into the contours of a sexual fantasy. Gaultier likewise takes the loose, flimsy western kimono-as-dressing-gown and makes it aggressively sexy. Through his clothes, Madonna projects her sexuality as though it were a kind of weapon.

Nor does Madonna passively play out the male fantasy of the fetishised female, the woman who is attributed masculine power to disguise from the eyes of the fetishist the horror of her sexual difference, that is to say, her lack of a phallus which suggests the mutilation of the male physique, thereby triggering castration anxiety in the fetishist. Rather than looking at fetishes as a male attempt to mould women to fit in with a masculine sexual fantasy, Amanda Fernbach in her study *Fantasies of Fetishism: From Decadence to the Post-Human* (2002) suggests that it is the dominatrix who fantasises herself into the image of an all-mighty, uncastratable 'Goddess figure' in rejection of women's disempowered ('castrated') state within society.[7] In the music video of 'Nothing Really Matters', Madonna first appears as a dark goddess-like figure. Enveloped in a black vinyl kimono, she cradles a clear plastic bag sloshing with water, in a parody of motherhood, indeed of the Virgin Mary. Her acolytes consist of a group of Far-East Asian dancers crowded inside a stark, claustrophobic factory building. Lurching about in this post-industrial setting, they are unindividualised: their faces are dusted white and their bodies look grub-like in the shapeless white tunics in which they are swathed. Their limbs jerk and twitch; their heads loll on their shoulders. Their mouths hang open, and their eyes are unfocused. They are like blank marionettes manipulated by a clumsy puppeteer. In imitation of Madonna, they fumble with enormous plastic bags of water in their arms.

The song, written by Madonna together with Susan and Patrick Raymond Leonard, is about putting aside youth's self-centred quest for personal happiness and awakening to the insight 'That nobody wins' and that love is its own reward. The refrain, 'Nothing really matters/ Love is all we need', is punched out by Madonna in Gaultier's flaming orange-red kimono and matching leather 'obi', as she grooves in time to the pulsating music. The acolytes, meanwhile, literally see the light in the form of a rapidly revolving flame suspended at the end of a rope which is energetically whirled by one lithe, bare-chested male dancer. They gape and raise their eyes ceiling-ward. More eastern women dance around a black-kimonoed Madonna, reverently gesticulating. Apparently freed now from their spasms, one man levitates, while another breaks out into a furious gyration. A trio of women stick out their tongues and pant.

The intentionally graceless, disjointed, juddering movements of the dancers (and their white make-up) owe their inspiration at least partly to earlier forms of the Japanese avant-garde performance-art/dance known as *butoh*, which experiments with different modes of physical expression that break away from the aesthetic expectations of dance traditions both Japanese and western. One might very well be tempted to 'interpret' the dancers in the Madonna video as expressing, first, an apocalyptic vision of alienation, followed by an instance of collective inspiration – a Pentecostal moment, to use a Christian allusion. Yet one cannot ignore the contrast they present, compared to Madonna. They might represent humankind reduced to toys of fate, but this condition does not apply to Madonna herself. She alone is individualised, despite her orientalised straight black hair and kohled eyes. She is vibrantly alive and sexy, especially in her fiery orange outfit – she is alternately kittenish, coy and brazen. Of course she is the famous singer, the star. However, it is difficult to avoid the impression that the Asians, as though ignorant of the meaning of love, yet again have to be taught about love, this time by Madonna.

In her guise as an 'oriental' woman, Madonna is able to play out camp fantasies about female subordination and sexual submissiveness, which seem to go against everything feminist activists in the west have been fighting for on behalf of women for the past forty years. For her rendition of 'Nobody's Perfect' in her Drowned World concert, she shuffles after a male dancer playing the part of the imperious lover, trying to placate him. At length, she offers herself up to the sweep of his samurai sword. As for the lover (dressed inexplicably in a kimono with girlish long *furisode*-length sleeves and grimacing in a manner that is presumably supposed to be kabuki-like), he howls, rolls his eyes, and slashes at Madonna with his sword, finally slicing off a lock of her hair, which trophy he triumphantly clenches in his fist. In the performance Madonna gave at the Palace of Auburn Hills in Auburn Hills, Michigan, on 26 August 2001 (which was recorded for video distribution), this role of the male lover was played by a black dancer, thereby making it appear that non-Caucasians, whether of Asian or African descent, were all to be swept into this category of primitive man. 'Nobody's Perfect' was followed in the concert by large-screen projections of photos of Madonna's white geisha face battered, bruised and bleeding. These images project the idea of the Asian woman as victim of masculine violence. Then, in the subsequent sequence, Madonna gets her revenge, comic-book/anime style, as she sings 'Sky Fits Heaven' kitted out in blood-red martial arts gear. She flies through the air in a harness and karate-kicks her hapless male adversaries, while meaningless Japanese lettering explodes on a screen whenever she lands a blow, in a manner familiar from cult American television shows of the 1960s such as *Batman*, which parodied the conventions of American superhero comics.

The *Boston Phoenix* observed acerbically of the music video of 'Nothing Really Matters' that Madonna 'erases the objects of her alleged identification and inspiration': 'Geishaphilia keeps them [Asian women] silent, powerless, and crazy – their mouths taped shut, their bodies out of control' (18–25 March 1999).[8] A similar imperiousness characterised the manner in which Madonna concluded the 'geisha' segment of the Drowned World show. Finishing the last verses of 'Mer Girl', Madonna whipped off her black wig to reveal a full head of blonde hair. She then took a rifle and (in anticipation, perhaps, of her next character in the show, a guitar-toting cowgirl) shot her stage doppelgänger, an Asian dancer, who had been seen earlier fluttering (in a muddle of Asian motifs) to a vaguely Bali-style musical accompaniment.[9] Pamela Robertson, in *Guilty Pleasures: Feminist Camp from Mae West to Madonna* (1996), has suggested that while Madonna has associated herself with various subcultures both in America and abroad, her stardom has meant that she has always been able to dissociate herself from them when it suited her to drop them, so that her commitment has never gone very much deeper than the level of style.[10] In the Drowned World concert, female subservience is a fantasy which Madonna plays at. There is no sense that it is the reality which so many women are forced to endure the world over. When Madonna is finished with her geisha persona, she does not merely cast it off but rejects it emphatically. She goes so far as to symbolically eradicate the presence of Asian-ness from the stage.

Another pop superstar to experiment with a geisha persona was Kylie Minogue, who took a different approach from Madonna's. The music video of the electronic pop number 'GBI: German Bold Italic' (1998), directed by the French photographer Stéphane Sednaoui, who was Minogue's lover at the time, exaggerates the western stereotype of the geisha as a sex toy, puppet-like and blank-faced. In the video, Minogue, with the kittenish sexuality she has used to sell her image to the public, is repackaged as a sort of depersonalised sex doll in a kimono, an image which serves as an ironic comment on the commodification of the pop star. As the title of the song suggests, 'GBI', which was written by the Korean-Japanese DJ and music producer Towa Tei with lyrics by Minogue, likens a woman's attractiveness to the decorative effect of a printer's typeface. In the video, it is Minogue's costumes that provide the decorative effect. She is first seen barely clad in a skimpy red bikini, writhing sensuously in the bath – although a foaming bubble bath rather than a more traditional Japanese type of tub. She sings the refrain: 'You will like my sense of style'. On her head she sports a gigantic, silver-hued bouffant wig which bristles with spangles and pins topped with large figures of flying cranes. This wig makes her look curiously like Madame Butterfly camping it up as the sexually over-ripe Marschallin in Richard Strauss's *Der Rosenkavalier*. It does, however, save Minogue from the embarrassment of looking as though she is attempting to 'orientalise' her physical appearance, as Madonna does in her music video of 'Nothing Really Matters'. Abruptly the bath scene shifts to a street scene shot among New York's skyscrapers. Minogue shuffles demurely along the pavement, still wearing the same wig but now dressed in an ornate, iridescently coloured kimono with flowing *furisode* sleeves and an elaborately tied obi. Though, strictly speaking, she is not dressed in the style usually adopted by real geishas, her attire is enough to make most people in the west assume she is made up like one: the critic Peter Conrad, for instance, in the *Observer* newspaper, described Minogue as being dressed 'as a geisha' (9 July 2006). Minogue peers about her, stopping occasionally to strike angular 'Japanese' poses with her hands and make low obeisances to random passers-by. She moves like an automaton; her eyes are unfocused. Scenes of Minogue shuffling in a kimono around New York are offset by shots of Towa Tei wandering through the claustrophobic streets of inner-city Tōkyō, earphones clasped firmly over his ears like gigantic earmuffs. He peers at his surroundings through the enormous lenses of his black-rimmed spectacles. Unlike Minogue, he stares directly and unflinchingly into the camera. His expression always remains impassive.

As the camera moves between close-ups of Minogue's face and Tei's, it appears at times that Minogue is addressing the words of the song to Tei, as though issuing her invitations to him (though they never appear together in the same frame). Later in the video, Minogue is shown with a collar around her neck. This is attached to a lead held by a leering Japanese *sararīman*, or office worker, in a dark business suit. Minogue, who has commanded a wide public following in Japan since the late 1980s, is represented here as an object of the sexual fantasies of non-western men. Yet, at the same time, these non-westerners are presented in a manner so tongue in cheek that the possibility that they might pose an actual threat either to the virtue of Caucasian women or the virility of Caucasian men is virtually negated. They are as camp as Minogue is in her over-the-top 'geisha' wig. In the final section of the video, Minogue's co-artist Towa Tei sits primly on the edge of a hotel bed as he is caressed by two lithesome modern young Japanese women in stockinged-feet but otherwise dressed neatly in trim western-style office clothes. The camera cuts between shots of Minogue thrashing about in her kimono and those of one or the other of the two prim Japanese women on the bed in states of increasing undress, looking very knowingly straight at the camera, with confident, meaningful smiles on their lips. There is a swapping of western sexual stereotypes here: the western woman plays out the fantasy of being an oriental sex slave while the young Japanese women play at being the office siren. The video concludes as Tei dissolves into a girlish giggle, as though the whole thing was one long joke.

Since the influx of Japanese goods into the west from the middle of the nineteenth century onwards, dressing up as a Japanese has been a popular fancy-dress conceit, especially after the theatrical success of *The Mikado*, the musical comedy *The Geisha*, and Puccini's *Madama Butterfly*. Yoshihara Mari, a cultural historian, has argued that for many female actors and singers in America (and, indeed, in Europe), playing the role of a Japanese geisha on stage did not only not harm their career, but often had a positive effect on their reputation, establishing them as models of the 'New Woman', the modern independent woman who creates a life for herself outside the narrow confines of her immediate family. Yoshihara mentions the American actress Blanche Bates, who first created the role of Cho-Cho-San on stage in the New York production of David Belasco's play and went on to win acclaim in another Japanese-themed play co-written by John Luther Long and Belasco, *The Darling of the Gods* (1902). Other examples that might be added to the list include British stage stars of the day such as Marie Tempest (the first O Mimosa San in *The Geisha*), Letty Lind (who created the role of Molly Seamore / Roli-Poli likewise in *The Geisha*), Evelyn Millard (who created the role of Belasco's Cho-Cho-San in London), and Florence Smithson (who appeared as O Hana San, the temple-singing-girl-turned-geisha in the musical comedy *The Mousmé* (1911), produced by Robert Courtneidge and featuring his daughter Cicely in the role of another Japanese *mousmé*). In response to Yoshihara, W. Anthony Sheppard, a professor of music with a specialist interest in the field of oriental influences on western music, has written that he cannot really see how 'playacting as a subservient childlike geisha' helped to change American women's perception of their role and place in society.[11] It is true that in Puccini's opera Cio-Cio-San never develops to the point where she begins to question the basic assumptions which she had hitherto allowed to dictate her life, whereas playwrights such as Henrik Ibsen were depicting female characters who change through their interactions with the people around them. In *A Doll's House* (1879), for instance, Nora's growing understanding of both her husband and herself leads her to reassess their marriage and eventually to walk away from it, thus taking control of her own life. But female theatre audiences in the west continued to have a considerable appetite for fragile romantic heroines (and not just Japanese ones), notwithstanding the rise of this new naturalism movement in theatre. Cio-Cio-San has attracted the sympathy of female audiences in the west because she arouses a mixture of empathy arising from a sense of the commonalty of human experience and pity for those less fortunate than oneself. While western women can enjoy this experience of relating to Cio-Cio-San's sorrows, some of their enjoyment also derives from a sense of detachment – from the position of being (or believing oneself to be) unaffected by those cultural shackles of female servility with which women in non-western countries are commonly believed to be fettered. Both Madonna and Kylie Minogue donned Japanese-style costumes in order to play-act at being the subservient woman. Taking off those garments, they shake off that subservience. Whereas in the west kimonos are closely associated with geishas and by extension with ideas of female submissiveness, perhaps the time has come for ordinary Japanese women to reclaim the kimono for themselves, not as a symbol of the traditional role of women in Japanese society but as an expression of their sense of identity in the modern world. Avant-garde Japanese fashion designers such as Kawakubo Rei of Comme des Garçons, Issey Miyake and Yohji Yamamoto have been seeking to express this sense of modern-day Japan by bringing together traditional Japanese concepts in clothing with western ones, and in the process radically diverging from western stereotypes of the 'oriental' look, as well as the highly sexualised conventions of western feminine dress.[12]

Although Madonna and Kylie Minogue were merely play-acting at being geishas, Liza Crihfield Dalby, whose study of contemporary geisha society, first published in 1983, was reissued in 1998 in the wake of the interest in geishas generated by *Memoirs of a Geisha*, has had personal experience of appearing as a geisha at a Kyōto teahouse. Dalby's depiction of geishas in her book, which was based on the research she undertook in the late 1970s for her doctoral dissertation in anthropology at Stanford University, is not so much as sexualised beings; rather, she concentrates on the role they fulfil within the social gatherings that take place in teahouses and similar establishments. She had begun her fieldwork interviewing working geishas in Tōkyō, before moving to the Pontochō district of Kyōto, where she was based at the Mitsuba Ryokan, an establishment which provided traditional-style banqueting rooms and was licensed for geishas to entertain on its premises, though at the time it did not have any attached directly to it. Dalby relates that it was the mistress of the Mitsuba who suggested to her that if she really wanted a first-hand understanding of the life of a geisha, she should consider becoming one herself. The mistress of the Mitsuba had been an apprentice geisha, or *maiko*, in her youth, and her mother before her had run a teahouse in the same quarter in Kyōto. Liza Dalby made her debut as a geisha the day after the mistress of the Mitsuba – now Dalby's *okāsan*, or 'mother' – first presented the idea to, and gained the acquiescence of, the mistress of the Daiichi teahouse, one of the most influential in the Pontochō quarter and the one to which Dalby's *okāsan* had been affiliated during her time as a *maiko*. Dalby participated in the professional activities of the Pontochō geishas under the name Ichigiku. She did not formally join the community because it was understood she would be returning sooner or later to the United States. Neither did she accept any fees for her appearances in her professional capacity as a geisha.

It is remarkable how quickly Dalby felt she was able to assume the look and act the part of a geisha. Because of her age and circumstances, she did not undergo an apprenticeship as a *maiko*. She was, however, already highly skilled at the *shamisen*, and on the advice of her *okāsan*, she had started taking lessons in *kouta*, the style of traditional Japanese song which geishas are most frequently asked to perform. Dalby, however, ascribes her success at the first ever banquet she attended as a geisha not to her proficiency in Japanese music or any other esoteric Japanese art form, but – being fluent in Japanese – to the ease with which her American upbringing, ironically, allowed her to speak to men. She concludes that the special training supposedly required of *maiko* and geishas actually involved nothing more profound than learning to hold one's end up (albeit with wit and grace) in any sort of conversation one might find oneself engaged in with a member of the opposite sex. It appears that Dalby's American-style self-confidence, openness and candour made her a natural as a geisha, while, paradoxically, Japanese *maiko* seemed to need years to learn – and with considerable difficulty – to overcome their reticence around men, with which they had been inculcated by society since early childhood.[13]

Dalby writes that she mastered the proper way of moving in a kimono through careful imitation of her compeers. As a geisha, Dalby very rarely donned the full formal costume, which is comprised of white make-up, a wig done up in a traditional hairstyle, and the Japanese woman's formal black silk kimono embellished with the family crest (or, in the case of geishas, the crest of their geisha house) and decorated with a dyed or embroidered design near the hem of the garment. Dalby usually wore her own hair, which she had done at the hairdresser's in a large smooth bouffant like other geishas. She believes that when she was with her fellow geishas, her looks did not give her away as a non-Japanese. Not only did she have naturally dark hair, but her pale skin tone gave her an advantage in a profession in which many Japanese women have to resort to carefully applied cosmetics – whether of the traditional white kind or the modern, more natural looking (that is to say, less artificial looking) western type – in order to achieve that clear pale complexion which the Japanese have always prized in women.[14] The only feature which she feels made her stand out among her fellow geishas was her height. Dalby relates how she had once overheard Japanese passers-by making comments which made her realise they assumed she was a female impersonator, though an ' "awfully glamorous" ' one.[15] Dalby does not take offence at being taken for a man in a woman's kimono. If anything, it proves how successful she has been in appropriating the properties of Japanese womanhood. While a western drag artiste exaggerates with his use of costume and make-up particular features of a woman's sexuality (her breasts, her legs, her lips, her hair), the Japanese *onnagata*'s transformation does not involve parody. As Roland Barthes speculated, 'the Western transvestite wants to be a (particular) woman, the Oriental actor seeks nothing more than to combine the signs of Woman.'[16]

Dalby's confidence that she had been able to merge seamlessly into the company of the geishas of Pontochō is striking for its lack of any sense of inferiority. It is interesting to contrast this with the observations made by the playwright David Henry Hwang, the author of *M. Butterfly*, who has written of the feeling he believes he shares with many Asian-Americans that they are 'perpetual foreigners' in their own country. In his introduction to a collection of his plays *FOB and other Plays* (1990), Hwang writes how he, like many other Asian-Americans, had become conscious in childhood of skin colour as an inescapable marker of one's difference from the perceived norm, and how the impossibility of ridding oneself of such stigmatising markers of difference had given rise to feelings of self-loathing.[17] Dalby, in her account of her experiences as a geisha in Kyōto, does, however, give an example of how awareness of her difference (in her case her nationality) generated certain prejudices among some of her fellow geishas. Dalby recounts how exasperated and frustrated she felt when they would not believe that she, being a foreigner, could be any good on the *shamisen*, as though skill on a Japanese instrument depended on one's nationality rather than on dedication and hard work. Dalby's experience bears some similarity to that described by the Japanese-American anthropologist Dorinne Kondo. 'No matter how many generations Asian Americans are resident here [in the United States],' Kondo writes, 'no matter how articulate we seem, we inevitably attract the comment, "Oh, you speak English so well." ' In Kondo's example, however, racial appearance operates as the marker of otherness and this happens in Kondo's own country.[18]

Try as the likes of Liza Crihfield Dalby might to present geisha society as a guardian of elements of traditional Japanese culture, there will be people in the west who will not be persuaded that women who make it their profession to be pleasing to men would stop short of offering their bodies. If already on the slippery slope of acquiescing in servility for the sake of money, what would stop a woman from degrading herself that one step further? In the view of the columnist Barbara Ellen, for example, writing in the *Observer* in April 2001,[19] the geisha's cultural pretensions merely obfuscate the ugly fact that she is in reality the worst possible combination of 'companion, hostess, servant and whore'. 'Strip away all the trimmings, the beauty, grace and mystery of what Liza Dalby . . . called "the flower and willow world",' Ellen suggests, 'and you're left with the vulgar reality of . . . a glorified hostess, who is quite happy to bang their married john, and then pour him a nice post-coital cup of tea.'

As Barbara Ellen sees it, geishas are disingenuous, whereas western prostitutes at least do not equivocate about what they have to sell. The latter sell sex – and nothing more. Geishas are worse because they relinquish their 'essential self' – their individuality, their mind, their will – in order to make themselves pleasing to men. In Ellen's view, that a woman (whether in the east or the west) can in this day and age contemplate subordinating her wishes to those of a man in the deluded belief that this is a constructive step in the preservation of their relationship is nothing less than a betrayal of a principle which women have fought long and hard to establish – that of the right to self-determination. What is more, Ellen feels she can spot the modern western equivalent of Japanese geishas – not on the street corners of London, but in the comfortable homes of suburbia, where she suspects the retrogressive idea that one's independence is a price worth paying to keep a man is spreading insidiously among the ranks of ordinary women.

Getting the man of one's dreams is, when all is said and done, the theme of Arthur Golden's *Memoirs of a Geisha*. Although the novel combines several conventional genres in western popular fiction – the coming-of-age novel, as well as the business-success story, in which the entry-level hero/ine surmounts formidable obstacles to rise to the top of his/her profession – it is, after all, a traditional love story with a happy ending: girl gets boy, except that Golden's heroine, the geisha Sayuri, is content to become a mistress rather than a wife. This remains unexplained. It is true that the geisha world, as Golden portrays it, is so self-absorbed that it has very little time for, or interest in, people outside it. Nonetheless, Sayuri's complete indifference to the fact that the kindly gentleman she has adored for so long has been married all that time never becomes an issue in the novel. Since the object of Sayuri's infatuation – referred to throughout the novel by his company position, the Chairman – is seen only through Sayuri's eyes but remains beyond her ken for much of the novel (frustratingly for both Sayuri and the reader), her passion for him is never shown to develop or mature past the star-struck stage, leaving the denouement of the love-story aspect of *Memoirs* less than satisfying.

Apart from being a love story, Golden's novel purports to lay bare the inner workings of the geisha community from an insider's point of view – nothing whets the curiosity so much as the prospect of an exposé of a secretive society. To this end, *Memoirs of a Geisha* is presented as a set of recollections dictated by Sayuri and translated into English by an American academic with a chair in Japanese history at a university in New York. In this way the novel lays claim to a voice of authenticity. *Memoirs of a Geisha*, moreover, gives a modern twist to

34 'Au baiser je le reconnais,/Mon amoureux est un Français'. French early twentieth-century hand-tinted picture postcard.

the subject of geishas by showing it as a highly competitive profession: at first the heroine Sayuri's heart is not in it; she tries to escape, fails and suffers a fall from grace; she afterwards discovers a sense of purpose which gives her the motivation to claw her way to the top, pushing jealous rivals aside in the process. The 'newcomer to show business supplants established favourite as top star' plotline, in itself, is hardly a new one. The relationship between the up-and-coming geisha Sayuri and Hatsumomo, a geisha at the zenith of her popularity, is reminiscent of the rivalry at the heart of the Hollywood film *All about Eve* (1950). Whereas Pierre Loti alleged in *Madame Chrysanthème* that he possessed no key with which he might have gained entry into the minds of the '*mousmés*' of Nagasaki as they sat twanging away at their *shamisen*, Golden has no such trouble. His women are greedy, grasping, jealous, spiteful and conniving, and they fight with each other with all the sophistication of cats. If anything, they conform to the western stereotype of the female sex in general (regardless of race) as being fundamentally impulsive and emotional, only Hatsumomo and the proprietress of the geisha house to which Sayuri belongs are both so extravagantly malevolent that, in the end, they lose their impact as villains. They are rather like the wicked stepmother and stepsister in the Cinderella story.

Despite the camp wickedness of Sayuri's tormentors, the geisha business as portrayed in *Memoirs of a Geisha* is a vicious one. Sayuri as a child (when she is still called Chiyo) is separated from her father and sister and sold against her will to a geisha house. She is harshly treated, bullied mercilessly and punished brutally. The reader is entitled to ask how a child like Chiyo/Sayuri comes to accept her circumstances. Chiyo/Sayuri is shown falling in with geisha society; yet the novel really does not engage with the question of how it is that a victim becomes part of the abusive system in which she is trapped. The devices of romantic fiction take over and Chiyo/Sayuri's motive for her volte-face and her sudden desire to become a geisha is ascribed to a love interest. Although she is still a child, she seems to be precociously conscious that if she wants to enjoy the society of nice gentlemen like the Chairman (whom she has just encountered in the company of a geisha), the quickest route would be to make use of her own sexuality and become a top geisha herself.

In *Memoirs of a Geisha* the geisha business is essentially about sex. That is what the male patrons of geishas are after. Golden's take on geisha society adheres to familiar western suspicions about what really goes on within its secretive confines. Golden is well aware that the spiciness of his material helps to sell his novel, as he hints in his choice of name for the fictitious professor of Japanese history who is supposed to have transcribed Sayuri's dictated recollections: Jakob Haarhuis. Christina B. Rosenberger reported in the Harvard University newspaper the *Harvard Crimson* that the author explained at a public appearance in

Boston that 'Haarhuis' was a play on the words 'whore house'.[20] Golden increases the shock value of his story by setting the action back in the pre-war and imme-diate post-war periods, when abuses were common. The novel's descriptions of the sordidness of living conditions in Japan – the stench, the overcrowding, the repulsive food people eat – are, however, more than just touches of realism. They serve as a metaphor for the corruption that lies at the heart not only of geisha society but of Japanese society in general. In this respect, Golden's novel has much in common with works of a previous era, such as Loti's *Madame Chrysanthème*, Mascagni's opera *Iris* and Paris's novel *Kimono*. All of these works share a fascination with – at the same time as revulsion for – that ornate artifice which the west has associated so closely with Japanese culture. This artifice is taken to be symptomatic of the decadence that is supposed to lie at the heart of Japanese life. *Memoirs of a Geisha* implies that all the layers of elaborate social ritual to which the geishas adhere, their polished music-making and dancing, their sumptuous clothes and ostentatious hairstyles held together by their exquis-itely fashioned, bejewelled ornaments only act to mask an underlying rank corruption – a moral turpitude arising from ennui and jaded sensuality. Yet, iron-ically, Golden's novel itself is more interested in wallowing in the decadent behaviour and lifestyle of the geishas and their patrons than in delving into the corruption. The problem comes back to Sayuri's characterisation. She herself suggests that she has inherited from her mother not only her unusual watery grey eyes, but a certain watery quality to her personality – a graceful adaptability to circumstances. Sayuri certainly adapts to geisha society. By the time she retires as a geisha to become the Chairman's mistress, she appears to have become thor-oughly immersed in the hedonistic, bitchy atmosphere of the geisha world, and it is with nostalgia that she looks back on the evenings she had spent on her rounds of professional engagements in the company of men (other than the Chairman), associating those occasions with pleasurable intrigues from which she is now excluded. This is all the more surprising since previously Sayuri has revealed that the average geisha party tended to be very dull.

It is never clear whether Sayuri's rise in the geisha world is to be read as a triumph of her will over a hostile world or as her gradual collusion with a corrupt one. Is the reader being asked to rejoice in her happiness in finally being united with the man she has adored for so long (as the formula of romantic fiction would seem to suggest), or lament that she has been moulded into a deferential, submissive kind of Japanese woman and that her horizons have thus been shrunk by the vicious and petty surroundings in which she has been raised? Then there is the disturbing revelation that the Chairman has, from a distance, been funding and directing Sayuri's training as a geisha all along. This Pygmalion gets, in the end, to possess the creature he has created. But Sayuri's reaction to this news is merely one of pleasure at discovering that the Chairman has cared for her since their very first meeting when she was still a child. Towards the end of the novel, there is a further example of moral ambivalence. When Sayuri finally severs all her links with the proprietress of the geisha house to which she has belonged since childhood, she relinquishes her claim to the business, to which, as the proprietress's adopted daughter, she had been designated the heir. But in exchange for dissociating herself from the geisha house, she makes sure – with the help of the Chairman's accountants – that she gets her share of its profits. Does this make Sayuri an astute businesswoman? She is, after all, about to leave for New York where she intends to open a small, exclusive teahouse of her own, as a kind of elegant meeting place for Japanese dignitaries and businessmen passing through the city (she has also decided that this would be the best way to avoid becoming an embarrassment to the Chairman, who is planning to marry his eldest legitimate daughter to a businessman he wants to make his heir). Or is she, in fact, guilty of turning a blind eye to the tainted nature of the money to which she lays claim? In many ways, *Memoirs* glamorises the victims of a business the abuses of which the novel supposedly sets out to expose. Perhaps this inherent contradiction is the key to the novel's popularity. In any case, the problem is also present in the Hollywood film version of *Memoirs*, which was released in the United States in December 2005. The camera lingers lovingly on the voluptuous beauty of the setting in which the geishas in the film lead their gilded lives. But, as Roger Ebert put it in the *Chicago Sun-Times*, 'if this movie had been set in the West, it would be perceived as about children sold into prostitution, and that is not nearly as wonderful as "being raised as a geisha" ' (16 December 2005).

It should be borne in mind that *Memoirs of a Geisha* is, after all, a work of fiction. It is no more an ethnological or anthropological study of the Japanese people than *Madama Butterfly* is. They are both constructs of the creative imagination, which takes fragmentary perceptions of the world as it finds them and builds them into a picture of its own creation. Writers and artists have never allowed themselves to be restricted in their subject material to their own direct, personal experiences. The imagination seeks entry into the unfamiliar and yet unknown: it ranges freely over both the forgotten past and the projected future; it crosses the gender divide and penetrates into the often jealously guarded cultural domain of different social classes and different ethnic groups. Such incursions may be deeply resented by those on the receiving end, and offence taken that those considered to be, in some way or another, outsiders should appropriate, as it were, elements of one's own culture for their own, albeit creative, ends. The feeling that one's culture is being misrepresented, either wilfully or through a lack of understanding, can be bewildering, at times irritating, and on occasions upsetting. Puccini's *Madama Butterfly* makes a point about how insensitive and cavalier Pinkerton is towards Japanese culture, and yet how many times have Japanese opera lovers shuddered to see western productions of the opera in which the Japanese characters blithely ignore strongly held Japanese taboos, such as not trampling over indoor *tatami*-mat flooring in outdoor footwear, and not wearing kimonos right side over the left, regardless of whether the wearer is a man or woman, because only the dead are dressed in that way.

The first version of *Madama Butterfly*, which opened in 1904 in Milan, contained at least one gratuitously negative racial stereotype of the Japanese as a figure of fun: Yakusidé, a drunkard uncle of Cio-Cio-San's, whose antics at the wedding reception in Act I are received with indulgent amusement by his fellow guests. Racial stereotyping was considerably toned down in Puccini's subsequent reworkings of the opera, and by the 1906 Paris version Yakusidé's scene had disappeared. Nevertheless, the fundamentally negative light in which Cio-Cio-San's relations and friends are portrayed in the wedding scene in the first act did not change. They are universally calculating, material-minded and spiteful. Cio-Cio-San's friends are hardly friends at all. The women exchange snide remarks about Pinkerton's looks (he is unattractive), the possible reasons why Cio-Cio-San has accepted him (he may not be good-looking but at least he has some money), and the chances of the relationship prospering (she is already losing her beauty, so he is bound to cast her aside). A cousin claims she had been offered Pinkerton first, but had turned the proposition down. It really comes as no surprise that these people turn their backs on Cio-Cio-San after her uncle the Bonze accuses her of renouncing her own people and her religion by going to the Christian mission. Cio-Cio-San is the one pure and innocent soul among a welter of conniving natives. She is an exception among her own people. Cio-Cio-San is a damsel in distress who needs rescuing by an enlightened outsider from those who are beneath her. This is, to say the least, a less than flattering picture of the Japanese race.

Is this something to be offended by, that a woman whose unworldliness is so extreme that it makes her virtually a simpleton should be put on a pedestal as the ideal Japanese? But there is another way of looking at the question of Cio-Cio-San's naïvety. Cio-Cio-San *is* a holy fool. Puccini's music transforms her love into something sublime. Cio-Cio-San's love becomes that love which burns away all worldly sin, all imperfections, in a holy union that transforms two loving souls into one being. This is the love of Wagner's Tristan and Isolde. Isolde's *Liebestod*, with which Wagner's opera ends, is one of the greatest, as well as one of the last, expressions of this western romantic ideal of transcendent love. What *Madama Butterfly* portrays is the unsustainability of this romantic ideal. The love duet between

Cio-Cio-San and Pinkerton at the climax of Act I is a declaration of such love: a love that excludes all others, that is mutual and all-encompassing, an overwhelming love that has no care for the concerns of mundane existence, such as having enough money to live on and finding a way of jogging along from day to day with one's partner. There is no comparable scene in either Long's novella or Belasco's stage play. It was a stroke of Puccini's genius to give this quality to Cio-Cio-San and Pinkerton's love: Long's Pinkerton is too cynical to harbour such emotions, and Belasco's play dwells exclusively on the fallout of Pinkerton's abandonment of Butterfly.

Puccini follows Belasco's sequence of events in the second half of his opera, thereby depicting the inexorable destruction by reality of this dream of transcendent love. Such transcendent love belongs, perhaps, only in the realm of fable. Cio-Cio-San and Pinkerton's union descends into the realm of contracts and legalities. Even Cio-Cio-San invokes American law to argue she is Pinkerton's legitimate wife. Isolde's love for Tristan is sublimated in death, but *Madama Butterfly* substitutes what is, in the end, nothing but a shabby domestic suicide, the onanistic *petit mort* of a solitary woman. Cio-Cio-San might protest as much as she likes that she is armed with her father's dagger. In the end, she turns its blade not on Goro and definitely not on Pinkerton, but on herself. In killing herself, Cio-Cio-San has, after all, been very obliging. For all the sympathy Puccini's first audiences may have extended to the poor little Japanese geisha, many would no doubt have agreed that it would have been socially unacceptable for Cio-Cio-San to have gone to the United States as Pinkerton's wife. (Katō Yuki, for example, a former geisha of Kyōto who in 1904 married George Denison Morgan, a nephew of John Pierpont Morgan, the American financier, received a very cold welcome from most members of his family, as well as from New York society as a whole.) It was all for the best that the Pinkertons should take the child themselves (especially since the boy takes after his father and not his mother in looks), while Cio-Cio-San has been able to prove her spirit of self-sacrifice and self-abnegation, her bravery, her Japanese-ness. The Orient redeems itself in spite of its ridiculousness in an act of exaggerated bravado. There is, though, a futility associated with Cio-Cio-San's father's dagger, the symbol of Japanese virility. By wielding the dagger, Cio-Cio-San oversteps the bounds of her sex. She usurps her father's masculine power, and yet what has he used it for in the first place but to kill himself in atonement for failure? Cio-Cio-San, for her part, dies for love: her death by means of the phallic dagger is meant as an act of love; and in her death, her love is supposed to triumph for ever. But there is no exaltation in Puccini's music. Pinkerton, of course, does not join her in death. In the final reckoning, Cio-Cio-San's triumph rings hollow.

Then there is Pinkerton's return from the heights of transcendental love to the resumption of a life spent in pursuit of honour and glory in the service of the American navy. There has always existed in the human mind, in the west as in the east, the opposition between the contemplative life and the active life, a life that finds its ultimate fulfilment in a transcendent love (whether for a woman or for God) versus a life dedicated to the achievement of glorious deeds in the name of one's country and people. The active hero in Greek mythology rejects the exotic siren, the sweet pleasures of personal happiness for the sake of his manly duties. Jason discards Medea, and Theseus leaves Ariadne behind on the island of Naxos. Likewise, Virgil in the *Aeneid* has his hero Aeneas abandon Dido, queen of Carthage, so that the Trojan prince might go on to fulfil his destiny of conquering Latium and founding the Roman race. According to the narrative of conquest and empire building, all these women are redundant once they have served their brief purpose of helping their heroes attain an immediate goal. Yet the human spirit seemingly has felt the need to propitiate – to placate – the wrath of women abandoned in this way. Medea's rage and bloody revenge became the subject of tragedies by Euripides, Seneca and Ovid; legend rewarded Ariadne for her suffering with a union with the god Dionysus; and Virgil composed heart-wrenchingly beautiful lines on Dido's noble despair.

It is tempting to read the Madame Butterfly story as an indictment of nineteenth-century western imperialist attitudes towards other races. At the same time, as the character Song Liling suggests in Hwang's *M. Butterfly*, the story is based on the assumption that it is apt that it should be the weaker oriental woman who worships, and kills herself for the sake of the strong, virile westerner, even though it turns out he is unworthy of her. 'Consider it this way,' Song says to the French diplomat Gallimard,

> what would you say if a blonde homecoming queen fell in love with a short Japanese businessman? He treats her cruelly, then goes home for three years, during which time she prays to his picture and turns down marriage from a young Kennedy. Then, when she learns he has remarried, she kills herself. Now, I believe you would consider this girl to be a deranged idiot, correct?[21]

But in the Japanese novelist Mori Ōgai's novella *Maihime* (1890), this reversal more or less does take place. It is the Japanese man who falls in love with, then betrays and ultimately ruins, a trusting, innocent German girl. The exotic western woman becomes the Japanese man's object of desire; her fragility makes him all the more manly; yet her seductiveness ultimately threatens to emasculate him and he ends up casting her aside. The protagonist of Mori Ōgai's novella is a high-flying Japanese civil servant named Ōta, who is posted to

Berlin and becomes involved in a doomed love affair with a beautiful, fatherless local girl. Ōta's sojourn in an unfamiliar world stimulates his intellect and his aesthetic sensibilities, and he valiantly comes to the aid of a helpless dancing girl, Elise, whom a Berlin theatre proprietor is trying to force into becoming his mistress. Ōta and Elise strike up a warm friendship. Ōta becomes increasingly alienated from the Japanese community in Berlin, and is drawn closer and closer to Elise. He becomes the centre of malicious gossip among his Japanese compatriots, and is dismissed from his civil-service position by his superiors. He and Elise find solace in one another. They become lovers and set up house together, although they do not have much money. Elise falls pregnant. She trusts Ōta will eventually marry her. Ōta, however, has not been able to entirely let go of his professional ambitions. His friends, meanwhile, have been working secretly on his behalf so he can return to Japan and resume his career. They expect him, in exchange, to leave Elise. Ōta is unable to face telling her he has accepted a new posting on the understanding that he will break off his relationship with her. He prevaricates and succumbs to a high fever. While he is dangerously ill, a close Japanese friend of his takes it upon himself to inform Elise of Ōta's decision. The shock is too much for her and she goes mad. Ōta, on the other hand, recovers. He returns with his friend to Japan, leaving behind some money for Elise.

The story was partially autobiographical. Mori, who was not only a writer of great eminence but a military doctor who served with the Japanese army, spent four years in Germany in the 1880s. There had been a real-life Elise in Mori's life, a dancer like the fictional Elise. But unlike her, this Elise had not gone mad on Mori's departure. She followed him all the way to Tōkyō. It was said of her that she was fully prepared to support herself, if necessary, as a seamstress in order to remain in Japan. Mori's relations, anxious for his reputation and his career, persuaded her, however, to return to Europe.

The enterprise, the resolve and the courage of the real-life Elise disappear from Mori's novella. For Ōta, the Berlin episode is like a dream, an all too brief moment of freedom from the demands of a man's career and his duties, both social and familial. His love affair with Elise, in the end, has been no more substantial than a hallucination that might have flickered through the mad Elise's imagination. In a similar manner, Cio-Cio-San is sacrificed so that Pinkerton and his wife can get on with their lives – and so that the audience can go home to theirs. The exotic 'Other' is like the poet's vision of the Abyssinian maid in Coleridge's 'Kubla Khan' – the 'damsel with a dulcimer' – whose song of wondrous joy is doomed to be irretrievably lost. The lacquer-haired geisha is another of the dream women that haunt the western imagination. An object of western desire, she shimmers into view, swirls the hem of her richly embroidered kimono, and then is gone once more.

Notes

Introduction

1. Basil Hall Chamberlain, *Things Japanese, Being Notes on Various Subjects Connected with Japan*, 2nd, rev. and enlarged edn (London: Kegan Paul, Trench, Trübner; and Yokohama, Shanghai, Hong Kong, Singapore: Kelly & Walsh, 1891), p. 453.

Chapter 1: Were They or Weren't They?

1. Henry Norman, *The Real Japan: Studies of Contemporary Japanese Manners, Morals, Administration, and Politics* (London: T. Fisher Unwin, 1892), p. 177. Norman left journalism in 1899. In the following year, he was elected to parliament, and was later knighted.
2. Henry T. Finck, *Lotos-time in Japan* (London: Lawrence and Bullen, 1895), p. 74.
3. Engelbert Kaempfer, *The History of Japan: Giving an Account of the Antient and Present State and Government of that Empire; of its Temples, Palaces, Castles, and other Buildings; of its Metals, Minerals, Trees, Plants, Animals, Birds and Fishes; of the Chronology and Succession of the Emperors, Ecclesiastical and Secular; of the Original Descent, Religions, Customs, and Manufactures of the Natives, and of their Trade and Commerce with the Dutch and Chinese. Together with a Description of the Kingdom of Siam*, trans. J.G. Scheuchzer (London: Thomas Woodward and Charles Davis, 1727), I, 260–61. Kaempfer's *History* was first published posthumously in 1727 in an English translation by John Gaspar Scheuchzer of his original manuscript written in German.
4. Li Yannian's poem is found in the Chinese book *Hanshu*, an historical account of the Western Han dynasty which was written in the first century AD.
5. Kaempfer, I, 332–33; Charles Peter Thunberg, *Travels in Europe, Africa, and Asia. Performed between the Years 1770 and 1779* (London: W. Richardson, Cornhill, and J. Egerton, 1795), III, 74–75.
6. [M. M. Busk (ed.)], *Manners and Customs of the Japanese in the Nineteenth Century: From Recent Dutch Visitors of Japan, and the German of Dr. Ph. Fr. Von Siebold* (London: John Murray, 1841), pp. 27–28; Kaempfer, II, 438. Caron's account of Japan, *Beschrijvinghe van het machtigh Coninckrijcke Japan*, which Caron based on a report he sent to the Dutch East India Company office in Batavia in 1636, was published in Amsterdam in 1648. An English translation by Captain Roger Manley was published in London in 1663.
7. Yoshida Tsunekichi, *Tōjin O-Kichi: Bakumatsu gaikō hishi* (Tōkyō: Chūō Kōronsha, 1966), pp. 122–28; Nakazato Kian, *Bakumatsu kaikō rashamen jōshi* (Tōkyō: Sekirokaku Shobō, 1931), pp. 140–42; Yokohama Kaikō Shiryōkan (ed.), *Meiji no Nippon: Yokohama shanshin no sekai*, expanded edn (Yokohama: Yūrindō, 2003), p. 29.

8. Edward Barrington De Fonblanque, *Niphon and Pe-che-li; or, Two Years in Japan and Northern China* (London: Saunders, Otley, 1862), pp. 44–45.

9. C. Pemberton Hodgson, *A Residence at Nagasaki and Hakodate in 1859–1860: with an Account of Japan generally* (London: Richard Bentley, 1861), p. 243.

10. Hodgson, pp. 230, 243; De Fonblanque, pp. 44–45.

11. Hodgson, p. 230.

12. Ibid., p. 243. The very top class of courtesan did not appear behind this type of window. *Harimise* in Tōkyō's Yoshiwara quarter originally took place during the daytime, between noon and four in the afternoon. It was only after the brothel quarter moved to its new – more inconvenient – location in 1657 that evening *harimise* was allowed. The time of evening *harimise* occurred was between six and ten at night (it was later extended to midnight). It was not until 1916 that the custom of *harimise* was finally banned in Tōkyō. Miyamoto Yukiko, 'Kao wo misete kyaku wo hiku', in Nishiyama Matsunosuke (ed.), *Yūjo* (1979; repr. Tōkyō: Tōkyōdō Shuppan, 1994), pp. 28–29, 256.

13. Hodgson, p. 230; Rodolphe Lindau, *Un Voyage autour du Japon* (Paris: Hachette, 1864), p. 194. Lindau was in Japan in 1859, and again between 1861 and 1862. His account first appeared in the French journal *La Revue des deux mondes*, and was widely consulted by subsequent French visitors to the country. He served as Swiss consul in Yokohama between 1864 and 1866.

14. Lindau, pp. 193–94; Aimé Humbert, *Le Japon illustré* (Paris: Hachette, 1870), II, 279.

15. Hodgson, pp. 239–41.

16. Humbert, II, 248–49.

17. Lindau, pp. 61–63, 66 fn. 1.

18. Comte Raymond de Dalmas, *Les Japonais: Leur pays et leurs mœurs* (Paris: E. Plon, Nourrit et Cie, 1885), pp. 150–51.

19. Michael Cooper (ed.), *They Came to Japan: An Anthology of European Reports on Japan, 1543–1640* (London: Thames and Hudson, 1965), p. 46.

20. Kaempfer, II, 438–39; Thunberg, III, 125.

21. Kaempfer, I, 260; II, 438–39.

22. Usami Misako, *Shukuba to meshimori-onna* (Tōkyō: Dōseisha, 2000), pp. 12–23, 67–78. Apprehended illegal prostitutes were given a term of five years; from the 1720s onwards, this was reduced to three (Hayashi Yoshikazu, *Jidai fūzoku kōshō jiten* (Tōkyō: Kawade Shobō Shinsha, 1977), p. 453).

23. Hodgson, p. 240.

24. George Smith, *Ten Weeks in Japan* (London: Longman, Green, Longman, and Roberts, 1861), pp. 276–77. George Smith, who had worked as a missionary in China, was the first Anglican bishop of the newly created diocese of Victoria (Hong Kong).

25. J. J. Rein, *Japan nach Reisen und Studien im Auftrage der Königlich Preussischen Regierung* (Leipzig: Verlag von Wilhelm Engelmann, 1881), I, 496; trans. as *Japan: Travels and Researches Undertaken at the Cost of the Prussian Government* (London: Hodder & Stoughton, 1884), p. 428. Rein refers to the serving girl as '*nesan*' (sister), a term by which Japanese men themselves would most likely have addressed such women. Johannes Justus Rein was commissioned by the Prussian Ministry of Commerce to look into the state of trade and industry in Japan. He spent nearly two years in Japan, between 1874 and 1875, and after his return to Germany became professor of geography at Marburg.

26. Hodgson, p. 237.

27. Common alternative spellings for *musume* included '*moosme*', '*mousmee*' (under which the word is found in the *Oxford English Dictionary*), '*musumé*', and '*mousmé*' (as the word was often rendered in French texts).

28. Lindau, pp. 59, 68 fn, 135 fn 1.

29. Isabella L. Bird, *Unbeaten Tracks in Japan: An Account of Travels in the Interior, including Visits to the Aborigines of Yezo and the Shrines of Nikkô and Isé* (London: John Murray, 1880), I, 86–87.

30. Dōke Seiichirō, *Baishunfu ronkō: Baishō no enkaku to genjō* (Tōkyō: Shishi Shuppansha, 1928), pp. 92–95.

31. Women customarily tied their obi in front until the late eighteenth century, when the obi became much broader and the bow more cumbersome. Only courtesans then continued to wear elaborate bows in front.

32. Usami, pp. 3–7, drawing upon Igarashi Tomio, *Meshimori-onna: Shukuba no shōfutachi* (Tōkyō: Shin Jinbutsu Ōraisha, 1981); Sekiguchi Hiroko, 'Yūkō suru onnatachi', in Sōgō Joseishi Kenkyūkai (ed.), *Nippon josei no rekishi: Sei, ai, kazoku* (Tōkyō: Kadokawa Shoten, 1992), pp. 54–62, and Fukutō Sanae, 'Yūkō-jofu kara yūjo e', in Joseishi Sōgō Kenkyūkai (ed.), *Nippon josei seikatsushi* (Tōkyō: Tōkyō Daigaku Shuppan, 1990), I, 217–46; Yoshida Hidehiro, *Nippon baishun shikō: Hensen to sono haikei* (Tōkyō: Jiyūsha, 2000), p.44.

33. Fukagawa also had clandestine courtesans. Like the geishas, these prostitutes belonged to various houses (*okiya*), and they were summoned to attend clients at teahouses in the area. They had male attendants, who carried the boxes in which their costume for the evening was stored. They would change into their finery when they arrived at their destination. Prostitutes who did not belong to a pleasure quarter, officially sanctioned or not, were called *yotaka* ('nighthawks') in Edo, *tsujigimi* in Kyōto and *sōka* in Ōsaka. They were often to be found near bridges and on the banks of rivers, where they set up temporary shelters constructed out of reed mats which they carried about with them. Idealised pictures of *yotaka* frequently turn up in *ukiyoe* prints. They can be identified by the towel draped over their heads.

34. Blackening the teeth was an ancient custom practised by both men and women of the ruling classes; it was gradually taken up by women throughout the rest of society. In the fifteenth and sixteenth centuries, girls belonging to high-ranking samurai families blackened their teeth to indicate they had reached marrigeable age. From the seventeenth century onwards, women did not begin blackening their teeth until they were married. Male members of the imperial family continued to blacken their teeth (and shave off their eyebrows) until the 1860s.

35. Laurence Oliphant, *Narrative of the Earl of Elgin's Mission to China and Japan in the Years 1857, '58, '59* (Edinburgh and London: William Blackwood, 1859), II, 201–202.

36. Lindau, pp. 61, 135, 220. Dalmas, too, employed the word '*djoréa*' in his book to denote '*maisons de prostitution*'. On a visit to Kyōto, Dalmas discovered that his hotel, the one designated for westerners, was located in the middle of the Gion quarter, which he describes in his book as that city's counterpart to Tōkyō's Shin-yoshiwara. But access to *djoréa*, he reported, was strictly forbidden to foreigners, so he had been unable to gain first-hand experience of one of those institutions, or meet one of the famed inmates of Gion, who he had been assured were '*les plus appétissantes*' in the entire country (Dalmas, pp. 153, 255, 327).

37. The court subsequently ruled that the contracts by which the men were bound were invalid, and ordered the men to be handed over to their country's representatives. The Peruvians sued for damages, and the affair was not concluded until 1875, when the case was settled in Japan's favour under mediation from the Russians. Obinata Sumio, 'Nippon kindai kokka no seiritsu to baishō mondai', in Sōgō Joseishi Kenkyūkai (ed.), *Sei to shintai* (Tōkyō: Yoshikawa Kōbunkan, 1998), pp. 75–109; Abe Yasushi, 'Meiji go-nen Inoue Kaoru no yūjo "kaihō" kengi no kōan', *Shiryū* (Sapporo: Hokkaidō Kyōiku Daigaku Shigakukai), 36 (1996), 73–91. See also Morita Tomoko, 'Maria-Rūsu-gō jiken to geishōgi kaihōrei', in Ōkuchi Yūjirō (ed.), *Onna no shakaishi 17–20 seiki: Ie to jendā wo kangaeru* (Tōkyō: Yamakawa Shuppansha, 2001), pp. 245–64, and her study of the implications the Maria Luz case had on the question of extraterritoriality in Japanese treaty ports, *Kaikoku to chigaihōken: Ryōjisaiban seido no un'yō to Maria-Rūsu-gō jiken* (Tōkyō: Yoshikawa Kōbunkan, 2005). There is also an account of this episode in Harold S. Williams, *Shades of the Past; or, Indiscreet Tales of Japan* (Rutland, VT and Tōkyō: Charles E. Tuttle, 1959), pp. 140–44.

38. Nakano Eizō, *Kuruwa no seikatsu* (1968; repr. Tōkyō: Yūzankaku, 1981), pp. 52–54, 79–80.

39. Humbert, II, 284, 252.

40. The term *oiran* did not come into usage in Japan until the very end of the eighteenth century, after the disappearance of the most exclusive *tayū* class of courtesan. According to the memoirs of Fukuda Toshiko, the owner of the restaurant Matsubaya in the former Shin-yoshiwara pleasure district where she grew up, the term *oiran* was applied to all the

courtesans of the quarter. Born in 1920, Fukuda Toshiko was adopted at the age of three by the proprietress of the Matsubaya, when it was a still a *hikitejaya* (Fukuda Toshiko, *Yoshiwara wa konna tokoro de gozaimashita – kuruwa no onnatachi no Shōwashi* (1993; repr. Tōkyō: Bungensha, 2004), p. 38).

41. *Kamuro* were from eight to twelve or thirteen years of age. Only those who showed potential were taken from the courtesans upon whom they waited as servants, and carefully trained up by the brothel proprietor to become high-status *oiran*.

42. J.E. De Becker, *The Nightless City, or, the History of the Yoshiwara Yûkwaku*, 5th, rev. edn (1901; repr. New York: ICG Muse, 2000), pp. 30–36.

43. Norman, pp. 298–302.

44. Humbert, II, 283.

45. Aihara Kyōko, *Kyōto maiko to geiko no okuzashiki* (Tōkyō: Bungei Shunjū, 2001), pp. 37–39, 48, 80–86. These days, establishments to which geishas belong are referred to as *okiya*. In Kyōto, they are called *yakata*. Trainee (apprentice) geishas, or *maiko*, lodge there, as do newly fledged geishas, who work for their *okiya* for about five years without formal pay (although they are given an allowance) while they reimburse their *okiya* for the training, clothes and board they received during their apprenticeship.

46. Nakano, *Kuruwa no seikatsu*, pp. 108–12; Dōke, p. 151; Hanazono Utako, *Geigi-tsū* (Tōkyō: Shiroku Shoin, 1930), pp. 162–64.

47. Norman, pp. 219–24, 235.

48. Finck, pp. 75–76, 78; Pierre Loti, *Madame Chrysanthème* (1887; repr. Paris: Édouard Guillaume, 1888), p. 241; trans. Laura Ensor (1889; repr. London, Manchester and New York: George Routledge & Sons, 1897), p. 251.

49. [Busk (ed.)], *Manners and Customs*, p. 57.

50. Basil Hall Chamberlain, and W.B. Mason, *A Handbook for Travellers in Japan, including the Whole Empire from Yezo to Formosa*, 5th, rev. and enlarged edn (London: John Murray; Yokohama: Kelly & Walsh, 1899), p. 131.

51. T. Philip Terry, *Terry's Guide to the Japanese Empire*, rev. edn (Boston and New York: Houghton Mifflin; London: Constable, 1928); repr. in Harold S. Williams, *Foreigners in Mikadoland* (Rutland, VT and Tōkyō: Charles E. Tuttle, 1963), p. 283.

52. William Elliot Griffis, *The Mikado's Empire* (New York: Harper and Brothers, 1876), p. 556 fn; and Norman, p. 305.

53. Charles Jérôme Lecour, *La Prostitution à Paris et à Londres, 1789–1877* (1872; 3rd edn, Paris, 1882), p. 145; reproduced in translation in Charles Bernheimer, *Figures of Ill Repute: Representing Prostitution in Nineteenth-century France* (Cambridge, MA and London: Harvard University Press, 1989), p. 90.

54. Griffis, p. 556 fn.

55. See Jill Harsin's study of the history of regulated prostitution in Paris, in *Policing Prostitution in Nineteenth-century Paris* (Princeton: Princeton University Press, c.1985). Bernheimer, p. 89.

56. See Bernheimer, pp. 16–20.

57. Dalmas, p. 155; Norman, p. 289; Nishiyama Matsunosuke, 'Kenbai', in Nishiyama (ed.), pp. 46–47.

58. Oliphant, II, 494; Lindau, p. 65; Hodgson, pp. 237–38, 242–43; De Fonblanque, pp. 139–40; Kaempfer, I, 261. George Smith also deplored 'the government regulation of houses of infamy' and the 'public revenue accruing from the systematic licensing and control of these resorts of the dissolute'. 'Young females of handsome appearance', the bishop wrote indignantly, 'are sold by their venal parents, and consigned at an early age to a life of degradation.' He was appalled, furthermore, that such girls, after their term of service had concluded, were 'not infrequently taken in marriage by the middle class of Japanese, who regard it as no disgrace to select their wives from such institutions' (Smith, p. 104).

59. William Acton, *Prostitution, Considered in its Moral, Social, & Sanitary Aspects, in London, and other Large Cities* (London: John Churchill, 1857), p. 64.

60. Alexandre Dumas, *fils*, *Théâtre complet de Alexandre Dumas Fils*, I (Paris: Michel Lévy Frères, 1868), 22–28.

61. Kaempfer, I, 260; Thunberg, III, 77.
62. Henry Knollys, *Sketches of Life in Japan* (London: Chapman & Hall, 1887), pp. 222–24.
63. Pierre Loti, *Japoneries d'automne* (Paris: Calmann-Lévy, 1889), pp. 77, 85–86; Kondō Tomie, *Rokumeikan kifujinkō* (Tōkyō: Kōdansha, 1980), p. 155.
64. Sir Edwin Arnold, *Seas and Lands*, new edn (London: Longmans, Green, 1892), p. 324. The essays in this book, written as reportage of his stay in Japan from November 1889 to November 1890, originally appeared in the *Daily Telegraph*. In 1893, the twice-widowed Sir Edwin, on his second visit to Japan, married a young Japanese woman Kurokawa Tama as his third wife.
65. Imaizumi Mine, *Nagori no yume* (Tōkyō: Nagasaki Shobō, 1941), referred to in Kondō, *Rokumeikan kifujinkō*, p. 45. Mine was the daughter of a physician trained in Dutch (western) medicine. Her husband Imaizumi Toshiharu came from the same part of Japan as Ōkuma Shigenobu. He is said to have negotiated for Ayako on behalf of the latter.
66. Sara Jeannette Duncan, *A Social Departure: How Orthodocia and I Went round the World by Ourselves* (London: Chatto & Windus, 1890), p. 176. The book was first serialised in the *Lady's Pictorial* and later published as a single volume in 1890.
67. Haga Tōru et al. (eds), *Bigot. Recueil d'illustrations humoristiques I: Études de mœurs* (Tōkyō: Iwanami Shoten, 1989), p. 129.
68. Alice Mabel Bacon, *Japanese Girls and Women* (Boston and New York: Houghton, Mifflin, 1891), pp. 288–89.
69. Duncan, *A Social Departure*, pp. 110–11.
70. Douglas Sladen and Norma Lorimer, *More Queer Things about Japan* (London: Anthony Treherne, 1904), pp. 36–41, 44–45.
71. Humbert, II, 249–52; John La Farge, *An Artist's Letters from Japan* (London: T. Fisher Unwin, 1897), pp. 189–90; Dalmas, p. 161.
72. Arthur Diósy, *The New Far East* (London: Cassell, 1898), p. 246.
73. John Binny's article was entitled 'Prostitute Thieves'. Henry Mayhew, *London Labour and the London Poor. Extra Volume: Those That Will Not Work, by Several Contributors* (London: Griffin, Bohn, 1862), p. 357; *Saturday Review*, 13 (1862), 124–25; Michael Mason, *The Making of Victorian Sexuality: Sexual Behaviour and its Understanding* (Oxford and New York: Oxford University Press, 1994), pp. 96–98; Arsène Houssaye, *Confessions*, 2nd edn (1885), II, 297–305, trans. in *Man about Paris: The Confessions of Arsène Houssaye*, ed. Henry Knepler (London: Victor Gollancz, 1972), pp. 73–80.
74. Rein, *Japan: Travels and Researches*, p. 428.
75. Loti, *Madame Chrysanthème*, pp. 85–86 (Ensor, pp. 93–94); Dalmas, p. 136.
76. La Farge, p. 35; Humbert, II, 111–12; Mortimer Menpes, *Japan, a Record in Colour*, transcribed by Dorothy Menpes (London: Adam and Charles Black, 1901), p. 95.
77. Cooper (ed.), pp. 43–44; Kaempfer, II, Appendix, p. 59; Thunberg, III, 257; Rein, *Japan: Travels and Researches*, p. 419; De Fonblanque, p. 162; Rutherford Alcock, *The Capital of the Tycoon: A Narrative of a Three Years' Residence in Japan* (London: Longman, Green, Longman, Roberts, & Green, 1863), I, 301–2; Alcock, II, 257. The Jesuit priest Alessandro Valignano noted how people of all classes – down to labourers and peasants – expected to be treated with respect and courtesy (Cooper (ed.), p. 42). Alcock was surprised to see much less servility among the lower classes than he had expected (Alcock, I, 199). Rutherford Alcock was appointed the first British consul-general to Japan in 1858. He returned to Britain on leave in 1862, and was knighted that same year. He was back in Japan in 1864, but left the following year upon being appointed minister-plenipotentiary to Beijing.
78. Francis L. Hawks, *Narrative of the Expedition of an American Squadron to the China Seas and Japan, Performed in the Years 1852, 1853, and 1854, under the Command of Commodore M. C. Perry, United States Navy, by Order of the Government of the United States* (Washington: 1856), p. 405; George Henry Preble, *The Opening of Japan: A Diary of Discovery in the Far East, 1853–1856*, ed. Boleslaw Szczesniak (Norman: University of Oklahoma Press, 1962), p. 126 (journal entry for 25 February 1854); Alcock, II, 284; Raphael Pumpelly, *Across America and Asia: Notes of a Five Years' Journey around the World and of Residence in Arizona, Japan and*

China (London: Sampson Low, Son and Marston, 1870), pp. 109, 141. Such stones as Pumpelly describes represented the *konseijin*, a god of reproduction. In the brothel quarters, representations of the phallus, made of paper on a wooden frame and weighed down with lead, were worshipped in indoor shrines (Nakano Eizō, *Yūjo no seikatsu*, enlarged edn (Tōkyō: Yūzankaku, 1996), pp. 160–61). These kinds of phallic representation were banned by the Meiji government in 1872. J.J. Rein wrote in 1884 that 'Phallus-worship', together with 'its symbols formerly so numerous and widely spread', had been banished since the beginning of the reign of Emperor Meiji 'as a result of foreign influence' (Rein, *Japan: Travels and Researches*, p. 432). The stones were in fact banned six years into the new era, in 1873. Photographs of such objects were published in Friedrich S. Krauss's *Das Geschlechtleben in Glauben, Sitte, Brauch und Gewohnheitrecht der Japaner*, 2nd, rev. edn (Leipzig, 1911). Phallus-worship in Japan was a subject of great interest in the west, as is evident from the list of publications in Roger Goodland's *A Bibliography of Sex Rites and Custom* (London: G. Routledge and Sons, 1931). Less obviously shaped stones are still found (coupled with a stone representing female genitalia) in many large formal gardens built by *daimyō* (regional lords) under the Tokugawa Shogunate.

79. Pumpelly, p. 141; Dalmas, pp. 158–59.
80. Baron Joseph Alexander von Hübner, *Promenade autour du monde 1871*, 2nd edn (Paris: Hachette, 1873), I, 353–54; Smith, pp. 112–13.
81. Humbert, II, 249–50; Christopher Dresser, *Japan, its Architecture, Art and Art Manufactures* (London: Longmans, Green 1882), pp. 29–30; Bird, I, 256–57.
82. Smith, p. 88; Alcock, I, 231. Laurence Oliphant observed that many women relaxing in their homes, which were thrown wide open to public view from the street because of the warm weather, would be stripped to their waists (Oliphant, II, 19).
83. Cooper (ed.), p. 238.
84. Thunberg, III, 77; De Fonblanque, pp. 132–33; Hodgson, p. 251.
85. Sherard Osborn, *A Cruise in Japanese Waters*, 2nd edn (Edinburgh and London: William Blackwood and Sons, 1859), pp. 57, 173. A decorated naval officer who had previously taken part in a British naval expedition to the Arctic and had seen active service in the Crimean War, Captain Osborn commanded HMS *Furious*, which took the British plenipotentiary to China, Lord Elgin (James Bruce, 8th Earl of Elgin), to Japan in 1858. Osborn was made rear-admiral in 1873.
86. Dresser, p. 80; La Farge, pp. 179–80; Hodgson, p. 252.
87. I am indebted to Professor Jane Stevenson for pointing out this reference.
88. Georges Duby (ed.), *A History of Private Life: Vol. II Revelations of the Medieval World*, trans. Arthur Goldhammer (Cambridge, MA and London: Belknap Press, 1988), pp. 602–607. See also William M. Shepherd, *The Life of Poggio Bracciolini* (Liverpool: J. M'Creery; London: T. Cadell, Jun. and W. Davies, 1802), pp. 66–76. The twentieth-century sociologist Norbert Elias charts the course of these changes in his study *Über den Prozess der Zivilisation* (*The Civilizing Process*), originally published in Basel in 1939.
89. Alcock, I, 371; Hodgson, pp. 257–58.
90. Alcock, I, 253; De Fonblanque, p. 133. De Fonblanque was also alluding in his oblique manner to male homosexuality, which the Jesuits back in the seventeenth century reported was prevalent in Japan and uncensored. See Cooper (ed.), pp. 46, 47 nn. 49–50.
91. Dalmas, p. 155; Hübner, I, 353–54.
92. Smith, pp. 102, 104, 112, 122. Humbert felt that a tacit convention existed among the Japanese that nakedness should remain, morally speaking, a matter of indifference (Humbert, II, 115).
93. Smith, pp. 106–107; Rein, *Japan: Travels and Researches*, p. 428; [Busk (ed.)], *Manners and Customs*, p. 170; De Fonblanque, p. 136; Hodgson, p. 243.
94. Bacon, p. 217; Amos S. Hershey and Susanne W. Hershey, *Modern Japan: Social-Industrial-Political* (Indianapolis: Bobbs-Merrill, 1919), p. 43. Amos and Susanne Hershey relate an anecdote about a Japanese wife who had lived in the United States with her husband for five years. On returning to their homeland, the husband was invited to a dinner given by a family

friend. The husband, being westernised and modern, insisted that the guests should all be accompanied by their wives. The women, however, ended up spending the evening sitting silently together along one side of the room, politely listening to the entertainment which was being given by geishas, who had been summoned, according to custom, to liven up the proceedings. The men flirted with the geishas, also in accordance with custom. Arriving home after the party, the husband reproached his wife for her reticence throughout the evening, upon which she replied, ' "I have not forgotten that a Japanese woman must be silent in public if she wishes to be respected" ' (Hershey and Hershey, pp. 34–35).

95. Osborn, *A Cruise in Japanese Waters*, p. 56; Hawks, p. 397; De Fonblanque, pp. 135–36.
96. Basil Hall Chamberlain, *Things Japanese, Being Notes on Various Subjects Connected with Japan* (London: Kegan Paul, Trench, Trübner; Tōkyō: The Hakubunsha; Yokohama, Shanghai, Hong Kong, Singapore: Kelly & Walsh, 1890), p. 366; 2nd, rev. and enlarged edn (1891), p. 463. In *Things Japanese*, Basil Hall Chamberlain gives a translation of precepts for model female behaviour set out at the beginning of the eighteenth century by the Japanese Confucian scholar Kaibara Ekiken, which were widely disseminated through books known as *Onna daigaku* (which title Isabella Bird translated as '*Woman's Great Learning*' (Bird, I, 223)). Chamberlain's translation first appeared in his article 'Educational Literature for Japanese Women', *Journal of the Royal Asiatic Society of Great Britain*, 10:3 (July 1878) (*Things Japanese*, pp. 367–76; 2nd edn, pp. 454–63).
97. Griffis, pp. 559–60.
98. Norman, p. 180; [Busk (ed.)], *Manners and Customs*, p. 171; Hodgson, pp. 241–42. Some commentators, however, did ascribe the existence of concubinage in Japan as much to the desire for male heirs as to the promiscuity and licentiousness of Japanese sexual habits.
99. See 'The Modern Notion of Happiness', in Denis de Rougemont, *Love in the Western World*, trans. Montgomery Belgion, rev. edn (New York: Pantheon Books, 1956), pp. 280–81; Janet Todd, *Sensibility: An Introduction* (London and New York: Methuen, 1986), pp. 19–21; and 'Chapter One: Two Currents of Love' in Peter Gay, *The Bourgeois Experience: Victoria to Freud. Vol. 2: The Tender Passion* (New York and London: Oxford University Press, 1986).
100. Rein, *Japan: Travels and Researches*, p. 430; Percival Lowell, *The Soul of the Far East* (1888; repr. New York: Macmillan 1911), pp. 91, 125, 213–17. Lowell travelled to Japan on three separate occasions. He later dedicated himself to astronomy and is probably best remembered now for having supported the theory that there are canals on the planet Mars.
101. De Fonblanque, p. 139; Chamberlain, *Things Japanese*, 2nd edn, p. 452; Smith, p. 104. Henry Norman noted that there was no language of 'romantic love' in Japan, and hence, not surprisingly, no romantic love itself (Norman, p. 181). See also Hawks, p. 397.
102. Acton, pp. 65, 163. See James F. McMillan, *Housewife or Harlot: The Place of Women in French Society, 1870–1940* (Brighton: Harvester Press, 1981), pp. 30–35; also Theodore Zeldin, 'Marriage and Morals', in *France 1848–1945: Ambition and Love* (Oxford: Oxford University Press, 1979), pp. 285–309.
103. Bacon, p. 34; Griffis, p. 560.
104. Hershey and Hershey, p. 33; Diósy, pp. 259, 263; Lindau, p. 63.
105. Lafcadio Hearn, *Japan: An Attempt at Interpretation* (New York: Macmillan, 1904), pp. 394, 397–98.
106. Loti, *Madame Chrysanthème*, pp. 85–86.
107. La Farge, p. 190.
108. Rein, *Japan: Travels and Researches*, p. 432; [Busk (ed.)], *Manners and Customs*, p. 58. Laurence Oliphant maintained that it was not considered dishonourable for a man to take female family members with him to enjoy the music, dance and conversation of the courtesans of the Shinagawa quarter, since these courtesans, though technically prostitutes, were 'considered the most highly accomplished of their sex' (Oliphant, II, 494).

109. Lewis H. Morgan, *Ancient Society: or, Researches in the Lines of Human Progress from Savagery through Barbarism to Civilization* (Chicago: Charles H. Kerr, [1877]), pp. 486–87. See also pp. 482–86 for a discussion of how women were treated in ancient Greece and Rome.
110. Norman, pp. 224, 295–96; Humbert, II, 283; Bacon, pp. 288–89.
111. Griffis, p. 556 fn.
112. Nakano, *Yūjo no seikatsu*, pp. 160–61.
113. See Michael Ashkenazi and Robert Rotenberg, 'Cleansing Cultures: Public Bathing and the Naked Anthropologist in Japan and Austria', in *Sex, Sexuality, and the Anthropologist*, ed. Fran Markowitz and Michael Ashkenazi (Urbana and Chicago: University of Illinois Press, 1999), pp. 92–114, for an entertaining first-hand account by a western anthropologist of his experience of Japanese mixed bathing.
114. Kanno Satomi, *Shōhisareru ren'airon: Taishō chishikijin to sei* (Tōkyō: Seikyūsha, 2001), pp. 40–43. See also Harald Fuess, *Divorce in Japan: Family, Gender and the State, 1600–2000* (Stanford: Stanford University Press, 2004).

Chapter 2: Geishas as Artefact

1. Norman, p. 302. The high, three-toothed, black-lacquered *geta* (pattens) for which the high-status *oiran* were famous were only adopted in Kyōto and Ōsaka from the 1730s onwards, and do not seem to have been introduced to the Shin-yoshiwara pleasure quarter of Edo until the 1750s (Hayashi, p. 450).
2. James McNeill Whistler, 'Mr. Whistler at Cheyne Walk', *World*, 22 May 1878, reproduced as 'The Red Rag' in *The Gentle Art of Making Enemies* (1890; repr. London: William Heinemann, 1994), p. 127.
3. Oscar Wilde, 'The Decay of Lying: An Observation', in *Intentions* (London: James R. Osgood McIlvaine, 1891), pp. 10, 45–46. The essay, which first appeared in *Nineteenth Century*, 25: 143 (January 1889), was revised for its inclusion in *Intentions*.
4. Menpes, p. 132.
5. Ibid., pp. 125, 126, 131; Dresser, p. 24.
6. Menpes, pp. 126, 130.
7. Ibid., pp. 129–32; Wilde, p. 46.
8. Other early enthusiasts for Japanese art included the ceramist Camille Moreau, Marc-Louis-Emanuel Solon, the director of the Sèvres porcelain factory, and Frédéric Villot, curator of the Louvre. A shop named A l'Empire Chinois appears to have sold Japanese artefacts in the 1850s. Another shop among the first in Paris to sell Chinese and Japanese curios during the 1860s was La Porte Chinoise at 36 rue Vivienne. This emporium had started out in 1826 as a *salon de thé*. La Jonque Chinoise, another shop popular among Japonistes, opened in 1862 at 220 rue de Rivoli; this was run by M and Mme Desoye. By the 1870s Japanese prints were available for sale at the department store Bon Marché (Gabriel P. Weisberg, 'Japonisme: Early Sources and the French Printmaker 1854–1882', in *Japonisme: Japanese Influence on French Art 1854–1910* (Cleveland: Cleveland Museum of Art, 1975–76), p. 4). Important dealers in Japanese art included Philippe and Auguste Sichel, Hayashi Tadamasa, and Matsuki Bunkio in Boston. Hayashi had originally come to Paris as an interpreter attached to the Japanese delegation responsible for organising the Japanese government's exhibits at the 1878 Paris Exposition Universelle. Hayashi stayed on in France after the exposition ended, and in 1884 established himself as an art dealer based in Paris. He and the Sichel brothers were friends of Edmond de Goncourt.
9. Other important showcases for Japanese art were the international exhibitions held at Paris in 1867, 1878, 1889 and 1900; the one held in Vienna in 1873, and the exhibitions held in Philadelphia in 1876, and in St Louis in 1904. Japanese wares were among the exhibits shown by the British East India Company at the Great Exhibition of 1851 held at the Crystal Palace, and Japanese *objets* belonging to Dutch collectors had been exhibited at the Paris International Exhibition of 1855. According to Ellen P. Conant, Japan was represented in thirty-six of the eighty-eight international exhibitions held between 1862 and 1910, in which year a Japan–British Exhibition was held at Shepherd's Bush, London, to celebrate

diplomatic as well as economic ties between Britain and Japan after the Anglo-Japanese Alliance had been forged in 1902. See Ellen P. Conant, 'Refractions of the Rising Sun: Japan's Participation in International Exhibitions 1862–1910', in Satō Tomoko and Watanabe Toshio (eds), *Japan and Britain: An Aesthetic Dialogue 1850–1930* (London: Lund Humphries, 1991), pp. 79–92.

10. William Michael Rossetti (ed.), *Dante Gabriel Rossetti: His Family Letters, with a Memoir by William Michael Rossetti* (London: Ellis and Elvey, 1895), II, 180.

11. In a more restricted sense, the term *kosode* refers to a silk garment which is thinly padded with cotton and has medium-sized square sleeves. The *furisode*, also formerly padded (though not in modern times), has very long square sleeves reaching down almost below the wearer's knees. The gaily patterned, long-sleeved *furisode* first appeared in the seventeenth century as dancers' costumes. It was soon adopted by fashionable young women, and it remains to this day the formal wear of unmarried women. During the eighteenth century, young men up to the age of fourteen or fifteen also wore long-sleeved kimonos, although the sleeves were usually not as long as those worn by young women. However, boys known as *wakashū*, who sold sexual favours to men, were distinguishable by their very long sleeves. The unlined, silk *kosode* for summer wear was called *tan'i*. Linen, unpadded summer kimonos were known as *katabira*. A *nunoko* was a padded winter kimono made either of cotton or linen. The *awase* was an unpadded, but lined, silk kimono worn during the spring and summer. (Nagasaki Iwao, *Nippon no bijutsu 8: No. 435 Kosode kara kimono e* (Tōkyō: Nippon No Bijutsu, 2002), pp. 30–31; Kanazawa Yasutaka, *Edo fukushokushi*, rev. edn (Tōkyō: Seiabō, 1998), pp. 82–87, 228–30). In cold weather, both men and women often wore another delicately patterned, lined kimono called *shitagi* ('underclothing') under their *kosode*. There were elaborate, unwritten rules about which combinations of patterns and colours between the two garments were acceptable. The garment worn next to the skin was (and still is) called the *jiban* (more commonly *juban*), a term that evolved from the Portuguese word *gibāo*. This was formerly a short garment, but it eventually became floor length and was known as the *naga* ('long') *jiban*. The *jiban* too had a decorative purpose, as its collar and the edges around its sleeves could be seen under the *kosode* and *shitagi*. It was the fashion in the eighteenth and into the nineteenth century for women to put a wide collar (*han'eri* or *kake'eri*) made of a contrasting fabric, colour and pattern to that of the *kosode* around the neck of their *juban* (Kanazawa, pp. 179–87, 230).

12. Hanazono, pp. 3, 25,172.

13. Diósy, p. 268 fn.

14. Norman, pp. 198–99.

15. Loti, *Madame Chrysanthème*, p. 206 (Ensor, p. 216).

16. Bird, I, 76, 77; De Fonblanque, pp.14, 109.

17. Arnold, *Seas and Lands*, p. 175.

18. The *yamatoe* tradition of courtly painting, also referred to as the 'Tosa'-style in nineteenth-century western works of reference on Japanese art, evolved from the ninth century onwards. The guardianship of the tradition was held by members of the Tosa school from the beginning of the fifteenth century to the middle of the nineteenth. See Chapter 3, 'Painting – The Older Traditions', in Lawrence Smith, Victor Harris and Timothy Clark, *Japanese Art: Masterpieces in the British Museum* (London: British Museum Publications, 1990), pp. 50–52.

19. Marcus B. Huish, *Japan and its Art*, 2nd, rev. edn (London: Simpkin, Marshall, Hamilton, Kent; Yokohama, Shanghai and Hong Kong: Kelly & Walsh, 1892), p. 86; William Anderson, *The Pictorial Arts of Japan* (London: Sampson Low, Marston, Searle & Rivington, 1886), p. 234. Whilst Anderson did not care much for *yamatoe* painting, he did appreciate Japanese woodblock prints. He put together his own private collection of Japanese illustrated woodblock-printed books in the seven years he spent in Japan between 1873 and 1880, serving as medical officer to the British legation in Tōkyō and teaching anatomy and surgery at the recently established Japanese naval academy. This collection, consisting of almost 2,000 volumes, was eventually acquired by the British Library. For essays on Marcus B. Huish and William Anderson, see the Japan Society's *Britain and Japan: Biographical Portraits,*

vol. 5, ed. Hugh Cortazzi (London: Global Orient, 2004). Huish was the sixth chairman of the Japan Society; Anderson its first.

20. Thick white face powder was worn in Japan by aristocratic women since the seventh century, and was de rigueur for all women in the eighteenth and nineteenth centuries, until western fashions began to spread through Japanese society. Kuge Tsukasa, *Keshō* (Tōkyō: Hōsei Daigaku Shuppan, 1970), p. 211.

21. Alcock, I, 192, 466; Sladen and Lorimer, p. 429.

22. Alcock, I, 242.

23. Anderson, pp. 230–31, 234.

24. For a discussion of the ways in which physical beauty was associated with moral beauty in western thought since the sixteenth century, see Chapter 5, 'The Cult of Physiognomy: Physical Beauty as the Cipher of Moral Excellence', in Robert E. Norton, *The Beautiful Soul: Aesthetic Morality in the Eighteenth Century* (Ithaca and London: Cornell University Press, 1995), pp. 176–209.

25. Edmond de Goncourt, *L'Art japonais au XVIIIᵉ siècle: Outamaro, le peintre des maisons verts* (1891; repr. Paris: Fasquelle/Flammarion, n.d.), pp. 112–14.

26. Likewise, Arita porcelain figurines of *bijin* ('beautiful women') have wonderful flowing lines which convey a sense of physical ease and freedom of movement. Such figurines were produced at the end of the seventeenth century and exported to Europe, entering collections such as the one housed in the Kina Pavilion (the Chinese Pavilion) at the Swedish royal palace of Drottningholm. See John Ayers, Oliver Impey and J.V.G. Mallet, *Porcelain for Palaces: The Fashion for Japan in Europe 1650–1750* (London: Oriental Ceramics Society, 1990), pls. 165, 166.

27. Dalmas, pp. 130–31. Two British officers, R. Mounteney Jephson and Edward Pennell Elmhirst, were of the same opinion with regard to the revealing qualities of the kimono. They thought the kimono had an advantage over western dress in that it revealed the gracefulness of the physical form without the aid of any of the 'meretricious deceptions of civilisation' (*Our Life in Japan* (London: Chapman and Hall, 1869), p. 132). Most other writers wrote disparagingly of the way in which the tightly wrapped kimono and obi, to say nothing of the wooden pattens (*geta*), hampered the movement of Japanese women. Sir Edwin Arnold, however, was another admirer of the slender fingers of Japanese women.

28. Pumpelly, p. 82.

29. Hübner, p. 398.

30. Humbert, II, 116; Sir Edwin Arnold, *Japonica* (London and New York: James R. Osgood, McIlvaine, 1892), p. 52; Dalmas, pp. 134–35. Arnold's essays in *Japonica* originally appeared in *Scribner's Magazine*.

31. Alcock, I, 224; II, 254; William Michael Rossetti, *Fine Art, Chiefly Contemporary* (London: Macmillan, 1867), pp. 386–87.

32. Huish, p. 88; James Jackson Jarves, *A Glimpse at the Art of Japan* (New York: Hurd and Houghton; Cambridge: The Riverside Press, 1876), p. 13; La Farge, p. 156; Menpes, p. 61. For a discussion of the nude in 'high' art and pornographic depictions of the human body, see Lynda Nead, *The Female Nude: Art, Obscenity and Sexuality* (London and New York: Routledge, 1992), pp. 22–25; and Allison Pease, *Modernism, Mass Culture, and the Aesthetics of Obscenity* (Cambridge: Cambridge University Press, 2000), pp. 4–29.

33. Gary Levine, Robert R. Preato and Francine Tyler, *La Femme: The Influence of Whistler and Japanese Print Masters on American Art 1880–1917* (New York: Grand Central Art Galleries, 1983), pp. 36–37.

34. The painting is in the collection of the Musée des Beaux-Arts, Dijon.

35. See Satō and Watanabe (eds), p. 111.

36. Quoted in Klaus Berger, *Japonismus in der westlichen Malerei 1860–1920*, trans. David Britt as *Japonisme in Western Painting from Whistler to Matisse* (Cambridge: Cambridge University Press, 1992), p. 16.

37. Charles Baudelaire, 'The Painter of Modern Life', in *The Painter of Modern Life and Other Essays*, trans. Jonathan Mayne (London: Phaidon, 1964), pp. 31–34, 38.

38. Humbert, II, 283.
39. Rossetti, *Fine Art*, p. 386.
40. Geneviève Lacambre et al., *Le Japonisme*, exhibition catalogue (Paris: Éditions de la Réunion des musées nationaux, 1988), p. 312; also see Geneviève Lacambre, 'Hokusai and the French Diplomats: Some Remarks on the Collection of Baron de Chassiron', trans. Yvonne M.L. Weisberg, in Gabriel P. Weisberg, Laurinda S. Dixon et al. (eds), *The Documented Image: Visions in Art History* (Syracuse: Syracuse University Press, 1987), pp. 71–72.
41. Kenneth Clark, *The Nude: A Study of Ideal Art* (London: John Murray, 1956), p. 7.
42. Richard Thomson, *Degas: The Nudes* (London: Thames and Hudson, 1988), p. 11. Degas also owned works by, among others, Nishikawa Sukenobu (1671–1750) and Utamaro; and he studied Hokusai's *Manga* (Weisberg, Japonisme: Early Sources and the French Printmaker 1854–1882', pp. 12–13).
43. Georges Jeanniot, 'Souvenirs de Degas', *La Revue universelle* (15 October and 1 November 1933); trans. in *Degas by Himself*, ed. Richard Kendall (1987; repr. London: Time Warner Books UK, 2004), p. 191. Kenneth Clark, despite his dismissal of the technique of Japanese *ukiyoe* artists, had no trouble bestowing unreserved praise upon Degas for the energy and vividness with which he depicted human movement. Clark felt of Degas's art that it possessed a 'life-enhancing completeness', a quality which made the viewer forget that the depiction of the human body he was looking at was in no way classically beautiful (Clark, *The Nude*, p. 212).
44. Octave Mirbeau, 'Exposition de peinture, 1 rue Lafitte', *La France* (21 May 1886), p. 2; trans. in Thomson, p.135. In the late 1870s, Degas experimented with monotype to produce his studies of nudes. In the early 1880s he reworked several of these monotypes in pastel; by the middle of the decade, he was working predominantly in pastel to create his nudes.
45. John Keay, *The Honourable Company: A History of the English East India Company* (1991; repr. London: HarperCollins, 1993), p. 60. This episode is recounted in Samuel Purchas, *Purchas His Pilgrimes in Japan, Extracted from Hakluytus Posthumus, Or Purchas His Pilgrimes, Contayning a History of the World in Sea Voyages and Lande Travells by Englishmen and others*, ed. Cyril Wild (Kōbe: J.L. Thompson; London: Kegan Paul, Trench, Trubner, [1939]), p. 131 fn 1.
46. Hawks, p. 405; Alcock, II, 246; Eduard Hildebrandt, *Reise um die Erde* (Berlin: Otto Janke, 1867), II, 167.
47. The influential art dealer Siegfried Bing was instrumental in bringing Utamaro to the attention of the public. Bing began dealing in Japanese art in Paris in the 1870s, opening his first gallery in 1875. In 1888 he put on his first exhibition of *ukiyoe* prints from his own private collection; a predominant proportion of the exhibited pieces were by Utamaro. An exhibition of prints by Utamaro and Hiroshige which Bing showed in 1893 is said to have made a particular impression on Monet, who extensively collected works by both of these artists (Berger, pp. 73, 90). In December 1895, Bing opened his newly refurbished emporium dedicated to objects of decorative art in the up and coming art nouveau style. By the early years of the new century, it was becoming increasingly difficult to make money selling Japanese art. Meanwhile, the Japanese government appointed Hayashi Tadamasa *commissaire-générale* for the Japanese exhibition at the 1900 Exposition Universelle in Paris. Responsibilities such as these made it increasingly difficult for Hayashi to continue with his business dealing in art. He wound it up in 1902, leaving his unsold merchandise with Bing to be auctioned off. Bing's own Maison Art Nouveau closed in 1904 and, after he died in the following year, the art nouveau movement rapidly waned in France.
48. Goncourt, *Outamaro*, pp. 134–35.
49. Ibid., pp. 144–46. Asano and Clark describe the print as 'Lovers in the private second-floor room of a tea-house' (Asano Shūgō and Timothy Clark, *The Passionate Art of Kitagawa Utamaro: Text* (Tōkyō: Asahi Shinbunsha; London: British Museum Press, 1995), p. 279).
50. Goncourt, *Outamaro*, pp. 136–38. The first plate in Utamaro's erotic album *Utamakura* also features two *ama*. Goncourt discusses this composition in his study of the artist.
51. It is also used as the subject of erotic *netsuke*. Netsuke were toggles used on a cord to secure a small container (*inrō*) to the wearer's obi. They were made of either wood or ivory, and often elaborately carved.

52. The print is reproduced in Woldemar von Seidlitz, *Geschichte des japanischen Farbholzschnitts* (Dresden: Verlag von Gerhard Kühtmann, 1897), p. 105; trans. Anne Heard Dyer and Grace Tripler as *A History of Japanese Colour-prints* (London: William Heinemann, 1910), opposite p. 98. According to Klaus Berger, Vever began collecting Japanese art in 1881. After the First World War, his collection passed to his friend Matsukata Kojirō, who subsequently presented it to the National Museum, Tōkyō (Berger, p. 179).

53. Katsukawa Shunshō, colour woodblock print of an abalone diving girl and an amorous octopus, dated *c*.1773/74, private collection, Paris. Reproduced in Jack Hillier, *The Art of Hokusai in Book Illustration* (London: Sotheby Parke Bernet; Berkeley and Los Angeles: University of California Press, 1980), p. 170.

54. J-K. Huysmans, 'Félicien Rops', in *Certains* (Paris: Librairie Plon, 1908), pp. 89–90.

55. Ibid., p. 81.

56. Ibid., p. 88.

57. J-K. Huysmans, *A Rebours* (1884; 6th edn, Paris: Bibliothèque-Charpentier, 1895), p. 136; trans. as *Against Nature* by Robert Baldick (London: Penguin, 1959), p. 109.

58. Huysmans, *A Rebours*, pp. 126–31 (Baldick, pp. 103–106).

59. Huysmans, 'Félicien Rops', p. 88.

60. Baudelaire, p. 37, Huysmans, 'Félicien Rops', p. 89.

61. Illica had conceived the idea of a Japanese opera as early as July 1894. André Messager's operatic version of Loti's *Madame Chrysanthème* had been produced only the year before. Illica first presented his proposal to Alberto Franchetti, with whom he had worked previously, but the composer turned it down. Illica then offered it to Mascagni, who had shot to fame in 1890 with *Cavalleria rusticana*. Illica provided Mascagni with the first instalment of his libretto in June 1896, and by October of the following year Mascagni had finished the first act and most of the second. Mascagni did not begin setting the final, third act until March 1898, finishing it in October. The opera was premiered on 22 November 1898, at the Teatro Costanzi in Rome under the baton of the composer himself.

62. In the puppet play, the maiden Dhia is cruelly treated by her callous father, who neglects her and then decides to sell her off to a rich merchant from Shimonoseki, simply because he has grown tired of supporting her. He thinks she is useless and unfilial, and resents the food he has to give her. Dhia threatens to kill herself and prays for succour to the Goddess of Goodness. Jor appears and takes her with him to Nirvana. The puppet play recasts Iris's own relationship with her blind father (who is totally reliant on her filial devotion) in terms of exploitation of the child by the parent. While Iris is moved to pity by the portrayal of Dhia's sufferings – and is spellbound by the image of Jor – she actually ends up in the power of Kyoto and Osaka, not through any action of her own, prompted or not by the play, but simply by being physically overpowered by Kyoto's henchmen, as she stares at the spectacle in stupefied admiration. Three whirling geishas (representing Beauty, Death and Vampire) conceal her from view with their swirling veils as they whisk her away. When Iris awakens from her drugged sleep in a Yoshiwara brothel, she mistakes the place for Jor's paradise.

63. Goncourt, *La Fille Élisa* (1877; repr. Paris: G. Charpentier, 1879), pp. 93, 105.

64. Goncourt, *Outamaro*, p. 100.

65. 'Charming *geishas* at dinner – the correct serving of a Japanese meal, Tokyo, Japan', stereograph, Underwood & Underwood.

66. Baudelaire, p. 37.

67. Prostitutes working in *maisons de tolérance* were obliged to wear shifts, suggesting that Degas's scenes are imaginary.

68. Seidlitz, *Geschichte des japanischen Farbholzschnitts*, p. 149 (*A History of Japanese Colour-prints*, p. 138).

69. Toulouse-Lautrec gave the address of this brothel to the art dealer Paul Durand-Ruel, who believed it to be the address of the artist's studio. Durand-Ruel only found out the truth when he had himself driven there by his coachman. The regulations which governed the running of *maisons de tolérance* may have actually made it difficult for Toulouse-Lautrec to take up residence in one of these establishments, as he claimed he was doing.

70. Ozawa Takeshi, 'Bijo wo utsushita bakumatsu Meiji no shashinshitachi', in Ozawa Takeshi (ed.), *Furuzashin de miru bakumatsu Meiji no bijin zukan* (Tōkyō: Sekai Bunkasha, 2001), p. 39.
71. Loti, *Madame Chrysanthème*, p. 241 (Ensor, pp. 250–51).
72. In the *Kurobune emaki* (Black Ship Scroll), a sequence of ink-and-watercolour pictures of the Americans at Shimoda in 1854, produced by an anonymous contemporary Japanese artist (and later copied and circulated in the form of a woodblock book), there is a scene showing Brown and his assistants photographing a courtesan at Daian Temple in Shimoda. The courtesan is drawn conventionally, and wears four long hairpins in her coiffure. The caption to the picture refers to the courtesan (*yūjo*) as being local (although Shimoda did not actually have an official brothel quarter and therefore, technically, no *yūjo*), and the accompanying text informs the reader that when the Americans expressed their wish to photograph some women, government officials ordered singing girls to be chosen as subjects. Eleanor M. Hight, 'The Many Lives of Beato's "Beauties"', in Eleanor H. Hight and Gary D. Sampson (eds), *Colonialist Photography: Imag(in)ing Race and Place* (London: Routledge, 2002), p. 133. See also Oliver Statler, *The Black Ship Scroll* (Tōkyō: John Weatherhill, 1963).
73. Loti, *Madame Chrysanthème*, p. 143 (Ensor, p. 151).
74. Finck, p. 263.
75. Nakano, *Kuruwa no seikatsu*, p. 98; De Becker, p. 157.
76. Ozawa (ed.), p. 43.
77. Shimo'oka had his studio in Yokohama until some time around 1876, after which he moved to Tōkyō and eventually abandoned photography.
78. In 1862 Wirgman set up *Japan Punch*, an English-language satirical magazine published in Yokohama.
79. Felice Beato's photograph of a young woman with a pipe, sitting beside a brazier (*hibachi*), is mistakenly captioned '*Geisha con pipa per l'oppio*' in Claudia Gabriele Philipp, Dietmar Siegert, and Rainer Wick (eds), *Felice Beato: Viaggio in Giappone 1863–1877*, trans. Simonetta Bertoncini (Milan: Federico Motta Editore, 1991), p. 183. This same photograph, however, was provided by Beato with a descriptive paragraph (probably by James William Murray) explaining the Japanese way of smoking tobacco. Japanese smoking customs featured frequently in travelogues relating to Japan. In the title to Beato's photograph, the woman is referred to as a 'Young Lady', although the *shamisen* in the background suggests she is a geisha. There was a strict ban on the import of opium into Japan, and although smuggling appears to have taken place at ports open to foreign shipping, the custom of smoking opium did not spread in Japan as it did through China (Yokohama Kaikō Shiryōkan (ed.), *F. Beato bakumatsu Nippon shashin shū* (Yokohama: Yokohama Kaikō Shiryō Fukyū Kyōkai, 1987), p.165).
80. Women who were not geishas and the like did not begin to appear in public photographs until 1908, when the Japanese newspaper *Jiji Shinpō* decided to take part in a worldwide photographic beauty contest sponsored by a Chicago newspaper. *Jiji Shinpō* invited applications from all over the country, but explicitly excluded women who made their living by entertaining men. See Ozawa (ed.), p. 96. The American artist John La Farge reported that, once hired, the geishas he engaged seemed to think no more of posing for him than of singing and dancing and pouring *sake* (La Farge, p. 190).
81. Comte Ludovic de Beauvoir, *Pékin, Yeddo, San Francisco: Voyage autour du monde III* (Paris: Henri Plon, 1872), p. 260; trans. Agnes and Helen Stephenson as *Peking, Jeddo, and San Francisco: The Conclusion of a Voyage round the World* (London: John Murray, 1872), pp. 210, 212. Born in 1846, the count accompanied the equally youthful Pierre d'Orléans, Duke of Penthièvre, on a round-the-world voyage which lasted from 1865 to 1867, and took in Australia, Java, Thailand, China, Japan and America. He subsequently produced an account of this journey in three volumes. The count arrived in Yokohama on 21 April 1867, and left Japan from the same port on 25 May. He later became a marquis.
82. Humbert, II, 280; Clive Holland, *Old and New Japan* (London: J.M. Dent; New York: E.P. Dutton, 1907), p. 153.
83. Walter del Mar, *Around the World through Japan* (London: Adam and Charles Black, 1903), pp. 240–41. The five verses consisted of *chon kina*, sung seated; *chon tate*, sung standing up

and dancing to the music; *chon nuge*, in which the loser of the forfeit took off a piece of clothing; *chon nezō*, which required the loser to assume a sleeping position; and finally *chon aiko*, in which the loser had to imitate the movements of the winner of the forfeit.

84. For a chronology of the careers of Beato, Stillfried and Farsari, see John Clark, *Japanese Exchanges in Art 1850s to 1930s with Britain, Continental Europe, and the USA* (Sydney: Power Publications, 2001).

85. See Ishiguro Keishichi, *Utsusareta bakumatsu: Ishiguro Keishichi korekushon* (Tōkyō: Akashi Shoten, 1990), p. 28, and Ishiguro Keishō (ed.), *Meijiki no porunogurafi* (Tōkyō: Shinchōsha, 1996). Two such photographs are also reproduced in Nakano Eizō's *Kuruwa no seikatsu*.

86. According to John Lemprière's eighteenth-century *Classical Dictionary*, the Three Graces were portrayed nude by the ancients because the three young women presided over human kindness, and 'kindnesses ought to be conferred with sincerity and candor'. See under 'Charites'.

87. Philipp, Siegert and Wick (eds), pp. 185, 206.

88. *The Studio*, 9 (1896), 208. See Ayako Ono, 'George Henry and E.A. Hornel's Visit to Japan and *Yokohama Shashin*: The Influence of Japanese Photography', *Apollo*, 150: 453 (n.s.) (November 1999), 11–18, and Bill Smith, *Hornel: The Life and Work of Edward Atkinson Hornel* (Edinburgh: Atelier Books, 1997), pp. 83–98.

89. Ozawa (ed.), p. 32; Yokohama Kaikō Shiryōkan (ed.), *Meiji no Nippon*, p. 29.

90. Douglas Sladen, *The Japs at Home* (London: Hutchinson, 1892), p. 44.

91. Karl Lewis was in the postcard business in Yokohama from 1902 to 1916.

92. Annette Kuhn, *The Power of the Image: Essays on Representation and Sexuality* (London: Routledge & Kegan Paul, 1985), pp. 37–38, and Leigh Summers, *Bound to Please: A History of the Victorian Corset* (Oxford and New York: Berg, 2001), pp. 198–203.

93. Kurt Gänzl, *The British Musical Theatre I: 1865–1914* (Basingstoke: Macmillan, 1986), p. 297.

94. Del Mar, p. 241.

Chapter 3: Madame Butterfly's Antecedents

1. Loti, *Madame Chrysanthème*, pp. 1–2 (Ensor, p. 8).

2. Arthur Groos, 'Madame Butterfly: The Story', *Cambridge Opera Journal* 3:2 (1991), 125–58.

3. John Luther Long, *Madame Butterfly; Purple Eyes; a Gentleman of Japan and a Lady; Kito; Glory* (New York: Century, 1898), p. 56. Long's novella is also reprinted in the English National Opera Guide to Puccini's opera (Nicholas John (ed.), *Madam Butterfly/Madama Butterfly* (London: John Calder; New York: Riverrun Press, 1984), pp. 25–59).

4. Long, p. 8.

5. Ibid. p. 13.

6. In law, marriages are required to be registered at the town hall. No wedding ceremony – or exchange of vows – is necessary to make a marriage legally binding.

7. Loti, *Madame Chrysanthème*, pp. 59–61 (Ensor, pp. 67–69).

8. Preble, p. 125 (journal entry for 24 February 1854).

9. Walter LaFeber, *The Clash: US – Japanese Relations throughout History* (New York and London: W.W. Norton, 1997), p. 13.

10. The letter is translated in *Bokui ōsetsu roku*. Quoted in Yoshida Tsunekichi, pp. 22–23.

11. Ibid., p. 22.

12. Ibid., pp. 29–33.

13. The lunar calendar was in use in Japan until the solar calendar was adopted, and 3 December 1872, according to the old lunar calendar, was designated 1 January 1873.

14. Report dated 27 May (local date) to the Council of Elders signed by the magistrates Inoue Shina-no-kami Kiyonao and Nakamura Dewa-no-kami Toki'tsumu. Ibid., p. 73.

15. According to a petition Kichi's mother and brother submitted to the local authorities in the town of Shimoda in the summer of 1857, Kichi had initially been told to stay at home because she was suffering from some kind of inflammation. When Harris became ill himself, Kichi was told to continue staying away. She was never reinstated as his attendant. Kichi's mother

and brother were petitioning for financial help, claiming that Kichi's association with the Americans had made her so unpopular that they were no longer able to support themselves as before by taking in washing. Ibid. pp. 84–86.

16. Nakazato, pp. 214–24. Oliphant received his first official appointment in 1861 as first secretary to the British legation in Japan under Britain's first consul-general in that country, Rutherford Alcock. But Oliphant had been in the capital Edo for little more than a week when he was seriously wounded in the attack on the legation. Henry Heusken was assassinated by *shishi* on the night of 15 January 1861 (5 December local date), as he was making his way back to the American legation on horseback from a meeting with a Prussian diplomatic delegation, which was in Edo to negotiate a trade treaty with the Shogunate.

17. Nakazato, pp. 113, 118–19.

18. The story is related in *Rashamen kikigaki* (Nakazato, pp. 185–86).

19. Kitagawa Morisada, *Ruishū kinsei fūzokushi* (1908), vol. 2, p. 166; quoted as preface to Jūichiya Gisaburō's *Tōjin O-Kichi* (Tōkyō, 1929). Kitagawa's work was an encyclopaedic account of contemporary customs, compiled in the middle of the nineteenth century.

20. Nakazato, pp. 101–10.

21. Nishiyama Matsunosuke, 'Roshia jorōshi', in Nishiyama (ed.), pp. 132–33.

22. Hugh Cortazzi, *Victorians in Japan: In and around the Treaty Ports* (London and Atlantic Highlands, NJ: Athlone Press, 1987), p. 278.

23. Ibid., p. 277.

24. Ibid., pp. 277, 278.

25. Loti, *Madame Chrysanthème*, pp. 40–41 (Ensor, p. 49).

26. It was not until 1872, the year in which the new Meiji government overhauled the old system of indentured courtesans, that the stipulation that women intending to become mistresses of foreigners had to register with a brothel was formally dropped.

27. Del Mar, p. 365.

28. Humbert, II, 376–77.

29. Nicolas Serban, *Pierre Loti : Sa vie, son œuvre* (Paris: Les Presses Françaises, 1924), p. 97; Funaoka Suetoshi, *Pierre Loti et l'Extrême-Orient: Du journal à L'œuvre* (Tōkyō: France Tosho, 1988), p. 105.

30. Funaoka, p. 37.

31. Loti, *Madame Chrysanthème*, p. 180 (Ensor, p. 190).

32. Ibid., p. 316 (Ensor, p. 326).

33. Ibid., p. 271 (Ensor, p. 282).

34. Ibid., p. 280 (Ensor, p. 290).

35. Ibid., p. 68 (Ensor, p. 76).

36. Chrysanthème's mother makes an appearance in Loti's novel as very much a character in her own right.

37. André Messager, Georges Hartmann, and André Alexandre, *Madame Chrysanthème: Comédie lyrique en quatre actes, une prologue et un épilogue* (Paris: Choudens, 1893), p. 264.

38. Régamey provided the illustrations for both volumes of Guimet's travelogue *Promenades japonaises* (1878, 1880).

39. Félix Régamey, *Le Cahier rose de Madame Chysanthème* (Paris: Bibliothèque artistique et littéraire, 1894), p. 20.

40. Ibid., pp. 36–37.

41. Funaoka, pp. 107–108.

42. Ibid.; Pierre Loti, *La Troisième Jeunesse de Madame Prune* (Paris: Calmann-Lévy, 1905), pp. 40, 73; trans. S.R.C. Plimsoll as *Madame Prune* (London: T. Werner Laurie, 1919), pp. 14, 25–26, 31, 55–56.

43. Loti, *Madame Prune*, pp. 35–39, 197 (Plimsoll, pp. 27–30, 143–46); Funaoka, pp. 109–15.

44. Long, p. 8.

45. Ibid., p. 82.

46. David Belasco, *Six Plays* (New York: Little, Brown, 1928), p. 28.

47. Mosco Carner, *Puccini: A Critical Biography* (London: Gerald Duckworth, 1958), pp. 380–81; Julian Budden, *Puccini: His Life and Works* (Oxford and New York: Oxford University Press, 2002), pp. 256–57, 266–70.

48. Osman Edwards, *Japanese Plays and Playfellows* (London: William Heinemann, 1901), p. 65.

49. The Satsuma Rebellion provides the historical backdrop to the 2003 Tom Cruise vehicle *The Last Samurai*, which eulogises the samurai, turning the rebels into noble heroes forced to launch a last defence of their way of life based on simplicity, discipline and honour against the imperial government's new faceless, westernised army. This sort of exaltation of an exotic 'old Japan' over contemporary Japan is nothing new.

50. Loti, *Madame Chrysanthème*, p. 37 (Ensor, p. 46).

51. A.B. Mitford, *Tales of Old Japan* (London: Macmillan, 1871), I, 40. The first two chapters of Mitford's book initially appeared as articles in the *Fortnightly Review* in 1870. Algernon Bertram Mitford (later Freeman-Mitford) was attached to the British legation in Japan from 1866 to 1870. He was created Baron Redesdale in 1902. He was the paternal grandfather of the six famous Mitford sisters.

52. Yokoyama Toshio notes that the idea of the 'imitative Japanese' started to appear in Britain in the 1870s (Yokoyama Toshio, *Japan in the Victorian Mind: A Study of Stereotyped Images of a Nation 1850–80* (Basingstoke: Macmillan, 1987), pp. 106–108). For a later newspaper article which discusses this common western prejudice about Japan, see the article on 'The Japanese Man in the Street', *World* (12 September 1905).

53. Michele Girardi, *Giacomo Puccini: L'arte internazionale di un musicista italiano* (Venice: Marsilio Editori, 1995), p. 241.

54. Long, p. 84.

55. Catherine Clément, *L'Opéra, ou La défaite des femmes* (1979), trans. Betsy Wing as *Opera, or, The Undoing of Women* (1988; repr. London and New York: I.B. Tauris, 1997), pp. 46, 47.

56. See Nitobe Inazō, 'The Institution of Suicide and Redress', in *Bushido, the Soul of Japan* (Tōkyō: The Student Company, 1905), pp. 100–20. *Bushido, the Soul of Japan* was first published in Philadelphia by Leeds and Biddle in 1900. A revised and enlarged tenth edition, with an introduction by William Elliot Griffis, was published in 1905 separately by G.P. Putnam's Sons, New York, and The Student Company in Tōkyō.

57. Kasaya Kazuhiko, *Bushidō sono meiyo no okite* (Tōkyō: Kyōiku Shuppan, 2001), p. 98.

58. Nitobe, p. 113.

59. Ibid., pp. 29, 93–94.

60. Nakazato, pp. 51–52. The novelist Ariyoshi Sawako took a line from Kiyū's poem for the title of her novel about her: *Furu amerika ni sode wa nurasaji* [I will not wet my sleeve in falling American rain] (1970).

61. See the discussion of Nogi's suicide in the first chapter of Robert Jay Lifton, Katō Shūichi, and Michael R. Reich, *Six Lives, Six Deaths: Portraits from Modern Japan* (New Haven: Yale University Press, 1979).

62. Albert Tracy, *Rambles through Japan without a Guide* (London: Sampson Low, 1892), p. 8. Albert Tracy was the pseudonym of Albert Leffingwell, an American physician who later became known in his country as a supporter of the need for vivisection reform.

63. After Van Nieuwenrode's death, Cornelia's mother eventually married a local Japanese man. Cornelia remarried after Cnoll's death; this second marriage seems to have been very stormy and became the subject of much gossip in Batavia. Iwao Seiichi, *Zoku: Nan'yō Nihonmachi no kenkyū* (Tōkyō: Iwanami Shoten, 1987), pp. 14, 144. The painting is reproduced in *Imitation and Inspiration: Japanese Influence on Dutch Art*, ed. Stefan Van Raay (Amsterdam: D'ARTS, 1989), p. 11.

64. François Caron, *Nippon daiōkokushi*, Japanese trans. and commentary by Kōda Shigetomo (Tōkyō: Heibonsha, 1967), pp. 25–27.

65. Yoshida Tsunekichi, pp. 151–52.

66. Arlette Kouwenhoven and Matthi Forrer, *Siebold to Nippon: Sono shōgai to shigoto*, Japanese trans. by Kuniko Forrer (Leiden: Hotei, 2000), pp. 24–25, 46–47. Siebold remained in Japan until 1862, lecturing on the natural sciences and acting as adviser to the Tokugawa Shogunate on diplomatic

matters. On his departure, Alexander stayed behind, having found a position as interpreter with the British legation. He later became a diplomat in the service of the Japanese government.

67. Yoshida Tsunekichi, pp. 153–56.
68. Ibid., p. 175; Murakami Kazuhiro, *Nippon kindai kon'inhō shiron* (Kyōto: Hōritsu Bunkasha, 2003), p. 36.
69. Shimizu Isao, *Bigō ga mita Nipponjin: Fūshiga ni egakareta Meiji* (Tōkyō: Kōdansha, 2001), p. 19.
70. Olive Risley Seward (ed.), *William H. Seward's Travels Around the World* (New York: D. Appleton, 1873), pp. 100–101. The American William Seward went on a round-the-world trip for his health in 1870. He arrived in Yokohama on 25 September and departed Nagasaki on 14 October.
71. It was turned into both a play and a film, neither of which did well.
72. Onoto Watanna, *A Japanese Nightingale* (New York and London: Harper and Brothers, 1901), p. 18.
73. 'The Half Caste', originally published in *Conkey's Home Journal* (November 1898); reprinted in Onoto Watanna, *'A Half Caste' and Other Writings*, ed. Linda Trinh Moser and Elizabeth Rooney (Urbana and Chicago: University of Illinois Press, 2003), p. 150.
74. Onoto Watanna, *The Heart of Hyacinth* (1903; repr. Seattle and London: University of Washington Press, 2000), p. 57.
75. Ibid., p. 145.
76. Ibid., pp. 233, 235.
77. Onoto Watanna, *Sunny-San* (Toronto: McClelland & Stewart; New York: George H. Doran, 1922), pp. 30, 34.
78. Yoshida Tsunekichi, pp. 118–19.
79. In 1930, Muramatsu Shunsui's own book on the subject, *Jitsuwa Tōjin O-Kichi*, was published by Heibonsha in Tōkyō.
80. *Tōjin O-Kichi* was first published in the journal *Chūō Kōron*, and appeared in novel form in 1929. *Toki no haisha Tōjin O-Kichi* was first published as a serialisation in the *Tōkyō-Asahi* newspaper, and appeared in book form in 1930.
81. According to the memoirs of Heusken's Japanese servant Sukezō, Kichi was a good-looking, fair-skinned geisha in her early twenties, who was already quite popular with boatmen and well known locally as an accomplished performer of a type of song called the *shin'nai-bushi*. Related in *Ishin hishi nichibei gaikō no shinsō*. See Yoshida Tsunekichi, p. 87.
82. Ibid., pp. 119–20.
83. Okayama Mariko, *Karatachi no michi: Yamada Kōsaku* (Tōkyō: Shinya Sōshosha, 2002), pp. 139–66.
84. Sir Edwin Arnold fashioned his play *Adzuma, or, The Japanese Wife* (London: Longmans, Green, 1893) around the Japanese story of a faithful samurai wife who decides the only way she can establish her innocence in the face of unwanted advances from another man would be by substituting herself in her husband's bed on the night she knows her vile pursuer intends to make a dastardly attempt on her husband's life. The assassin does not realise his mistake until it is too late. Like the Roman matron Lucretia, Adzuma is only able to prove her innocence by demonstrating that she is unwilling to live even with a shadow of a stain on her reputation.
85. This is pure fantasy: the treaty was hurriedly signed on board the USS *Powhatan* on 29 July 1858, with Harris urging haste on account of the possibility of an imminent invasion by a joint Anglo-French fleet emboldened by the humiliation of the Chinese by their combined armies and the signing of the Treaty of T'ienchin. Even more fantastical is Robert Payne's suggestion in his novelisation of Ellis St Joseph's screenplay that the Japanese translator Moriyama Einosuke (a historical figure, incidentally) was in reality one of the highest-born nobles of the land. In Payne's novel, Moriyama masterminds not only the (fictitious) attempt on Harris's life, and later, the (factual) assassination of his interpreter Heusken, but also the final disappearance of O-Kichi, who is shown as a permanent fixture at the American diplomatic compound at Edo, doted upon by Harris.

Chapter 4: Hara-Kiri!

1. The first act involved the rivalry between two samurai for the affections of Katsuragi. One of these two samurai, Katsuragi's former patron Banza, insults her current lover Nagoya. The act culminated with Katsuragi throwing herself between the rivals in order to save Nagoya, with whom she is deeply in love. The situation (as well as the names of the three main characters) was taken from the famous last act of the kabuki play *Inazuma-zōshi* by Tsuruya Nanboku, first performed in 1823. The highlight of this act, known as *Saya'ate*, was the scene in which the hero Nagoya Sanza and the villainous Fuwa Banzaemon, rivals for the love of the *tayū* Katsuragi, come to the brink of a duel as a consequence of Fuwa's insulting gesture of knocking the scabbard of his sword against Nagoya's.

2. 'The Theaters', *Grand Rapids Herald* (12 November 1899), quoted in Shelley C. Berg, 'Sada Yacco: The American Tour, 1899–1900', *Dance Chronicle*, 16:2 (1993), 159; 'Mme. Yacco', *Boston Post* (24 December 1899), in Berg, 'Sada Yacco: The American Tour', 179.

3. Yamaguchi Reiko, *Joyū Sadayakko* (1982; repr. Tōkyō: Asahi Shinbunsha, 1993), p. 46.

4. Judith Gautier, 'Sada Yacco', *Femina: Le Théâtre et la Femme* (1901–2), 324.

5. Kawajiri Sei'tan, *Engei meika no omokage* (Tōkyō: Uchūdō, 1910), p. 47. In an autobiographical article published in the *Kyūshū Shinbun* on 10 May 1913, Sadayakko maintained that she had been adopted at the age of seven, but her own adopted daughter Kawakami Tomiji remembered Sadayakko reminiscing about how she had run away at the age of four to be with Hamada Kame, the woman who became her adoptive parent.

6. According to the researches of Yamaguchi Reiko, the geishas of Yoshichō, along with those of Nihonbashi, Shintomi and Sukiyabashi, were ranked next down in terms of expensiveness from those of Yanagibashi and Shinbashi. Below them were the geishas of Karasumori and the Shin-yoshiwara. Then came the geishas of Fukagawa and Kagurazaka, and on the lowest rung were those of the Akasaka district (Yamaguchi, pp. 23, 30–31, 33).

7. Matsunaga Goichi, *Kawakami Otojirō: Kindaigeki, hatenkō na yoake* (Tōkyō: Asahi Shinbunsha, 1988), pp. 38–39, 41, 44–46; Inoue Seizō, *Kawakami Otojirō no shōgai* (Fukuoka: Ashi Shobō, 1985), pp.15–21.

8. Matsunaga, pp. 40–42.

9. Ibid., pp. 47, 52; Inoue, pp. 24–26.

10. Matsunaga, p. 59; Inoue, pp. 32–33.

11. He secured this engagement through a belligerent *sōshi* named Fukui Shigebei. A year later, Fukui joined Otojirō's troupe as an *onnagata*. Matsunaga, pp. 66–67.

12. Inoue, pp. 50–53; Matsunaga, pp. 102, 111-12; Ōzasa Yoshio, *Nippon gendai engekishi: Meiji, Taishōhen* (Tōkyō: Hakusuisha, 1985), p. 53.

13. The niece and the dog returned to Tōkyō with Hamada Kame, who was summoned to Yokosuka, when the boat blundered into the naval port there. Yokosuka is not very far from Yokohama. Matsunaga, pp. 142–43; Yamaguchi, pp. 90, 92.

14. Kanao Tanejirō, *Kawakami Otojirō ōbei manyūki* (Ōsaka: Kanao Bun'endō, 1901), p. 2. In 1901 Kanao published two accounts of the Kawakamis' western tour: *Otojirō ōbei manyūki* roughly followed the form of a journal, while *Kawakami Otojirō Sadayakko manyūki* (Ōsaka: Kanao Bun'endō, 1901) was presented as an interview with the couple.

15. Inoue, pp. 62–63; Matsunaga, pp. 149–50, 165; Kanao, *Otojirō ōbei manyūki*, pp. 23, 34.

16. Kawajiri, pp. 54–55; Kawakami Sadayakko, 'Hajimete joyū ni natta koro – intai ni saishite', *Shin Engei* 2:11 (November 1917), 102–103; Fujii Sōtetsu (ed.), *Jiden Otojirō Sadayakko* (Tōkyō: San'ichi Shobō, 1984), pp. 195–96; Inoue, p. 62; Yamaguchi pp. 101–102.

17. Kanao, *Otojirō ōbei manyūki*, p. 16.

18. Ibid., pp. 9, 16.

19. 'Japanese Players at the Coronet Theatre', *The Times* (24 May 1900), 106.

20. *Chicago Times Herald* (3 November 1899), quoted Berg, 'Sada Yacco: The American Tour', 173; Kanao, *Otojirō ōbei manyūki*, pp. 19–20.

21. The plot of Otojirō's adaptation of *The Merchant of Venice* was given in the July 1903 issue of *Kabuki*, quoted Yamaguchi, p. 111.

22. Kanao, *Otojirō Sadayakko manyūki*, p. 30.

23. Kanao, *Otojirō ōbei manyūki*, p. 36.
24. The show was closed down on 5 March after 29 performances. Nethersole was arrested along with her agent, her co-star Hamilton Revelle, and the manager of the theatre. Their trial was held between 3 and 5 April, and the play reopened on the 7th. Kanao, *Otojirō Sadayakko manyūki*, pp. 37–38.
25. Ibid., pp. 40–41.
26. Ibid., pp. 35–36; Fujii (ed.), p. 85. *Otojirō ōbei manyūki* only relates he had told Hay that he found western theatre thrilling and beautiful to watch (p. 60).
27. Kanao, *Otojirō ōbei manyūki*, p. 44.
28. On 13 June 1900, *The Times* noted that the run had been extended twice already, and reviewed the troupe's new offering, *Kesa*. On the 16th, the paper ran a short notice of four more matinées to be put on in the following week in response to popular demand.
29. In some newspapers and journals, for example the *Sketch*, the play continued to be called *The Royalist*, but the theatre synopsis gives the title as *The Loyalist*.
30. Some contemporary accounts reported the venue as Marlborough House, while Otojirō in his memoirs maintained that the troupe had entertained the Prince of Wales at Buckingham Palace (Shelley C. Berg, 'Sada Yacco in London and Paris, 1900: Le Rêve Réalisé', *Dance Chronicle*, 18:3 (1995), 365; Kanao, *Otojirō ōbei manyūki*, p. 46).
31. Kanao, *Otojirō Sadayakko manyūki*, p. 71.
32. Kanao, *Otojirō ōbei manyūki*, pp. 48–55, 57–58.
33. The story of Kesa is found in Book 18 of the thirteenth-century historical epic *Genpei jōsuiki*. Sir Edwin Arnold used the same legend as the basis of his play *Adzuma* (1893). Kesa Gozen's given name was Azuma.
34. The plot is summarised in the London *Times* review of 13 June 1900.
35. Kanao, *Otojirō ōbei manyūki*, p. 45; Kanao, *Otojirō Sadayakko manyūki*, pp. 58–59, 76. Otojirō said that hara-kiri scenes received more rapturous applause in Paris than in either London or America.
36. Kanao, *Otojirō ōbei manyūki*, pp. 37, 48–49; Kanao, *Otojirō Sadayakko manyūki*, pp. 74–76.
37. Eleven of the twenty had performed *seppuku* before the French minister to Japan (who had demanded in the first place that the culprits should be punished by death) felt too ill to continue viewing the proceedings. The surviving nine were thereupon reprieved. Ōkuma Miyoshi, *Seppuku no rekishi* (1973; repr. Tōkyō: Yūzankaku, 1995), pp. 220–31.
38. Henry Fouquier, 'Sada Yacco', *Le Théâtre*, 44 (October, 1900).
39. Kanao, *Otojirō Sadayakko manyūki*, p. 35; Arthur Symons, *Plays, Acting, and Music* (London: Duckworth, 1903), p. 77.
40. Lady Colin Campbell, 'A Woman's Walks: In Far Japan', *World*, 13 June, 1900, pp. 13–14.
41. Luigi Rasi, *La Duse* (1901; repr. Roma: Bulzoni, 1986), p. 127; Louis Fournier, *Kawakami and Sada Yacco* (Paris: Brentano's, 1900), pp. 10, 31; Kanao, *Otojirō Sadayakko manyūki*, p. 76; André Gide, 'Lettres à Angèle: VII. Sada Yacco', in *Prétextes: Reflexions sur quelques points de littérature et de morale* (1903; 4th edn, Paris: Mercure de France, 1913), p. 141.
42. *World* (10 July 1901).
43. *Stage* (20 June 1901).
44. Symons, pp. 76–77.
45. *World* (10 July 1901).
46. Charles Ricketts, *Self-Portrait*, compiled by T. Sturge Moore, ed. Cecil Lewis (London: Peter Davies, 1939), p. 39 (journal entry for 22 June 1900).
47. Symons, p. 76.
48. *World* (24 July 1901).
49. Ibid., (10 July 1901).
50. 'The Exposition Theatres' (dated 7 September), *New York Times* (16 September 1900), p. 18.
51. *World* (24 July 1901).
52. John L. Stoddard began giving lectures based on his foreign travels in 1879. These lectures were collectively published for the first time in 1897–98. *John L. Stoddard's Lectures* (Boston: Balch Brothers; Chicago: Geo. L. Shuman, 1904), III, 64–65.

53. Marcelle A. Hincks, *The Japanese Dance* (London: William Heinemann, 1910), p. 7.
54. Ibid., pp. 8–9.
55. Lady Colin Campbell, 13; Judith Gautier, *Les Musiques bizarres à l'Exposition de 1900. La Musique japonaise* (Paris: Société d'Éditions littéraires et artistiques, Librairie Paul Ollendorff, Enoch & Cie, 1900), p. 16; Judith Gautier, *Les Parfums de la pagode* (Paris: Librairie Charpentier et Fasquelle, 1919), pp. 224–27.
56. Max Beerbohm, 'Almond Blossom in Piccadilly Circus' (22 June 1901); repr. in *Around Theatres* (London: William Heinemann, 1924), I, 277.
57. Ibid., pp. 277–78.
58. Kanao, *Otojirō ōbei manyūki*, p. 10.
59. Symons, p. 76.
60. Max Beerbohm, 'Incomparables Compared' (29 June 1901); repr. in *Around Theatres*, I, 282.
61. Helen Martin (née Faucit), *On Some of Shakespeare's Female Characters* (Edinburgh: William Blackwood, 1885), p. 437, quoted in William Archer, *Masks or Faces? A Study of the Psychology of Acting* (London: Longmans, Green, 1888), p. 122.
62. Katherine Metcalf Roof, 'Concerning the Japanese Players', *The Impressionist*, 8 (June 1900), quoted in Berg, 'Sada Yacco in London and Paris, 1900: Le Rêve Réalisé', 355.
63. Edwards, pp. 82–83.
64. Beerbohm, 'Almond Blossom in Piccadilly Circus', I, 276–77.
65. Max Beerbohm, 'The Sicilian Entertainment' (22 February 1908); repr. in *Around Theatres*, II, 361.
66. Symons, pp. 76–77.
67. Gide, pp. 135–41.
68. Having set off for home in November 1900, after their triumphant appearance at the Paris Exposition, the troupe arrived in Kōbe in January of the New Year. In April, however, Otojirō and Sadayakko were back on ship heading for a second tour of Europe. They performed in London in the summer, moving on to Paris in September. They then toured to Berlin, Leipzig, Munich, Vienna, Budapest, Warsaw, St Petersburg, Milan, Venice, Rome, Madrid and Lisbon.
69. Suzanne Shelton, *Divine Dancer: A Biography of Ruth St Denis* (Garden City, NY: Doubleday, 1981), p. 41.
70. Isadora Duncan, 'The Dance of the Future' (1902 or 1903), in *The Art of the Dance*, ed. Sheldon Cheney (1928; repr. New York: Theatre Arts Books, 1969), p. 54; 'The Philosopher's Stone of Dancing' (1920), ibid., pp. 51–53
71. Duncan, 'Depth', ibid., p. 99.
72. Ibid., p. 100.
73. Ricketts, p. 39.
74. 'Bringing Temple Dances from the Orient to Broadway', *New York Times* (15 March 1906), quoted in Shelton, p. 98.
75. Duncan, 'The Dance of the Greeks', in *The Art of the Dance*, p. 95. This essay has been translated from Duncan's surviving manuscript in French.
76. Duncan, 'Dancing in Relation to Religion and Love' (1927), ibid., pp. 121–22.
77. Hugo von Hofmannsthal, *Reden und Aufsätze 1: 1891–1913, Gesammelte Werke in zehn Einzelbänden VIII*, ed. Bernd Schoeller (Frankfurt am Main: Fischer Taschenbuch Verlag, 1979), pp. 476, 498–99; see Philip Ward, *Hofmannsthal and Greek Myth: Expression and Performance*, British and Irish Studies in German Language and Literature, 24 (Oxford, Bern, Berlin, Brussels, Frankfurt am Main, New York and Vienna: Peter Lang, 2002), pp. 169, 174, 183–84, 189.
78. Hofmannsthal, *Reden und Aufsätze 1: 1891–1913*, p. 473; see Ward, p. 180. Julius Hart, 'Die Japaner im "Bunten Theater" ', *Der Tag* (12 December 1901); reproduced in Peter Pantzer (ed.), *Japanischer Theaterhimmel über Europas Bühnen: Kawakami Otojiro, Sadayakko und ihre Truppe auf Tournee durch Mittel- und Osteuropa 1901/1902* (Munich: Iudicium, 2005), pp. 178–81. The article was quoted with approbation by the Viennese critic Hermann Bahr in his review on 8 February of the Kawakami troupe for *Neues Wiener Tagblatt* (Pantzer, pp. 904–906).
79. Max Beerbohm, 'Duse at the Lyceum' (26 May 1900); repr. in *Around Theatres*, I, 144–45.

80. Beerbohm, 'Incomparables Compared', I, 280–82.
81. Loie Fuller, *Fifteen Years of a Dancer's Life* (London: Herbert Jenkins, 1913), pp. 207–209. The troupe's repertory on this occasion included *La Dame aux camélias* (of which the novelist Jules Renard observed in his journal that Sadayakko's portrayal of the last stages of consumption was much too explicit to be to the Parisian taste), *The Geisha and the Knight*, *Kesa*, the court scene from *The Merchant of Venice*, and a hara-kiri piece, *The Shōgun*, which also featured a mad scene by Sadayakko.
82. Arthur Groos, 'Cio-Cio-San and Sadayakko: Japanese Music-Theater in *Madama Butterfly*', *Monumenta Nipponica*, 54:1 (Spring 1999), 50–51.
83. 'Madame Hanako' (Ōta Hisa), 'Geisha de yōkō shi joyū de kaeru made no nijū'nen', *Shin Nippon*, 7:1 (January 1917), 87–88.
84. 'Madame Hanako,' 88.
85. Yamaguchi, p. 16; Kurata Yoshihiro, *Geinō no bunmeikaika: Meiji kokka to geinō kindaika* (Tōkyō: Heibonsha, 1999), pp. 320–26; Ōzasa, p. 61.
86. 'Madame Hanako', 88–89.
87. Sukenobu Isao, *Rodan to Hanako: Yōroppa wo kaketa Nipponjin joyū no shirarezaru shōgai* (Tōkyō: Bungeisha, 2005), pp. 21–24.
88. 'Madame Hanako', 89–92. In this autobiographical essay of 1917, Hanako wrote that it was a Belgian trader, not a Danish one, who had been looking for people to appear at his Copenhagen attraction, and that she left Japan for Europe in 1901 ('Madame Hanako', 91–92), but the researches of Sukenobu Isao have clarified the more probable sequence of events (Sukenobu, pp. 25–27).
89. 'Madame Hanako', 93–96; Sawada Suketarō, *Petite Hanako*, trans. Michiko Ina (Frasne: Canevas Éditeur, 1997), pp. 24–26.
90. 'Madame Hanako', 94–96.
91. Sawada, p. 36.
92. 'Madame Hanako', 96; Fuller, pp. 208–10.
93. Fuller, pp. 209–10. Since Fuller, in her memoirs, describes giving this new ending to a play already in the troupe's repertoire, one which, in her opinion, had no real climax, it appears she is suggesting that it was the original play featuring the characters Akoya and Kagekiyo which was transformed into the play *Hara-Kiri*. However, in a surviving synopsis for *Hara-Kiri* in the archives of the Victoria and Albert Museum's Theatre Collections, London, Akoya does not die at the end but, together with her lover Kagekiyo, renounces the secular world and enters the path of Buddha (see Sawada, p. 30).
94. Donald Keene, 'Hanako', *New Japan*, 14 (1962); repr. in *Appreciations of Japanese Culture* (Tōkyō and New York: Kodansha International, 1981), p. 251.
95. In *Hara-Kiri*, Kagekiyo, a loyal retainer of the defeated Heike clan, plots to take the life of the chief of the victorious rival Genji clan, Minamoto no Yoritomo. Kagekiyo is pursued by samurai in the service of Yoritomo. Kagekiyo's faithful aged servant Tomotada desperately tries to shield Kagekiyo from his pursuers by engaging them in battle. It is Tomotada who commits *seppuku* when he realises he is about to be overcome by his master's enemies. Hanako played Akoya, a geisha beloved by Kagekiyo.
96. Sawada, pp. 30, 41–46; Fuller, p. 215; *Gifu Nichi-nichi Shinbun* (January 1925), quoted Sawada, p. 57; *Des Moines Register* (3 November 1907), quoted Keene, p. 253; Sukenobu, pp. 52–54.
97. 'Madame Hanako', 97–98.
98. Ibid., 98; Sawada, pp. 51–57; Fuller, p. 215.
99. 'Madame Hanako', *Gifu Nichi-nichi Shinbun* (6–10 January 1925).
100. Frederic V. Grunfeld, *Rodin: A Biography* (1987; repr. New York: Da Capo Press, 1998), p. 214 fn.
101. Richard Nelson Current and Marcia Ewing Current, *Loie Fuller: Goddess of Light* (Boston: Northeastern University Press, 1997), pp. 122–27, 142; Isadora Duncan, *My Life* (New York: Boni and Liveright, 1927), pp. 90–91, quoted in Grunfeld, p. 414; Ruth St Denis, *Ruth St Denis, an Unfinished Life: An Autobiography* (New York and London: Harper and Brothers, 1939), p. 86, quoted in Grunfeld, pp. 513–14.

102. Judith Cladel, *Rodin: The Man and his Art, with Leaves from his Note-book*, trans. S.K. Star, intro. by James Huneker (New York: Century, 1918), p. ix.

103. Shizuoka Kenritsu Bijutsukan, and Aichi Kenritsu Bijutsukan (eds), *Rodin et le Japon*, exhibition catalogue (Tōkyō: Gendai Chōkoku Sentā, 2001), pp. 284–85.

104. Anne-Marie Bonnet, *Auguste Rodin: Erotic Drawings*, trans. Michael Robertson (London: Thames and Hudson, 1995), pp. 16, 22–23.

105. For example, when the artist Kuroda Seiki (1886–1924), the leading contemporary Japanese exponent of western-style painting, showed one of his nude studies at an art exhibition in Tōkyō in October 1901, the chief of the local police precinct ordered the subject's pubic area to be covered with a black cloth. This sparked off a debate in the Japanese press over the propriety of paintings of nudes, as well as the use by artists of nude models. The cloth, incidentally, was removed on the occasion of a visit to the exhibition on 24 October by the eminent statesman and diplomat, the Marquis (later Prince) Saionji Kinmochi (1849–1940), who as a young man had lived in France for nearly ten years, and had studied at the Sorbonne. See also Sawada, p. 69.

106. For example, Musée Rodin (Paris), D.1134, D.1135, D.1136, D.1141, D.1145; also D.1138 and D.1144. See Shizuoka Kenritsu Bijutsukan, and Aichi Kenritsu Bijutsukan (eds), pp. 44–49.

107. Ruth St Denis, 'How Dancing Develops a Beautiful Figure' (1913), quoted Shelton, p. 104.

108. Auguste Rodin, *L'Art: Entretiens réunis par Paul Gsell* (Paris: Bernard Grasset, 1911), p. 152; trans. Mrs Romilly Fedden as *Rodin on Art and Artists. Conversations with Paul Gsell* (1912; repr. New York: Dover, 1981), p. 48.

109. Rodin, *L'Art*, p. 226 (Fedden, p. 71).

110. Cladel, p. 162.

111. Gaston Varenne, 'Bourdelle inconnu', *La Revue de France* (1 October 1934), 450, mentioned in Shizuoka Kenritsu Bijutsukan, and Aichi Kenritsu Bijutsukan (eds), p. 58; John L. Tancock, *The Sculpture of Auguste Rodin: The Collection of the Rodin Museum, Philadelphia* (Philadelphia: Philadelphia Museum of Art, 1976), p. 546. Tancock draws upon Georges Grappe, *Catalogue du Musée Rodin I – Hôtel Biron*, 5th edn (Paris: Musée Rodin, 1944), no. 372.

112. Shizuoka Kenritsu Bijutsukan, and Aichi Kenritsu Bijutsukan (eds), p. 60.

113. Musée Rodin, S. 568 and Ph.1992. Shizuoka Kenritsu Bijutsukan, and Aichi Kenritsu Bijutsukan (eds), pp. 59–60, 65.

114. Cladel, p. 165.

115. Maurice Barrès, *Mes Cahiers* (Paris, 1931), IV, 124–27, trans. in Grunfeld, pp. 475–76.

116. Cladel, p. 142.

117. 'Madame Hanako,' 101–102; Sukenobu, pp. 203–205, 262. James R. Brandon notes that Hanako's fierce squint, which Rodin managed to capture after much effort in the mask *La Tête d'angoisse de la mort*, was probably her attempt at a kabuki facial expression called *nirami*, which involves turning one eye inward while glaring straight out with the other (*nirami* comes from the verb *niramu*, which means 'to glare' or 'to glower'). But if Hanako was indeed performing a *nirami*, it was not in the traditional dramatic context in which it is usually performed. A *nirami* forms part of a pose indicating a stand of righteous defiance against a manifestation of evil, and it is a special pose belonging to the traditions of the Ichikawa acting dynasty. See James R. Brandon, 'On *Little Hanako*', *Asian Theatre Journal*, 5:1 (Spring 1988), 92–93.

118. 'Madame Hanako,' 101.

119. Konstantin Stanislavsky, *My Life in Art*, trans. J.J. Robbins, 4th edn (London: Geoffrey Bles, 1945), p. 507.

120. Isadora Duncan, 'The Philospher's Stone of Dancing' (1920), in *The Art of the Dance*, p. 51; Stanislavsky, pp. 466–67.

121. Akimoto Ai, *Hanako no kubi: Rodan to Sutanisurafusukī wo miryō shita joyū* (Tōkyō: Kōdansha, 2000), p. 313; Ban'nai Tokuaki and Kameyama Ikuo, 'Roshia no Hanako', in Yasui Ryōhei (ed.), *Kyōdōkenkyū Nippon to Roshia* (Tōkyō: Waseda Daigakubu Bungakubu Yasui Ryōhei Kenkyūshitsu, 1987), pp. 129–31.

122. 'Madame Hanako,' 100; Sawada, pp. 99–100. Sawada translates the synopsis from a copy of the programme in the Raymond Mander and Joe Mitchenson Theatre Collection.
123. Nikolai Evreinov, 'Lyubovnaya reklama', *Teatr i iskusstvo*, 49 (1909), 110–11, trans. in Ban'nai and Kameyama, pp. 127–28.
124. Sawada, pp. 113–15. Sawada, a professor of American literature, is married to the daughter of Hanako's adopted son.
125. V. Yur'ev, 'Gostrol' Ganako', *Rampa i zhizn*, 4 (1913), 11, trans. in Ban'nai and Kameyama, p. 129.
126. Three references to Hanako occur in Meierkhol'd's 1925 report concerning A. Faiko's *Bubus the Teacher* and the use of music in theatre (Vsevolod Meierkhol'd, *Stat'i, Techi, Pis'ma* (1968), II, 84–92). According to Ban'nai and Kameyama, Hanako's dance, which Meierkhol'd remembered, would have been in *Otake*. It can be inferred from his references to Hanako that he had also seen *Ki-musume*. Ban'nai and Kameyama, pp. 133–34.
127. Sukenobu, pp. 198–202. Osanai Kaoru's memoirs of his trip to Europe *Hokuō tabi nikki* was published in 1917.
128. Edward Gordon Craig, 'Kingship: Some Thoughts Concerning Hanako the Actress: Japan: India: Friendship and the King', *The Mask* (January 1914), 238; Craig, *The Theatre – Advancing* (Boston: Little, Brown, 1919), p. 232.
129. *Ki-musume* was based loosely on the famous Japanese legend *Sarayashiki*, in which a lady-in-waiting, who has been punished with death for losing an expensive and precious plate belonging to her master, comes back to haunt, with her ghostly voice, the castle well into which her body has been cast. In eighteenth-century stage adaptations of the legend (it was turned into both a *jōruri* narrative song and a kabuki play), the lady-in-waiting was framed for the loss of the plate by a political enemy of her husband. Hanako's version, which removed the supernatural element of the tale, along with the political intrigue, was no longer about a restless ghost who seeks retribution for her cruel and unjust punishment/murder. Instead it reduced the plot to a simple-minded story about a suitor who engineers the downfall of the woman after whom he lusts because she has spurned him. It concluded melodramatically with the lady's self-immolation out of a sense of responsibility for the loss of the plate.
130. Sawada, pp. 130, 149–53; Sukenobu, pp. 85–89. In 1912 Rodin gave Hanako a mask he had made of her, but this work was lost in Berlin. Rodin and Hanako had subsequently discussed the possibility of a gift of two more pieces, but the First World War intervened, and after his death Hanako had to enter into lengthy negotiations for the works with the French state. She received a bronze mask in 1918 and a terracotta head in 1921. The two works are still together and are currently in the collection of the Niigata City Art Museum.
131. Yamaguchi Reiko believes Sadayakko did not appear in the play Otojirō staged in Japan between their two tours to the west. The play was in two sections, the first based on the troupe's experiences in Chicago and the second on the deaths of two members of the troupe later in Boston. Lesley Downer, on the other hand, writes that Sadayakko did perform in this play. Yamaguchi, p. 15; Lesley Downer, *Madame Sadayakko: The Geisha who Seduced the West* (London: Review, 2003), p. 195.
132. Matsunaga, p. 191.
133. Kurata, pp. 332–37; Ōzasa, pp. 61–69.
134. Kawakami Sadayakko, 'Joyū toshiteno watashi no kakugo', *Bungei Gahō* (November 1913), 49–52.
135. Hasegawa Shigure, *Kindai bijinden* (Tōkyō: Sairensha, 1936), pp. 49–50, 55. Her chapter on Sadayakko is dated March 1920.
136. Ibid., pp. 41–42; Ashikami Shū, 'Kawakami Sadayakko no geijutsu: Fu Kawakami Sadayakko Nagoya kōgyō no koto', *Shin Shōsetsu*, 19:6 (June 1914 suppl.), 78; 'Hanjō', 'Man'nen musume Kawakami Sadayakko no kaibō', *Shin Shōsetsu*, 21:8 (August 1916 suppl.), 54–55.
137. Yamaguchi, pp. 235–37, 243–45, 249, 255–56, 262.
138. Ibid., pp. 299–301, 306–307, 314.
139. *Turandot* was based on a 1762 play by Carlo Gozzi, who had found the story of the Chinese princess in *Les Contes persans*, an early eighteenth-century French collection of tales set in

the fabulous Orient, compiled by Pétis de la Croix. The opera was left incomplete at Puccini's death in 1924.

140. The proposed 1892 London staging of Wilde's *Salome*, with Bernhardt in the title role, had to be abandoned when the Lord Chamberlain refused to issue a licence for its performance due to its biblical theme. Wilde's play was first printed, in the original French version, in Paris in 1893. It finally had its stage premiere in 1896 in Paris. Richard Strauss based his libretto for his opera *Salome* on a German translation of Wilde's play by Hedwig Lachmann. Composed between the end of 1904 and the first half of 1905, it was premiered in Dresden on 9 December 1905.

141. Arsène Alexandre, 'Les Pantomimes japonaises, au Théâtre de la Loïe Fuller', *Le Théâtre*, 41 (September 1900), 18.

142. Ricketts, p. 39.

143. 'Kin'eijo' (Okada Yachiyo), 'Kawai no O-Tsuma to Sadayakko no Sarome', *Shin Shōsetsu*, 20:6 (June 1915 suppl.), 79.

Chapter 5: From Foe to Friend

1. Loti, *Madame Chrysanthème*, p. 176 (Ensor, p. 184); Loti, *Madame Chrysanthème*, p. 280 (Ensor, p. 290).

2. 'Racial Discrimination and Immigration', written by Frank Ashton-Gwatkin, dated 10 October 1921 (Public Record Office: FO 371/6684). Quoted in Paul Gordon Lauren, *Power and Prejudice: The Politics and Diplomacy of Racial Discrimination*, 2nd edn (Boulder, CO and Oxford: Westview Press, 1996), pp. 109–10.

3. Quoted Frank Füredi, *The Silent War: Imperialism and the Changing Perception of Race* (London: Pluto Press, 1998), p. 4.

4. I am indebted to Keith Hamilton's entry in the *Oxford Dictionary of National Biography* (2004) for information concerning the life of Frank Ashton-Gwatkin. From the 1930s onwards, Ashton-Gwatkin's main brief at the Foreign Office was economic affairs and trade, with special reference to policies affecting central Europe. He participated in a series of British negotiations with Germany that led up to the German annexation of the Sudetenland. During the Second World War he played a major role in the reorganisation of the various branches of the British diplomatic service and the Foreign Office. He retired from the Foreign Office in 1947, after which he took up the post of associate director of studies at the Royal Institute of International Affairs. He renewed his association with Japan, and was involved in the re-establishment of the Japan Society of London after the war. In 1974 he visited Japan on the occasion of the golden wedding anniversary of the Shōwa Emperor (Hirohito) and his empress, Nagako.

5. In 1882 the US Congress imposed restrictions on immigration from China, but by the beginning of the twentieth century, it was immigration from Japan that was fuelling 'yellow peril' sentiments in northern California. A 'Gentleman's Agreement' between the United States and Japan in 1900, and again in 1907, sought to rein in immigration from Japan. Nonetheless, in 1913 California went ahead and passed legislation banning Japanese immigrants from owning land in the state.

6. Michael Banton, *The International Politics of Race* (Cambridge: Polity Press, 2002), p. 23; LaFeber, pp. 87–89, 104–106, 144–46.

7. It was superseded by the Four-Power Treaty, by which the signatories – the United States, Britain, France and Japan – agreed to respect each other's territories in the Pacific region.

8. John Paris, *Kimono* (New York: Boni and Liveright, 1922), pp. 25, 28–29. Not much is made in the novel of any specific French characteristics she might have assimilated during her childhood in France.

9. Ibid., p. 15.

10. Ibid., p. 34.

11. Ibid., p. 75.

12. Ibid., p. 245

13. Ibid.

14. Ibid., p. 258.
15. Ibid., p. 295.
16. Ibid., pp. 43–44.
17. Ibid., p. 276.
18. Ibid.
19. Ibid., p. 193.
20. Ibid., p. 320.
21. Ibid., p. 254.
22. Ibid., p. 298.
23. Eguchi Keiichi, *Futatsu no taisen* (1989; repr. Tōkyō: Shōgakukan, 1993), pp. 406–12; John W. Dower, *War without Mercy: Race and Power in the Pacific War* (London: Faber and Faber, 1986), p. 286.
24. Sheila K. Johnson, *The Japanese through American Eyes* (Stanford: Stanford University Press, 1988), pp. 8–10; Clayton R. Koppes and Gregory D. Black, *Hollywood Goes to War: How Politics, Profits, and Propaganda Shaped World War II Movies* (1987; repr. London: I.B. Tauris, 1988), pp. 234–36.
25. Koppes and Black, pp. 250–51; Dower, *War without Mercy*, pp. 83–84.
26. Ernie Pyle, *Last Chapter* (New York: H. Holt, [1946]), p. 5.
27. Dower, *War without Mercy*, pp. 84–93.
28. Ibid., pp. 62–73.
29. Ibid., pp. 304–305.
30. Masayo Duus, *Haisha no okurimono: Tokushuianshisetsu RAA wo meguru senryōshi no sokumen* (Tōkyō: Kōdansha, 1985), pp. 19–20, 24–25. The first contingent of American soldiers arrived at Atsugi Air Base to the west of Yokohama on 28 August. Two days later General Douglas MacArthur, Supreme Commander for the Allied Powers, landed at Atsugi and, on the same day, the first troops of marines came on shore at Yokosuka.
31. Fujime Yuki, *Sei no rekishigaku* (Tōkyō: Fuji Shuppan, 1997), p. 326; Duus, pp. 29–30.
32. Fukuda, p. 16.
33. Fujime, pp. 322–23; Takemae Eiji, *Senryō sengoshi* (1980), trans. and adapted by Robert Ricketts and Sebastian Swan as *The Allied Occupation of Japan and its Legacy* (2002; repr. New York and London: Continuum, 2003), p. 254.
34. Duus, pp. 44, 57–58, 72–73.
35. Kobayashi Daijirō and Murase Akira, *Min'na wa shiranai: Kokka baishun meirei* (Tōkyō: Yūzankaku, 1961), p. 52; Duus, pp. 94, 106.
36. Takemae, pp. 67–68; Kobayashi and Murase, pp. 31–34, 74; Duus, pp. 77–85, 97, 119, 150; Fujime, pp. 327, 332; Sumimoto Toshio, *Senryō hiroku* (Tōkyō: Mainichi Shinbunsha, 1952), I, 65–72; Fukuda, pp. 142–43, 147, 150–52.
37. Duus, pp. 89, 111–12; Kobayashi and Murase, p. 30; Fukuda, p. 151.
38. Duus, pp. 141, 175, 177, 212–13; Fujime, p. 327; Kobayashi and Murase, pp. 83–84.
39. Duus, p. 214; Kobayashi and Murase, p. 68.
40. Duus, p. 183; Williams, *Shades of the Past*, p. 349. Williams had lived in Japan since 1919. He left the country during the Second World War to serve with the Australian army, and returned after the war as a member of the occupation forces.
41. Duus, p. 247, 275; Kobayashi and Murase, pp. 157, 199.
42. Duus, pp. 233–34, 238–49; Fujime, pp. 328–29.
43. Duus, p. 229.
44. The designation of these establishments changed yet again in July 1948, from which time they were called 'special cafés' (*tokushu kafe*).
45. Fujime, pp. 384–85; Kobayashi and Murase, p. 150; Yoshida Hidehiro, p. 165.
46. Fujime, pp. 387–90, 394–96; Fukuda, pp. 209–12. The Anti-Prostitution Act was proclaimed on 24 May 1956, and came into effect on 1 April 1957. Pleasure quarters, however, were given an extra year of grace before legal penalties were applied for infringements of the law. This provision was granted so that brothels and teahouses had sufficient time either to wind up or transform their businesses, and the women to organise their future plans. The

Shin-yoshiwara pleasure quarter officially closed on 28 February 1958, by agreement of the businesses which belonged to the quarter (Fukuda, p. 206).

47. Elliott Chaze, *The Stainless Steel Kimono* (New York: Simon & Schuster, 1947), p. vii.
48. Ibid., p. 120.
49. Ibid., pp. 71–73.
50. Ibid., pp. 60–61.
51. Ibid., p. 150.
52. Ibid., pp. 37–39, 43–50.
53. Ibid., pp. 167–71.
54. Each group of islands comprising the Ryūkyū archipelago had its own military government. The principle that these blocks of islands should be governed separately was maintained until at least the autumn of 1951.
55. John Patrick, *The Teahouse of the August Moon* (New York: G.P. Putnam's Sons, 1952), p. 8.
56. Ibid., p. 23.
57. Eguchi, pp. 429–32; George H. Kerr, *Okinawa: The History of an Island People* (Rutland, VT and Tōkyō: Charles E. Tuttle, 1959), pp. 468–72.
58. Uehara Eiko, *Tsuji no hana: Sengohen* (Tōkyō: Jiji Tsūshinsha, 1989), I, 222.
59. Ibid., I, 79.
60. On other islands the old Japanese yen remained in use. The B-yen scrip became the single currency of the Ryūkyū Islands in July 1948, and remained so for the next ten years. The B-yen scrip was never used in mainland Japan. Nakano Yoshio and Arasaki Moriteru, *Okinawa sengoshi* (Tōkyō: Iwanami Shoten, 1976), p. 20.
61. Vern J. Sneider, *The Teahouse of the August Moon* (New York: G.P. Putnam's Sons, 1951), p. 28.
62. Patrick, p. 68.
63. Ibid., p. 93. See also Sneider, p. 61.
64. Sneider, p. 66.
65. Ibid., p. 65.
66. Ibid., p. 67.
67. Ibid., p. 110.
68. Ibid., pp. 233–34.
69. Patrick, pp. 165–67.
70. Ibid., pp. 158–60.
71. Ibid., pp. 174, 177–79.
72. Nicholas Evan Sarantakes, *Keystones: The American Occupation of Okinawa and US–Japanese Relations* (College Station: Texas A&M University Press, 2000), pp. 36–39.
73. Uehara, *Tsuji no hana: Sengohen*, I, 74, 78.
74. Uehara Eiko, *Tsuji no hana: Kuruwa no onnatachi* (Tōkyō: Jiji Tsūshinsha, 1976), pp. 7–11, 58–64.
75. Ibid., pp. 167–74.
76. Sarantakes, pp. 37–38.
77. Uehara, *Tsuji no hana: Sengohen*, I, 44
78. Ibid., 129, 189, 218.
79. Ibid., 222, 228–29.
80. Ibid., 283.
81. Ibid., 131–37, 163–65.
82. Kyō had established her reputation in the west in such highly acclaimed films as Kurosawa Akira's *Rashōmon* (1950), Mizoguchi Kenji's *Ugetsu monogatari* (1953) and Kinugasa Teinosuke's *Jigokumon* (1953). The last was based on the legend of *Kesa Gozen*, which Sadayakko had made one of her roles.
83. Nakano and Arasaki, pp. 14–20; Ryūkyū Shinpōsha (ed.), *Okinawa konpakuto jiten* (Naha: Ryūkyū Shinpōsha, 2003), pp. 88, 212, 314–15, 444.
84. The Republic of Korea was declared in the south on 15 August 1948, followed by the proclamation of the new People's Democratic Republic of Korea in the north on 9 September.

85. Bill Hume, *Babysan: A Private Look at the Japanese Occupation*, with commentary by John Annarino and Bill Hume (Tōkyō: Kasuga Bōeki K.K., 1953), p. 6.

86. Ibid., p. 10.

87. Ibid., p. 36.

88. Ibid., p. 7.

89. George J. Becker, *James A. Michener* (New York: Frederick Ungar, 1983), p. 50.

90. The 1957 film version of *Sayonara* substituted a fictional theatrical company called Matsubayashi for the Takarazuka company, and its girls were played by members of the Shōchiku Kagekidan Girls Review (SKD). The SKD was the Tōkyō sister company of the Ōsaka Shōchiku Kagekidan (currently known as OSK Nippon Kagekidan). The beginnings of the OSK go back to 1922, when it was set up as a rival to the Takarazuka. Its troupe based in Tōkyō was started six years later. After the Second World War, the Tōkyō troupe was relaunched as the SKD, and it remained in business until 1996. While Michener's novel ends with Hana-ogi merely being ordered to go to Tōkyō, the film has her being sent to the Japanese capital to work with another troupe. Kawasaki Kenko suggests that the Matsubayashi company in the film was based on the OSK rather than on the Takarazuka Revue Company, and that the plot change was a reference to the existence of the OSK's sister company in Tōkyō (Kawasaki Kenko, *Takarazuka to yū yūtopia* (Tōkyō: Iwanami Shoten, 2005), pp. 109–11). Kyō Machiko, who starred in the movie *The Teahouse of the August Moon*, trained with the OSK, and she was given ample opportunity in that film to demonstrate her mastery of traditional Japanese dance.

91. James A. Michener, *Sayonara* (New York: Random House, 1954), p. 17.

92. Ibid., p. 119.

93. Ibid., pp. 51–52.

94. Ibid., p. 94.

95. Ibid., p. 146.

96. Ibid., p. 224.

97. Ibid., p. 205.

98. Ibid., pp. 181, 204.

99. George Campbell, *Cry for Happy* (New York: Harcourt, Brace, 1958), pp. 42–43.

100. Ibid., pp. 18–20.

101. Ibid., p. 148.

102. Ibid., pp. 174–75.

103. For example, Murakami Yumiko, *Ierō feisu: Hariuddo eiga ni miru ajiajin no shōzō* (Tōkyō: Asahi Shinbunsha, 1993), p. 169.

Chapter 6: Bunny-boiler or Like a Virgin

1. 'East-West Twain Find a Meeting in MacLaine', *LIFE* 50:7 (17 February 1961), 91–96.

2. Sheridan Prasso, *The Asian Mystique: Dragon Ladies, Geisha Girls, and our Fantasies of the Exotic Orient* (New York: Public Affairs, 2005), p. 136; David Henry Hwang, 'Afterword', *M. Butterfly* (New York: Plume, 1989), pp. 98–99.

3. Prasso, p. 140; Karen Kelsky, *Women on the Verge: Japanese Women, Western Dreams* (Durham, NC: Duke University Press, 2001), pp. 165, 169. Karen Kelsky refers to Takahashi Fumiko's account in *Gaikokujin dansei to tsukiau hō* (How to Date a Foreign Man) (1989) of how pleased she was on hearing a similar saying from a Singaporean friend. Takahashi seems to have taken it as a compliment to Japanese women (Kelsky, p. 165).

4. Long, p. 80.

5. Tony Parsons, 'Pretty Ethnics: The Death of the White Woman', *Arena* (Spring 1991), 20–21.

6. 'Like a Geisha', *Harper's Bazaar* (February 1999), 126–35.

7. Amanda Fernbach, *Fantasies of Fetishism: From Decadence to the Post-Human* (New Brunswick, NJ: Rutgers University Press, 2002), p. 212.

8. 'Kimono Lisa? The Material Girl's New Look', *Boston Phoenix* (18–25 March 1999).

9. This conclusion to the geisha sequence was changed after the terrorist attacks of 11 September, which occurred towards the very end of Madonna's tour schedule. Instead of shooting the dancer, Madonna dropped her gun and embraced him.

10. Pamela Robertson, *Guilty Pleasures: Feminist Camp from Mae West to Madonna* (Durham, NC: Duke University Press, 1996), p. 135.

11. Yoshihara Mari, *Embracing the East: White Women and American Orientalism* (New York: Oxford University Press, 2003), p. 78; W. Anthony Sheppard, 'Cinematic Realism, Reflexivity and the American "Madame Butterfly" Narratives', *Cambridge Opera Journal*, 17:1 (2005), 80 fn.48.

12. Dorinne Kondo, *About Face: Performing Race in Fashion and Theater* (New York and London: Routledge, 1997), pp. 55, 69, 123–24.

13. Liza Crihfield Dalby, *Geisha*, new edn (London: Vintage, 2000), pp. 28, 103–13, 134. Although it was widely publicised at the time Dalby's book was reissued that she was the first westerner to become a geisha, other western women before Dalby had been attracted to, and did enter, the Japanese geisha community. Back in 1914, a short article from Reuters's Tōkyō correspondent was published in the London *Times* reporting that an Englishwoman who had formerly served as a teacher with the governor-general of Korea and also as an interpreter with the Sapporo police department had just become a geisha, the first white woman to do so (17 January 1914). The geisha Hanazono Utako, writing of the profession in 1930, identified the first foreigner to become a Japanese *geiki*, or geisha, as an American who, under the professional name of Hanako, appeared in the first public performances ever held by *geiki* in Kyōto. This had been in 1872, and these performances, originally part of a two-year programme of events intended to attract visitors back to the erstwhile capital of Japan, became an annual event and evolved into the Gion Kōbu district's Miyako Odori (known in English as the Cherry Dance) and the Pontochō district's Kamogawa Odori. While Hanazono Utako believes that most foreign women who subsequently claimed to be geishas were in reality no better than curiosities or common prostitutes, she gives a recent example of one who was a serious artist. This geisha, called Takeko, belonged to a geisha house called Wakekikuyoshi in the Asakusa district of Tōkyō in the years preceding the great Tōkyō earthquake of 1923 (Hanazono, p. 120).

14. Dalby, pp. 119–21.

15. Ibid., p. 140.

16. Roland Barthes, *L'Empire des signes* (1970), trans. Richard Howard as *Empire of Signs* (New York: Hill and Wang, 1982), p. 91.

17. From David Henry Hwang's introduction to his collection *FOB and other Plays* (New York: Plume, 1990), pp. x–xi.

18. Dalby, p. 140; Kondo, *About Face*, p. 191.

19. Barbara Ellen, 'Lie Back and Think of Japan', *The Observer* (1 April 2001).

20. Christina B. Rosenberger, 'The Book: Memoirs of a Geisha. Performers. Ice Divas. Queens. Goddess. Geisha', *Harvard Crimson*, 26 February 1999, 14 June 2005, <http://www.thecrimson.com/article/1999/2/26/the-book-memoirs-of-a-geisha/>.

21. David Henry Hwang, *M. Butterfly*, p. 17.

Select Bibliography

Acton, William. *Prostitution, Considered in its Moral, Social, & Sanitary Aspects, in London and other Large Cities*, London, John Churchill, 1857

Adachi Naorō. *Yūjo fūzokushi saimi* [Examination of the customs and manners of the courtesan] (1962); repr. Tōkyō, Tenbōsha, 1976

Aihara Kyōko. *Kyōto maiko to geiko no okuzashiki* [Inside the private quarters of the *maiko* and *geiko* of Kyōto], Tōkyō, Bungei Shunjū, 2001

Aketa Tetsuo. *Nippon hanamachishi* [The history of Japanese pleasure districts], Tōkyō, Yūzankaku, 1990

Akimoto Ai. *Hanako no kubi: Rodan to Sutanisurafusukī wo miryō shita joyū* [The head of Hanako: the actress who fascinated Rodin and Stanislavsky], Tōkyō, Kōdansha, 2000

Alcock, Sir Rutherford. *Art and Art Industries in Japan*, London, Virtue, 1878

——. *The Capital of the Tycoon: A Narrative of a Three Years' Residence in Japan*, 2 vols, London, Longman, Green, Longman, Roberts & Green, 1863

Alexandre, Arsène. 'Les Pantomimes japonaises, au Théâtre de la Loïe Fuller', *Le Théâtre*, 41 (September 1900), 16–19

Anderson, William. *The Pictorial Arts of Japan*. London, Sampson Low, Marston, Searle & Rivington, 1886

Araki Seizō. *Rashamen: Nippon hatten no ura ni himerareta yōshō no hiwa* [*Rashamen*, the women who became mistresses to westerners: the secret story behind Japan's modern development], Tōkyō, Tairiku Shobō, 1982

Archer, William. *Masks or Faces? A Study of the Psychology of Acting*, London, Longmans, Green, 1888

Arnold, Sir Edwin. *Adzuma, or, The Japanese Wife: A Play in Four Acts*, London, Longmans, Green, 1893

——. *Japonica*, London and New York, James R. Osgood, McIlvaine, 1892

——. *Seas and Lands*, new edn, London, Longmans, Green, 1892

Asahara Sumi. *Ozashiki asobi: Asakusa hanamachi geisha no iki wo dō tanoshimuka* [Geisha entertainment: appreciating the wit of the geishas of the Asakusa pleasure district], Tōkyō, Kōbunsha, 2003

Asano Shūgo and Timothy Clark. *The Passionate Art of Kitagawa Utamaro*, 2 vols, Tōkyō, Asahi Shinbunsha; London, British Museum Press, 1995

Ashikami Shū. 'Kawakami Sadayakko no geijutsu: Fu Kawakami Sadayakko Nagoya kōgyō no koto' [Kawakami Sadayakko's art: regarding Kawakami Sadayakko's performances in Nagoya], *Shin Shōsetsu*, 19:6 (June 1914 suppl.), 76–80

Ashkenazi, Michael, and Robert Rotenberg. 'Cleansing Cultures: Public Bathing and the Naked Anthropologist in Japan and Austria', in Fran Markowitz and Michael Ashkenazi (eds), *Sex, Sexuality, and the Anthropologist*, Urbana and Chicago, University of Illinois Press, 1999

Ayers, John, Oliver Impey, and J.V.G. Mallet. *Porcelain for Palaces: The Fashion for Japan in Europe 1650–1750*, London, Oriental Ceramics Society, 1990

Bacon, Alice Mabel. *Japanese Girls and Women*, Boston and New York, Houghton, Mifflin, 1891

Banta, Melissa, and Susan Taylor (eds). *A Timely Encounter: Nineteenth-century Photographs of Japan: An Exhibition of Photographs from the Collection of the Peabody Museum of Archaeology and Ethnology and the Wellesley College Museum*, Cambridge, MA, Peabody Museum Press; Wellesley, MA, Wellesley College Museum, 1988

Banton, Michael. *The International Politics of Race*, Cambridge, Polity Press, 2002

Barthes, Roland. *L'Empire des signes* (Geneva, 1970); trans. Richard Howard as *Empire of Signs*, New York, Hill and Wang, 1982

Bataille, Georges. *L'Érotisme* (Paris, 1957); trans. Mary Dalwood as *Eroticism* (1962); repr. London, Penguin, 2001

Baudelaire, Charles. *Le Peintre de la vie moderne* (1863); ed. and trans. Jonathan Mayne as *The Painter of Modern Life and other Essays*, London, Phaidon, 1964

Beasley, W.G. *Great Britain and the Opening of Japan 1834–1858* (1951); repr. Folkestone, Japan Library, 1995

Beauvoir, Ludovic de, comte. *Pékin, Yeddo, San Francisco: Voyage autour du monde III*, Paris, Henri Plon, 1872; trans. Agnes and Helen Stephenson as *Pekin, Jeddo, and San Francisco. The Conclusion of a Voyage round the World*, London, John Murray, 1872

Becker, George J. *James A. Michener*, New York, Frederick Ungar, 1983

Beek, Peter ten. *Die Japanerin: Geishas. Kirschblüten. Kimonos*, Düsseldorf, Hellas-Verlag, 1959

Beerbohm, Max. *Around Theatres*, 2 vols, London, William Heinemann, 1924

Belasco, David, *Six Plays*, New york, Little, Brown, 1928

Berg, Karl Georg. *Giacomo Puccinis Opern: Musik und Dramaturgie*, Kassel, Basel, London, New York, Bärenreiter, 1991

Berg, Shelley C. 'Sada Yacco in London and Paris, 1900: Le Rêve Réalisé', *Dance Chronicle*, 18:3 (1995), 343–404

——. 'Sada Yacco: The American Tour, 1899–1900', *Dance Chronicle*, 16:2 (1993), 147–96

Berger, Klaus. *Japonismus in der westlichen Malerei 1860–1920* (Munich, 1980); trans. David Britt as *Japonisme in Western Painting from Whistler to Matisse*, Cambridge, Cambridge University Press, 1992

Bernardi, Daniel (ed.). *The Birth of Whiteness: Race and the Emergence of US Cinema*, New Brunswick, NJ, Rutgers University Press, 1996

Bernheimer, Charles. *Figures of Ill Repute: Representing Prostitution in Nineteenth-century France*, Cambridge, MA and London, Harvard University Press, 1989

Bhabha, Homi K. *The Location of Culture*, London and New York, Routledge, 1994

Biagi Ravenni, Gabriella, and Carolyn Gianturo (eds). *Giacomo Puccini: L'uomo, il musicista, il panorama europeo*, Lucca, Libreria musicale italiana, c.1997

Billy, André. *The Goncourt Brothers*, trans. Margaret Shaw, London, André Deutsch, 1960

Birchall, Diana. *Onoto Watanna: The Story of Winnifred Eaton*, Urbana and Chicago, University of Illinois Press, 2001

Bird, Isabella L. *Unbeaten Tracks in Japan: An Account of Travels in the Interior, including Visits to the Aborigines of Yezo and the Shrines of Nikkô and Isé*, 2 vols, London, John Murray, 1880

Birkett, Jennifer. *The Sins of the Fathers: Decadence in France 1870–1914*, London and New York, Quartet Books, 1986

Blackmer, Corinne E., and Patricia Juliana Smith (eds). *En Travesti: Women, Gender Subversion, Opera*, New York, Columbia University Press, 1995

Blundell, Sue. *Women in Ancient Greece*, London, British Museum Press, 1995

Bongie, Chris. *Exotic Memories: Literature, Colonialism, and the Fin de Siècle*, Stanford, Stanford University Press, 1991

Bonnet, Anne-Marie. *Auguste Rodin: Erotic Drawings*, trans. Michael Robertson, London, Thames and Hudson, 1995

Bornoff, Nicholas. *Pink Samurai: Love, Marriage and Sex in Contemporary Japan*, London, Grafton Books, 1991

Boscaro, Adriana, and Maurizio Bossi (eds). *Firenze, il Giappone e l'Asia orientale: Atti del Convegno internazionale di studi Firenze, 25–27 marzo 1999*, Florence, Leo S. Olschki, 2001

Boxer, C.R. *The Dutch Seaborne Empire 1600–1800* (London, 1965); repr. London, Penguin, 1973

Brown, Ron M. *The Art of Suicide*, London, Reaktion Books, 2001

Buckley, Sarah. 'Photojournal: Geisha', *BBC News Online*, 2004, 12 March 2005, <http://news.bbc.co.uk/1/shared/spl/hi/picture_gallery/04/asia_pac_geisha/html/1.stm>

Budden, Julian. *Puccini: His Life and Works*, Oxford and New York, Oxford University Press, 2002

Burns, Stanley B., and Elizabeth A. Burns. *Geisha: A Photographic History, 1872–1912*, Brooklyn, Powerhouse Books, 2006

Buruma, Ian. *The Missionary and the Libertine: Love and War in East and West*, London, Faber and Faber, 1996

[Busk, M.M. (ed.)]. *Manners and Customs of the Japanese, in the Nineteenth Century: From recent Dutch Visitors of Japan, and the German of Dr. Ph. Fr. Von Siebold*, London, John Murray, 1841

Butler, Ruth. *Rodin: The Shape of Genius*, New Haven and London, Yale University Press, 1993

Campbell, Lady Colin. 'A Woman's Walks: In Far Japan', *World*, 13 June 1900, 13–14

Campbell, George. *Cry for Happy*, New York, Harcourt, Brace, 1958

Carner, Mosco. *Puccini: A Critical Biography*, London, Gerald Duckworth, 1958

Carter, A.E. *The Idea of Decadence in French Literature 1830–1900*, Toronto, University of Toronto Press, 1958

Chamberlain, Basil Hall. *Things Japanese, Being Notes on Various Subjects Connected with Japan*, London, Kegan Paul, Trench, Trübner; Tōkyō, The Hakubunsha; Yokohama, Shanghai, Hong Kong, Singapore, Kelly & Walsh, 1890; 2nd, rev. and enlarged edn, London, Kegan Paul, Trench, Trübner; Yokohama, Shanghai, Hong Kong, Singapore, Kelly & Walsh, 1891

——, and W.B. Mason. *A Handbook for Travellers in Japan, including the Whole Empire from Yezo to Formosa*, 5th, rev. and enlarged edn, London, John Murray; Yokohama, Kelly & Walsh, 1899

Champsaur, Félicien. *Poupée japonaise* (Paris, 1900); repr. Paris, Librairie Charpentier et Fasquelle, 1912

Chaze, Elliott. *The Stainless Steel Kimono*, New York, Simon & Schuster, 1947

Cherniavsky, Felix. *The Salome Dancer: The Life and Times of Maud Allan*, Toronto, McClelland & Stewart, 1991

Chiba Yoko. 'Sada Yacco and Kawakami: Performers of Japonisme', *Modern Drama*, 35:1 (March 1992), 35–53

Cladel, Judith. *Rodin: The Man and his Art, with Leaves from his Note-book*, trans. S.K. Star, New York, Century, 1918

Clark, John. *Japanese Exchanges in Art 1850s to 1930s with Britain, Continental Europe, and the USA*, Sydney, Power Publications, 2001

Clark, Kenneth. *The Nude: A Study of Ideal Art*, London, John Murray, 1956

Clark, T.J. *The Painting of Modern Life: Paris in the Art of Manet and his Followers*, rev. edn, London, Thames and Hudson, 1999

Clark, Timothy, Anne Nishimura Morse, Louise E. Virgin, and Allen Hockley. *The Dawn of the Floating World 1650–1765: Early Ukiyo-e Treasures from the Museum of Fine Arts, Boston*, exhibition catalogue, London, Royal Academy of Arts, 2001

Clément, Catherine. *L'Opéra, ou La défaite des femmes* (Paris, 1979); trans. Betsy Wing as *Opera, or, The Undoing of Women* (Minneapolis, 1988); repr. London and New York, I. B. Tauris, 1997

Cleto, Fabio (ed.). *Camp. Queer Aesthetics and the Perfoming Subject: A Reader*, Edinburgh, Edinburgh University Press, 1999

Cooper, Michael (ed.). *They Came to Japan: An Anthology of European Reports on Japan, 1543–1640*, London, Thames and Hudson, 1965

Corbin, Alain. *Les Filles de noce: Misère sexuelle et prostitution aux 19ᵉ et 20ᵉ siècles* (Paris, 1978); trans. Alan Sheridan as *Women for Hire: Prostitution and Sexuality in France after 1850*, Cambridge, MA and London, Harvard University Press, 1990

Cortazzi, Hugh. *Victorians in Japan: In and around the Treaty Ports*, London and Atlantic Highlands, NJ, Athlone Press, 1987

Current, Richard Nelson, and Marcia Ewing Current. *Loie Fuller: Goddess of Light*, Boston, Northeastern University Press, 1997

Dalby, Liza Crihfield. *Geisha*, new edn, London, Vintage, 2000

Dalmas, Raymond de, comte. *Les Japonais: Leur pays et leurs mœurs*, Paris, E. Plon, Nourrit et Cie, 1885

Davidson, James N. *Courtesans and Fishcakes: The Consuming Passions of Classical Athens*, London, HarperCollins, 1997

De Becker, J[oseph] E[rnest]. *The Nightless City, or, The History of the Yoshiwara Yûkwaku* (Yokohama, 1899); 5th, rev. edn, Yokohama and London, 1901; repr. New York and Tōkyō, ICG Muse, 2000

De Fonblanque, Edward Barrington. *Niphon and Pe-che-li; or, Two Years in Japan and Northern China*, London, Saunders, Otley, 1862

Del Mar, Walter. *Around the World through Japan*, London, Adam and Charles Black, 1903

Demel, Walter. *Come i cinesi divennero gialli: Alle origini delle teorie razziali*, trans. Michele Fiorillo, Milan, Vita e Pensiero, 1997

Desmond, Jane. 'Dancing Out the Difference: Cultural Imperialism and Ruth St. Denis's "Radha" of 1906', *Signs*, 17 (Autumn 1991), 28–49

Diósy, Arthur. *The New Far East*, London, Cassell, 1898

Dobson, Sebastian. *Art & Artifice: Japanese Photographs of the Meiji Era: Selections from the Jean S. and Frederic A. Sharf Collection at the Museum of Fine Arts, Boston*, Boston, MFA Publications; New York, Distributed Art Publishers, 2004

Dōke Seiichirō. *Baishunfu ronkō: Baishō no enkaku to genjō* [The prostitute: the history of prostitution and the present situation], Tōkyō, Shishi Shuppansha, 1928

Donaldson, Laura E. *Decolonizing Feminisms: Race, Gender, and Empire-building*, Chapel Hill, NC and London, University of North Carolina Press, 1992

Dower, John W. *Embracing Defeat: Japan in the Wake of World War II*, New York and London, W.W. Norton, 1999

——. *War without Mercy: Race and Power in the Pacific War*, London, Faber and Faber, 1986

Downer, Lesley. *Geisha: The Secret History of a Vanishing World*, London, Headline, 2000

——. *Madame Sadayakko: The Geisha who Seduced the West*, London, Review, 2003

Dresser, Christopher. *Japan, its Architecture, Art and Art Manufactures*, London, Longmans, Green, 1882

Duby, Georges (ed.). *A History of Private Life: Vol. II Revelations of the Medieval World*, trans. Arthur Goldhammer, Cambridge, MA and London, Belknap Press, 1988

Dumas, Alexandre, *fils*. *Théâtre complet de Alexandre Dumas Fils*, vol. 1, Paris, Michel Lévy Frères, 1868

Duncan, Isadora. *The Art of the Dance*, ed. Sheldon Cheney (New York, 1928); repr. New York, Theatre Arts Books, 1969

——. *My Life*, New York, Boni and Liveright, 1927

Duncan, Sara Jeannette, *A Social Departure: How Orthodocia and I Went round the World by Ourselves*, London, Chatto & Windus, 1890

Duus Masayo. *Haisha no okurimono: Tokushuianshisetsu RAA wo meguru senryōshi no sokumen* [Gifts of the vanquished: the role of special recreational facilities RAA in post-war history], Tōkyō, Kōdansha, 1985

Edel, Chantal (ed.). *Mukashi Mukashi, le Japon de Pierre Lotí* (Paris, 1984); repr. as *Japon fin de siècle. Photographies de Felice Beato et Raimund von Stillfried. Textes de Pierre Loti*, Paris, Arthaud, 2000

Edwards, Osman. *Japanese Plays and Playfellows*, London, William Heinemann, 1901

Eguchi Keiichi. *Futatsu no taisen* [The two world wars] (1989); repr. Tōkyō, Shōgakukan, 1993

Elias, Norbert. *Über den Prozess der Zivilisation*, 2 vols (1939, Basel); trans. Edmund Jephcott as *The Civilizing Process, Sociogenetic and Psychogenetic Investigations*, revised by Eric Dunning, Johan Goudsblom and Stephen Mennell, Oxford, Blackwell, 2000

Ernst, Earle. 'The Influence of Japanese Theatrical Style on Western Theatre', *Educational Theatre Journal*, 21:2 (May 1969), 127–38

Farrer, Reginald J. *The Garden of Asia: Impressions from Japan*, London, Methuen, 1904

Fernbach, Amanda. *Fantasies of Fetishism: From Decadence to the Post-human*, New Brunswick, NJ, Rutgers University Press, 2002

Finck, Henry T. *Lotos-time in Japan*, London, Lawrence and Bullen, 1895

Flitch, J.E. Crawford. *Modern Dancing and Dancers*, London, Grant Richards, and Philadelphia, J.B. Lippincott, 1912

Forbes-Winslow, D. *Daly's. The Biography of a Theatre*, London, W.H. Allen, 1944

Fouquier, Henry. 'Sada Yacco', *Le Théâtre*, 44 (October 1900), 10

Fournier, Louis. *Kawakami and Sada Yacco*, Paris, Brentano's, 1900

Frey, Julia. *Henri de Toulouse-Lautrec: A Life*, London, Weidenfeld & Nicolson, 1994

Fuess, Harald. *Divorce in Japan: Family, Gender and the State, 1600–2000*, Stanford, Stanford University Press, 2004

Fujii Sōtetsu (ed.). *Jiden Otojirō Sadayakko* [The story of Otojirō and Sadayakko in their own words], Tōkyō, San'ichi Shobō, 1984

Fujiki Hiroyuki et al. 'Zadankai: Kawakami Otojirō ichiza no kaigai kōen wo megutte' [Symposium: the Kawakami Otojirō troupe's foreign tour], *Nippon Engeki Gakkai Kiyō* (Bulletin of the Japanese Society for Theatre Research), 16 (1976), 74–94

Fujime Yuki. *Sei no rekishigaku: Kōshō seido, dataizai taisei kara Baishun Bōshi Hō, Yūsei Hogo Hō taisei e* [The study of the history of sex: from licensed prostitution and the criminalisation of abortion to the Anti-Prostitution and the Eugenic Protection Acts], Tōkyō, Fuji Shuppan, 1997

Fujimoto T[aizō]. *The Story of the Geisha Girl*, London, T. Werner Laurie, [1917]

Fukai Akiko, and Catherine Join-Diéterle (eds). *Japonisme et mode*, exhibition catalogue, Paris, Les musées de la Ville de Paris, 1996

——, et al. *Fashion: A History from the 18th to the 20th Century. The Collection of the Kyoto Costume Institute*, Cologne, Taschen, 2002

Fukuda Toshiko. *Yoshiwara wa konna tokoro de gozaimashita – kuruwa no onnatachi no Shōwashi* [Yoshiwara as it used to be – a history of the women of the pleasure quarter during the Shōwa era] (1993); repr. Tōkyō, Bungensha, 2004

Fuller, Loie. *Fifteen Years of a Dancer's Life*, London, Herbert Jenkins, 1913

Funaoka Suetoshi. *Pierre Loti et l'Extrême-Orient: Du journal à l'œuvre*, Tōkyō, France Tosho, 1988

Füredi, Frank. *The Silent War: Imperialism and the Changing Perception of Race*, London, Pluto Press, 1998

Gautier, Judith. *Les Musiques bizarres à l'Exposition de 1900. La Musique japonaise*, music transcribed by Benedictus, Paris, Société d'Éditions littéraires et artistiques, Librairie Paul Ollendorff, Enoch & Cie, 1900

——. *Les Parfums de la pagode*, Paris, Librairie Charpentier et Fasquelle, 1919

——. *Les Princesses d'amour*, Paris, Librairie Paul Ollendorff, 1900

Gay, Peter. *The Bourgeois Experience: Victoria to Freud. Vol. 2: The Tender Passion*, New York and London, Oxford University Press, 1986

Gide, André. *Prétextes: Réflexions sur quelques points de littérature et de morale* (Paris, 1903); 4th edn, Paris, Mercure de France, 1913

Girardi, Michele. *Giacomo Puccini: L'arte internazionale di un musicista italiano*, Venice, Marsilio Editori, 1995

Golden, Arthur. *Memoirs of a Geisha*, London, Chatto & Windus, 1997

Goncourt, Edmond de. *L'Art japonais au XVIIIe siècle: Hokousaï* (Paris, 1896); repr. Paris, Fasquelle/Flammarion, n.d.

——. *L'Art japonais au XVIIIe siècle: Outamaro, le peintre des maisons vertes* (Paris, 1891); repr. Paris, Fasquelle/Flammarion, n.d.

——. *La Fille Élisa* (Paris, 1877); repr. Paris, G. Charpentier, 1879

——. *La Maison d'un artiste*, 2 vols, Paris, G. Charpentier, 1881

——. *Pages from the Goncourt Journal*, ed. and trans. Robert Baldick, London, Oxford University Press, 1962

——. *Paris and the Arts, 1851 to 1896: From the Goncourt Journal*, ed. and trans. George J. Becker and Edith Philips, Ithaca, NY and London, Cornell University Press, 1971

Griffis, William Elliot. *The Mikado's Empire*, New York, Harper and Brothers, 1876

Groos, Arthur. 'Cio-Cio-San and Sadayakko: Japanese Music-Theater in *Madama Butterfly*', *Monumenta Nipponica*, 54:1 (Spring 1999), 41–73

——. 'Madame Butterfly: The Story', *Cambridge Opera Journal*, 3:2 (1991), 125–58

——. 'Return of the Native: Japan in *Madama Butterfly/Madama Butterfly* in Japan', *Cambridge Opera Journal*, 1:2 (1989), 167–94

Grunfeld, Frederic V. *Rodin: A Biography* (New York, 1987); repr. New York, Da Capo Press, 1998

Guimet, Émile. *Promenades japonaises*, 2 vols, Paris, G. Charpentier, 1878, 1880

Gulick, Sidney L. *Evolution of the Japanese, Social and Psychic*, New York, Fleming H. Revell, 1903

——. *Working Women of Japan*, New York, Missionary Education Movement of the United States and Canada, 1915

Haga Tōru et al. (eds). *Bigot. Recueil d'illustrations humoristiques*, 3 vols, Tōkyō, Iwanami Shoten, 1989

Hall, Francis. *Japan through American Eyes: The Journal of Francis Hall, Kanagawa and Yokohama, 1859–1866*, ed. and annotated by F.G. Notehelfer, Princeton, Princeton University Press, 1992

Hall, Stuart, and Paul du Gay (eds). *Questions of Cultural Identity*, London, SAGE Publications, 1996

Hanazono Utako. *Geigi-tsū* [Insights into the world of the *geigi*], Tōkyō, Shiroku Shoin, 1930

'Hanjō'. 'Man'nen musume Kawakami Sadayakko no kaibō' [Dissecting Kawakami Sadayakko, the eternal young girl], *Shin Shōsetsu*, 21:8 (August 1916 suppl.), 51–57

Harris, Townsend. *The Complete Journal of Townsend Harris, First American Consul and Minister to Japan*, ed. Mario Emilio Cosenza (New York, 1930); 2nd, rev. edn, Rutland, VT and Tōkyō, Charles E. Tuttle, 1959

Harrison, Michael. *Fanfare of Strumpets*, London, W.H. Allen, 1971

Harsin, Jill. *Policing Prostitution in Nineteenth-century Paris*, Princeton, Princeton University Press, c.1985

Hasegawa Shigure. *Kindai bijinden* [Stories of beautiful women of modern times], Tōkyō, Sairensha, 1936

Hawks, Francis L. *Narrative of the Expedition of an American Squadron to the China Seas and Japan, Performed in the Years 1852, 1853, and 1854, under the Command of Commodore M.C. Perry, United States Navy, by Order of the Government of the United States*, Washington, 1856

Hayashi Yoshikazu. *Jidai fūzoku kōshō jiten* [Encyclopaedic study of period customs and manners] Tōkyō, Kawade Shobō Shinsha, 1977

Hayes, John P. *James A. Michener: A Biography*, London, W.H. Allen, 1984

Hearn, Lafcadio. *Japan: An Attempt at Interpretation*, New York, Macmillan, 1904

Hershey, Amos S., and Susanne W. Hershey. *Modern Japan: Social-Industrial-Political*, Indianapolis, Bobbs-Merrill, 1919

Heusken, Henry. *Japan Journal 1855 to 1861*, trans. and ed. Jeannette C. van der Corput and Robert A. Wilson, New Brunswick, NJ, Rutgers University Press, 1964

Hight, Eleanor M., and Gary D. Sampson (eds). *Colonialist Photography: Imag(in)ing Race and Place*, London, Routledge, 2002

Hildebrandt, Eduard. *Reise um die Erde*, 2 vols, Berlin, Otto Janke, 1867

Hillier, Jack. *The Art of Hokusai in Book Illustration*, London, Sotheby Parke Bernet; Berkeley and Los Angeles, University of California Press, 1980

——. *Japanese Prints and Drawings from the Vever Collection*, 3 vols, London, Sotheby, 1976

Hincks, Marcelle A. *The Japanese Dance*, London, William Heinemann, 1910

Hoare, James E. *Japan's Treaty Ports and Foreign Settlements: The Uninvited Guests, 1858–1899*, Folkestone, Japan Library, 1994

Hodgson, C. Pemberton. *A Residence at Nagasaki and Hakodate in 1859–1860; with an Account of Japan generally*, London, Richard Bentley, 1861

Hokenson, Jan Walsh. *Japan, France, and East-West Aesthetics: French Literature, 1867–2000*, Madison, NJ, Fairleigh Dickinson University Press, 2004

Holland, Clive. *Old and New Japan*, London, J.M. Dent; New York, E.P. Dutton, 1907

Hübner, Joseph Alexander von, baron. *Promenade autour du monde 1871*, 2 vols (Paris, 1873); 2nd edn, 2 vols, Paris, Hachette, 1873

Huish, Marcus B. *Japan and its Art* (London, 1889); 2nd, rev. edn, London, Simpkin, Marshall, Hamilton, Kent; Yokohama, Shanghai and Hong Kong, Kelly & Walsh, 1892

Humbert, Aimé. *Le Japon illustré*, 2 vols, Paris, Librairie Hachette et Cie, 1870

Hume, Bill. *Babysan: A Private Look at the Japanese Occupation*, with commentary by John Annarino and Bill Hume, Tōkyō, Kasuga Boeki KK, 1953

Hunt, Lynn (ed.). *The Invention of Pornography: Obscenity and the Origins of Modernity, 1500 to 1800*, New York, Zone Books, 1993

Huysmans, Joris-Karl. *A Rebours* (1884); 6th edn, Paris, Bibliothèque-Charpentier, 1895; trans. Robert Baldick as *Against Nature*, London, Penguin, 1959

——. *Certains* (Paris, 1889); repr. Paris, Librairie Plon, 1908

——. *Le Drageoir aux épices, suivi de pages retrouvées* (Paris, 1874); repr. Paris, Les Éditions G. Crès et Cie, 1921

Hwang, David Henry. *FOB and other Plays*, New York, Plume, 1990

——. *M. Butterfly*, New York, Plume, 1989

Iikura Akira. *Ierō periru no shinwa: Teikoku Nippon to kōka no gyakusetsu* [The myth of the yellow peril: imperial Japan and the paradox of the yellow peril], Tōkyō, Sairyūsha, 2004

Inoue Seizō. *Kawakami Otojirō no shōgai* [The life of Kawakami Otojirō], Fukuoka, Ashi Shobō, 1985

Ishiguro Keishichi. *Utsusareta bakumatsu: Ishiguro Keishichi korekushon* [The last years of the Tokugawa Shogunate photographed: the Ishiguro Keishichi collection], Tōkyō, Akashi Shoten, 1990

Ishii Kanji. *Kaikoku to ishin* [The opening of Japan and the Meiji Reformation] (Tōkyō, 1989); repr. Tōkyō, Shōgakukan, 1993

Ito, Robert B. 'A Certain Slant: A Brief History of Hollywood Yellowface', *Bright Lights Film Journal*, March 1997, 6 May 2005, <http://www.brightlightsfilm.com/18/18_yellow.html>

Iwao Seiichi. *Zoku: Nan'yō Nihonmachi no kenkyū* [Further studies concerning Japanese communities in south-east Asia], Tōkyō, Iwanami Shoten, 1987

Iwasaki Mineko. *Geisha of Gion*, London, Simon & Schuster, 2002

Jarrassé, Dominique. *Rodin: La passion du mouvement*, Paris, Éditions Pierre Terrail, 1993

Jarves, James Jackson. *A Glimpse at the Art of Japan*, New York, Hurd and Houghton; Cambridge, The Riverside Press, 1876

Jephson, R. Mounteney, and Edward Pennell Elmhirst. *Our Life in Japan*, London, Chapman and Hall, 1869

John, Nicholas (ed.). *Madam Butterfly/Madama Butterfly*, English National Opera Guide 26, London, John Calder; New York, Riverrun Press, 1984

Johnson, Sheila K. *The Japanese through American Eyes*, Stanford, Stanford University Press, 1988

Joseishi Sōgō Kenkyūkai (The Research Society for Women's History) (ed.). *Nippon josei seikatsushi* [History of the daily lives of Japanese women], 5 vols, Tōkyō, Tōkyō Daigaku Shuppan (Tōkyō University Press), 1990

Jūichiya Gisaburō. *Tōjin O-Kichi* [O-Kichi the Foreigner] (Tōkyō, 1929); repr. Tōkyō, Shunyōdō, 1932

——. *Toki no haisha Tōjin O-Kichi.* [Defeated by history: O-Kichi the Foreigner] (Tōkyō, 1930); repr. Tōkyō, Shunyōdō, 1932

——. *Toki no haisha Tōjin O-Kichi zokuhen* [Defeated by history: The story of O-Kichi the Foreigner continued], Tōkyō, Shinchōsha, 1930

Jullian, Philippe. *Robert de Montesquiou. Un prince 1900* (Paris, [1965]); trans. John Haylock and Francis King as *Robert de Montesquiou, a Fin-de-siècle Prince*, London, Secker & Warburg, 1967

Kabbani, Rana. *Imperial Fictions: Europe's Myths of Orient*, rev. edn, London, Pandora, 1994

Kaempfer, Engelbert. *The History of Japan: Giving an Account of the Antient and Present State and Government of that Empire; of its Temples, Palaces, Castles, and other Buildings; of its Metals,*

Minerals, Trees, Plants, Animals, Birds and Fishes; of the Chronology and Succession of the Emperors, Ecclesiastical and Secular; of the Original Descent, Religions, Customs, and Manufactures of the Natives, and of their Trade and Commerce with the Dutch and Chinese. Together with a Description of the Kingdom of Siam, trans. J.G. Scheuchzer, 2 vols, London, Thomas Woodward and Charles Davis, 1727

Kanao Tanejirō. Kawakami Otojirō ōbei manyūki [An account of Kawakami Otojirō's tour of the United States and Europe], Ōsaka, Kanao Bun'endō, 1901

——. Kawakami Otojirō Sadayakko manyūki [An account of Kawakami Otojirō and Sadayakko's tour of the United States and Europe], Ōsaka, Kanao Bun'endō, 1901

Kanazawa Yasutaka. Edo fukushokushi [A history of dress and accessories during the Edo Period], rev. edn, Tōkyō, Seiabō, 1998

Kanno Satomi. Shōhisareru ren'airon: Taishō chishikijin to sei [Theories of love for consumption: sex and the intelligentsia of the Taishō era], Tōkyō, Seikyūsha, 2001

Kano Ayako. Acting Like a Woman in Modern Japan: Theater, Gender, and Nationalism, New York and Basingstoke, Palgrave, 2001

Kanzaki Kiyoshi. Baishun ketteiban: Kanzaki repōto [A definitive study of prostitution: the Kanzaki Report], Tōkyō, Gendaishi Shuppankai, 1974

——. Baishun: Kono jittai wo dōshitara iika [Prostitution: what can be done in the present period], Tōkyō, Aoki Shoten, 1955

——. Musume wo uru machi – Kanzaki repōto [The town where young women are sold – the Kanzaki Report], Tōkyō, Shinkō Shuppansha, 1952

——. Sengo Nippon no baishun mondai [The problem of prostitution in post-war Japan], Tōkyō, Shakai Shobō, 1954

Kasaya Kazuhiko, Bushidō sono meiyo no okite [The way of the samurai and the code of honour], Tōkyō, Kyōiku Shuppan, 2001

Katori Somenosuke. 'Sadayakko no intaigeki wo mite: Meijiza jūgatsu kyōgen' [On seeing Sadayakko's farewell performance: the October season at the Meijiza theatre], Shin Engei, 2:11 (November 1917), 100–101

Kawaguchi Yōko. 'Frau Schmetterling', in programme for Madam Butterfly, Cardiff, Welsh National Opera, 1995

——. 'Nagasaki Geisha', in programme for Madam Butterfly, Cardiff, Welsh National Opera, 2002

——. 'Turandot and the Fabulous East', in programme for Turandot, Cardiff, Welsh National Opera, 2000

Kawajiri Sei'tan. Engei meika no omokage [Images of celebrities of the theatre world], Tōkyō, Uchūdō, 1910

Kawakami Sadayakko. 'Hajimete joyū ni natta koro – intai ni saishite' [When I first became an actress – recollections on the eve of my retirement], Shin Engei, 2:11 (November 1917), 102–103

——. 'Joyū toshiteno watashi no kakugo' [My resolutions as an actress], Bungei Gahō (November 1913), 49–52

Kawasaki Kenko. Takarazuka to yū yūtopia [A utopia called Takarazuka], Tōkyō, Iwanami Shoten, 2005

Kawasaki Seirō. Bakumatsu no chūnichi gaikōkan ryōjikan [Foreign diplomats and consulates in Japan during the last years of the Tokugawa Shogunate], Tōkyō, Yūshōdō Shuppan, 1988

Keay, John. The Honourable Company: A History of the English East India Company, (London, 1991); repr. London, HarperCollins, 1993

Keene, Donald. Landscapes and Portraits: Appreciations of Japanese Culture (Tōkyō and Palo Alto, CA, 1971); repr. as Appreciations of Japanese Culture, Tōkyō and New York, Kodansha International, 1981

Kelsky, Karen. Women on the Verge: Japanese Women, Western Dreams, Durham, NC, Duke University Press, 2001

Kerr, George H. Okinawa: The History of an Island People, Rutland, VT and Tōkyō, Charles E. Tuttle, 1959

Kim Il-Myon. Yūjo, karayuki, ianfu no keifu [The lineage of courtesans, karayuki and comfort women], Tōkyō, Yūzankaku, 1997

'Kin'eijo'. 'Kawai no O-Tsuma to Sadayakko no Sarome' [O-Tsuma as played by Kawai and Sadayakko's Salome], *Shin Shōsetsu*, 20:6 (June 1915 suppl.), 77–80

Kipling, Rudyard. *Kipling's Japan: Collected Writings*, ed. Hugh Cortazzi and George Webb, London and Atlantic Highlands, NJ, The Athlone Press, 1988

Kirkbride, Ronald. *Tamiko*, London, Cassell, 1959

Knollys, Henry. *Sketches of Life in Japan*, London, Chapman & Hall, 1887

Kobayashi Daijirō, and Murase Akira. *Min'na wa shiranai: Kokka baishun meirei* [Nobody knows: the national prostitution order], Tōkyō, Yūzankaku Shuppan, 1961

Kobayashi Tadashi, Ōkubo Jun'ichi et al. *Ukiyoe no kanshō kiso chishiki* [Fundamental knowledge for the appreciation of *ukiyoe*], Tōkyō, Shibundō, 1994

Koestenbaum, Wayne. *The Queen's Throat: Opera, Homosexuality and the Mystery of Desire*, London, GMP Publishers, 1993

Koga Jūjirō. *Maruyama yūjo to tōkōmōjin* [The Chinese, Europeans and the courtesans of Maruyama], 2 vols, Nagasaki, Nagasaki Bunkensha, 1968–69

Kondo, Dorinne. *About Face: Performing Race in Fashion and Theater*, New York and London, Routledge, 1997

Kondō Tomie. *Rokumeikan kifujinkō* [On the ladies of the Rokumeikan], Tōkyō, Kōdansha, 1980

Konishi Shirō, and Oka Hideyuki (eds). *Hyaku'nen mae no Nippon: E.S. Morse Collection/ Photography, Peabody Museum of Salem* [Japan one hundred years ago], Tōkyō, Shōgakukan, 1983

Koppes, Clayton R., and Gregory D. Black. *Hollywood Goes to War: How Politics, Profits, and Propaganda Shaped World War II Movies* (New York and London, 1987); repr. London, I.B. Tauris, 1988

Krauss, Friedrich S. *Das Geschlechtleben in Glauben, Sitte, Brauch und Gewohnheitrecht der Japaner*, 2nd, rev. edn, Leipzig, 1911

Krips, Henry. *Fetish: An Erotics of Culture*, Ithaca, Cornell University Press, 1999

Kuhn, Annette. *The Power of the Image: Essays on Representation and Sexuality*, London, Routledge & Kegan Paul, 1985

Kurata Yoshihiro. *Geinō no bunmeikaika: Meiji kokka to geinō kindaika* [The cultural enlightenment and public entertainments: the Meiji state and the modernisation of public entertainments], Tōkyō, Heibonsha, 1999

Kurth, Peter. *Isadora: A Sensational Life*, Boston, New York and London, Little, Brown, 2001

Kusudo Yoshiaki, and Iwao Mitsuyo. *Bakumatsu ishin no bijo kōrui roku: Tokugawa Yoshinobu no jidai* [Record of the suffering of famous beauties of the last years of the Tokugawa Shogunate and the Meiji Revolution: the age of Tokugawa Yoshinobu], Tōkyō, Chūō Kōronsha, 1997

Lacambre, Geneviève et al. *Le Japonisme*, exhibition catalogue, Paris, Éditions de la Réunion des musées nationaux, 1988

La Farge, John. *An Artist's Letters from Japan*, London, T. Fisher Unwin, 1897

LaFeber, Walter. *The Clash: US–Japanese Relations throughout History*, New York and London, W.W. Norton, 1997

Lauren, Paul Gordon. *Power and Prejudice: The Politics and Diplomacy of Racial Discrimination*, 2nd edn, Boulder, CO and Oxford, Westview Press, 1996

Lee, Sang-Kyong. 'Edward Gordon Craig and Japanese Theatre', *Asian Theatre Journal*, 17:2 (Autumn 2000), 215–35

Lehmann, Jean-Pierre. *The Image of Japan: From Feudal Isolation to World Power, 1850–1905*, London, George Allen & Unwin, 1978

Leupp, Gary P. *Interracial Intimacy in Japan: Western Men and Japanese Women, 1543–1900*, New York and London, Continuum, 2003

Levine, Gary, Robert R. Preato, and Francine Tyler. *La Femme: The Influence of Whistler and Japanese Print Masters on American Art 1880–1917*, New York, Grand Central Art Galleries, 1983

Lindau, Rodolphe. *Un Voyage autour du Japon*, Paris, Hachette, 1864

Lindenberger, Herbert. *Opera in History: From Monteverdi to Cage*, Stanford, Stanford University Press, 1998

Littlewood, Ian. *The Idea of Japan: Western Images, Western Myths*, Chicago, Ivan R. Dee, 1996

Long, John Luther. *Madame Butterfly; Purple Eyes; A Gentleman of Japan and a Lady; Kito; Glory*, New York, Century, 1898

Loti, Pierre. *Japoneries d'automne*, Paris, Calmann-Lévy, 1889

———. *Madame Chrysanthème* (Paris, 1887); repr. Paris, Édouard Guillaume, 1888; trans. Laura Ensor (Paris and London, 1889); repr. London, Manchester and New York, George Routledge & Sons, 1897

———. *La Troisième Jeunesse de Madame Prune*, Paris, Calmann-Lévy, 1905; trans. S.R.C. Plimsoll as *Madame Prune*, London, T. Werner Laurie, 1919

Lowell, Percival. *The Soul of the Far East* (Boston and New York, 1888); repr. New York, Macmillan, 1911

Lucie-Smith, Edward. *Eroticism in Western Art* (London, 1972); repr. as *Sexuality in Western Art*, London, Thames and Hudson, 1991

Ma, Karen. *The Modern Madame Butterfly: Fantasy and Reality in Japanese Cross-cultural Relationships*, Rutland, VT and Tōkyō, Charles E. Tuttle, 1996

Mabuchi Akiko (ed.). *Japanese Art and Japonisme. Part I: Early Writings. Volume 1: A Glimpse at the Art of Japan*. Bristol, Ganesha, 1999

McClintock, Anne. *Imperial Leather: Race, Gender and Sexuality in the Colonial Contest*, New York and London, Routledge, 1995

McDowell, Colin. *Jean Paul Gaultier* (London, 1998); repr. London, Cassell, 2000

MacKenzie, John M. *Orientalism: History, Theory and the Arts*, Manchester, Manchester University Press, 1995

McMillan, James F. *Housewife or Harlot: The Place of Women in French Society, 1870–1940*, Brighton, Harvester Press, 1981

'Madame Hanako'. 'Geisha de yōkō shi joyū de kaeru made no nijū'nen' [On the twenty years between my leaving for the west as a geisha and my return as an actress], *Shin Nippon*, 7:1 (January 1917), 87–103

Maeda Shinjirō. *Baishun to jinshin baibai no kōzō* [The organisation of prostitution and human traffic], Kyōto, Dōbun Shoin, 1958

Maehder, Jürgen (ed.). *Esotismo e colore locale nell'opera di Puccini*, Pisa, Giardini, 1985

Mahling, Christoph-Hellmut. 'The "Japanese Image" in Opera, Operetta and Instrumental Music at the End of the 19th and during the 20th Century', in Tokumaru Yoshihiko et al., *Tradition and its Future in Music. Report of the 4th Symposium of the International Musicological Society, Ōsaka, 1990*, Ōsaka, Mita Press, 1991

Maki Hidemasa. *Jinshin baibai* [Human trafficking], Tōkyō, Iwanami Shoten, 1971

Maraini, Fosco. *L'Isola delle pescatrici*, Bari, Leonardo da Vinci Editrice, 1960

Marchetti, Gina. *Romance and the 'Yellow Peril': Race, Sex, and Discursive Strategies in Hollywood Fiction*, Berkeley, Los Angeles and London, University of California Press, 1993

Marcus, Steven. *The Other Victorians: A Study of Sexuality and Pornography in Mid-nineteenth-century England*, London, Weidenfeld & Nicolson, 1966

Martino, Daniele A. *Metamorfosi del femminino nei libretti per Puccini*, Turin, Book & Video, 1985

Mason, Michael. *The Making of Victorian Sexuality: Sexual Behaviour and its Understanding*, Oxford and New York, Oxford University Press, 1994

Matlock, Jann. *Scenes of Seduction: Prostitution, Hysteria, and Reading Difference in Nineteenth-century France*, New York, Columbia University Press, 1994

Matsumoto Ken'ichi. *Kaikoku, ishin: 1853–1871* [The opening of Japan and the Meiji Reformation 1853–71], Tōkyō, Chūō Kōronsha, 1998

Matsunaga Goichi. *Kawakami Otojirō: Kindaigeki, hatenkō na yoake* [Kawakami Otojirō: the sensational dawn of modern theatre], Tōkyō, Asahi Shinbunsha, 1988

Menpes, Mortimer. *Japan, a Record in Colour*, transcribed by Dorothy Menpes, London, Adam and Charles Black, 1901

Michener, James A. *The Bridges at Toko-ri*, New York, Random House, 1953

———. *The Floating World*, London, Secker & Warburg, 1954

———. *Sayonara*, New York, Random House, 1954

Miner, Earl. *The Japanese Tradition in British and American Literature*, Princeton, Princeton University Press, 1958

Minois, Georges. *Histoire du suicide: La société occidentale face à la mort volontaire* (Paris, 1995); trans. Lydia G. Cochrane as *History of Suicide: Voluntary Death in Western Culture*, Baltimore and London, Johns Hopkins University Press, 1999

Mitford, A. B. *Mitford's Japan: The Memoirs and Recollections, 1866–1906, of Algernon Bertram Mitford, the first Lord Redesdale*, ed. Hugh Cortazzi, London and Dover, NH, Athlone Press, 1985

——. *Tales of Old Japan*, 2 vols, London, Macmillan, 1871

Morgan, Lewis H. *Ancient Society; or, Researches in the Lines of Human Progress from Savagery through Barbarism to Civilization*, Chicago, Charles H. Kerr, [1877]

Mori Katsumi. *Jinshin baibai – kaigai dekasegi onna* [Human trafficking – women who go abroad to earn a living], Tōkyō, Shibundō, 1959

Mori Ōgai. *Maihime* (Tōkyō, 1890); repr. *Maihime; Sanshō Dayū, hoka yonhen* [The Dancing Girl; Sansho the Bailiff; and other stories], Tōkyō, Ōbunsha, 1966

Morita Tomoko. *Kaikoku to chigaihōken: Ryōjisaiban seido no un'yō to Maria-Rūsu-gō jiken* [The opening of Japan and extraterritoriality: the system of consular jurisdiction in practice and the *Maria Luz* incident], Tōkyō, Yoshikawa Kōbunkan, 2005

Morley, John David. *Pictures from the Water Trade: An Englishman in Japan*, London, André Deutsch, 1985

Motoyama Keisen. *Nagasaki hanamachihen* [The pleasure districts of Nagasaki], Tōkyō, Shunyōdō, 1928

——. *Nagasaki Maruyama banashi* [The story of the Maruyama district of Nagasaki], Tōkyō, Sakamoto Shoten, 1926

Murakami Yumiko. *Ierō feisu: Hariuddo eiga ni miru ajiajin no shōzō* [Yellow face: how Asians have been portrayed in Hollywood films], Tōkyō, Asahi Shinbunsha, 1993

[Musée Rodin (ed.).] *Rodin et l'Extrême-Orient*, exhibition catalogue, Paris, Musée Rodin, 1979

Nakano Eizō. *Kuruwa no seikatsu* [Life in the pleasure quarter] (Tōkyō, 1968); repr. Tōkyō, Yūzankaku, 1981

——. *Yūjo no seikatsu* [The life led by courtesans], enlarged edn, Tōkyō, Yūzankaku, 1996

Nakano Yoshio, and Arasaki Moriteru. *Okinawa sengoshi* [The history of post-war Okinawa], Tōkyō, Iwanami Shoten, 1976

Nakazato Kian. *Bakumatsu kaikō rashamen jōshi* [The romance of the *rashamen* of the last years of the Tokugawa Shogunate and during the opening of Japan], Tōkyō, Sekirokaku Shobō, 1931

Nead, Lynda. *The Female Nude: Art, Obscenity and Sexuality*, London and New York, Routledge, 1992

Netto, C[urt Adolph]. *Papier-Schmetterlinge aus Japan*, Leipzig, T.O. Weigel, 1888

Nishiyama Matsunosuke (ed.). *Yūjo* [The courtesan] (Tōkyō, 1979); repr. Tōkyō, Tōkyōdō Shuppan, 1994

Nitobe Inazo. *Bushido, the Soul of Japan* (Philadelphia, 1900); 10th, rev. and enlarged edn, Tōkyō, The Student Company, 1905

Nochlin, Linda. *The Politics of Vision: Essays on Nineteenth-century Art and Society* (New York, 1989); repr. London, Thames and Hudson, 1991

Norman, Henry. *The Real Japan: Studies of Contemporary Japanese Manners, Morals, Administration, and Politics*, London, T. Fisher Unwin, 1892

Norton, Robert E. *The Beautiful Soul: Aesthetic Morality in the Eighteenth Century*, Ithaca and London, Cornell University Press, 1995

O'Connell Davidson, Julia. *Prostitution, Power and Freedom*, Cambridge, Polity Press, 1998

Ōkubo Hasetsu. *Hanamachi fūzokushi* [A history of the customs of the pleasure districts] (Tōkyō, 1906); repr. Tōkyō, Nippon Tosho Sentā, 1983

Ōkuchi Yūjirō (ed.). *Onna no shakaishi 17–20 seiki: Ie to jendā wo kangaeru* [Social history of women in the 17th to the 20th centuries: investigating the concepts of family and gender], Tōkyō, Yamakawa Shuppansha, 2001

Ōkuma Miyoshi. *Seppuku no rekishi* [A history of *seppuku*] (Tōkyō, 1973); repr. Tōkyō, Yūzankaku, 1995

Oliphant, Laurence. *Narrative of the Earl of Elgin's Mission to China and Japan in the Years 1857, '58, '59*, 2 vols, Edinburgh and London, William Blackwood, 1859

Ono, Ayako. 'George Henry and E.A. Hornel's Visit to Japan and *Yokohama Shashin*: The Influence of Japanese Photography', *Apollo*, 150: 453 (n.s.) (November 1999), 11–18

——. *Japonisme in Britain: A Source of Inspiration. J. McNeill Whistler, Mortimer Menpes, George Henry, E.A. Hornel and Nineteenth-century Japan*, London, Routledge Curzon, 2003

Osada Masako. *Sanctions and Honorary Whites: Diplomatic Policies and Economic Realities in Relations between Japan and South Africa*, Westport, CT, Greenwood Press, 2002

Osborn, Sherard. *A Cruise in Japanese Waters* (1859); 2nd edn, Edinburgh and London: William Blackwood and Sons, 1859

——. *Japanese Fragments, with Facsimiles of Illustrations by Artists of Yedo*, London, Bradbury and Evans, 1861

Ōzasa Yoshio. *Nippon gendai engekishi: Meiji, Taishōhen* [The history of modern Japanese theatre: the Meiji and Taishō eras], Tōkyō, Hakusuisha, 1985

Ozawa Takeshi. *Bakumatsu Meiji no shashin* [Photography in the last decades of the Tokugawa Shogunate and the Meiji era], Tōkyō, Chikuma Shobō, 1997

—— (ed.). *Furuzashin de miru bakumatsu Meiji no bijin zukan* [An illustrated book of beautiful women of the last years of the Tokugawa Shogunate and into the Meiji era], Tōkyō, Sekaibunkasha, 2001

Pantzer, Peter (ed.). *Japanischer Theaterhimmel über Europas Bühnen: Kawakami Otojiro, Sadayakko und ihre Truppe auf Tournee durch Mittel- und Osteuropa 1901/1902*, Munich, Iudicium, 2005

Parent-Duchâtelet, Alexandre. *De la Prostitution dans la ville de Paris, considérée sous le rapport de l'hygiène publique, de la morale et de l'administration. . . .*, 2 vols, Paris, J.B. Ballière, 1836

Paris, John. *Kimono* (London, 1921); repr. New York, Boni and Liveright, 1922

Patrick, John. *The Teahouse of the August Moon*, New York, G.P. Putnam's Sons, 1952

Peabody Essex Museum (ed.). *Geisha: Beyond the Painted Smile*, New York, George Braziller, 2004

Pease, Allison. *Modernism, Mass Culture, and the Aesthetics of Obscenity*, Cambridge, Cambridge University Press, 2000

Philipp, Claudia Gabriele, Dietmar Siegert, and Rainer Wick (eds). *Felice Beato: Viaggio in Giappone 1863–1877*, trans. Simonetta Bertoncini, Milan, Federico Motta Editore, 1991

Pierrot, Jean. *L'Imaginaire décadent, 1880–1900* (Paris, 1977); trans. Derek Coltman as *The Decadent Imagination 1880–1900*, Chicago and London, University of Chicago Press, 1981

Pinet, Hélène. *Rodin et ses modèles: Le portrait photographié*, exhibition catalogue, Paris, Musée Rodin, 1990

Pinguet, Maurice. *La Mort volontaire au Japan* (Paris, 1984); trans. Rosemary Morris as *Voluntary Death in Japan*, Cambridge, Polity Press, 1993

Pinkerton, John. *A General Collection of the Best and Most Interesting Voyages and Travels in All Parts of the World*, vol. 7, London, Longman, Hurst, Rees, Orme and Brown; and Cadell and Davies, 1811

Porter, Roy, and Lesley Hall. *The Facts of Life: The Creation of Sexual Knowledge in Britain, 1650–1950*, New Haven and London, Yale University Press, 1995

Potts, Alex. *Flesh and the Ideal: Winckelmann and the Origins of Art History*, New Haven and London, Yale University Press, 1994

Powils-Okano, Kimiyo. *Puccinis 'Madama Butterfly'*, Bonn, Verlag für systematische Musikwissenschaft, 1986

Prasso, Sheridan. *The Asian Mystique: Dragon Ladies, Geisha Girls, and our Fantasies of the Exotic Orient*, New York, Public Affairs, 2005

Preble, George Henry. *The Opening of Japan: A Diary of Discovery in the Far East, 1853–1856*, ed. Boleslaw Szczesniak, Norman, University of Oklahoma Press, 1962

Pullen, Kirsten. *Actresses and Whores: On Stage and in Society*, Cambridge, Cambridge University Press, 2005

Pumpelly, Raphael. *Across America and Asia: Notes of a Five Years' Journey around the World and of Residence in Arizona, Japan and China*, London, Sampson Low, Son and Marston, 1870

Purchas, Samuel. *Purchas His Pilgrimes in Japan, Extracted from Hakluytus Posthumus, Or Purchas His Pilgrimes, Contayning a History of the World in Sea Voyages and Lande Travells by Englishmen and others*, ed. Cyril Wild, Kōbe, J.L. Thompson; London, Kegan Paul, Trench, Trubner [1939]

Put, Max. *Plunder and Pleasure: Japanese Art in the West 1860–1930*, Leiden, Hotei, c.2000

Raay, Stefan van (ed.). *Imitation and Inspiration: Japanese Influence on Dutch Art*, Amsterdam, D'ARTS, 1989

Ransome, Stafford. *Japan in Transition. A Comparative Study of the Progress, Policy, and Methods of the Japanese since their War with China*, London and New York, Harper and Brothers, 1899

Raspail, Jean. *Le Vent des pins* (Paris, 1958); trans. Jean Stewart as *Welcome, Honourable Visitors*, London, Hamish Hamilton, 1960

Reed, Sir Edward J. *Japan: Its History, Traditions, and Religions. With the Narrative of a Visit in 1879*, 2 vols, London, John Murray, 1880

Régamey, Félix. *Le Cahier rose de Madame Chysanthème*, Paris, Bibliothèque artistique et littéraire, 1894

Rein, J[ohannes] J[ustus]. *Japan nach Reisen und Studien im Auftrage der Königlich Preussischen Regierung*, 2 vols, Leipzig, Verlag von Wilhelm Engelmann, 1881, 1886; vol. 1 trans. as *Japan: Travels and Researches Undertaken at the Cost of the Prussian Government*, London, Hodder & Stoughton, 1884

Revers, Peter. *Das Fremde und das Vertraute: Studien zur musiktheoretischen und musikdramatischen Ostasienrezeption*, Stuttgart, F. Steiner, 1997

Richards, Jeffrey. *Imperialism and Music: Britain 1876–1953*, Manchester, Manchester University Press, 2001

Richardson, Joanna. *The Courtesans: The Demi-monde in 19th-century France*, London, Weidenfeld & Nicolson, 1967

Ricketts, Charles. *Self-Portrait*, compiled T. Sturge Moore, ed. Cecil Lewis, London, Peter Davies, 1939

Rij, Jan van. *Madame Butterfly: Japonisme, Puccini, and the Search for the Real Cho-Cho-San*, Berkeley, Stone Bridge Press, 2001

Robertson, Jennifer. *Takarazuka: Sexual Politics and Popular Culture in Modern Japan*, Berkeley, Los Angeles and London, University of California Press, 1998

Robertson, Pamela. *Guilty Pleasures: Feminist Camp from Mae West to Madonna*, Durham, NC, Duke University Press, 1996

Rodin, Auguste. *L'Art: Entretiens réunis par Paul Gsell*, Paris, Bernard Grasset, 1911; trans. Mrs Romilly Fedden as *Rodin on Art and Artists. Conversations with Paul Gsell* (London, 1912); repr. New York, Dover, 1981

———. *Erotic Watercolors*, intro. by Anne-Marie Bonnet, trans. Michael Robertson, New York, Stewart, Tabori and Chang, 1995

Rossetti, William Michael, *Fine Art, Chiefly Contemporary*, London, Macmillan, 1867

Rougemont, Denis de. *L'Amour et l'Occident* (Paris, 1939); trans. Montgomery Belgion as *Love in the Western World*, rev. edn, New York, Pantheon Books, 1956

Ryūkyū Shinpōsha (ed.). *Okinawa konpakuto jiten* [A compact encyclopaedia of Okinawa], Naha, Ryūkyū Shinpōsha, 2003

Said, Edward W. *Orientalism: Western Conceptions of the Orient* (New York, 1978); repr. London, Penguin, 1991

Saitō Takio. *Bakumatsu Meiji Yokohama shashinkan monogatari* [The story of photographic studios in Yokohama during the last years of the Tokugawa Shogunate and the Meiji era], Tōkyō, Yoshikawa Kōbunkan, 2004

Sarantakes, Nicholas Evan. *Keystone: The American Occupation of Okinawa and US–Japanese Relations*, College Station, Texas A&M University Press, 2000

Satō Tomoko, and Watanabe Toshio (eds). *Japan and Britain: An Aesthetic Dialogue 1850–1930*, London, Lund Humphries, 1991

Sawada Suketarō. *Petite Hanako*, trans. Michiko Ina, Frasne, Canevas Éditeur, 1997

Schwartz, William Leonard. *The Imaginative Interpretation of the Far East in Modern French Literature, 1800–1925*, Paris, H. Champion, 1927

Screech, Timon. *Sex and the Floating World: Erotic Images in Japan 1700–1820*, London, Reaktion Books, 1999

Seidlitz, Woldemar von, *Geschichte des japanischen Farbholzschnitts*, Dresden, Verlag von Gerhard Kühtmann, 1897; trans. Anne Heard Dyer and Grace Tripler as *A History of Japanese Colour-prints*, London, William Heinemann, 1910

Seward, Olive Risley (ed.). *William H. Seward's Travels around the World*, New York, D. Appleton, 1873

Shelton, Suzanne. *Divine Dancer: A Biography of Ruth St Denis*, Garden City, NY, Doubleday, 1981

Sheppard, W. Anthony. 'Cinematic Realism, Reflexivity and the American "Madame Butterfly" Narratives', *Cambridge Opera Journal*, 17:1 (2005), 59–93

Shimizu, Christine. *Le Japon du XIXᵉ siècle: La redécouverte*, Marseille, AGEP VILO, 1990

Shimizu Isao. *Bigō ga mita Nipponjin: Fūshiga ni egakareta Meiji* [The Japanese through Bigot's eyes: the Meiji era satirised], Tōkyō, Kōdansha, 2001

Shiraishi Hiroko. *Nagasaki Dejima no yūjo: kindai e no mado wo hiraita onnatachi* [The courtesans of the Dejima in Nagasaki: the women who opened a window upon the modern world], Tōkyō, Bensei Shuppan, 2005

Shirakura Yoshihiko, Tanaka Yūko, Hayakawa Monta, and Mihashi Osamu. *Ukiyoe shunga wo yomu* [Reading woodblock *shunga*], 2 vols, Tōkyō, Chūō Koron Shinsha, 2000

Shizuoka Kenritsu Bijutsukan, and Aichi Kenritsu Bijutsukan (Shizuoka Prefectural Museum of Art and Aichi Prefectural Museum of Art) (eds). *Rodin et le Japon*, exhibition catalogue, Tōkyō, Gendai Chōkoku Sentā (Contemporary Sculpture Centre), 2001

Sladen, Douglas. *The Japs at Home*, London, Hutchinson, 1892

——. *Queer Things about Japan*, London, Anthony Treherne, 1903

——, and Norma Lorimer. *More Queer Things about Japan*, London, Anthony Treherne, 1904

Smith, George. *Ten Weeks in Japan*, London, Longman, Green, Longman, and Roberts, 1861

Sneider, Vern J. *The Teahouse of the August Moon*, New York, G.P. Putnam's Sons, 1951

Sōgō Joseishi Kenkyūkai (The Society for Research on Women's History) (ed.). *Nippon josei no rekishi: Sei, ai, kazoku* [The history of Japanese women: sex, love, family], Tōkyō, Kadokawa Shoten, 1992

—— (ed.). *Sei to shintai* [Sex and the body], Tōkyō, Yoshikawa Kōbunkan, 1998

Stanislavsky, Konstantin. *My Life in Art*, trans. J.J. Robbins (Boston, 1924); 4th edn, London, Geoffrey Bles, 1945

Steinmetz, Andrew. *Japan and her People*, London, Routledge, Warnes and Routledge, 1859

Stewart, Frank Henderson. *Honor*, Chicago and London, University of Chicago Press, 1994

Stoddard, John L. *John L. Stoddard's Lectures. Vol. 3: Japan I, II, China* (Chicago, 1897); repr. Boston, Balch Brothers; Chicago, George L. Shuman, 1904.

Strange, Edward F. *Japanese Colour Prints*, London, HMSO, 1904

Sukenobu Isao. *Rodan to Hanako: Yōroppa wo kaketa Nipponjin joyū no shirarezaru shōgai* [Rodin and Hanako: the unknown life of the Japanese actress who blossomed in Europe], Tōkyō, Bungeisha, 2005

Sumimoto Toshio. *Senryō hiroku* [Secrets of the occupation], 2 vols, Tōkyō, Mainichi Shinbunsha, 1952

Suzuki Chikara. *Shinshin Nagasaki miyage* [A yet newer souvenir from Nagasaki] (Nagasaki, 1889); 2nd edn, Nagasaki, 1890

Sweetman, David. *Toulouse-Lautrec and the Fin de Siècle*, London, Hodder & Stoughton, 1999

Symons, Arthur. *Plays, Acting, and Music*, London, Duckworth, 1903

Takemae Eiji. *Senryō sengoshi* (Zushi, 1980); trans. and adapted by Robert Ricketts and Sebastian Swann as *The Allied Occupation of Japan and its Legacy* (New York, 2002); repr. New York and London, Continuum, 2003

Takigawa Masajirō. *Yūjo no rekishi* [History of the courtesan], Tōkyō, Shibundō, 1965

Thomas, Donald. *The Victorian Underworld*, London, John Murray, 1998

Thomson, Richard. *Degas: The Nudes*, London, Thames and Hudson, 1988

Thunberg, Charles Peter. *Travels in Europe, Africa, and Asia. Performed between the Years 1770 and 1779. Vol. III. Containing a Voyage to Japan, and Travels in Different Parts of that Empire, in the Years 1775 and 1776*, London, W. Richardson, Cornhill, and J. Egerton, 1795

Tracy, Albert. *Rambles through Japan without a Guide*, London, Sampson Low, 1892

Uehara Eiko. *Tsuji no hana: Kuruwa no onnatachi* [Flowers of the Tsuji Quarter: the women of the pleasure district], Tōkyō, Jiji Tsūshinsha, 1976

——. *Tsuji no hana: Sengohen* [Flowers of the Tsuji Quarter: the post-war years], 2 vols, Tōkyō, Jiji Tsūshinsha, 1989

Uemura Kōshō (ed.). *Nippon yūrishi* [History of Japanese pleasure quarters], Tōkyō, Bunka Seikatsu Kenkyūkai, 1929

Usami Misako. *Shukuba to meshimori-onna* [Posting inns and *meshimori-onna*], Tōkyō, Dōseisha, 2000

Walkowitz, Judith R. *Prostitution and Victorian Society: Women, Class, and the State*, Cambridge, Cambridge University Press, 1980

Ward, Philip. *Hofmannsthal and Greek Myth: Expression and Performance*, British and Irish Studies in German Language and Literature, 24, Oxford, Bern, Berlin, Brussels, Frankfurt am Main, New York and Vienna, Peter Lang, 2002

Watanabe Hiroshi. *Nippon bunka modan rapusode* [Japanese culture: a modern rhapsody], Tōkyō, Shunjūsha, 2002

Watanna, Onoto. *'A Half Caste' and other Writings*, ed. Linda Trinh Moser and Elizabeth Rooney, Urbana and Chicago, University of Illinois Press, 2003

——. *The Heart of Hyacinth* (New York, 1903); repr. Seattle and London, University of Washington Press, 2000

——. *A Japanese Nightingale*, New York and London, Harper and Brothers, 1901

——. *Sunny-San*. Toronto, McClelland & Stewart; New York, George H. Doran, 1922

——. *Tama*, New York and London, Harper and Brothers, 1910

Weeks, Jeffrey. *Sex, Politics and Society: The Regulation of Sexuality since 1800*, 2nd edn, London and New York, Longman, 1989

Weisberg, Gabriel P. et al. *Japonisme: Japanese Influence on French Art 1854–1910*, Cleveland, Cleveland Museum of Art, 1975–76

——, Laurinda S. Dixon et al. (eds). *The Documented Image: Visions in Art History*, Syracuse, Syracuse University Press, 1987

Whistler, James McNeill. *The Gentle Art of Making Enemies* (London, 1890); repr. London, William Heinemann, 1994

Wilde, Oscar. *Intentions*, London, James R. Osgood McIlvaine, 1891

Wilkinson, Endymion. *Misunderstanding* (Tōkyō, Chūō Kōronsha, 1981); rev. as *Japan versus Europe: A History of Misunderstanding*, Harmondsworth, Penguin, 1983

Williams, Harold S. *Foreigners in Mikadoland*, Rutland, VT and Tōkyō, Charles E. Tuttle, 1963

——. *Shades of the Past; or, Indiscreet Tales of Japan*, Rutland, VT and Tōkyō, Charles E. Tuttle, 1959

Winckelmann, Johann Joachim. *Gedanken über die Nachahmung der griechischen Werke in der Mahlerei und Bildhauerkunst* (1755); repr. Dresden and Leipzig, Im Verlag der Waltherischen Handlung, 1756

——. *Winckelmann: Writings on Art*, selected and ed. David Irwin, London, Phaidon, 1972

Wong, Eugene Franklin. 'On Visual Media Racism: Asians in the American Motion Pictures', Ph.D. dissertation, University of Denver, 1977; facsimile reproduction, New York, Arno Press, 1978

Yamaguchi Reiko. *Joyū Sadayakko* [The actress Sadayakko], (Tōkyō, 1982); repr. Tōkyō, Asahi Shinbunsha, 1993

Yamamoto Yūzō, *Nyo'nin aishi*, Tōkyō, Shiroku Shoin, 1931

Yanagida Kunio. *Meiji Taishōshi* [History of the Meiji and Taishō eras], 6 vols (Tōkyō, 1930–31); rev. as *Meiji Taishōshi: Sesōhen* [Aspects of life during the Meiji and Taishō eras], (Tōkyō, 1967); repr. Tōkyō, Chūō Kōron Shinsha, 2001

Yasui Ryōhei (ed.). *Kyōdōkenkyū Nippon to Roshia* [Japan and Russia], Tōkyō, Waseda Daigaku Bungakubu Yasui Ryōhei Kenkyūshitsu (Yasui Ryōhei Research Group, Faculty of Letters, Waseda University), 1987

Yokohama Kaikō Shiryōkan (Yokohama Historical Archive) (ed.). *F. Beato bakumatsu Nippon shashin shū* [F. Beato: a selection of his photographs of Japan in the last years of the Tokugawa Shogunate], Yokohama, Yokohama Kaikō Shiryō Fukyū Kyōkai, 1987

—— (ed.). *Meiji no Nippon: Yokohama shashin no sekai* [Japan in the Meiji era: the world of the Yokohama photograph], expanded edn, Yokohama, Yūrindō, 2003

Yokoyama Toshio. *Japan in the Victorian Mind: A Study of Stereotyped Images of a Nation, 1850–80*, Basingstoke, Macmillan, 1987

Yoshida Hidehiro. *Nippon baishunshikō: Hensen to sono haikei* [A study of the history of prostitution in Japan: its transformations and background], Tōkyō, Jiyūsha, 2000

Yoshida Tsunekichi. *Tōjin O-Kichi: Bakumatsu gaikō hishi* [Tōjin O-Kichi: a secret history of diplomacy during the last years of the Tokugawa Shogunate], Tōkyō, Chūō Kōronsha, 1966

Yoshihara Mari. *Embracing the East: White Women and American Orientalism*, New York, Oxford University Press, 2003

Zatlin, Linda Gertner. *Beardsley, Japonisme and the Perversion of the Victorian Ideal*, Cambridge, Cambridge University Press, 1997

Zeldin, Theodore. *France 1848–1945: Ambition and Love*, Oxford, Oxford University Press, 1979

Index